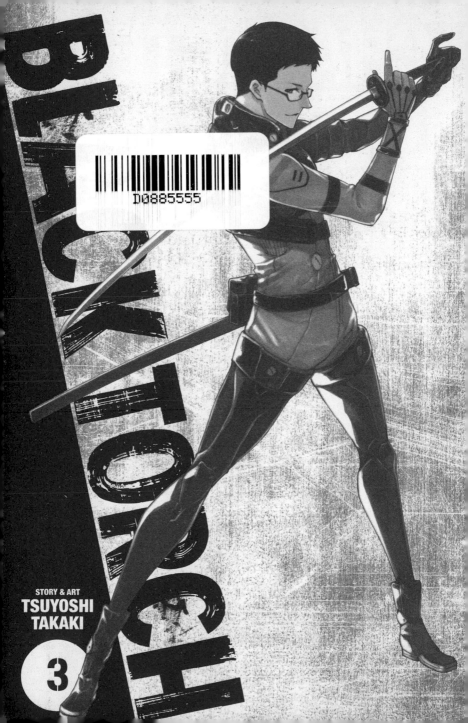

BLACK TORCH

STORY & ART
**TSUYOSHI
TAKAKI**

3

CHARACTER

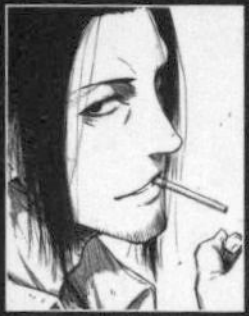

RYOSUKE SHIBA
Ninja, Bureau of Espionage

Chief of Special Operations Division 2 at the Bureau of Espionage, a secret national agency whose mission is the surveillance and disposal of mononoke. Founder of a new squad, code named: Black Torch.

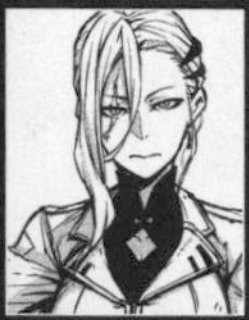

TOKO KUSUMI
Ninja, Bureau of Espionage

Shiba's co-worker and a coldly logical woman. She is the Chief of Special Operations Division 1, the largest and most influential division inside the Bureau of Espionage.

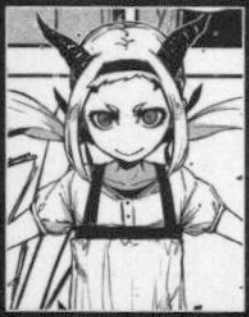

FUYO
Mononoke

A mononoke that looks like a little girl. Friendly with humans, she helps Shiba out with various training activities.

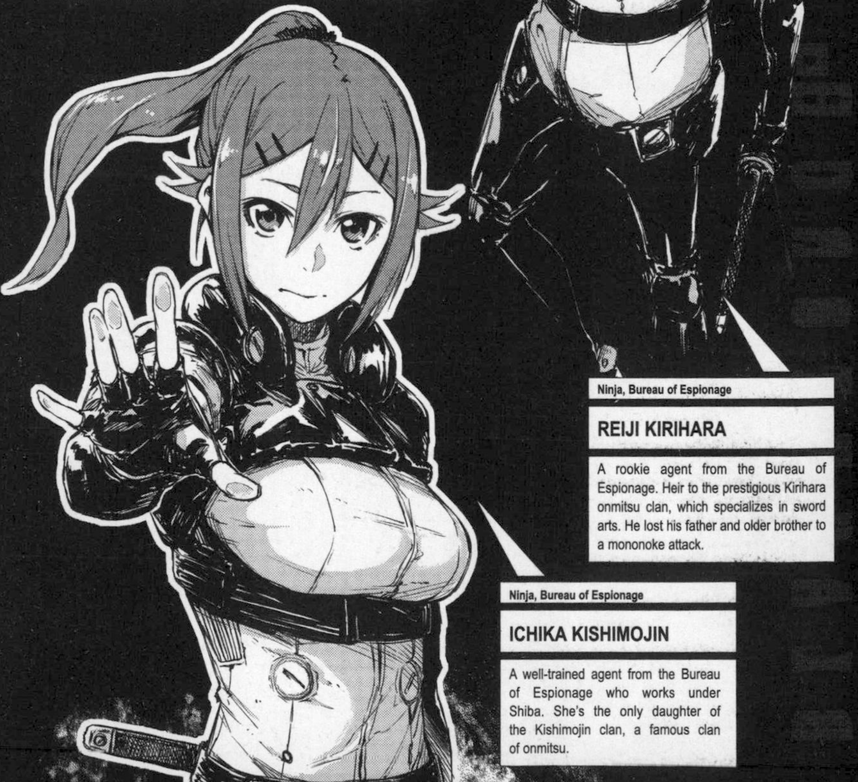

Ninja, Bureau of Espionage
REIJI KIRIHARA

A rookie agent from the Bureau of Espionage. Heir to the prestigious Kirihara onmitsu clan, which specializes in sword arts. He lost his father and older brother to a mononoke attack.

Ninja, Bureau of Espionage
ICHIKA KISHIMOJIN

A well-trained agent from the Bureau of Espionage who works under Shiba. She's the only daughter of the Kishimojin clan, a famous clan of onmitsu.

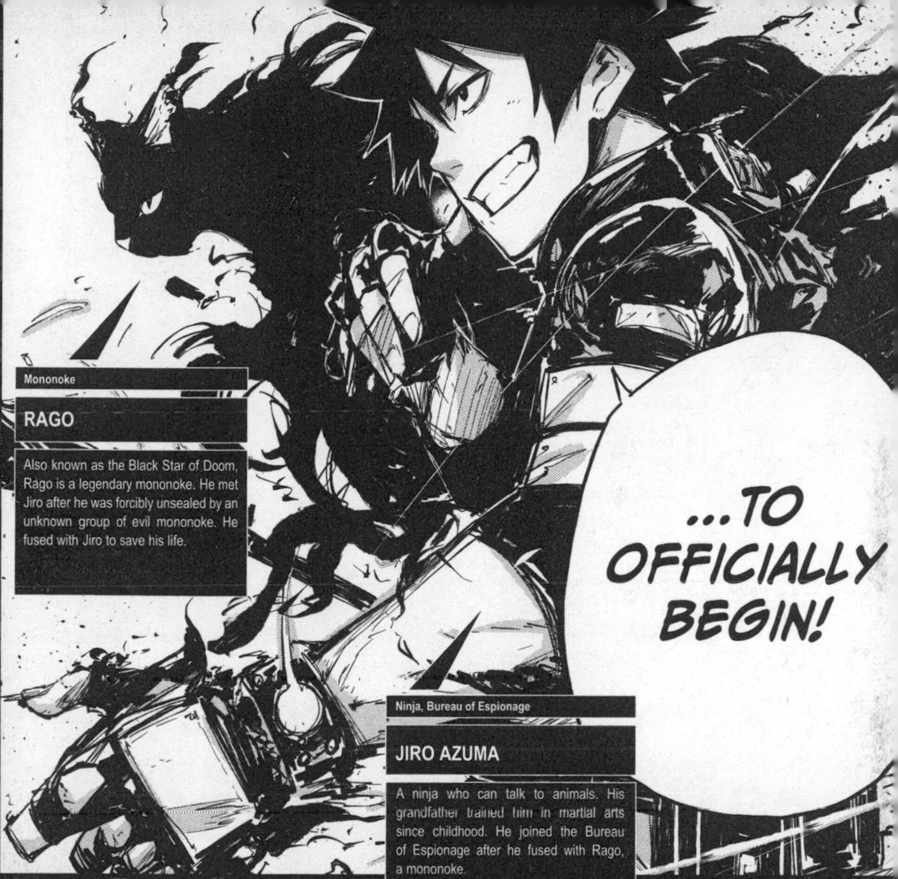
...TO OFFICIALLY BEGIN!
Mononoke
RAGO
Also known as the Black Star of Doom, Rago is a legendary mononoke. He met Jiro after he was forcibly unsealed by an unknown group of evil mononoke. He fused with Jiro to save his life.
Ninja, Bureau of Espionage
JIRO AZUMA
A ninja who can talk to animals. His grandfather trained him in martial arts since childhood. He joined the Bureau of Espionage after he fused with Rago, a mononoke.

STORY

Jiro Azuma, a ninja who can talk to animals and was raised by his grandfather, meets a mononoke named Rago. Mononoke are immortal demons with extraordinary supernatural powers. Rago is badly injured and Jiro, who has a soft spot for the animals he can talk to, treats Rago's wounds. Another mononoke attacks Rago and Jiro dies protecting him. Rago returns the favor by fusing with Jiro, bringing him back from death but forever changing his life forever. This fusion gives Jiro the power to crush his opponents with Rago's power, but he is no longer human.

Ryosuke Shiba invites Jiro and Rago to join the Bureau of Espionage, and together with Ichika Kishimojin and Reiji Kirihara, they form the new ninja squad code named: Black Torch! Their first mission leads them to the place where Rago had been sealed. They successfully fight off the mononoke there, but it leaves them with a cryptic message about Jiro's birth father.

Days later, the squad is brought together for some anti-mononoke training. Forced into an illusion courtesy of the human-friendly mononoke Fuyo, each member of the group confronts their own individual trials. Reiji faces his late elder brother Shinji, who was consumed by the sword Yamakaze. Ichika must battle with the stone statue that her mother had become. Both of them manage to surpass their challenges, safely emerging from Fuyo's illusion. Jiro and Rago, however, must do battle with a colossal black panther...?!

CONTENTS

3

BLACK TORCH

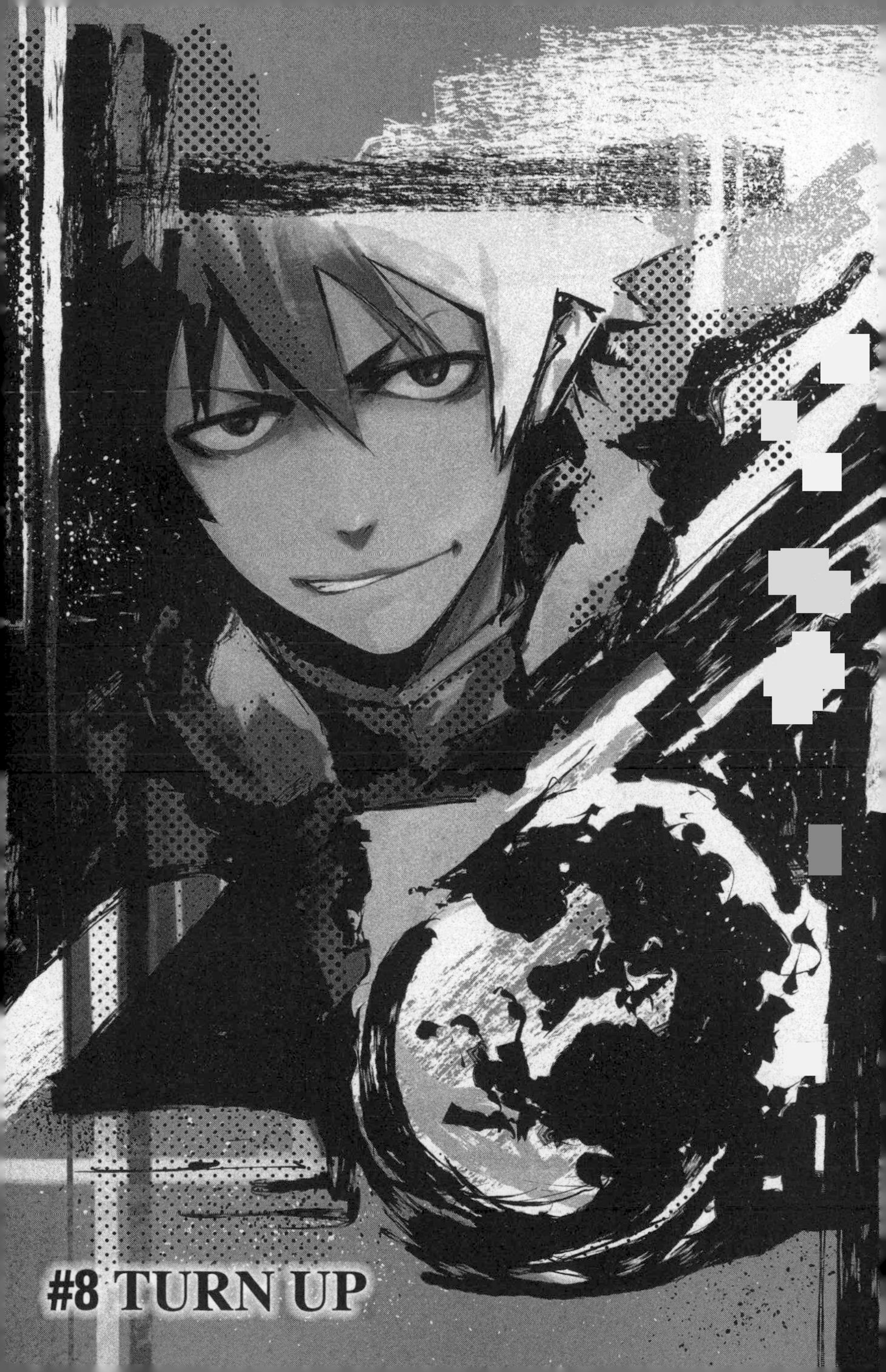
#8 TURN UP

BLACK TORCH

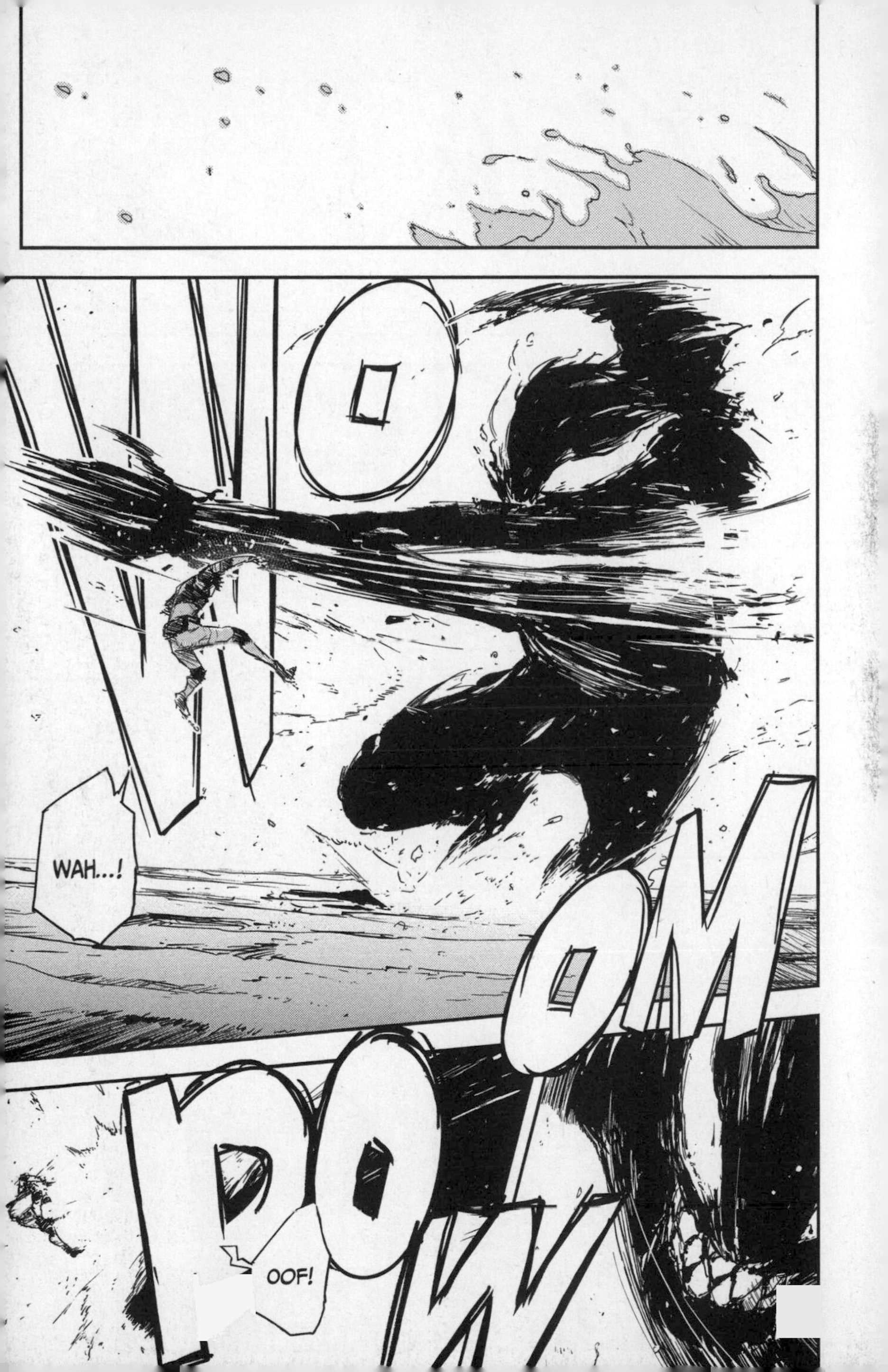
WAH...!
OOF!

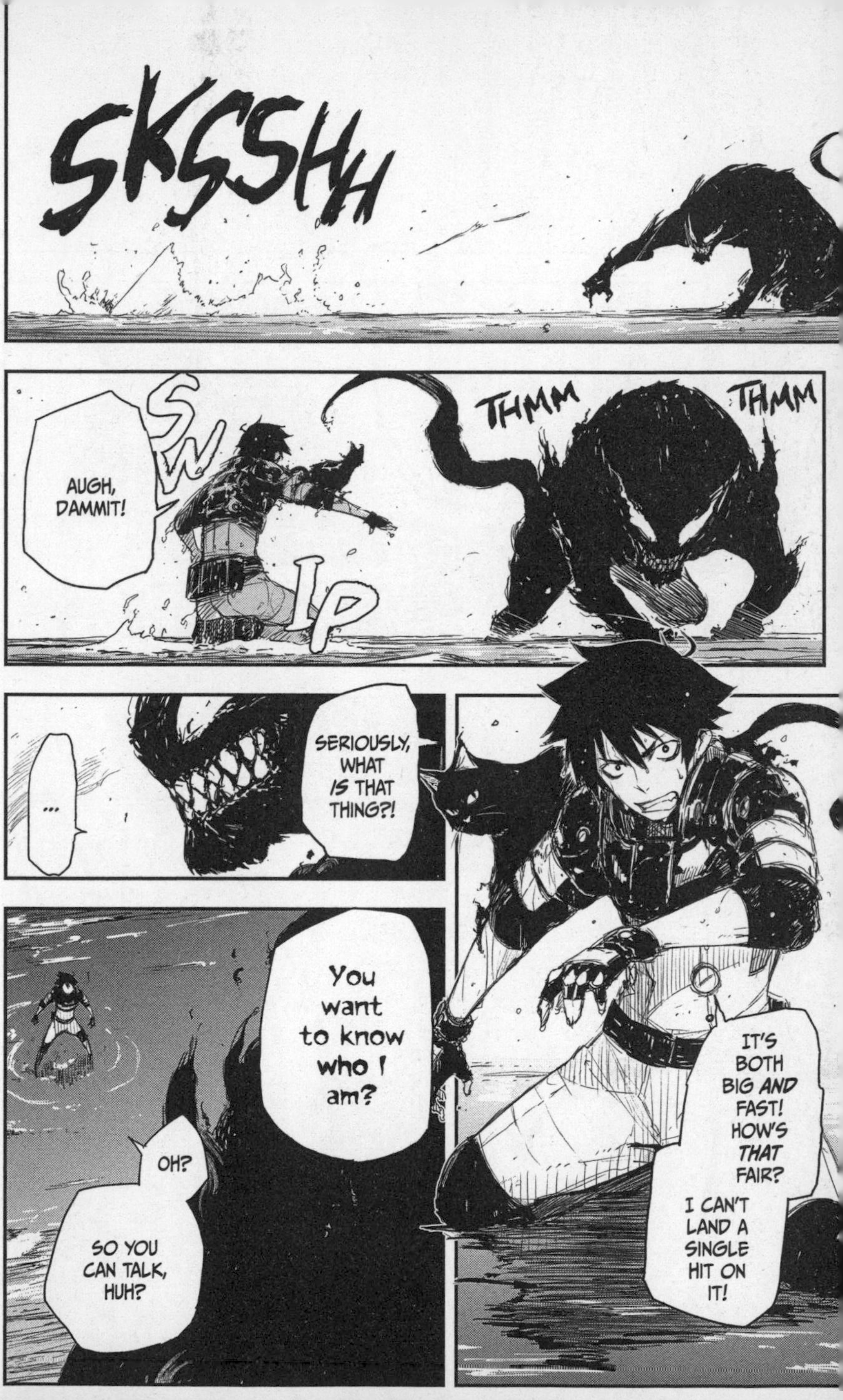
SKSHHH
THMM
THMM
SWIP
AUGH, DAMMIT!
IT'S BOTH BIG *AND* FAST! HOW'S *THAT* FAIR?
I CAN'T LAND A SINGLE HIT ON IT!
SERIOUSLY, WHAT *IS* THAT THING?!
...
You want to know who I am?
OH?
SO YOU CAN TALK, HUH?

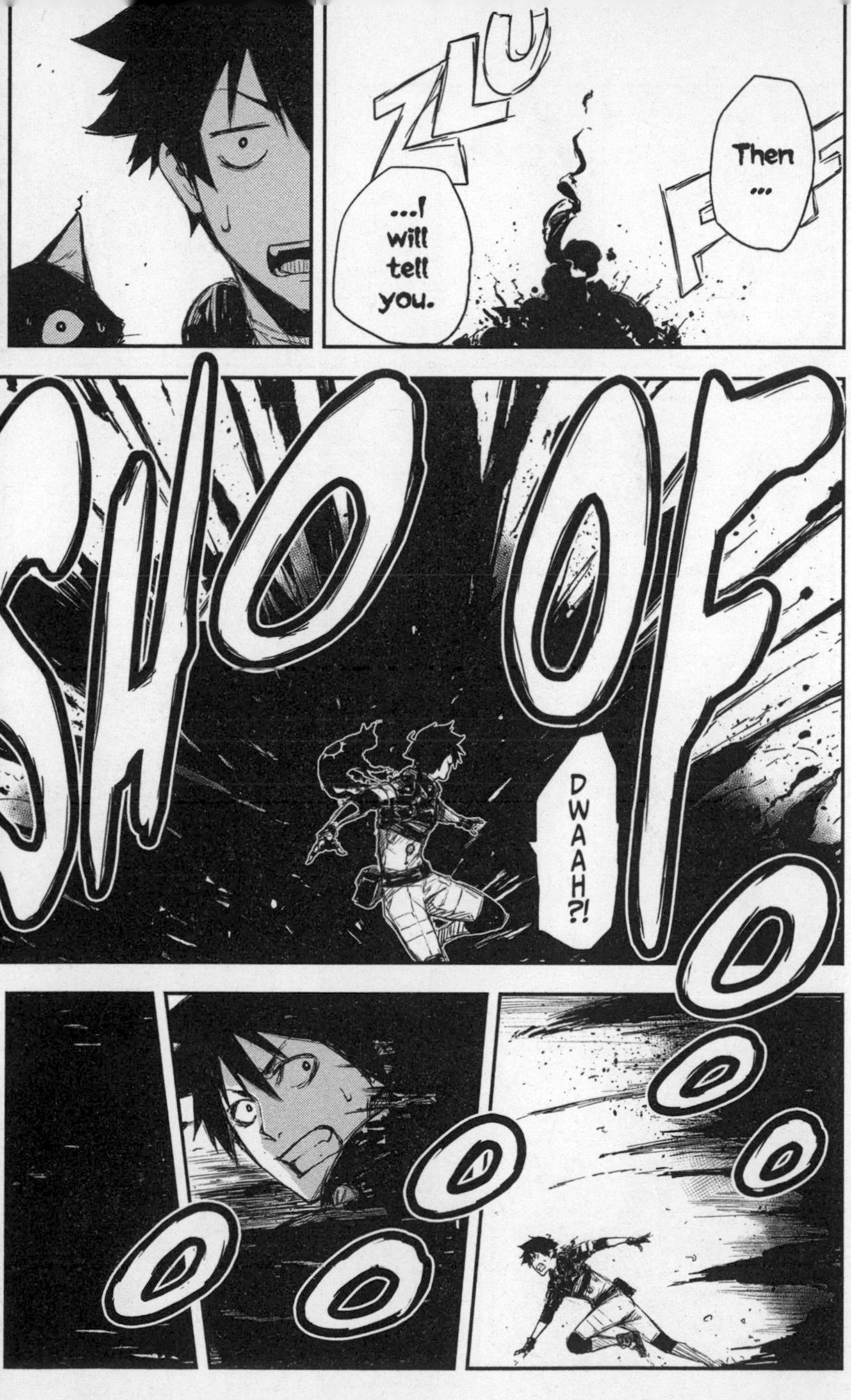
Then ...
ZZU
...I will tell you.
SHOOF
DWAAH?!

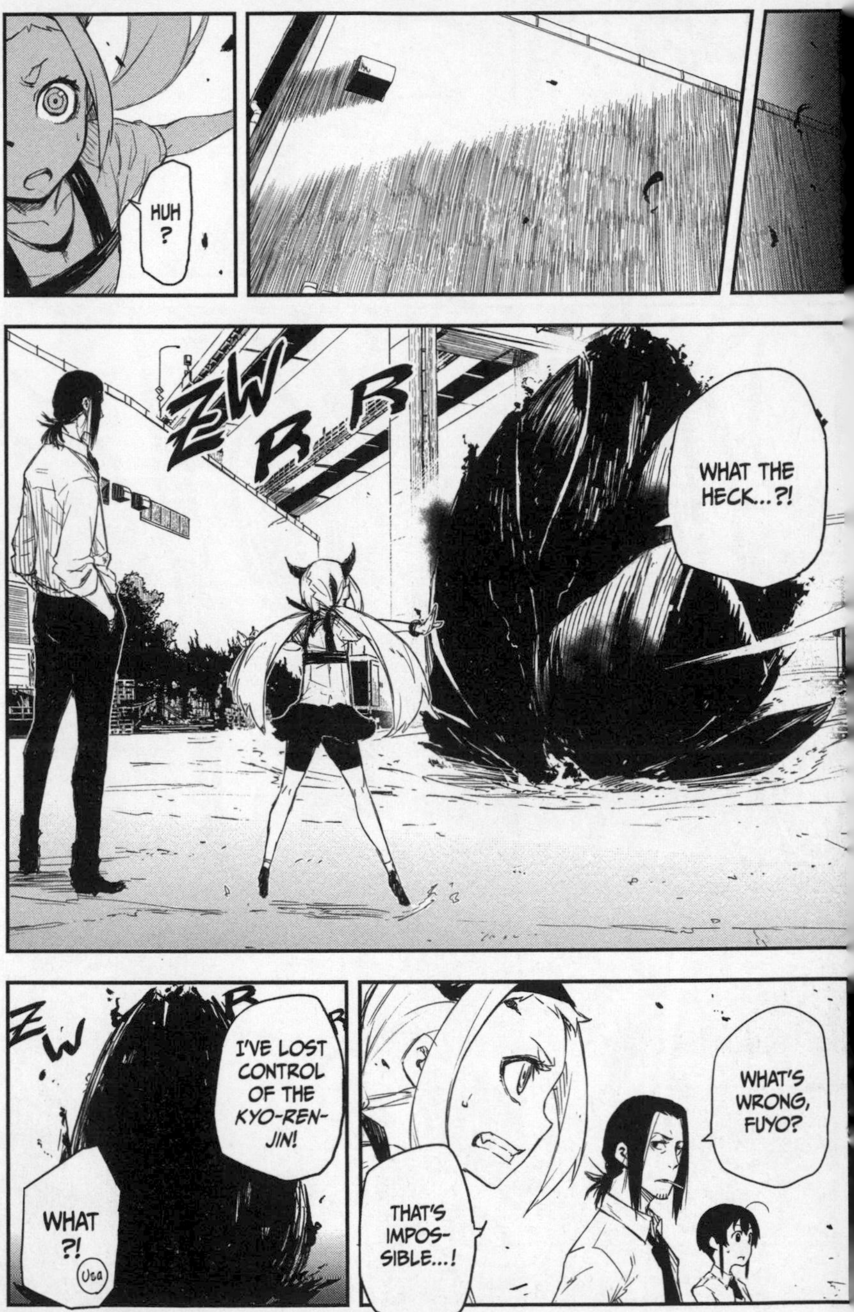
HUH?
WHAT THE HECK...?!
ZWRR
WHAT'S WRONG, FUYO?
THAT'S IMPOSSIBLE...!
ZWRR
I'VE LOST CONTROL OF THE KYO-REN-JIN!
WHAT?!
Usa

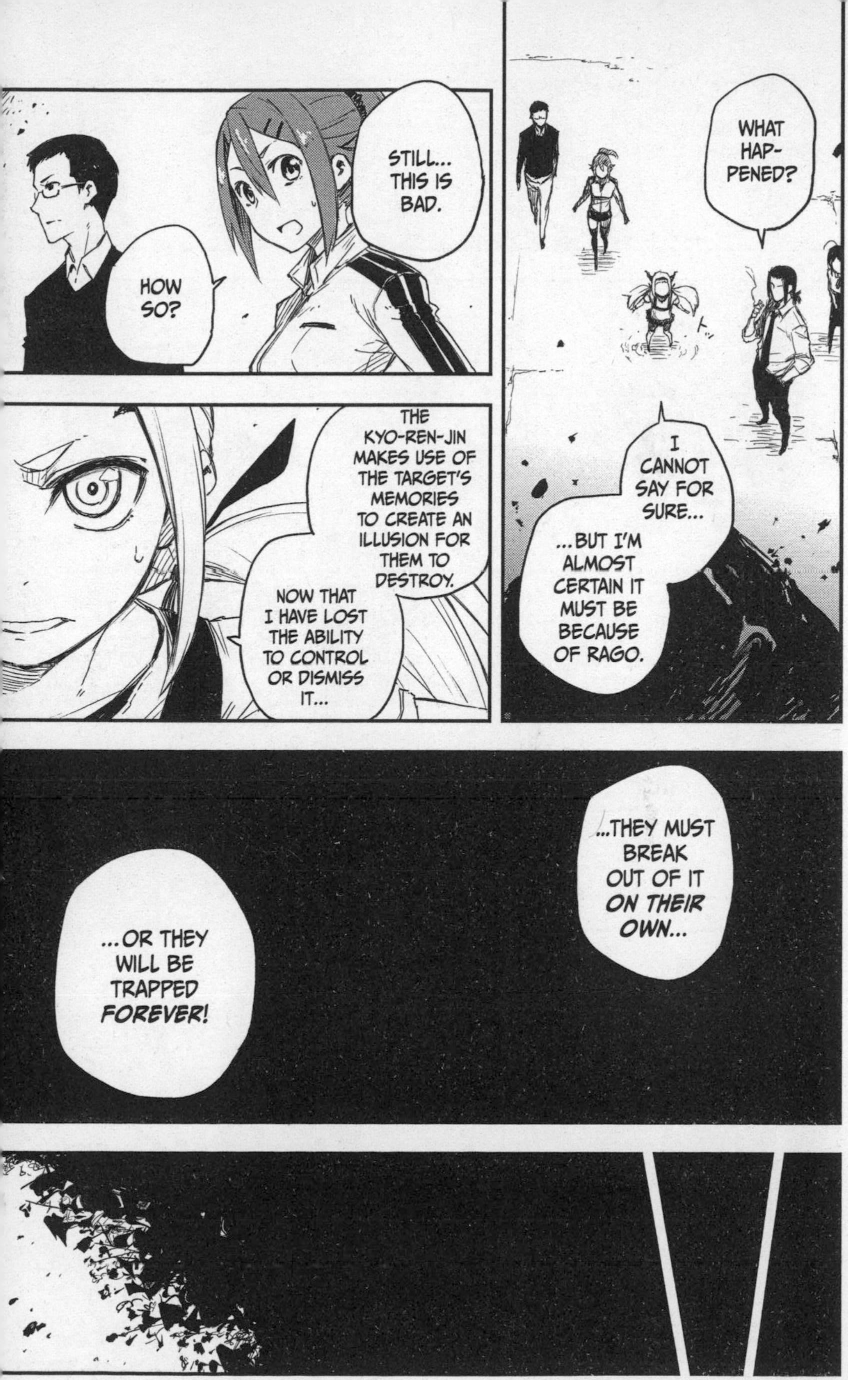
WHAT HAP-PENED?
I CANNOT SAY FOR SURE...
...BUT I'M ALMOST CERTAIN IT MUST BE BECAUSE OF RAGO.
STILL... THIS IS BAD.
HOW SO?
THE KYO-REN-JIN MAKES USE OF THE TARGET'S MEMORIES TO CREATE AN ILLUSION FOR THEM TO DESTROY.
NOW THAT I HAVE LOST THE ABILITY TO CONTROL OR DISMISS IT...
...THEY MUST BREAK OUT OF IT *ON THEIR OWN...*
...OR THEY WILL BE TRAPPED *FOREVER!*

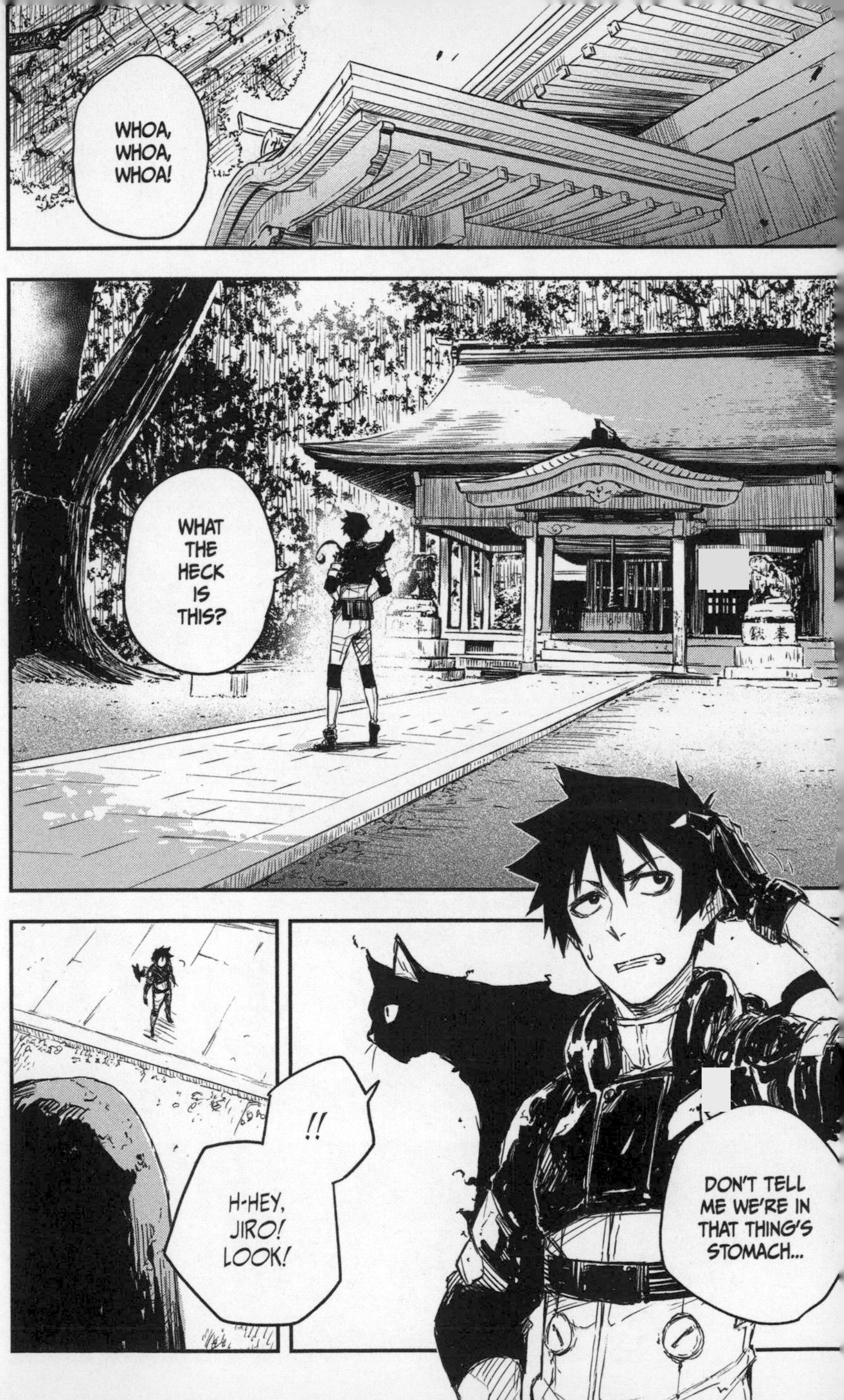
WHOA, WHOA, WHOA!
WHAT THE HECK IS THIS?
DON'T TELL ME WE'RE IN THAT THING'S STOMACH...
!!
H-HEY, JIRO! LOOK!

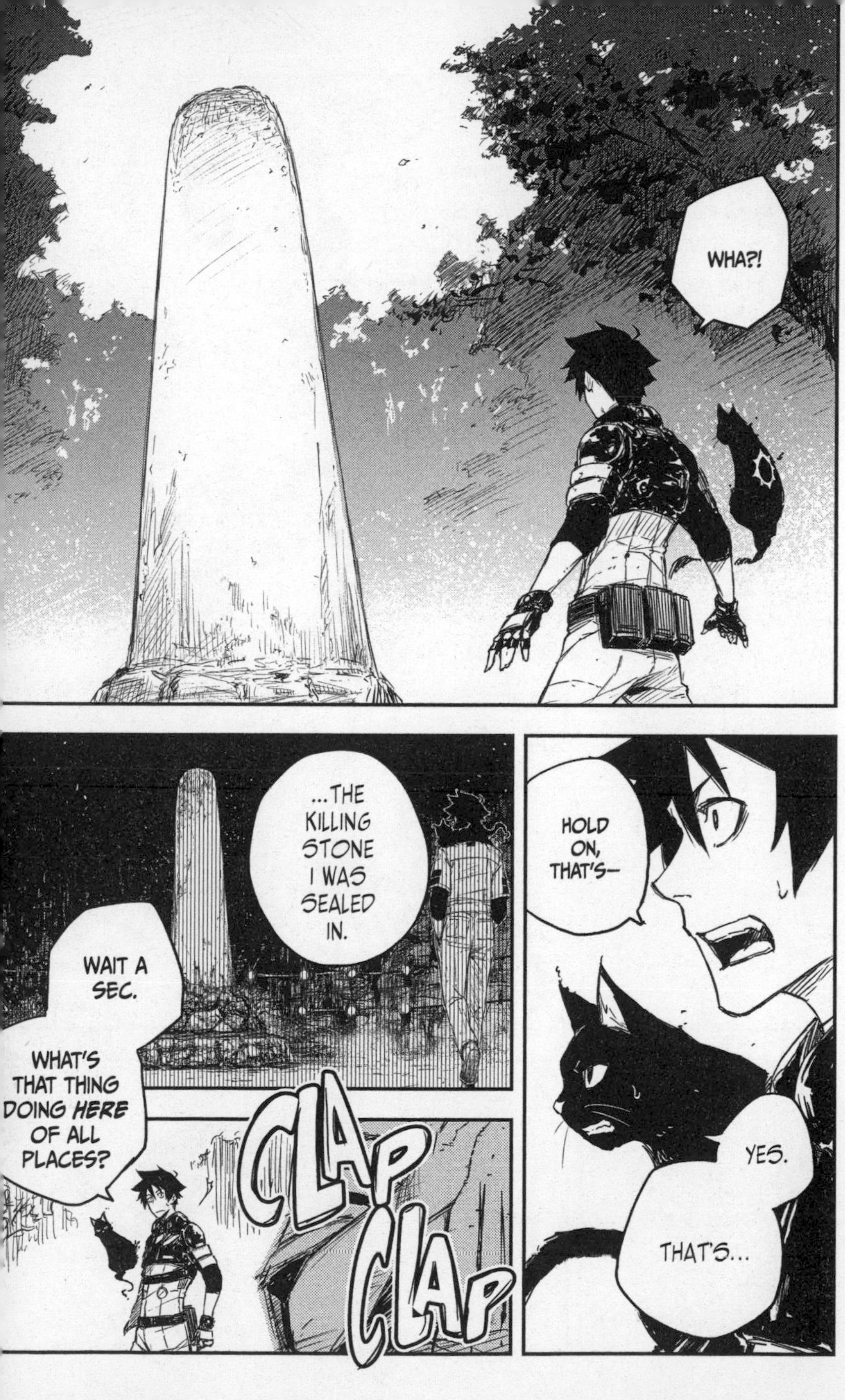
WHA?!
HOLD ON, THAT'S—
YES.
THAT'S...
...THE KILLING STONE I WAS SEALED IN.
WAIT A SEC.
WHAT'S THAT THING DOING *HERE* OF ALL PLACES?
CLAP CLAP

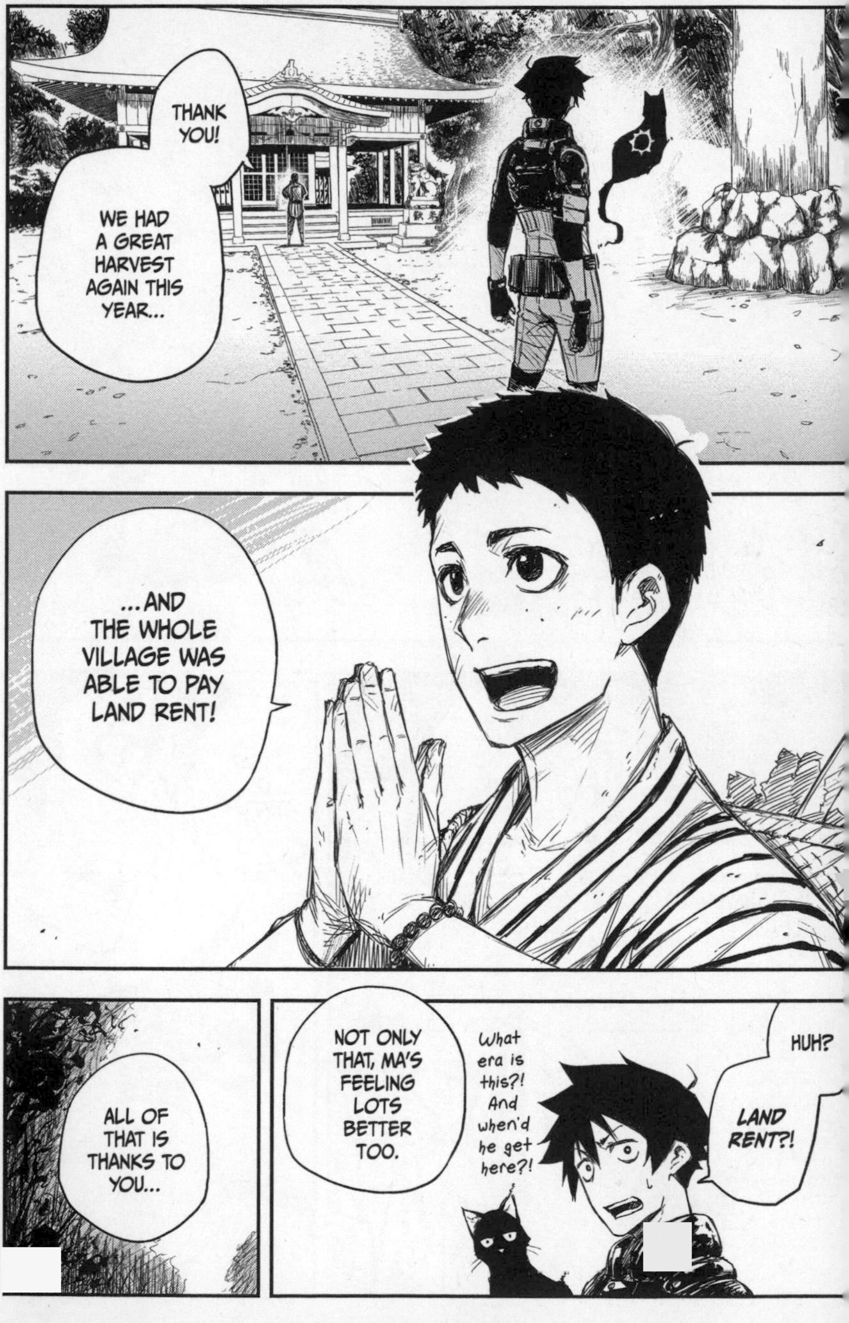
THANK YOU!
WE HAD A GREAT HARVEST AGAIN THIS YEAR...
...AND THE WHOLE VILLAGE WAS ABLE TO PAY LAND RENT!
HUH?
LAND RENT?!
NOT ONLY THAT, MA'S FEELING LOTS BETTER TOO.
What era is this?! And when'd he get here?!
ALL OF THAT IS THANKS TO YOU...

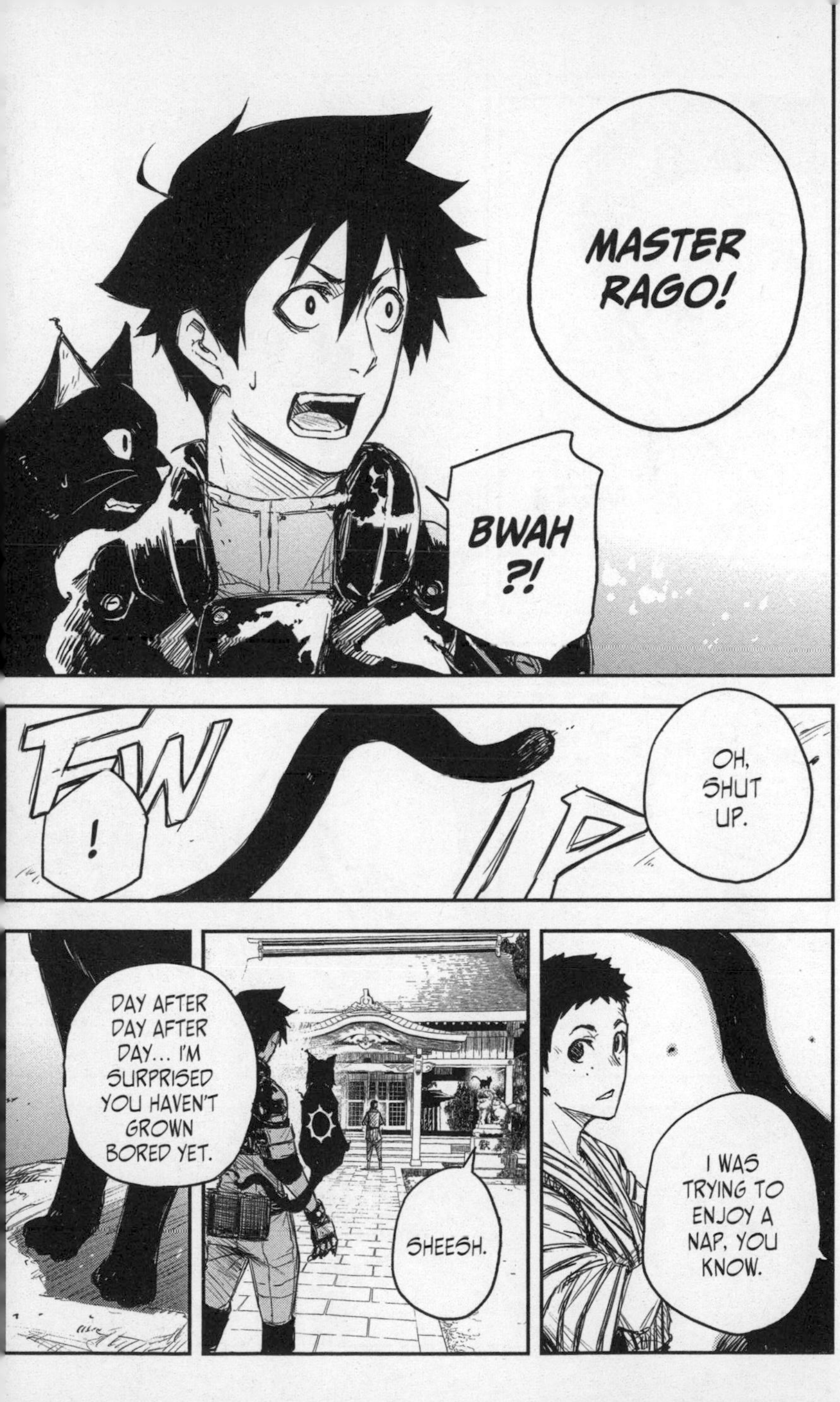
MASTER RAGO!
BWAH ?!
OH, SHUT UP.
FWIP
!
I WAS TRYING TO ENJOY A NAP, YOU KNOW.
SHEESH.
DAY AFTER DAY AFTER DAY… I'M SURPRISED YOU HAVEN'T GROWN BORED YET.

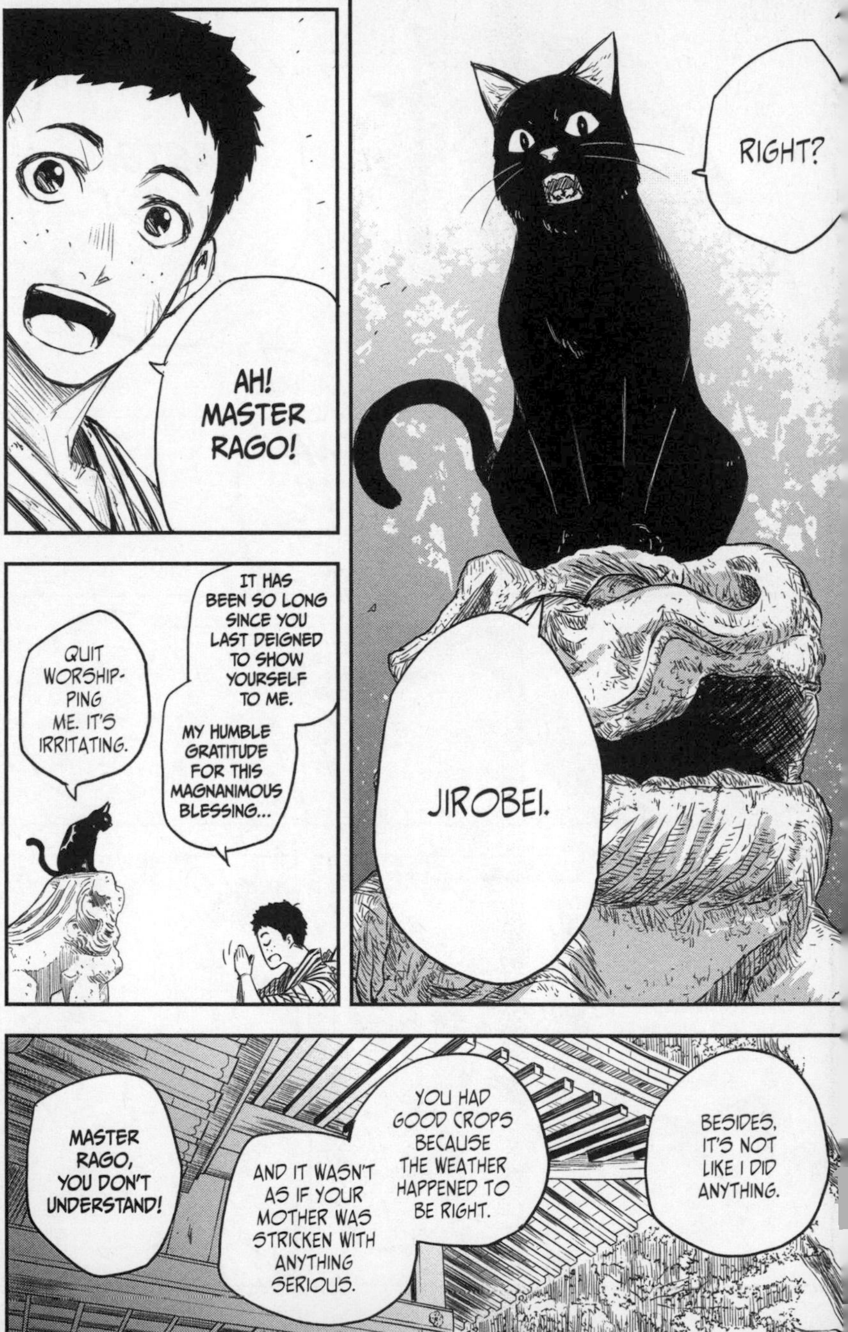
RIGHT?
JIROBEI.
AH! MASTER RAGO!
IT HAS BEEN SO LONG SINCE YOU LAST DEIGNED TO SHOW YOURSELF TO ME.
MY HUMBLE GRATITUDE FOR THIS MAGNANIMOUS BLESSING...
QUIT WORSHIP-PING ME. IT'S IRRITATING.
BESIDES, IT'S NOT LIKE I DID ANYTHING.
YOU HAD GOOD CROPS BECAUSE THE WEATHER HAPPENED TO BE RIGHT.
AND IT WASN'T AS IF YOUR MOTHER WAS STRICKEN WITH ANYTHING SERIOUS.
MASTER RAGO, YOU DON'T UNDERSTAND!

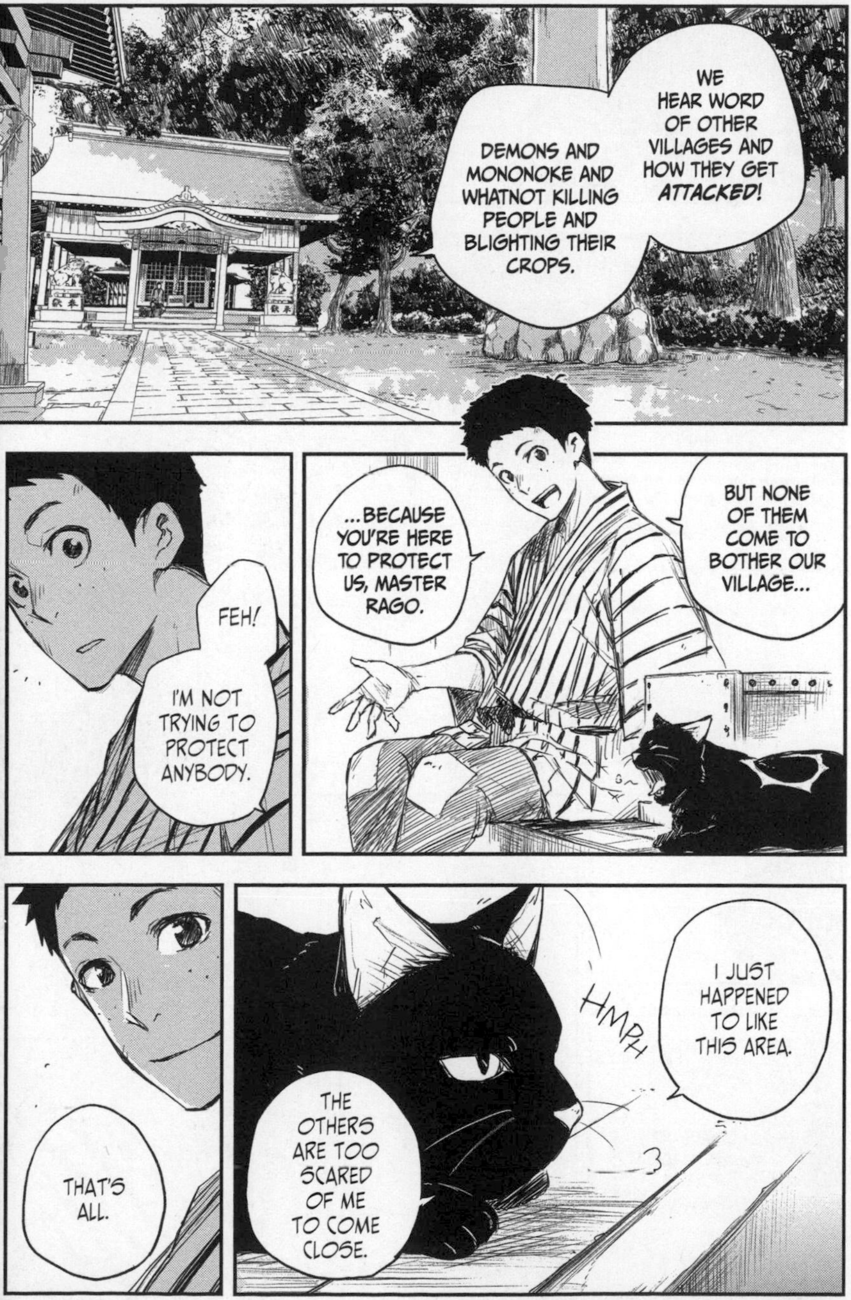
WE HEAR WORD OF OTHER VILLAGES AND HOW THEY GET *ATTACKED!*
DEMONS AND MONONOKE AND WHATNOT KILLING PEOPLE AND BLIGHTING THEIR CROPS.
BUT NONE OF THEM COME TO BOTHER OUR VILLAGE...
...BECAUSE YOU'RE HERE TO PROTECT US, MASTER RAGO.
FEH!
I'M NOT TRYING TO PROTECT ANYBODY.
I JUST HAPPENED TO LIKE THIS AREA.
HMPH
THE OTHERS ARE TOO SCARED OF ME TO COME CLOSE.
THAT'S ALL.

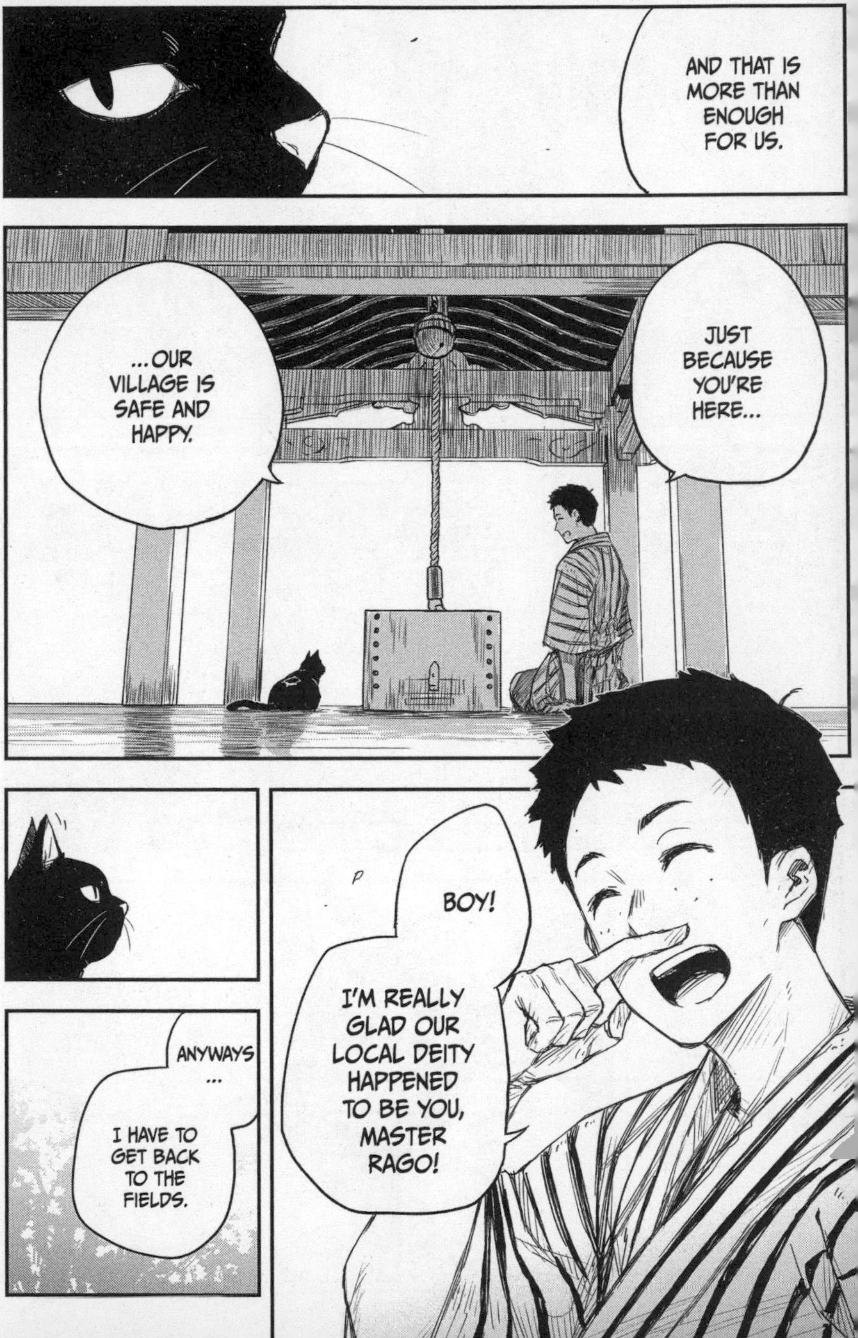
AND THAT IS MORE THAN ENOUGH FOR US.
JUST BECAUSE YOU'RE HERE...
...OUR VILLAGE IS SAFE AND HAPPY.
BOY!
I'M REALLY GLAD OUR LOCAL DEITY HAPPENED TO BE YOU, MASTER RAGO!
ANYWAYS...
I HAVE TO GET BACK TO THE FIELDS.

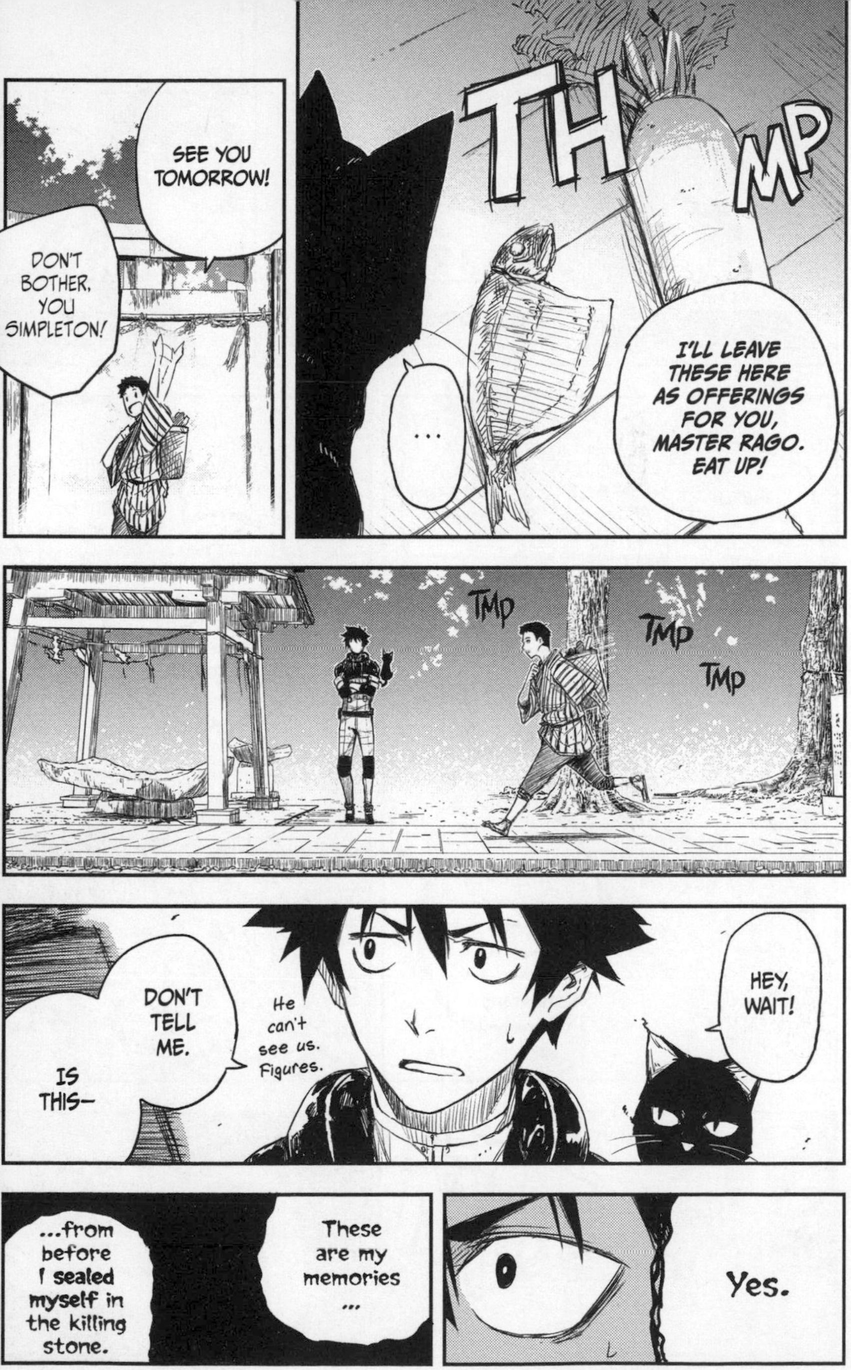
THOMP
I'LL LEAVE THESE HERE AS OFFERINGS FOR YOU, MASTER RAGO. EAT UP!
...
SEE YOU TOMORROW!
DON'T BOTHER, YOU SIMPLETON!
TMP
TMP
TMP
HEY, WAIT!
He can't see us. Figures.
DON'T TELL ME.
IS THIS—
Yes.
These are my memories...
...from before I sealed myself in the killing stone.

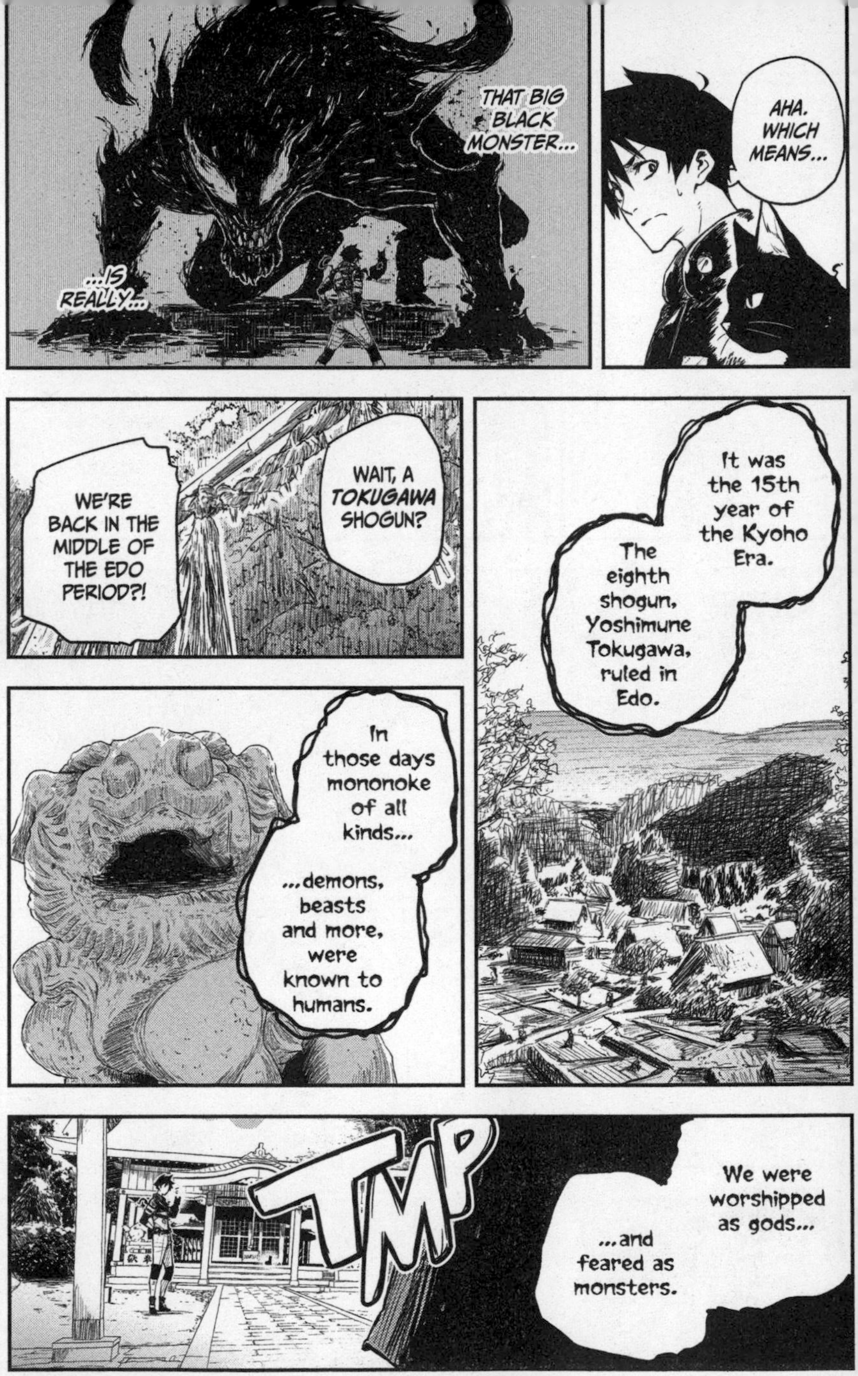
AHA. WHICH MEANS...
THAT BIG BLACK MONSTER...
...IS REALLY...
It was the 15th year of the Kyoho Era.
The eighth shogun, Yoshimune Tokugawa, ruled in Edo.
WAIT, A *TOKUGAWA* SHOGUN?
WE'RE BACK IN THE MIDDLE OF THE EDO PERIOD?!
In those days mononoke of all kinds...
...demons, beasts and more, were known to humans.
We were worshipped as gods...
...and feared as monsters.
TMP

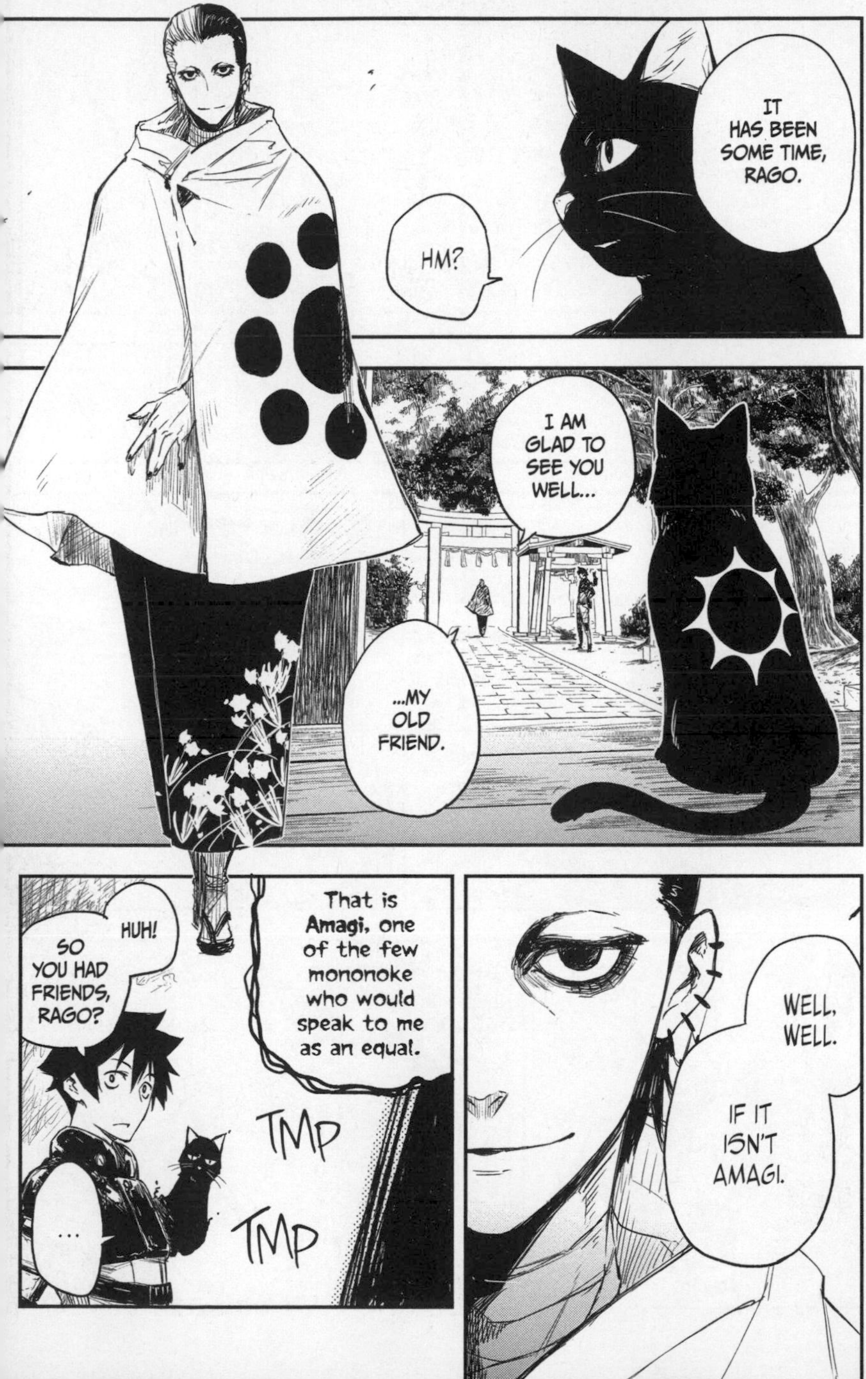
IT HAS BEEN SOME TIME, RAGO.
HM?
I AM GLAD TO SEE YOU WELL...
...MY OLD FRIEND.
WELL, WELL.
IF IT ISN'T AMAGI.
That is **Amagi**, one of the few mononoke who would speak to me as an equal.
HUH!
SO YOU HAD FRIENDS, RAGO?
TMP
TMP
...

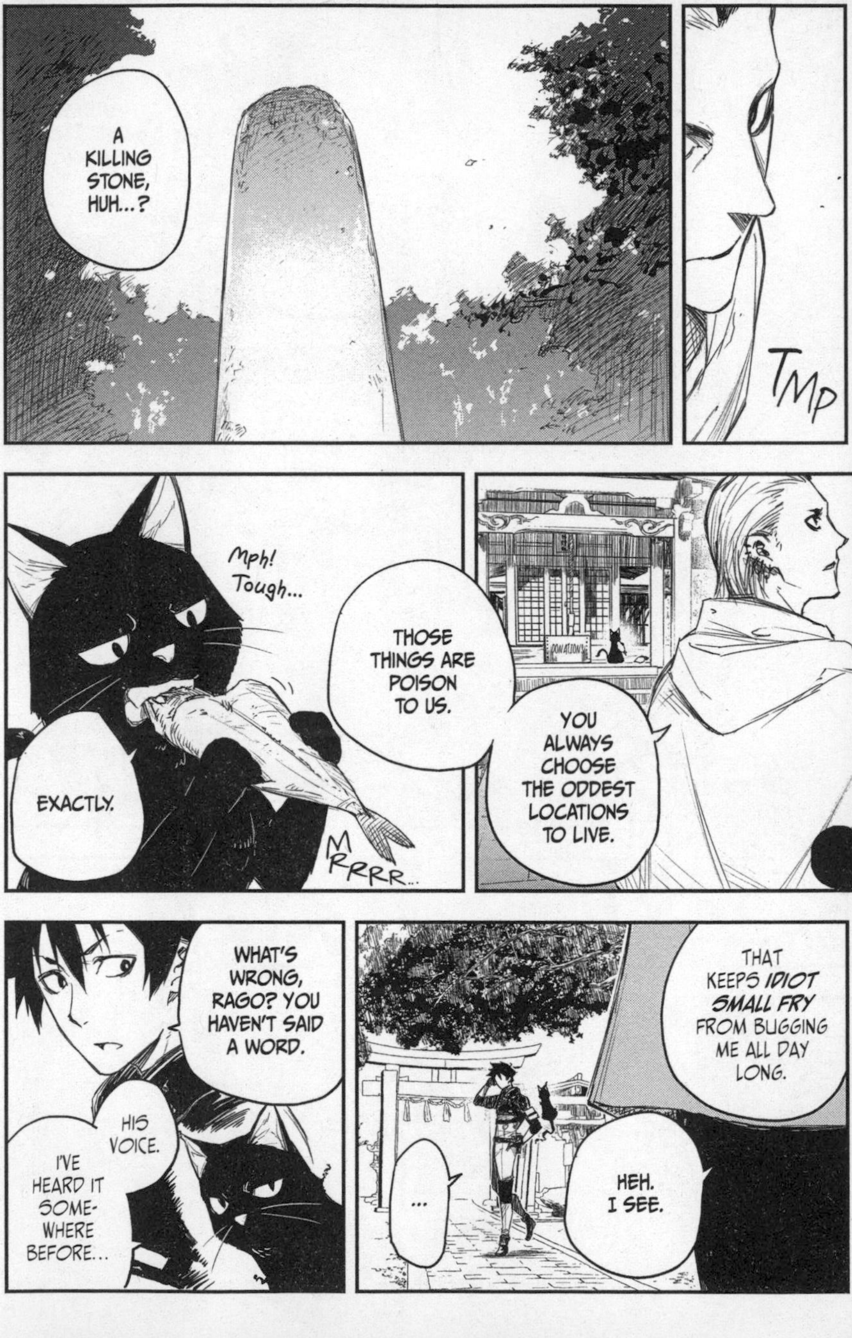
TMP
A KILLING STONE, HUH...?
DONATIONS
YOU ALWAYS CHOOSE THE ODDEST LOCATIONS TO LIVE.
Mph! Tough...
THOSE THINGS ARE POISON TO US.
EXACTLY.
MRRRR...
THAT KEEPS *IDIOT SMALL FRY* FROM BUGGING ME ALL DAY LONG.
HEH. I SEE.
...
WHAT'S WRONG, RAGO? YOU HAVEN'T SAID A WORD.
HIS VOICE.
I'VE HEARD IT SOME-WHERE BEFORE...

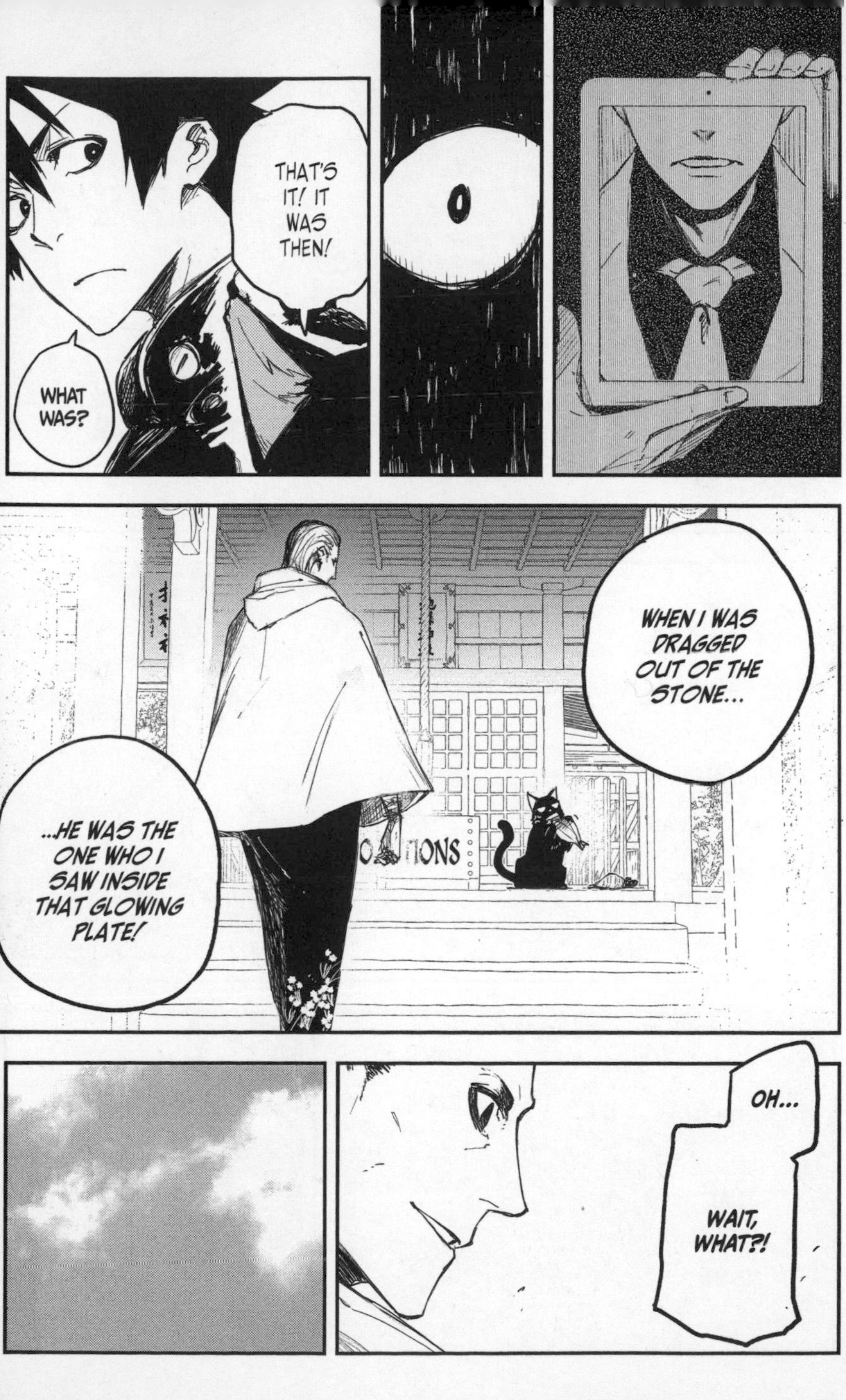
THAT'S IT! IT WAS THEN!
WHAT WAS?
WHEN I WAS DRAGGED OUT OF THE STONE...
...HE WAS THE ONE WHO I SAW INSIDE THAT GLOWING PLATE!
OH...
WAIT, WHAT?!

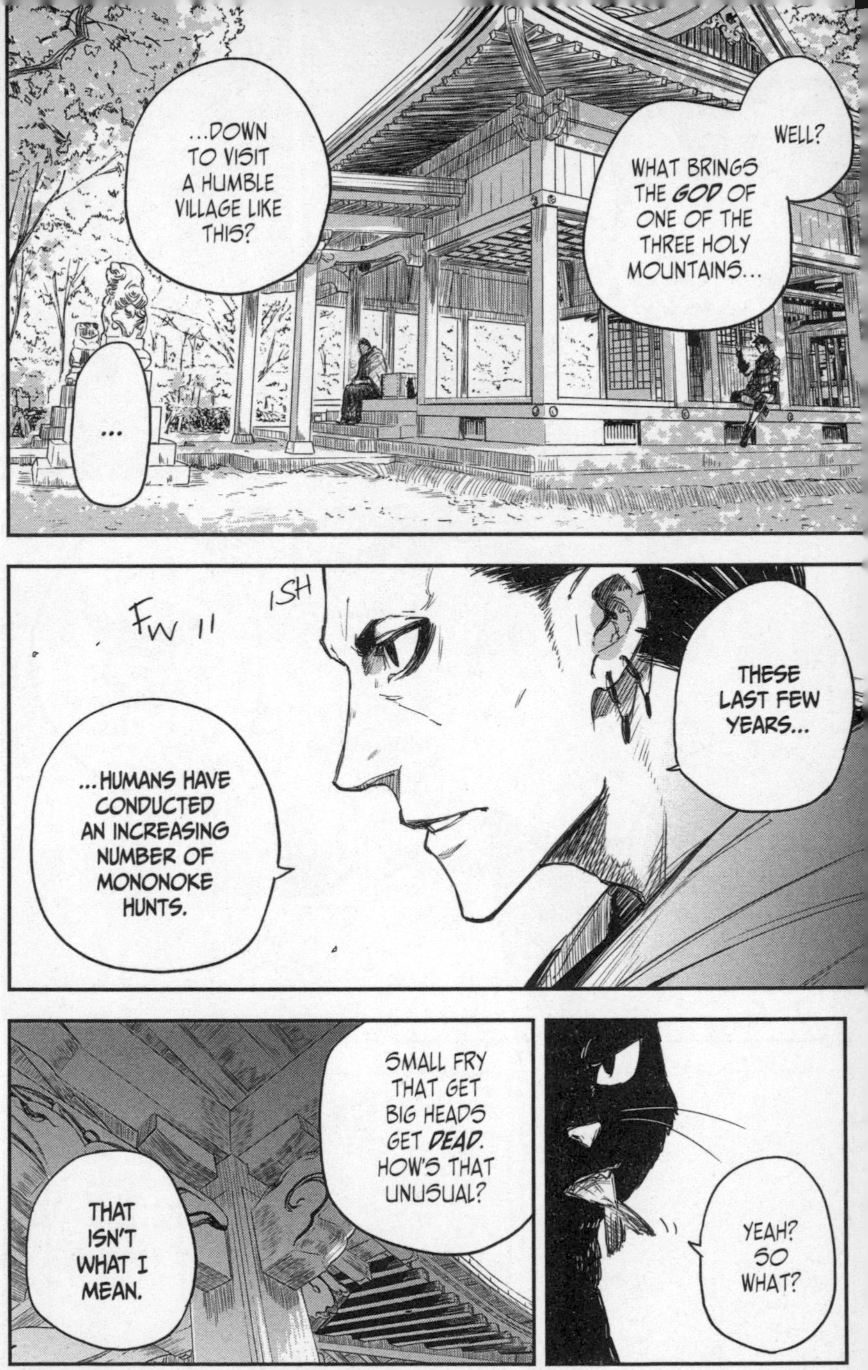
WELL?
WHAT BRINGS THE *GOD* OF ONE OF THE THREE HOLY MOUNTAINS...
...DOWN TO VISIT A HUMBLE VILLAGE LIKE THIS?
...
FWISH
THESE LAST FEW YEARS...
...HUMANS HAVE CONDUCTED AN INCREASING NUMBER OF MONONOKE HUNTS.
YEAH? SO WHAT?
SMALL FRY THAT GET BIG HEADS GET *DEAD*. HOW'S THAT UNUSUAL?
THAT ISN'T WHAT I MEAN.

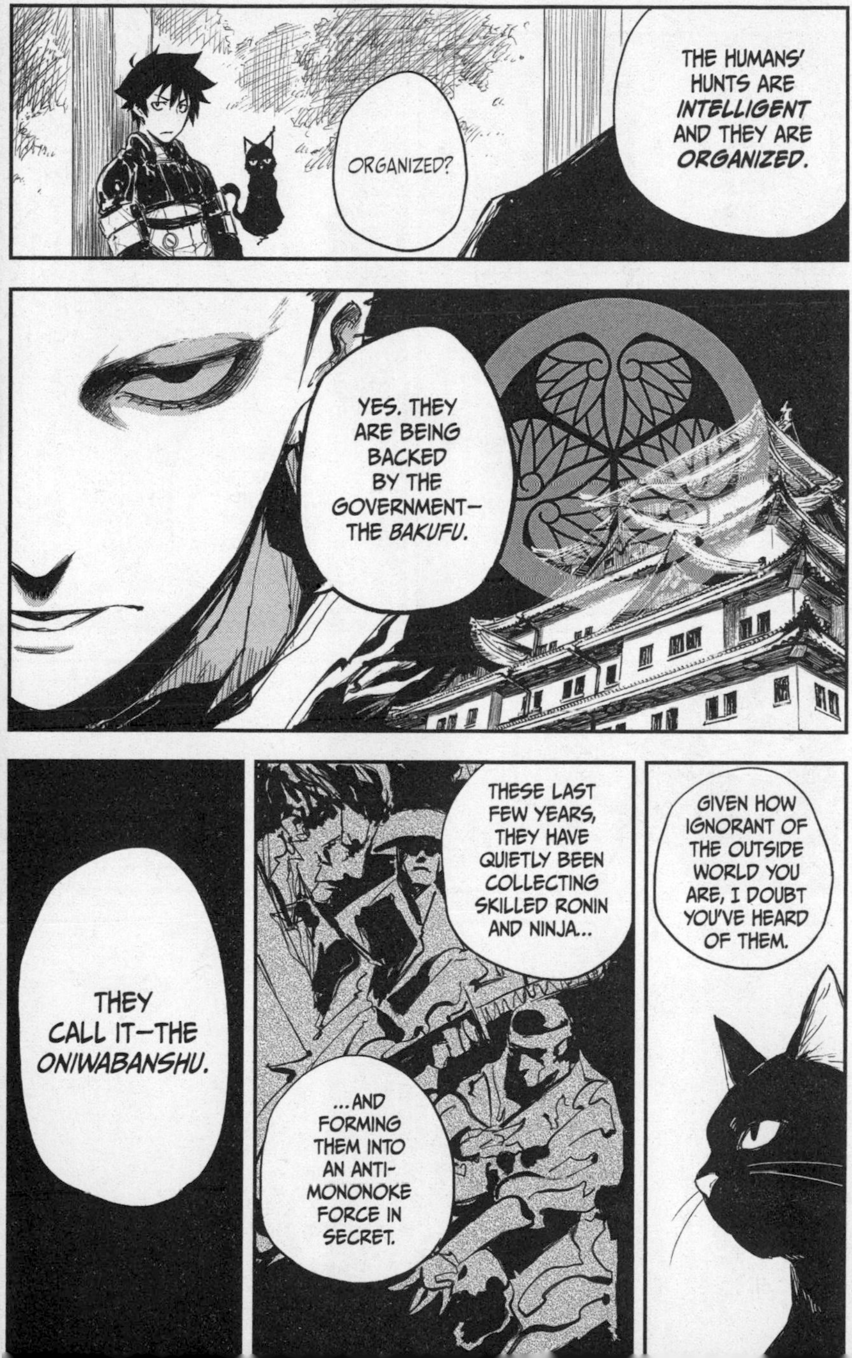
THE HUMANS' HUNTS ARE INTELLIGENT AND THEY ARE ORGANIZED.
ORGANIZED?
YES. THEY ARE BEING BACKED BY THE GOVERNMENT—THE BAKUFU.
GIVEN HOW IGNORANT OF THE OUTSIDE WORLD YOU ARE, I DOUBT YOU'VE HEARD OF THEM.
THESE LAST FEW YEARS, THEY HAVE QUIETLY BEEN COLLECTING SKILLED RONIN AND NINJA...
...AND FORMING THEM INTO AN ANTI-MONONOKE FORCE IN SECRET.
THEY CALL IT—THE ONIWABANSHU.

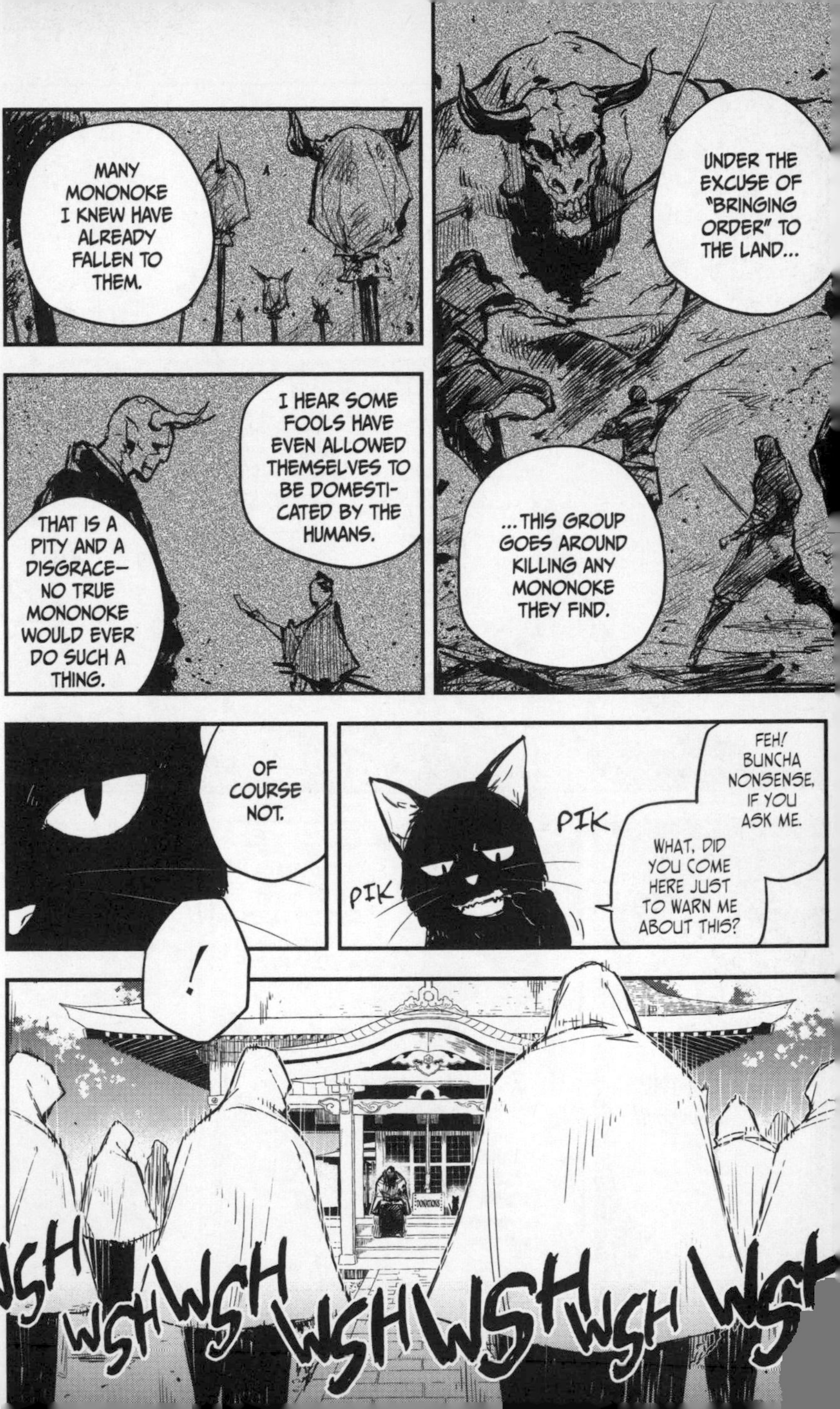
UNDER THE EXCUSE OF "BRINGING ORDER" TO THE LAND...
...THIS GROUP GOES AROUND KILLING ANY MONONOKE THEY FIND.
MANY MONONOKE I KNEW HAVE ALREADY FALLEN TO THEM.
I HEAR SOME FOOLS HAVE EVEN ALLOWED THEMSELVES TO BE DOMESTI-CATED BY THE HUMANS.
THAT IS A PITY AND A DISGRACE— NO TRUE MONONOKE WOULD EVER DO SUCH A THING.
FEH! BUNCHA NONSENSE, IF YOU ASK ME.
PIK
WHAT, DID YOU COME HERE JUST TO WARN ME ABOUT THIS?
PIK
OF COURSE NOT.
!
DONATIONS
WSH WSH WSH WSH WSH WSH WSH WSH

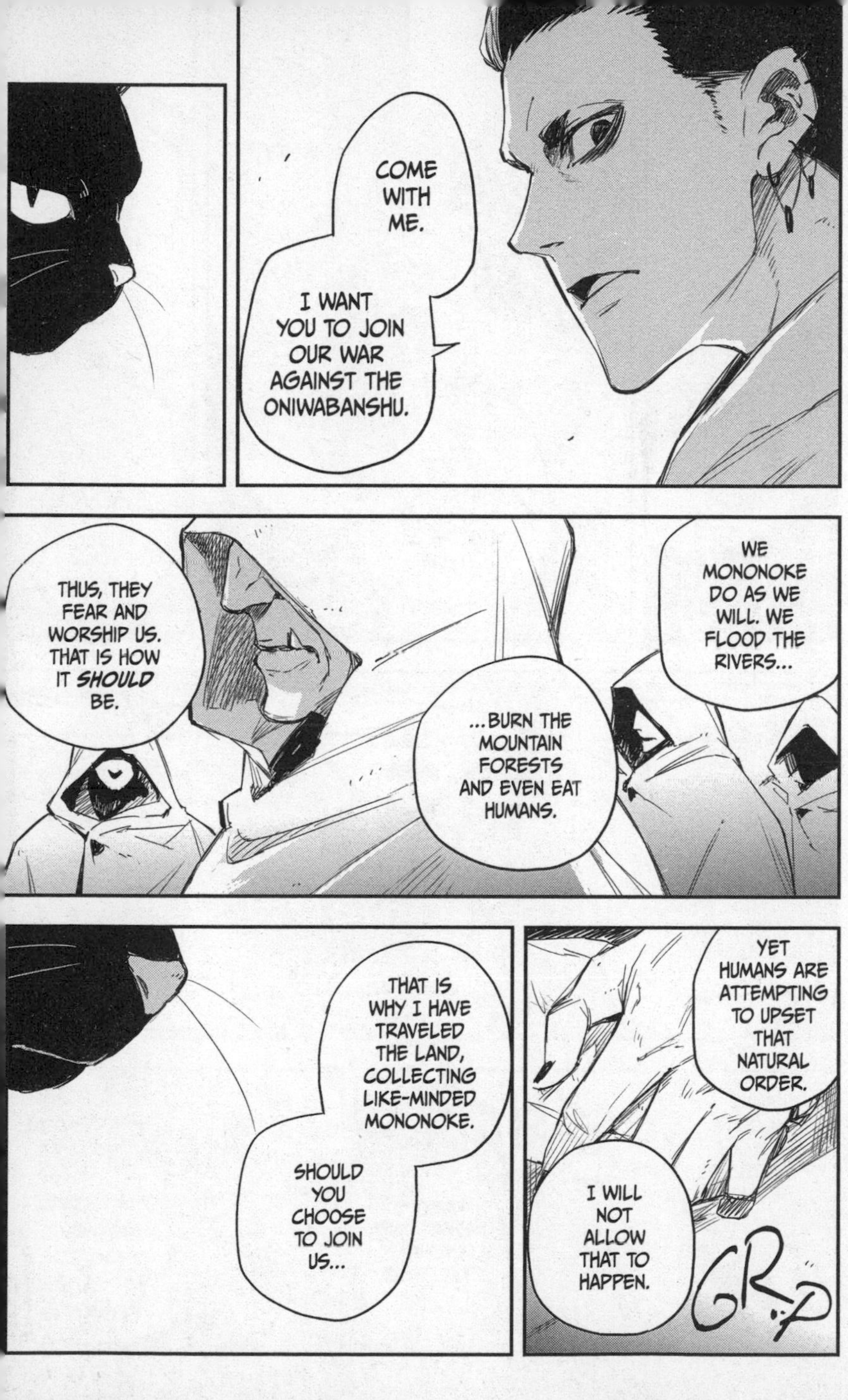
COME WITH ME.
I WANT YOU TO JOIN OUR WAR AGAINST THE ONIWABANSHU.
WE MONONOKE DO AS WE WILL. WE FLOOD THE RIVERS...
...BURN THE MOUNTAIN FORESTS AND EVEN EAT HUMANS.
THUS, THEY FEAR AND WORSHIP US. THAT IS HOW IT *SHOULD* BE.
YET HUMANS ARE ATTEMPTING TO UPSET THAT NATURAL ORDER.
I WILL NOT ALLOW THAT TO HAPPEN.
THAT IS WHY I HAVE TRAVELED THE LAND, COLLECTING LIKE-MINDED MONONOKE.
SHOULD YOU CHOOSE TO JOIN US...

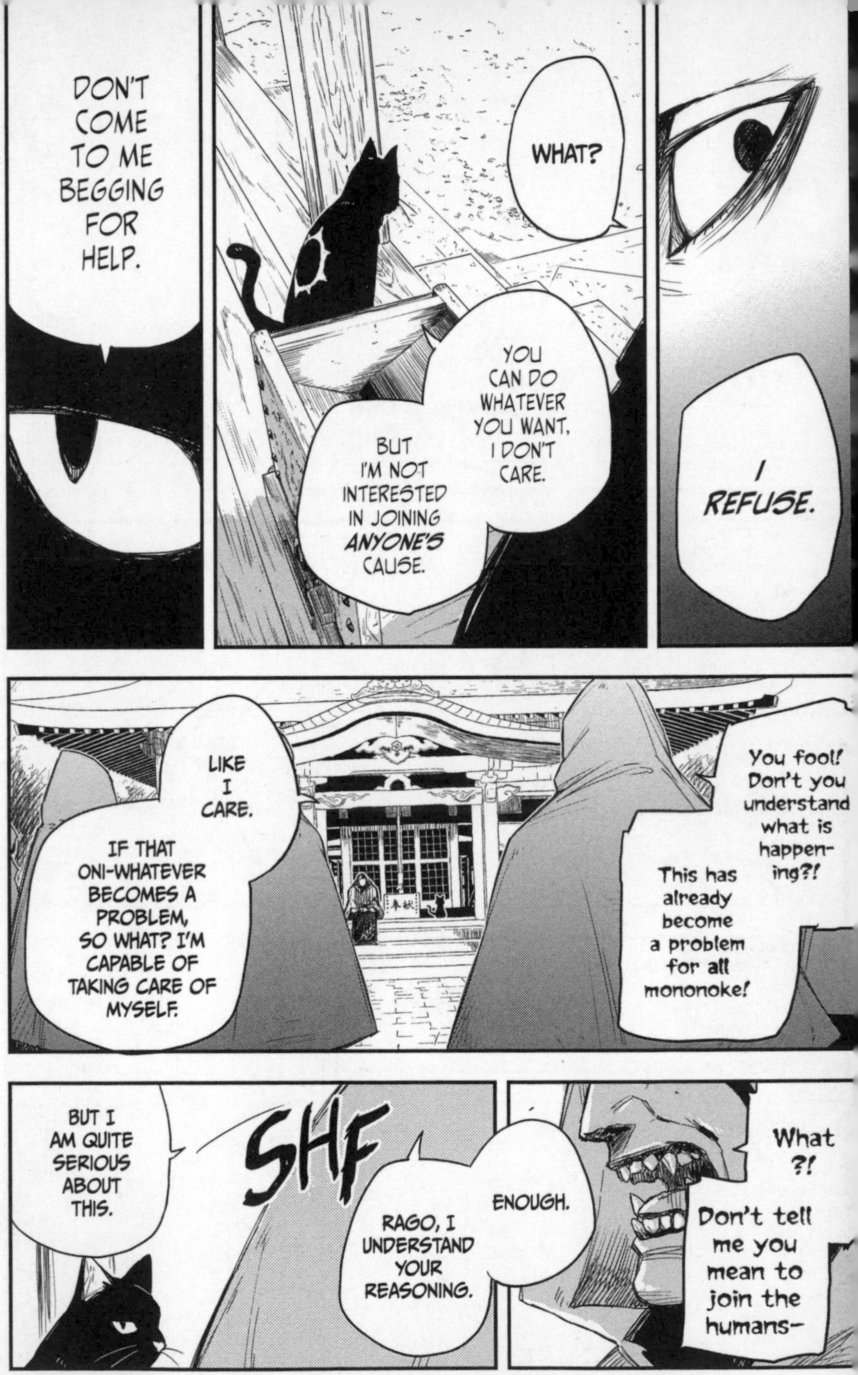
I REFUSE.
WHAT?
YOU CAN DO WHATEVER YOU WANT, I DON'T CARE.
BUT I'M NOT INTERESTED IN JOINING ANYONE'S CAUSE.
DON'T COME TO ME BEGGING FOR HELP.
You fool! Don't you understand what is happen-ing?!
This has already become a problem for all mononoke!
LIKE I CARE.
IF THAT ONI-WHATEVER BECOMES A PROBLEM, SO WHAT? I'M CAPABLE OF TAKING CARE OF MYSELF.
What ?!
Don't tell me you mean to join the humans-
SHF
ENOUGH.
RAGO, I UNDERSTAND YOUR REASONING.
BUT I AM QUITE SERIOUS ABOUT THIS.

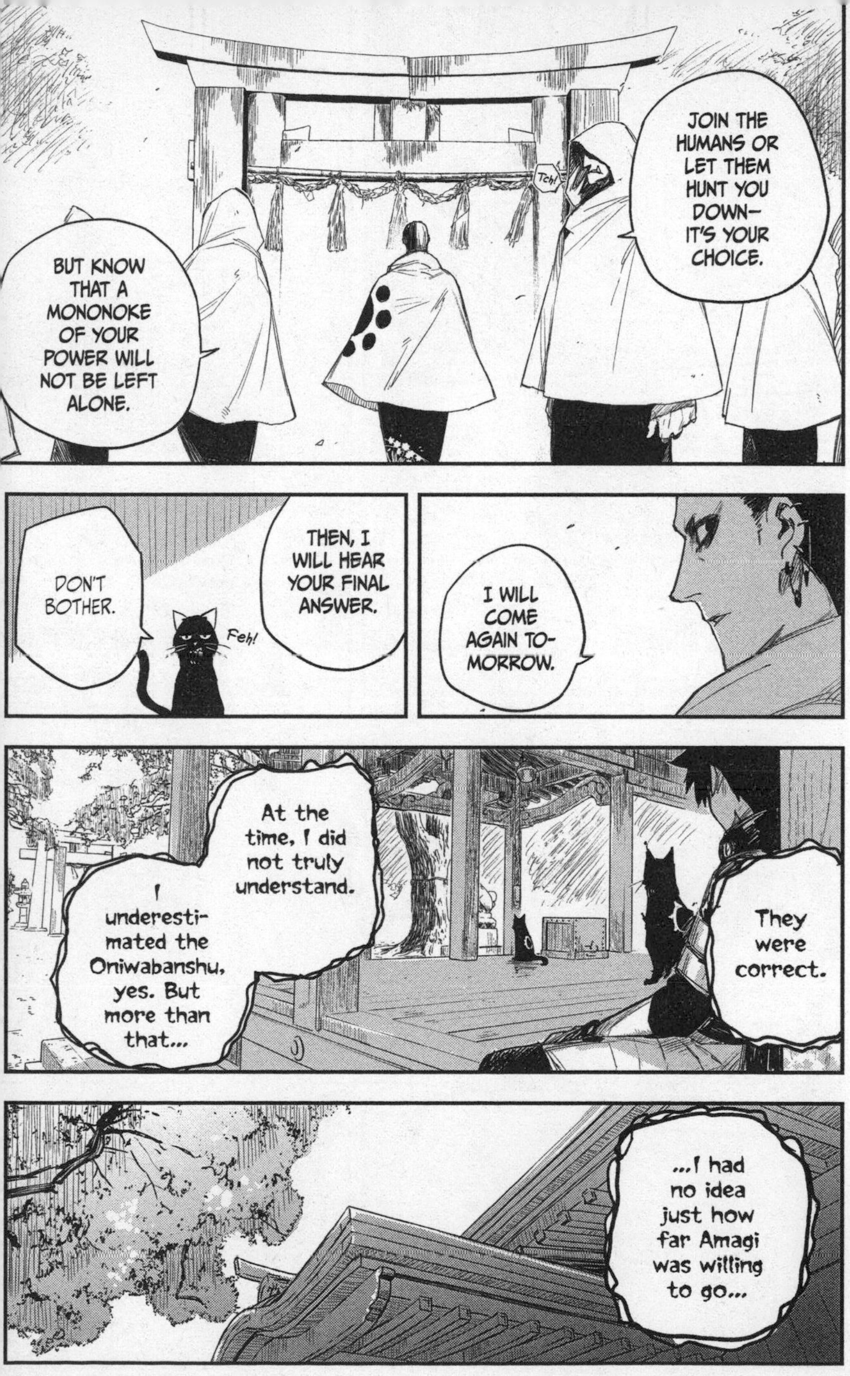
JOIN THE HUMANS OR LET THEM HUNT YOU DOWN— IT'S YOUR CHOICE.
Tch!
BUT KNOW THAT A MONONOKE OF YOUR POWER WILL NOT BE LEFT ALONE.
I WILL COME AGAIN TO-MORROW.
THEN, I WILL HEAR YOUR FINAL ANSWER.
DON'T BOTHER.
Feh!
They were correct.
At the time, I did not truly understand.
I underesti-mated the Oniwabanshu, yes. But more than that...
...I had no idea just how far Amagi was willing to go...

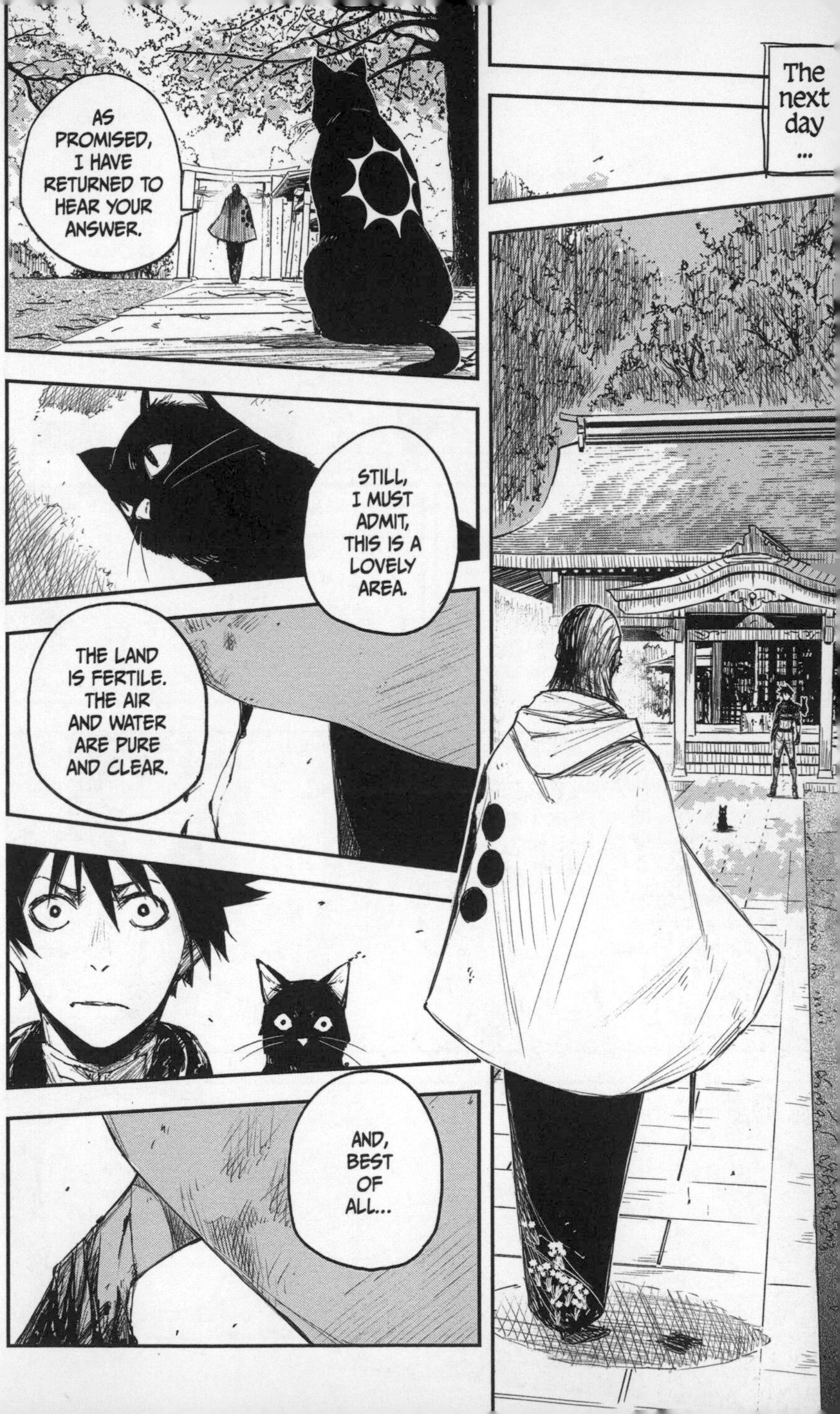
The next day ...
AS PROMISED, I HAVE RETURNED TO HEAR YOUR ANSWER.
STILL, I MUST ADMIT, THIS IS A LOVELY AREA.
THE LAND IS FERTILE. THE AIR AND WATER ARE PURE AND CLEAR.
AND, BEST OF ALL...

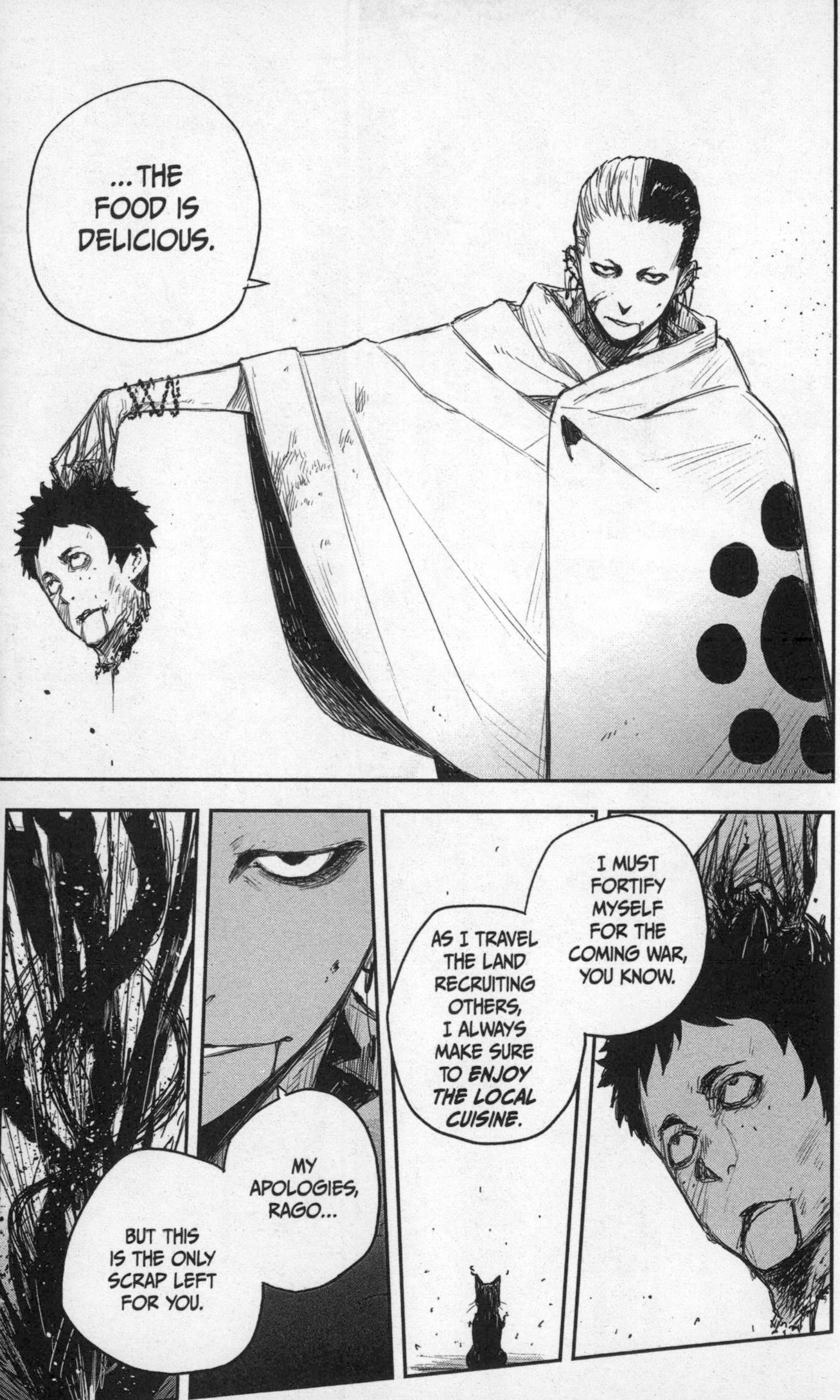
...THE FOOD IS DELICIOUS.
I MUST FORTIFY MYSELF FOR THE COMING WAR, YOU KNOW.
AS I TRAVEL THE LAND RECRUITING OTHERS, I ALWAYS MAKE SURE TO *ENJOY THE LOCAL CUISINE*.
MY APOLOGIES, RAGO...
BUT THIS IS THE ONLY SCRAP LEFT FOR YOU.

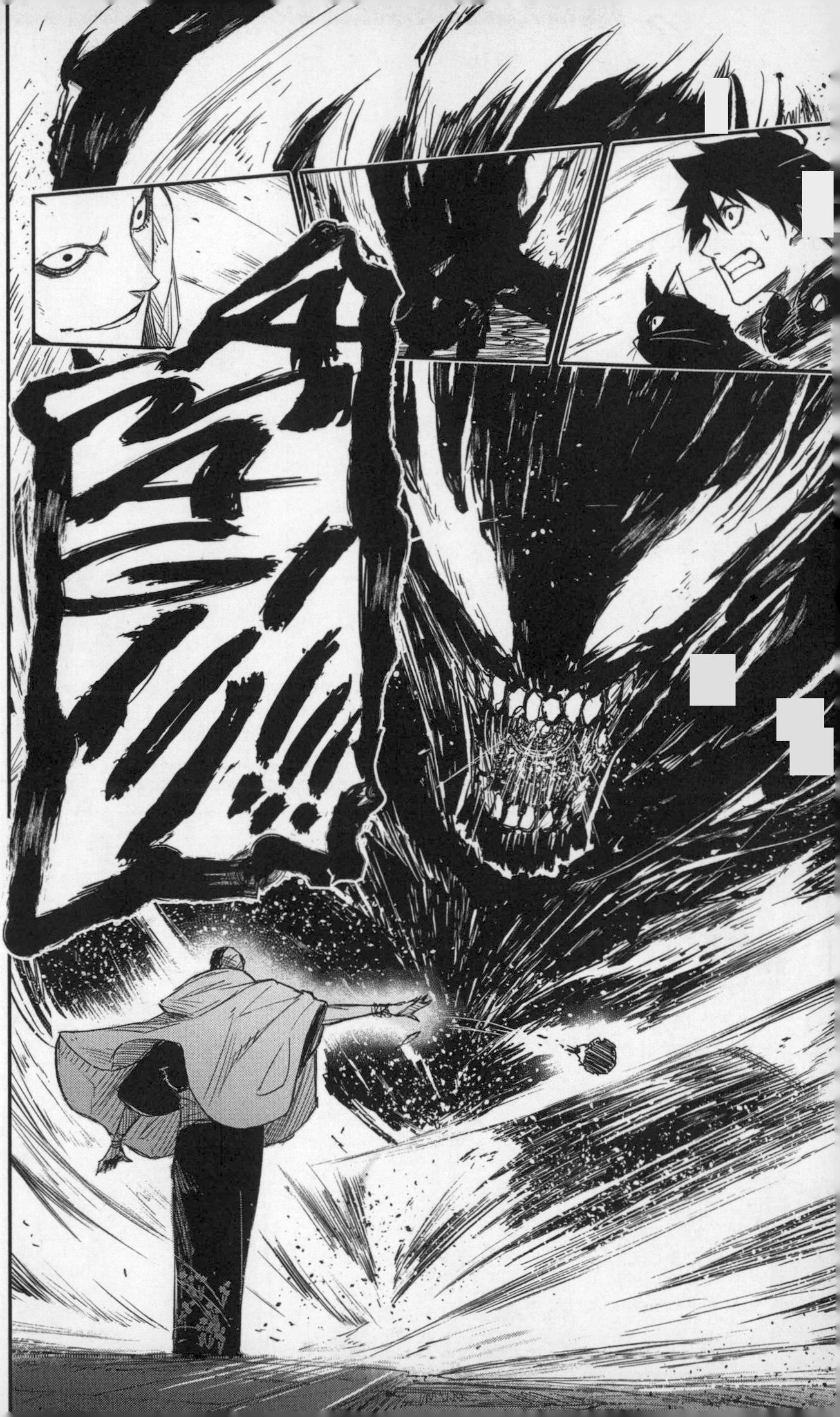

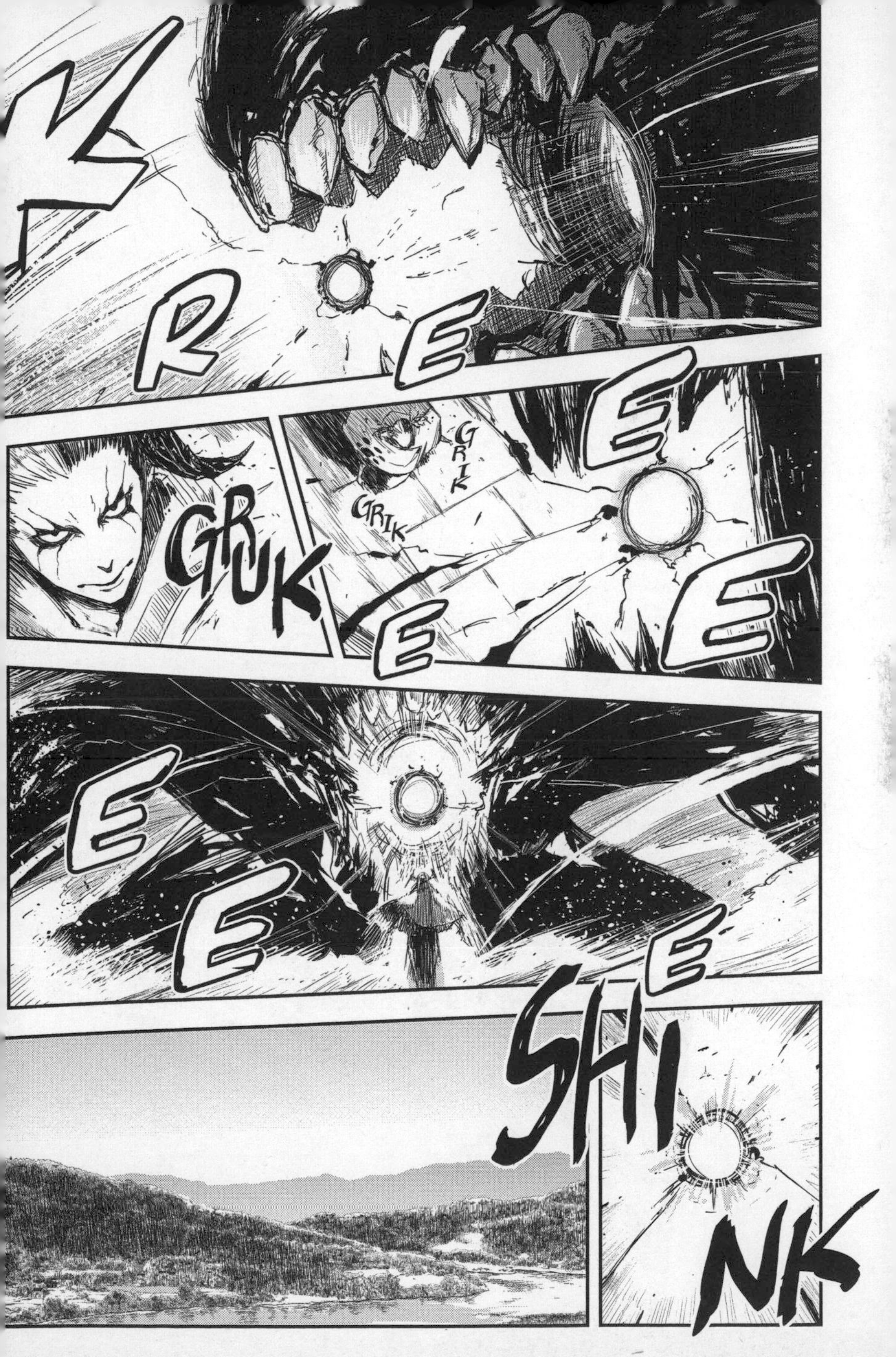

R
E
E
GRIK
GRIK
E
E
GRUK
E
E
E
SHI
NK

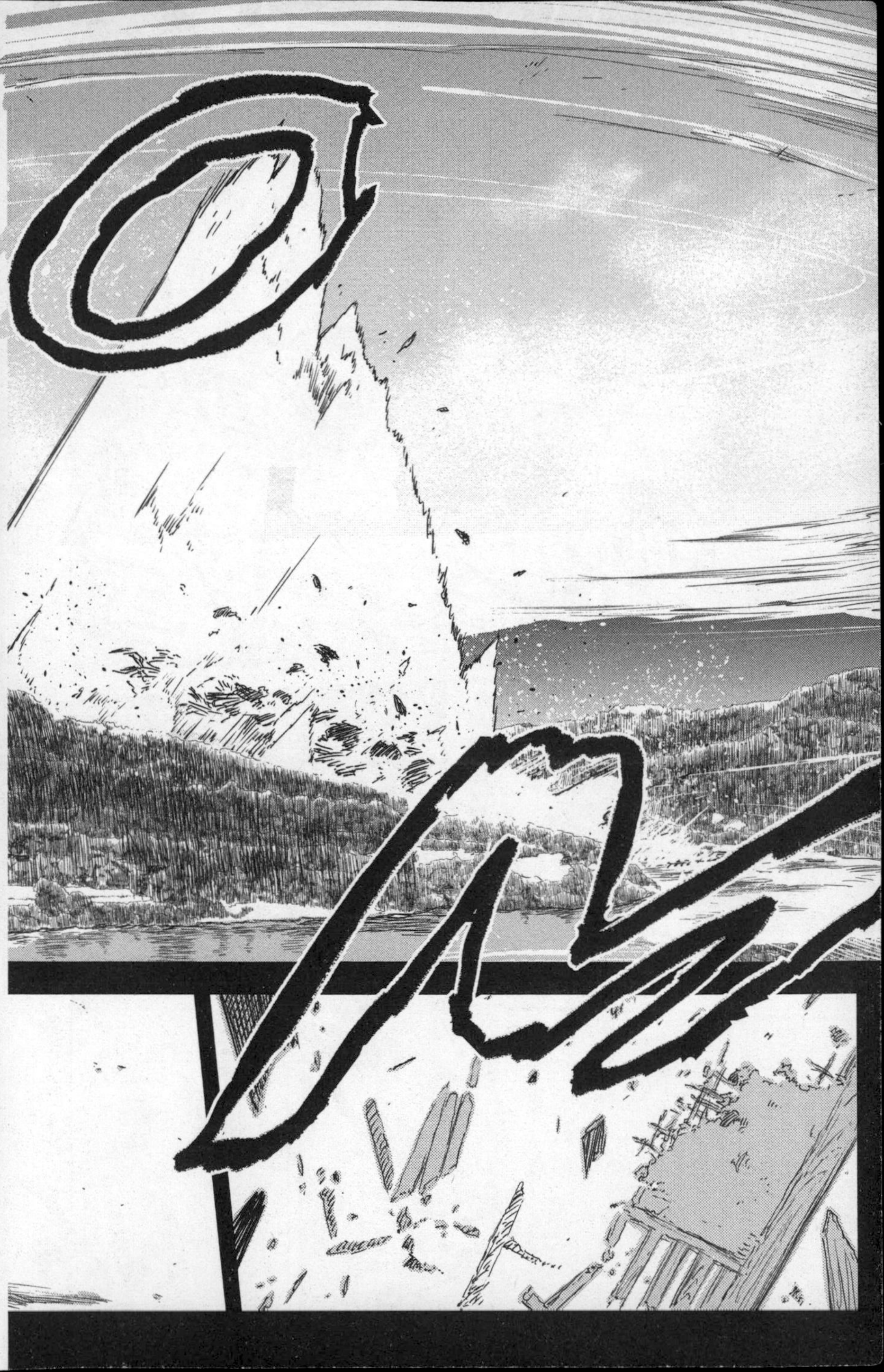

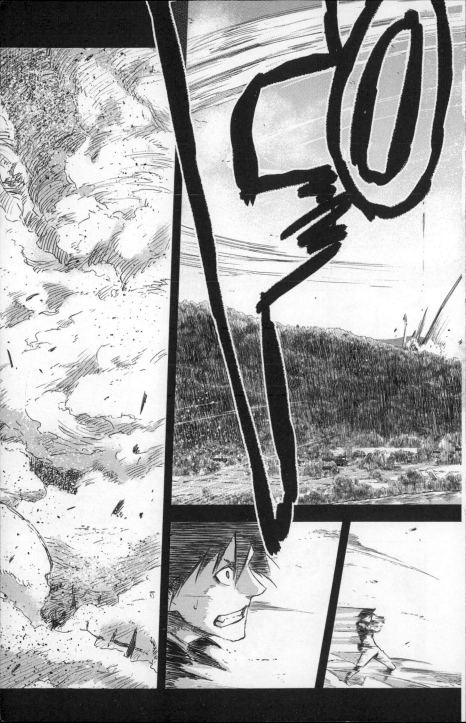

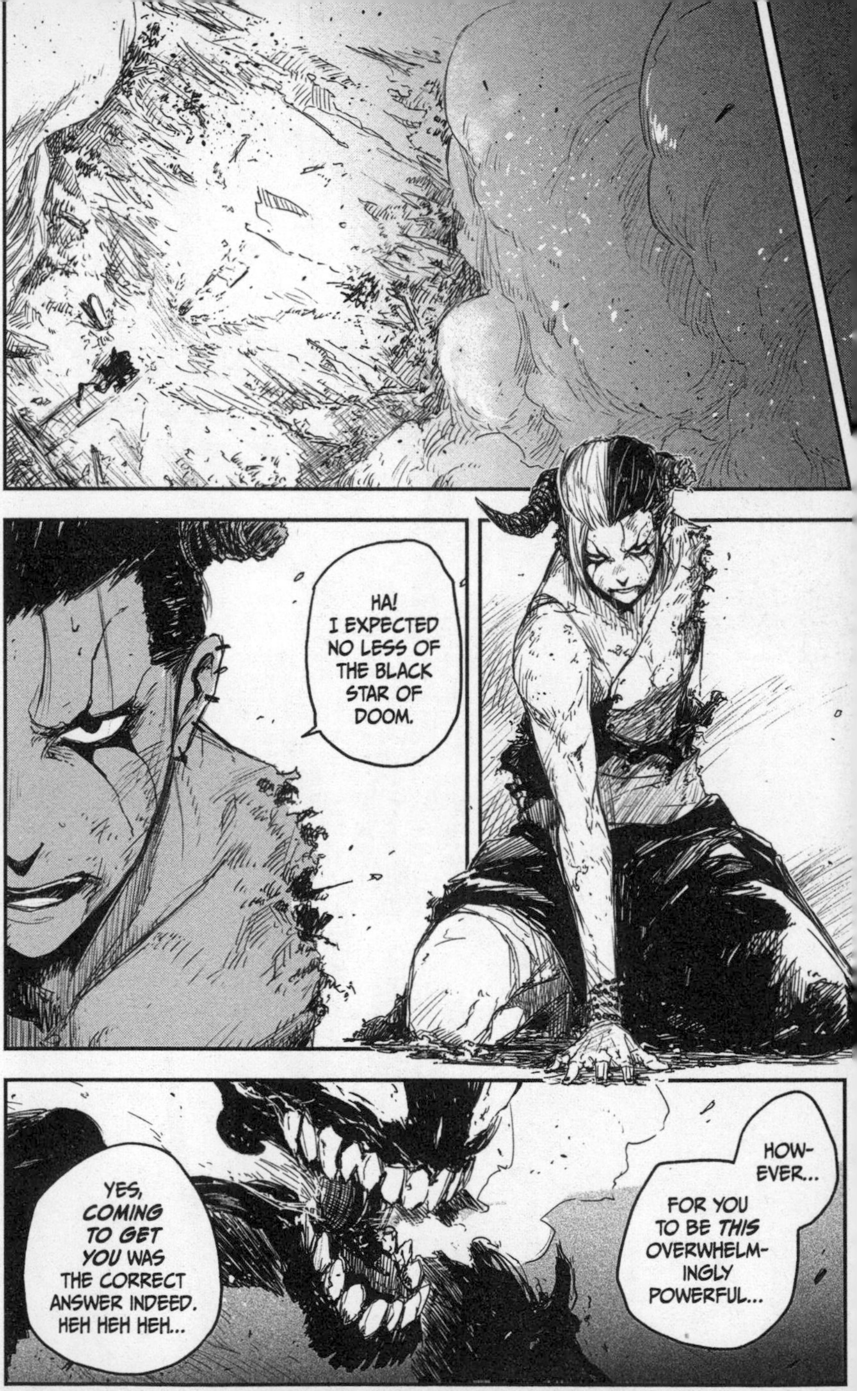
HA! I EXPECTED NO LESS OF THE BLACK STAR OF DOOM.
HOW-EVER...
FOR YOU TO BE *THIS* OVERWHELM-INGLY POWERFUL...
YES, *COMING TO GET YOU* WAS THE CORRECT ANSWER INDEED. HEH HEH HEH...

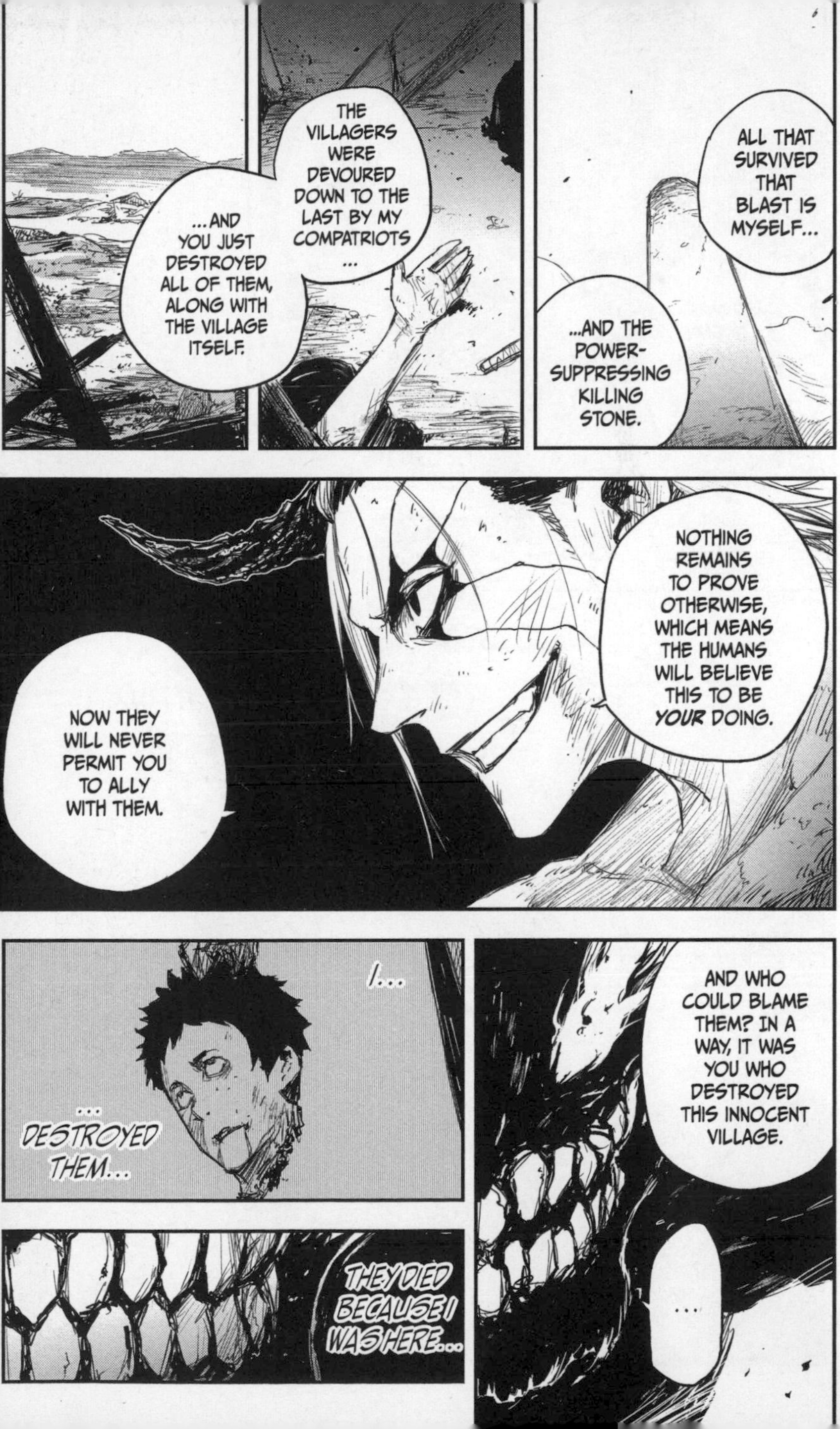
ALL THAT SURVIVED THAT BLAST IS MYSELF...
...AND THE POWER-SUPPRESSING KILLING STONE.
THE VILLAGERS WERE DEVOURED DOWN TO THE LAST BY MY COMPATRIOTS...
...AND YOU JUST DESTROYED ALL OF THEM, ALONG WITH THE VILLAGE ITSELF.
NOTHING REMAINS TO PROVE OTHERWISE, WHICH MEANS THE HUMANS WILL BELIEVE THIS TO BE *YOUR* DOING.
NOW THEY WILL NEVER PERMIT YOU TO ALLY WITH THEM.
AND WHO COULD BLAME THEM? IN A WAY, IT WAS YOU WHO DESTROYED THIS INNOCENT VILLAGE.
...
I...
...DESTROYED THEM...
THEY DIED BECAUSE I WAS HERE...

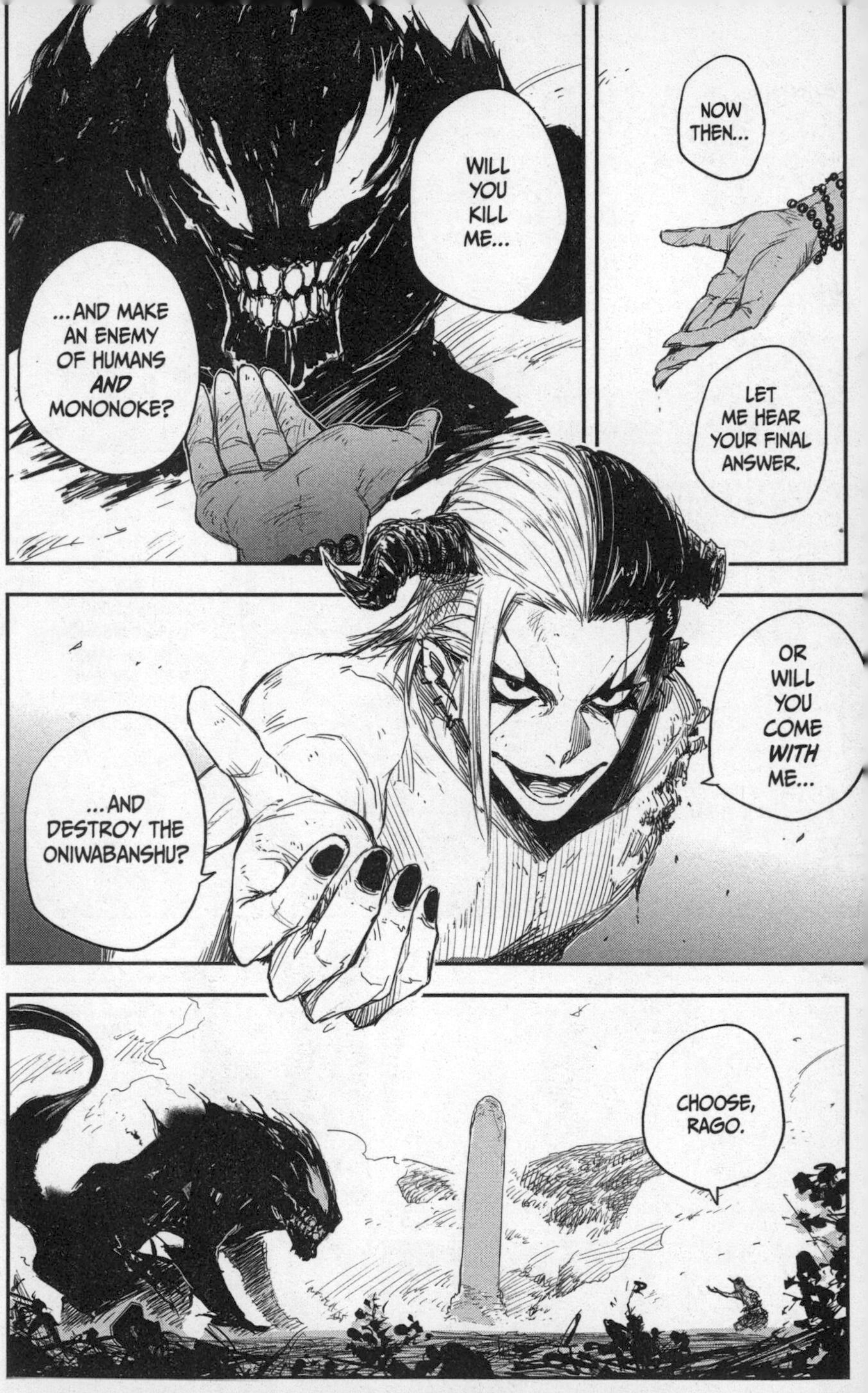
NOW THEN...
LET ME HEAR YOUR FINAL ANSWER.
WILL YOU KILL ME...
...AND MAKE AN ENEMY OF HUMANS *AND* MONONOKE?
OR WILL YOU COME *WITH* ME...
...AND DESTROY THE ONIWABANSHU?
CHOOSE, RAGO.

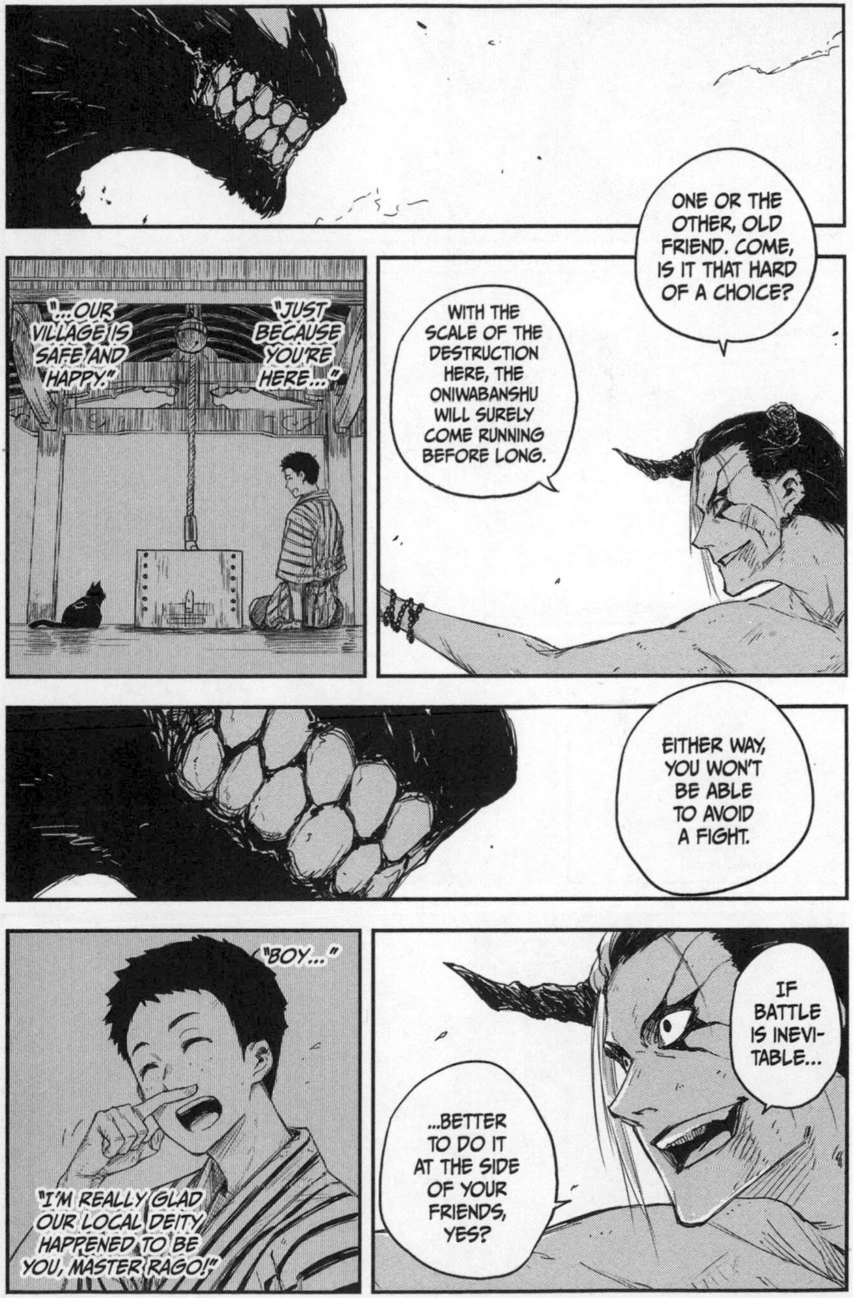
ONE OR THE OTHER, OLD FRIEND. COME, IS IT THAT HARD OF A CHOICE?
WITH THE SCALE OF THE DESTRUCTION HERE, THE ONIWABANSHU WILL SURELY COME RUNNING BEFORE LONG.
"JUST BECAUSE YOU'RE HERE..."
"...OUR VILLAGE IS SAFE AND HAPPY."
EITHER WAY, YOU WON'T BE ABLE TO AVOID A FIGHT.
IF BATTLE IS INEVI-TABLE...
...BETTER TO DO IT AT THE SIDE OF YOUR FRIENDS, YES?
"BOY..."
"I'M REALLY GLAD OUR LOCAL DEITY HAPPENED TO BE YOU, MASTER RAGO!"

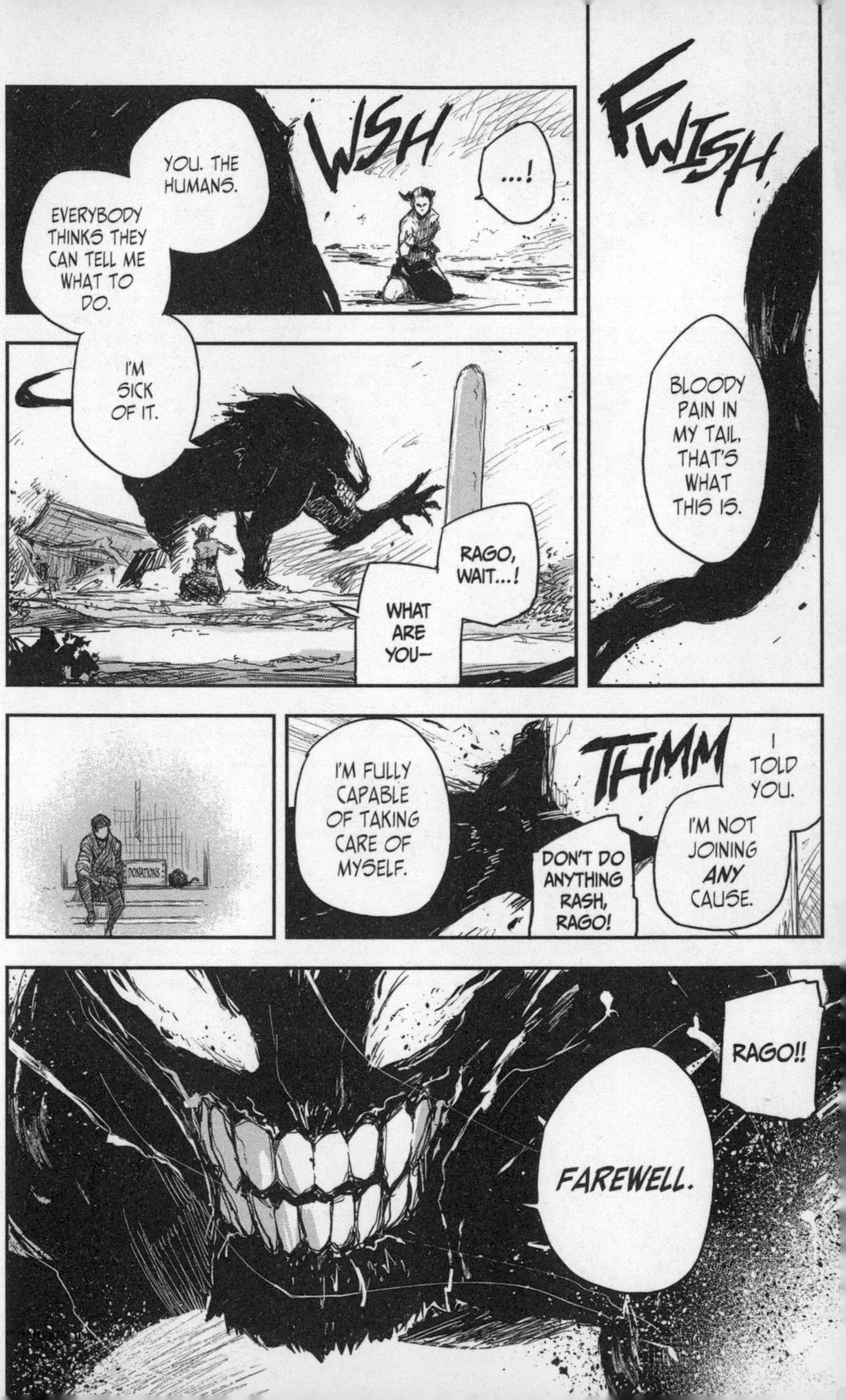
FWISH
BLOODY PAIN IN MY TAIL, THAT'S WHAT THIS IS.
...!
WSH
YOU. THE HUMANS.
EVERYBODY THINKS THEY CAN TELL ME WHAT TO DO.
I'M SICK OF IT.
RAGO, WAIT...!
WHAT ARE YOU—
I TOLD YOU.
I'M NOT JOINING *ANY* CAUSE.
THMM
DON'T DO ANYTHING RASH, RAGO!
I'M FULLY CAPABLE OF TAKING CARE OF MYSELF.
DONATIONS
RAGO!!
FAREWELL.

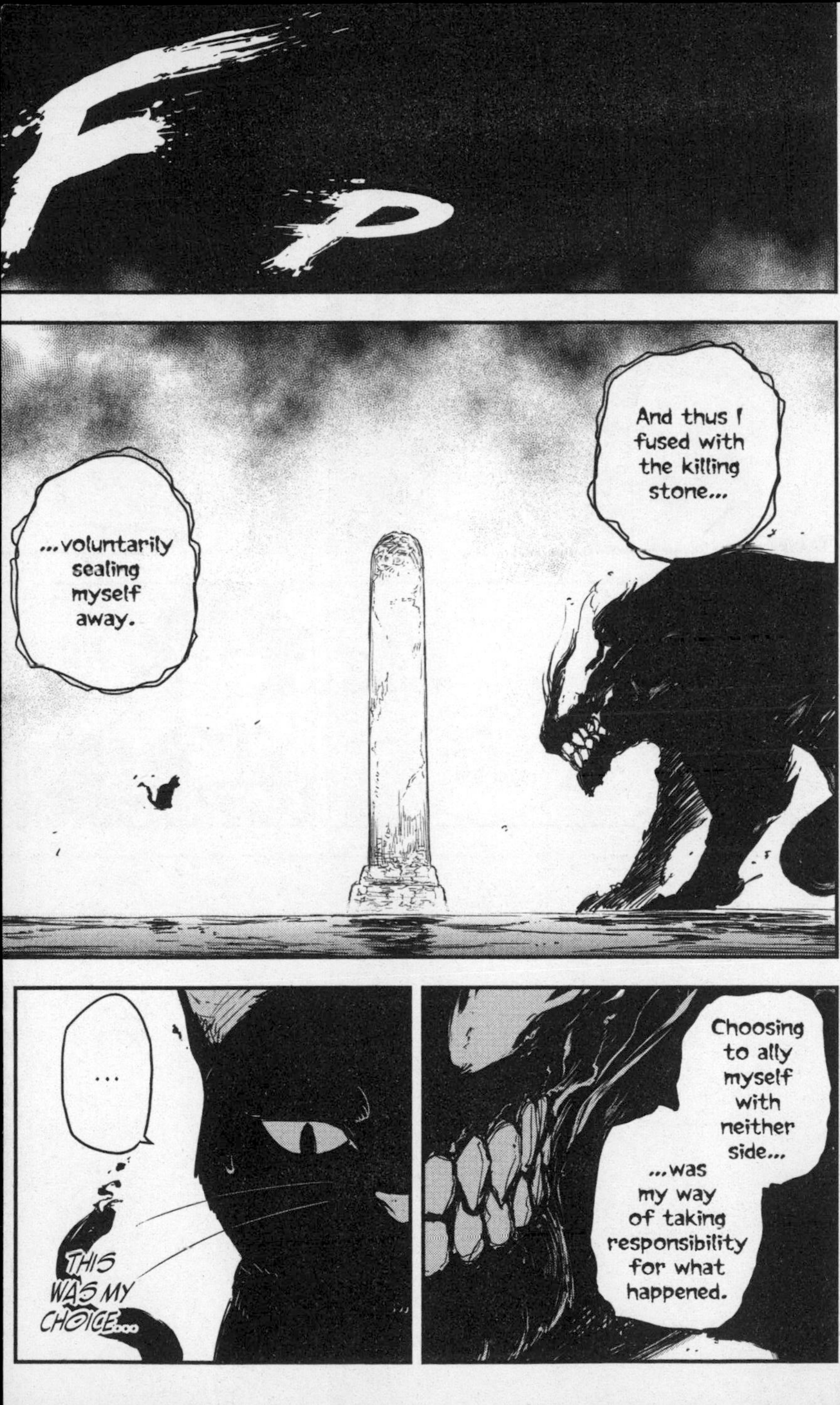

And thus I fused with the killing stone...
...voluntarily sealing myself away.
Choosing to ally myself with neither side...
...was my way of taking responsibility for what happened.
...
THIS WAS MY CHOICE...

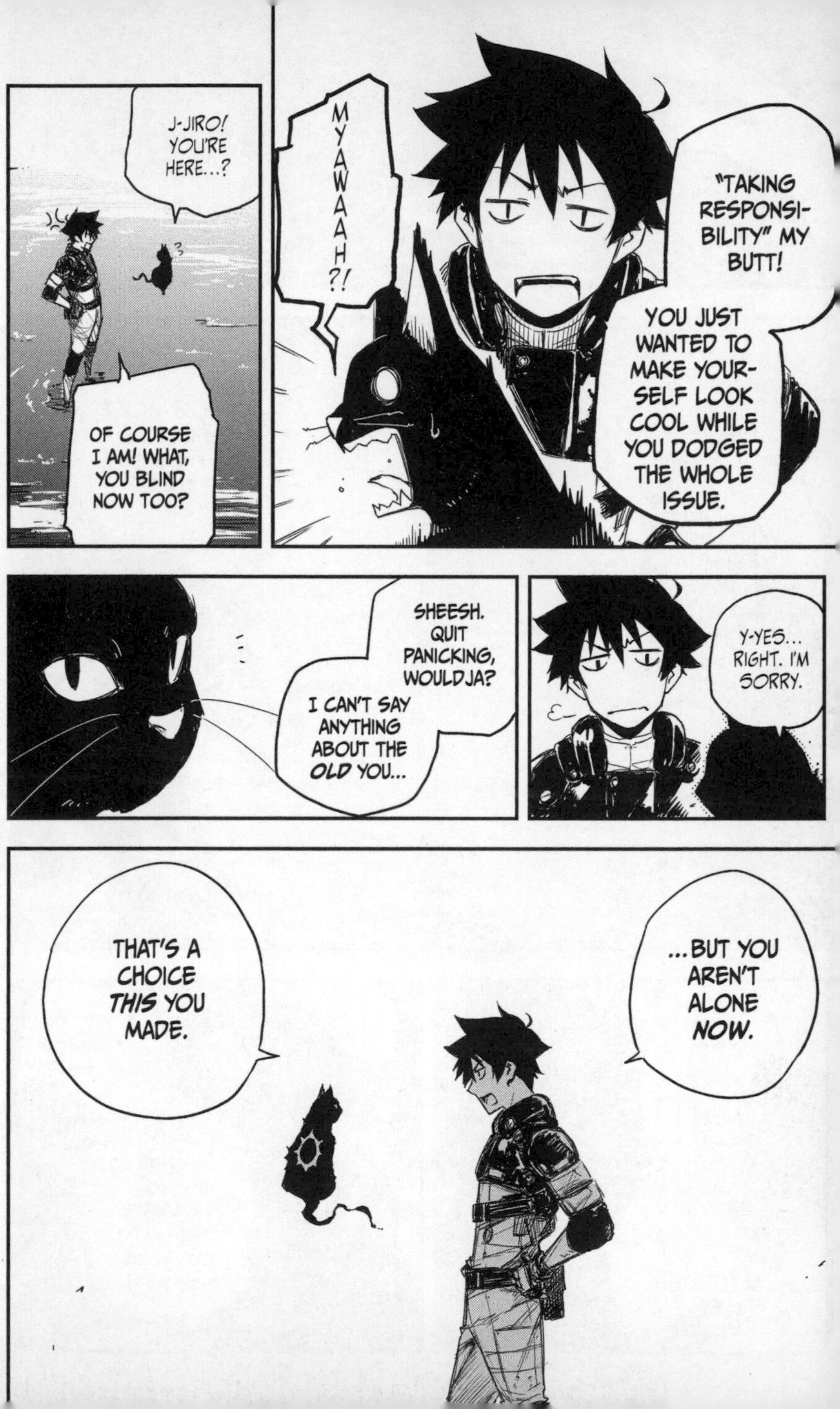
"TAKING RESPONSIBILITY" MY BUTT!
YOU JUST WANTED TO MAKE YOURSELF LOOK COOL WHILE YOU DODGED THE WHOLE ISSUE.
MYAWAAH?!
J-JIRO! YOU'RE HERE...?
OF COURSE I AM! WHAT, YOU BLIND NOW TOO?
Y-YES... RIGHT. I'M SORRY.
SHEESH. QUIT PANICKING, WOULDJA?
I CAN'T SAY ANYTHING ABOUT THE *OLD* YOU...
...BUT YOU AREN'T ALONE *NOW.*
THAT'S A CHOICE *THIS* YOU MADE.

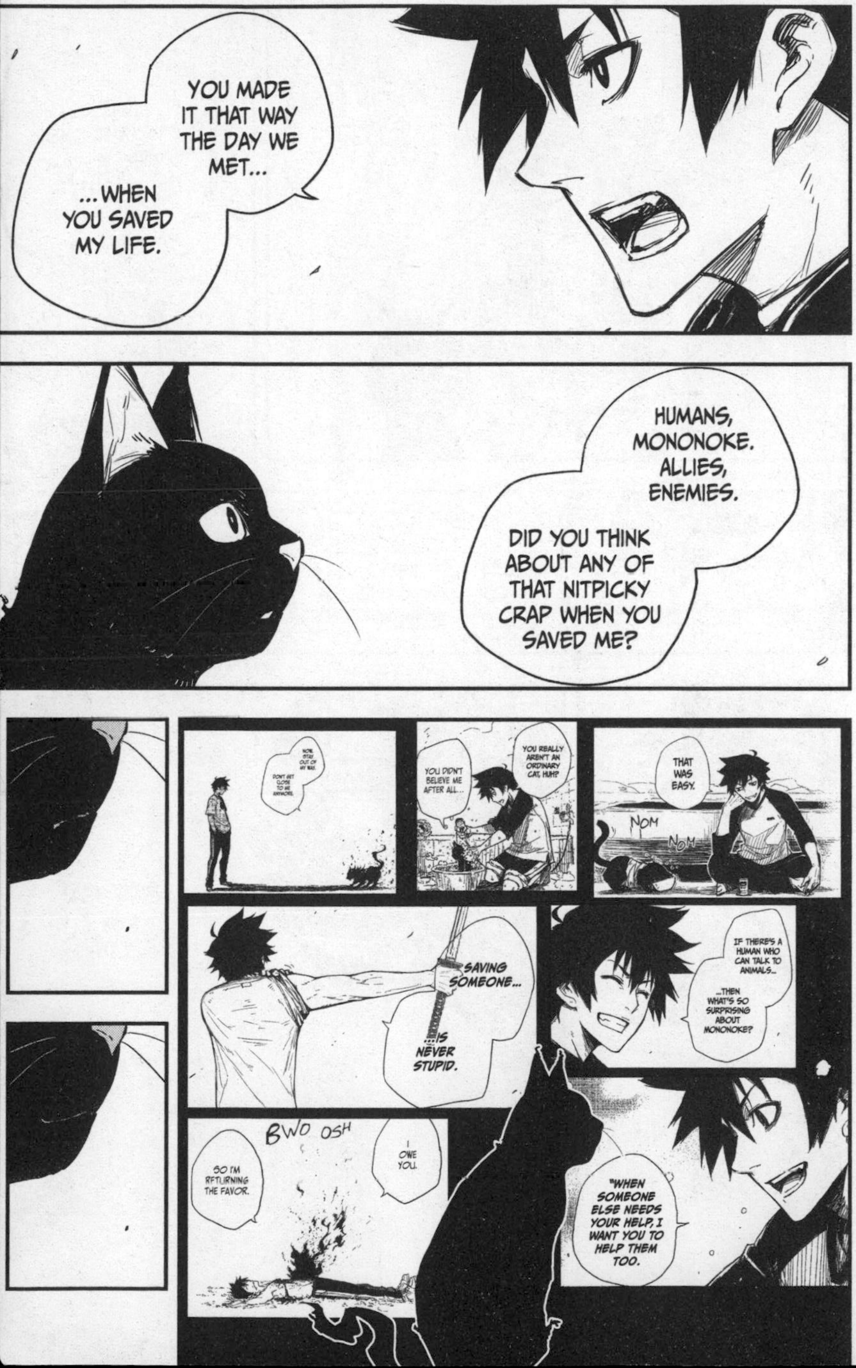
YOU MADE IT THAT WAY THE DAY WE MET...
...WHEN YOU SAVED MY LIFE.
HUMANS, MONONOKE. ALLIES, ENEMIES.
DID YOU THINK ABOUT ANY OF THAT NITPICKY CRAP WHEN YOU SAVED ME?
THAT WAS EASY.
NOM
NOM
YOU REALLY AREN'T AN ORDINARY CAT, HUH?
YOU DIDN'T BELIEVE ME AFTER ALL...
NOW, STAY OUT OF MY WAY.
DON'T GET CLOSE TO ME ANYMORE.
IF THERE'S A HUMAN WHO CAN TALK TO ANIMALS...
...THEN WHAT'S SO SURPRISING ABOUT MONONOKE?
SAVING SOMEONE...
...IS NEVER STUPID.
"WHEN SOMEONE ELSE NEEDS YOUR HELP, I WANT YOU TO HELP THEM TOO.
BWO OSH
I OWE YOU.
SO I'M RETURNING THE FAVOR.

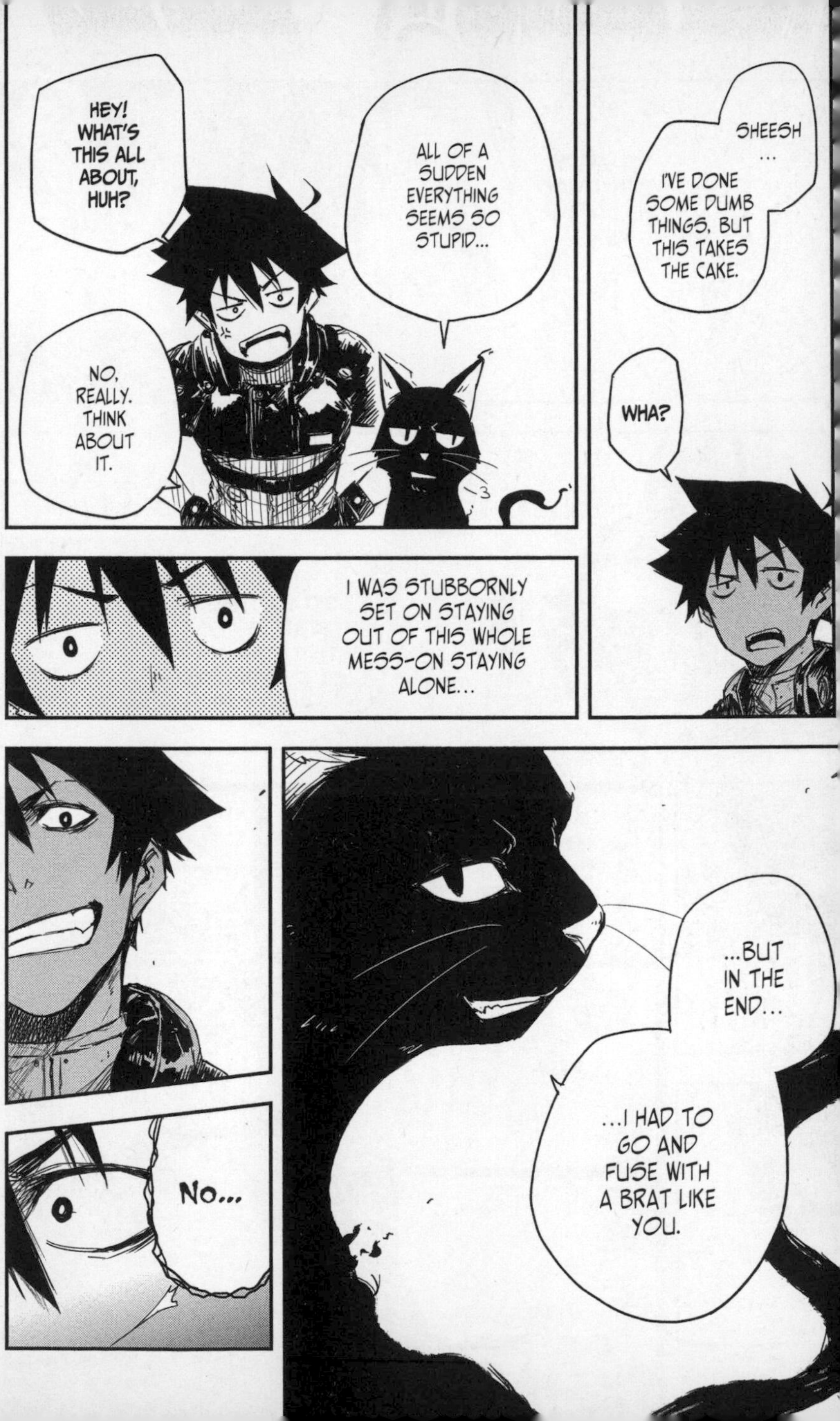
SHEESH ... I'VE DONE SOME DUMB THINGS, BUT THIS TAKES THE CAKE.
WHA?
ALL OF A SUDDEN EVERYTHING SEEMS SO STUPID...
HEY! WHAT'S THIS ALL ABOUT, HUH?
NO, REALLY. THINK ABOUT IT.
I WAS STUBBORNLY SET ON STAYING OUT OF THIS WHOLE MESS-ON STAYING ALONE...
...BUT IN THE END...
...I HAD TO GO AND FUSE WITH A BRAT LIKE YOU.
No...

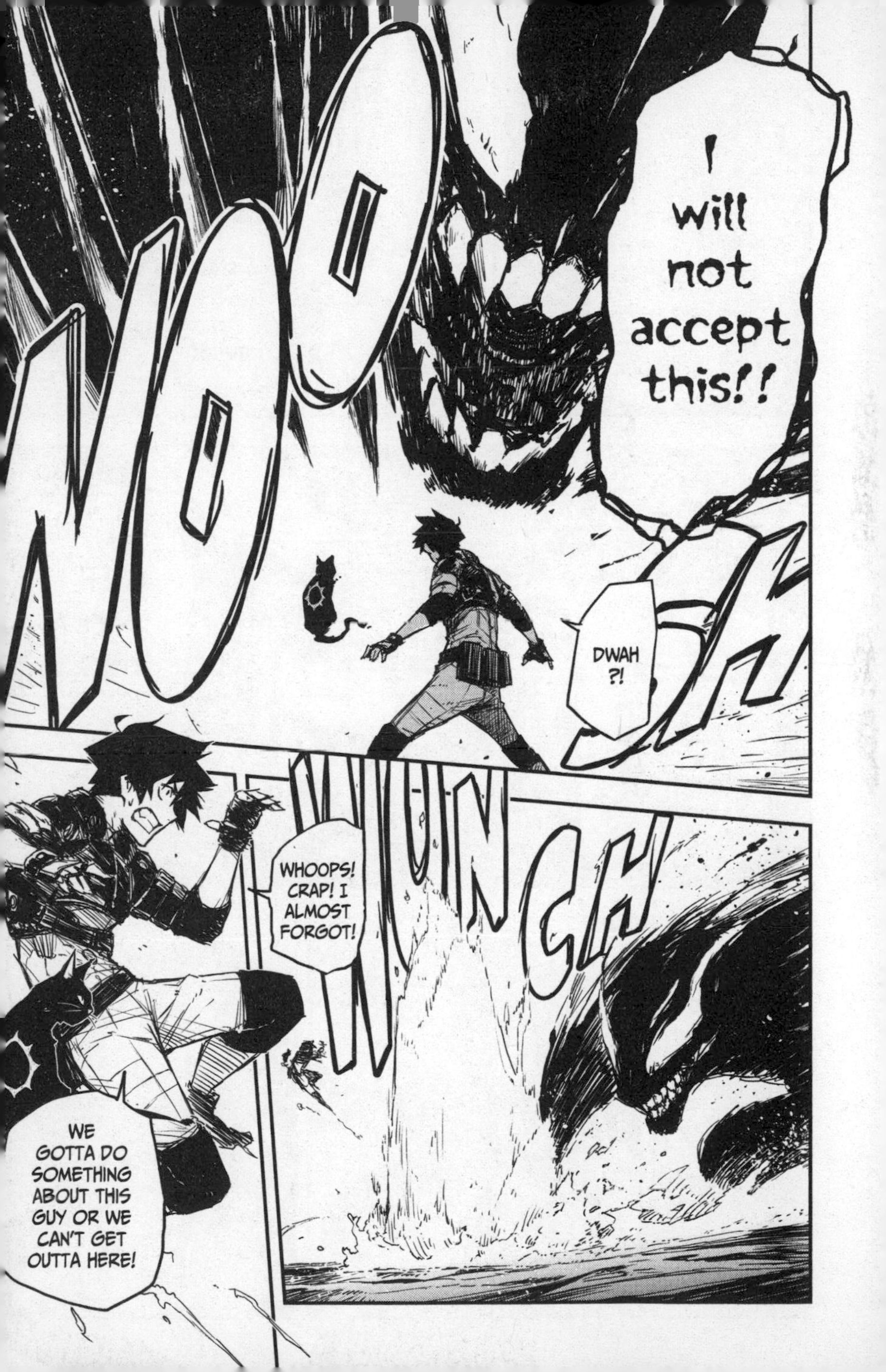
I will not accept this!!
NOOO
DWAH ?!
WHOOPS! CRAP! I ALMOST FORGOT!
WE GOTTA DO SOMETHING ABOUT THIS GUY OR WE CAN'T GET OUTTA HERE!

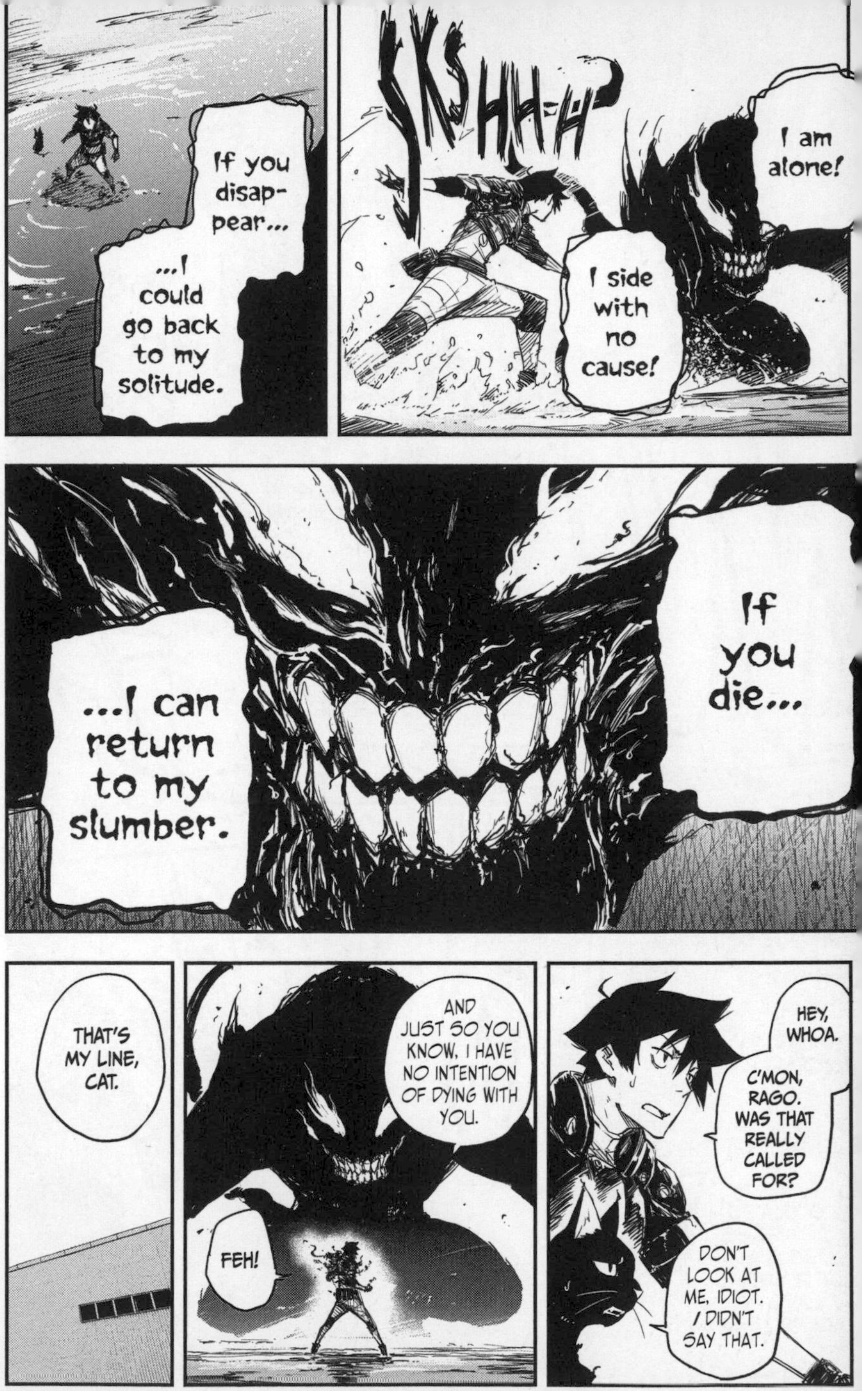
SKSHH-H
I am alone!
I side with no cause!
If you disap-pear...
...I could go back to my solitude.
If you die...
...I can return to my slumber.
HEY, WHOA.
C'MON, RAGO. WAS THAT REALLY CALLED FOR?
DON'T LOOK AT ME, IDIOT. I DIDN'T SAY THAT.
AND JUST SO YOU KNOW, I HAVE NO INTENTION OF DYING WITH YOU.
FEH!
THAT'S MY LINE, CAT.

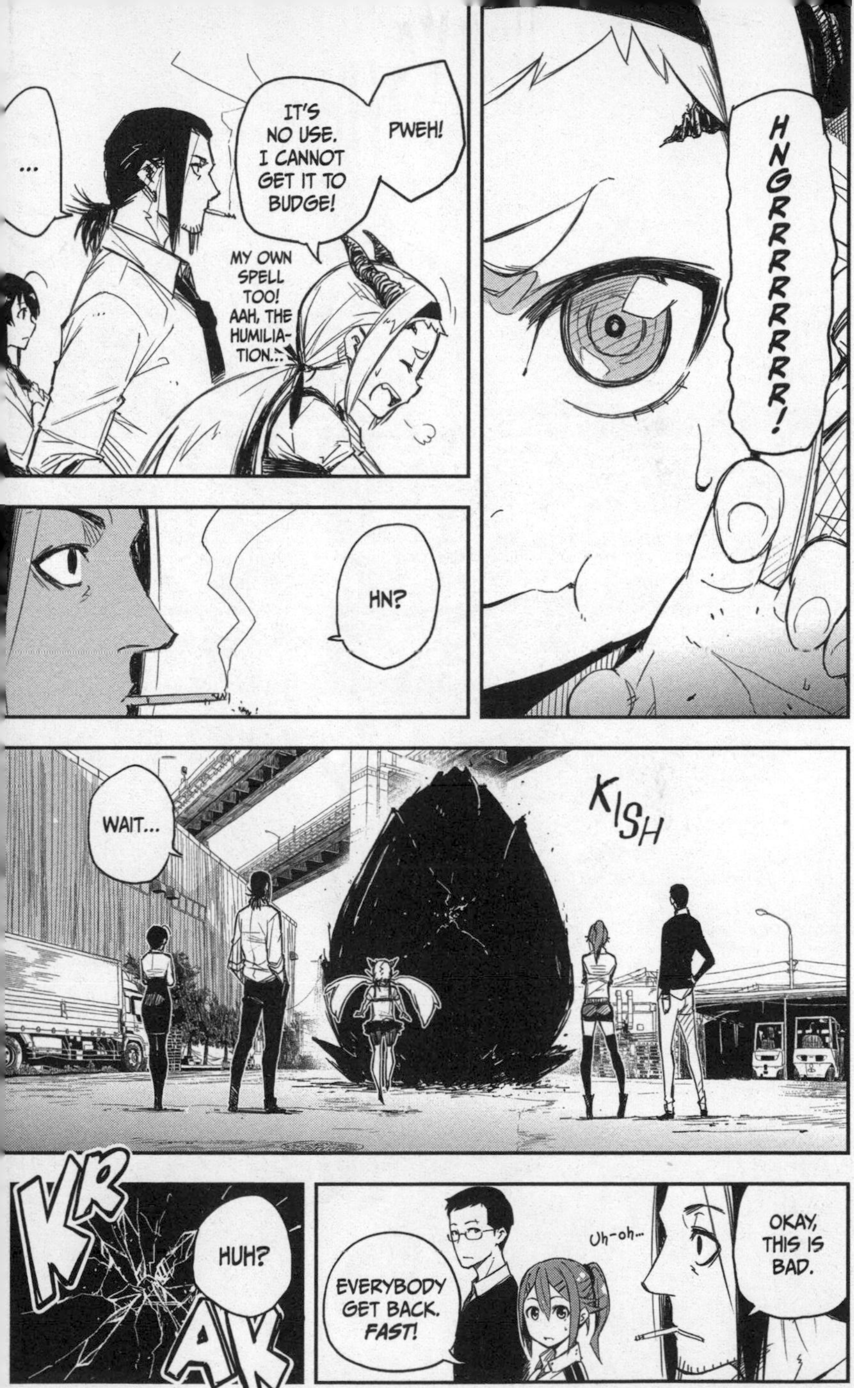
HNGRRRRRRR!
PWEH!
IT'S NO USE. I CANNOT GET IT TO BUDGE!
MY OWN SPELL TOO! AAH, THE HUMILIATION...
...
HN?
KISH
WAIT...
OKAY, THIS IS BAD.
Uh-oh...
EVERYBODY GET BACK. FAST!
HUH?
KRAK

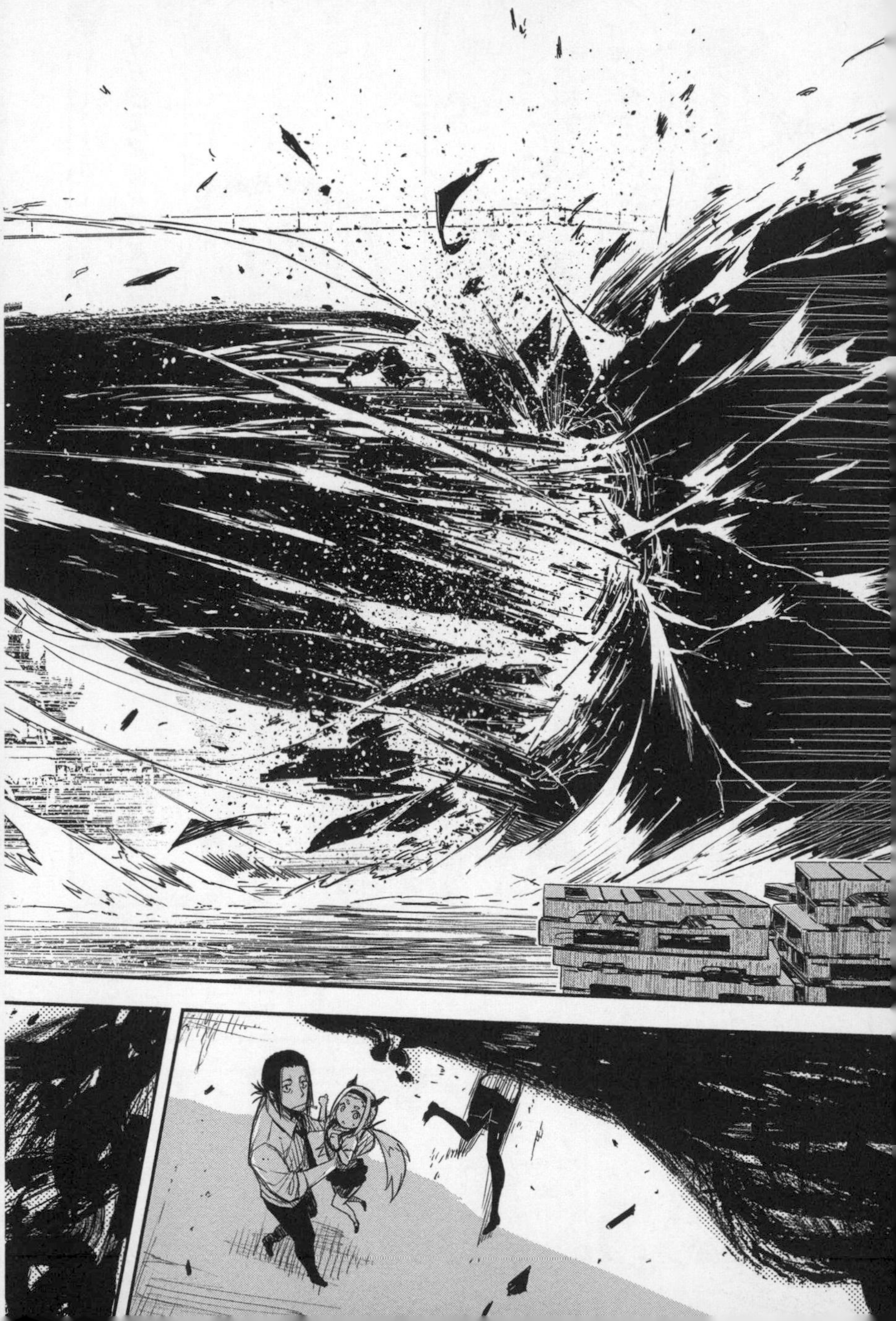

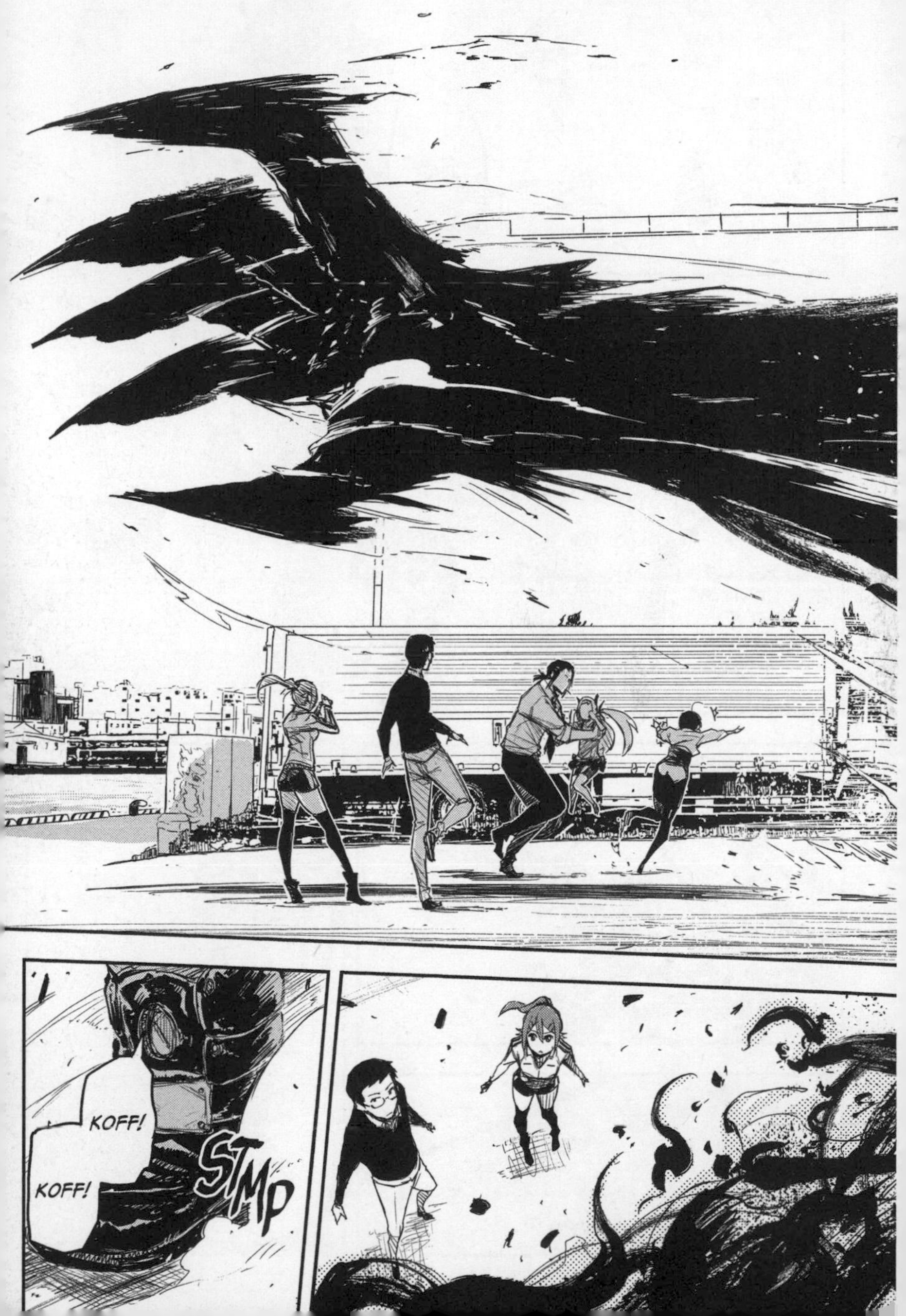

KOFF!
KOFF!
STMP

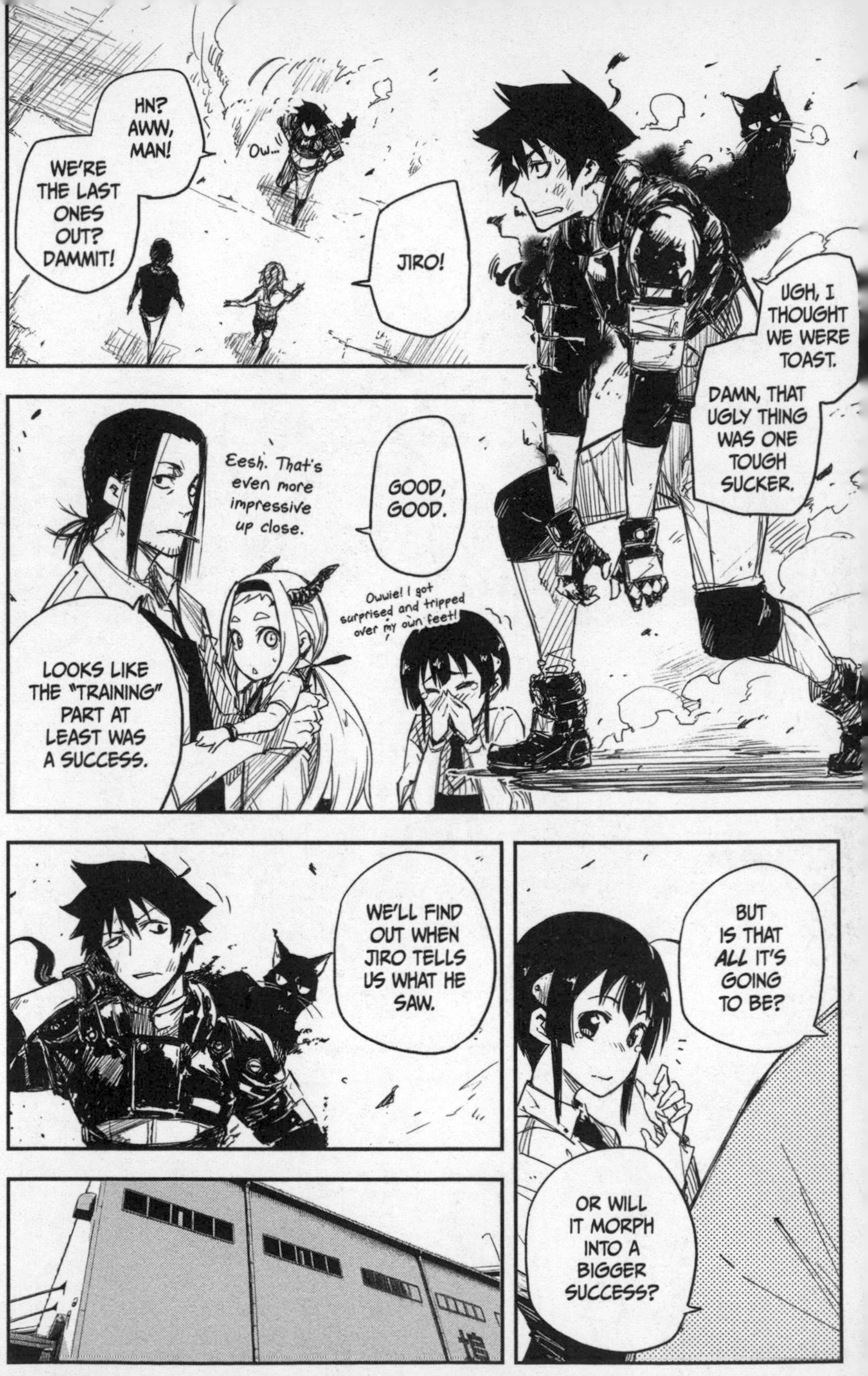
UGH, I THOUGHT WE WERE TOAST.
DAMN, THAT UGLY THING WAS ONE TOUGH SUCKER.
JIRO!
HN? AWW, MAN!
WE'RE THE LAST ONES OUT? DAMMIT!
Ow...
GOOD, GOOD.
Eesh. That's even more impressive up close.
Owwie! I got surprised and tripped over my own feet!
LOOKS LIKE THE "TRAINING" PART AT LEAST WAS A SUCCESS.
BUT IS THAT ALL IT'S GOING TO BE?
OR WILL IT MORPH INTO A BIGGER SUCCESS?
WE'LL FIND OUT WHEN JIRO TELLS US WHAT HE SAW.

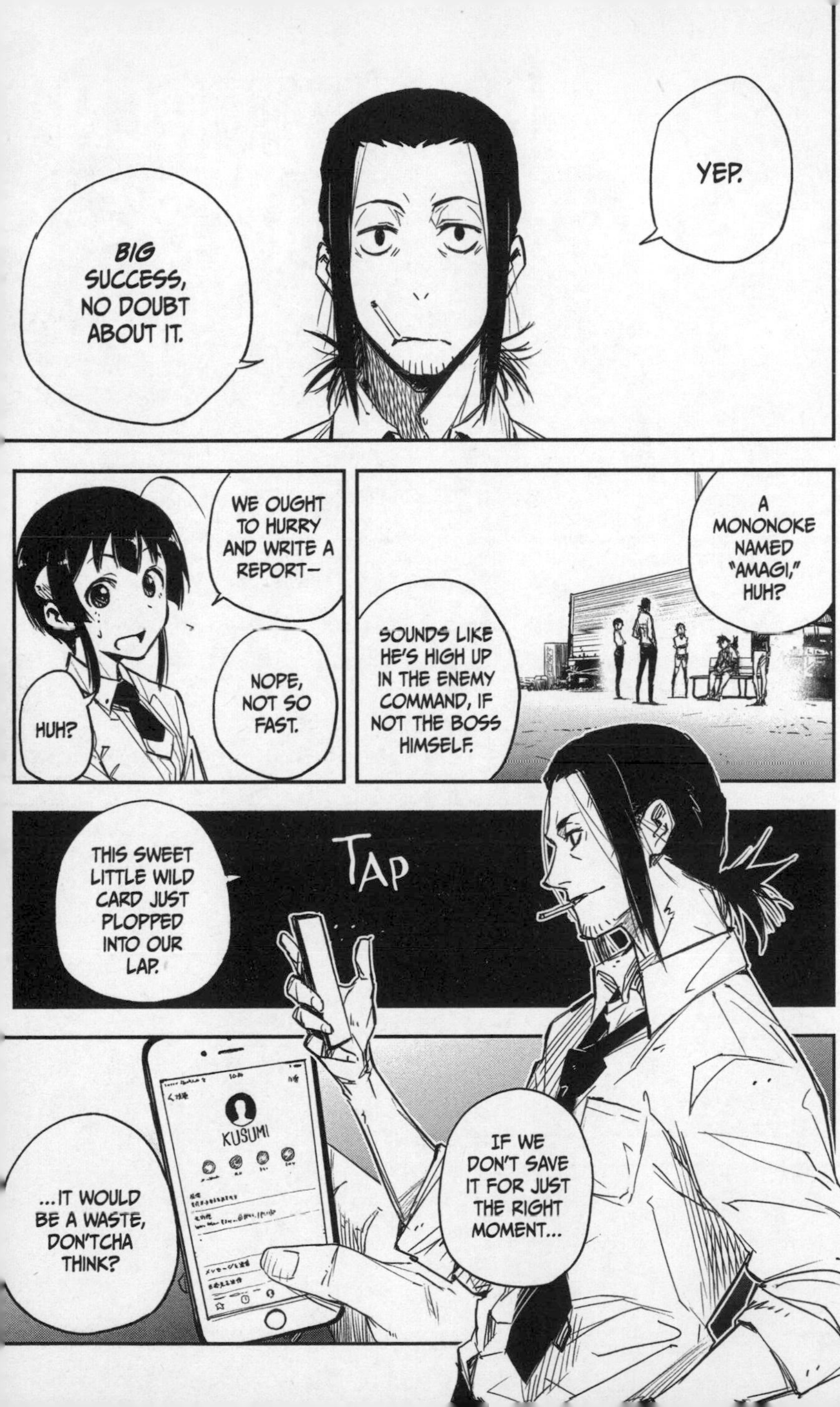
YEP.
BIG SUCCESS, NO DOUBT ABOUT IT.
A MONONOKE NAMED "AMAGI," HUH?
SOUNDS LIKE HE'S HIGH UP IN THE ENEMY COMMAND, IF NOT THE BOSS HIMSELF.
WE OUGHT TO HURRY AND WRITE A REPORT—
NOPE, NOT SO FAST.
HUH?
TAP
THIS SWEET LITTLE WILD CARD JUST PLOPPED INTO OUR LAP.
KUSUMI
IF WE DON'T SAVE IT FOR JUST THE RIGHT MOMENT...
...IT WOULD BE A WASTE, DON'TCHA THINK?

BLACK TORCH

#9 SPECIAL FORCE

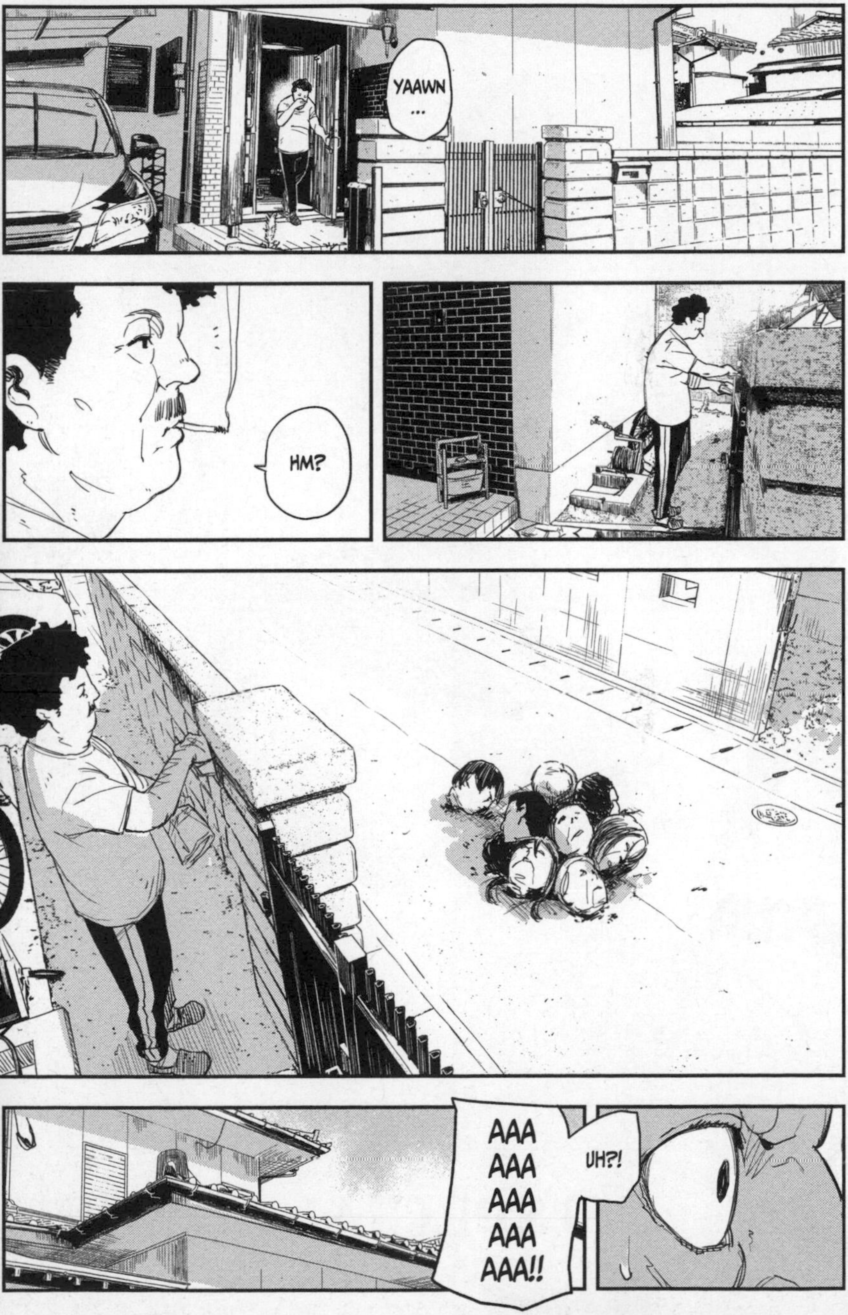
YAAWN ...
HM?
AAA AAA AAA AAA AAA!!
UH?!

#9 SPECIAL FORCE

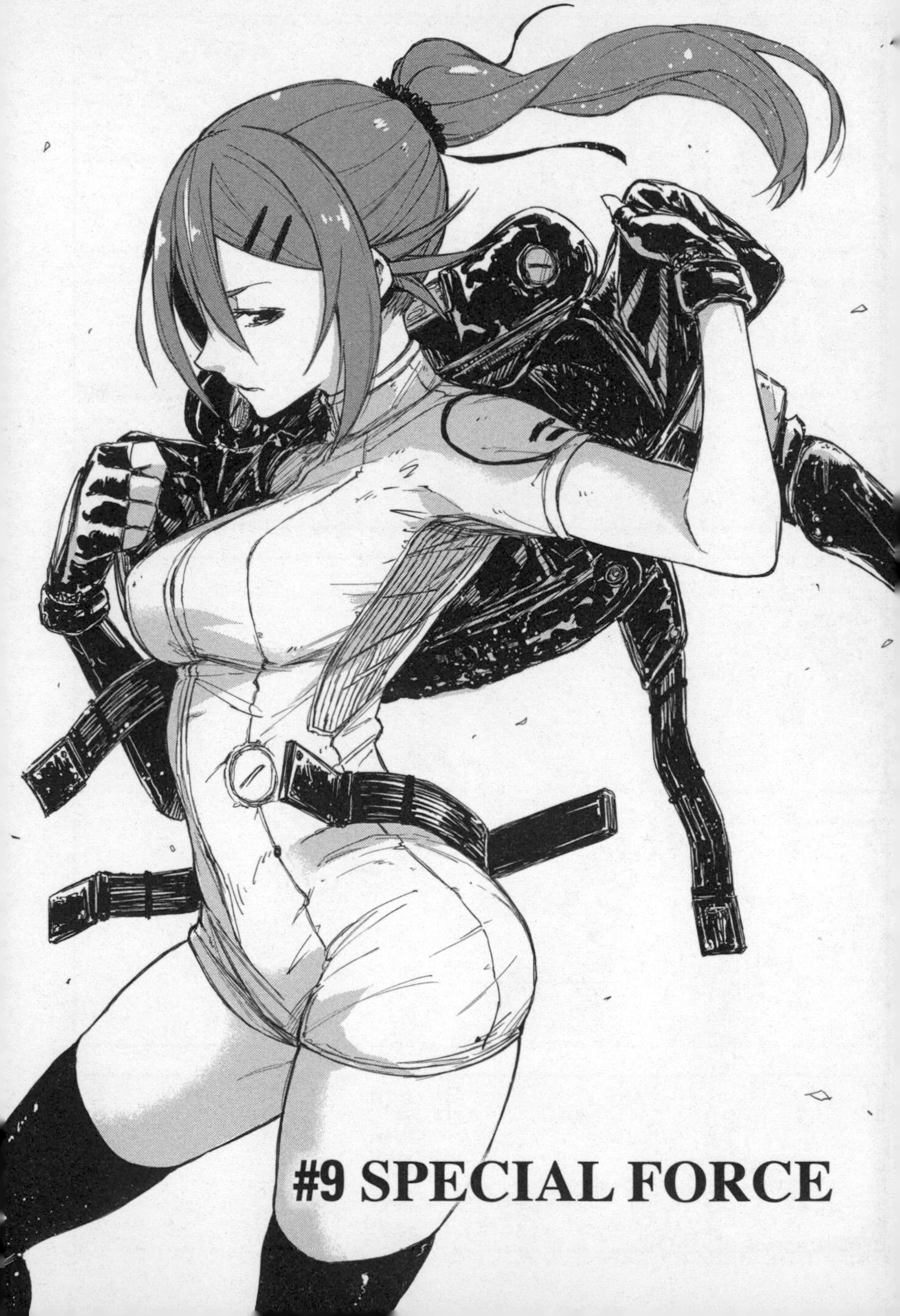

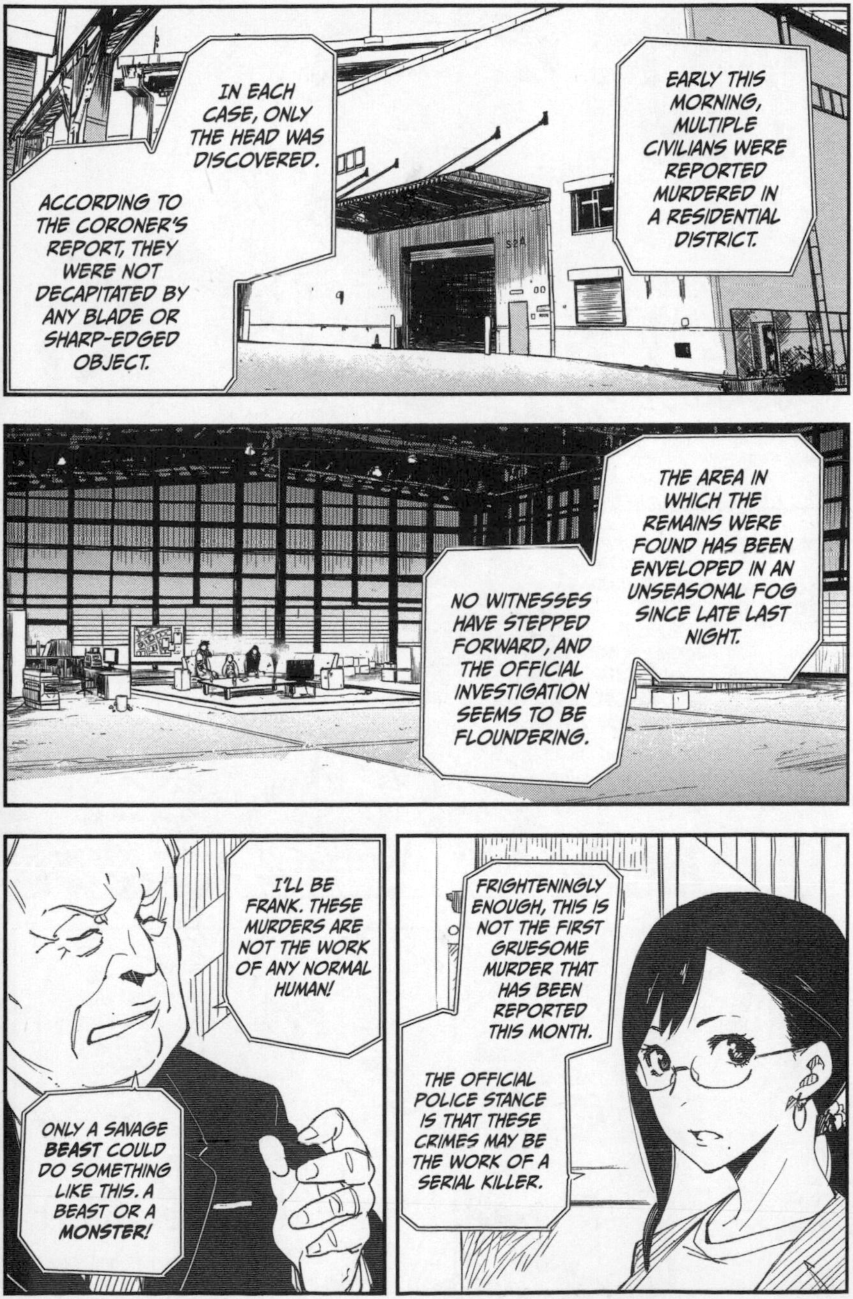
EARLY THIS MORNING, MULTIPLE CIVILIANS WERE REPORTED MURDERED IN A RESIDENTIAL DISTRICT.
IN EACH CASE, ONLY THE HEAD WAS DISCOVERED.
ACCORDING TO THE CORONER'S REPORT, THEY WERE NOT DECAPITATED BY ANY BLADE OR SHARP-EDGED OBJECT.
THE AREA IN WHICH THE REMAINS WERE FOUND HAS BEEN ENVELOPED IN AN UNSEASONAL FOG SINCE LATE LAST NIGHT.
NO WITNESSES HAVE STEPPED FORWARD, AND THE OFFICIAL INVESTIGATION SEEMS TO BE FLOUNDERING.
FRIGHTENINGLY ENOUGH, THIS IS NOT THE FIRST GRUESOME MURDER THAT HAS BEEN REPORTED THIS MONTH.
THE OFFICIAL POLICE STANCE IS THAT THESE CRIMES MAY BE THE WORK OF A SERIAL KILLER.
I'LL BE FRANK. THESE MURDERS ARE NOT THE WORK OF ANY NORMAL HUMAN!
ONLY A SAVAGE BEAST COULD DO SOMETHING LIKE THIS. A BEAST OR A MONSTER!

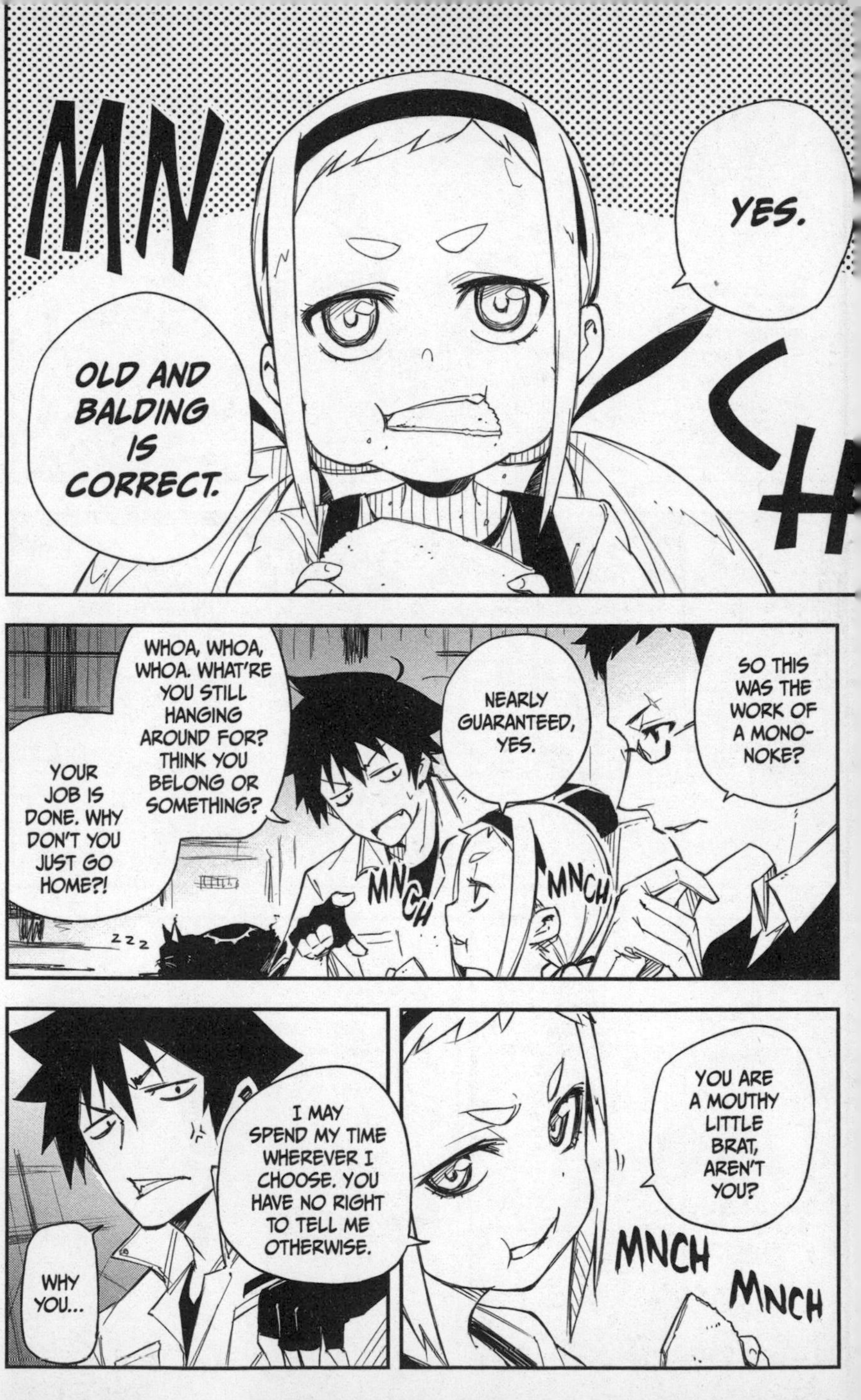
YES.
OLD AND BALDING IS CORRECT.
MN
CH
SO THIS WAS THE WORK OF A MONO-NOKE?
NEARLY GUARANTEED, YES.
WHOA, WHOA, WHOA. WHAT'RE YOU STILL HANGING AROUND FOR? THINK YOU BELONG OR SOMETHING?
YOUR JOB IS DONE. WHY DON'T YOU JUST GO HOME?!
MNCH
MNCH
ZZZ
YOU ARE A MOUTHY LITTLE BRAT, AREN'T YOU?
MNCH
MNCH
I MAY SPEND MY TIME WHEREVER I CHOOSE. YOU HAVE NO RIGHT TO TELL ME OTHERWISE.
WHY YOU...

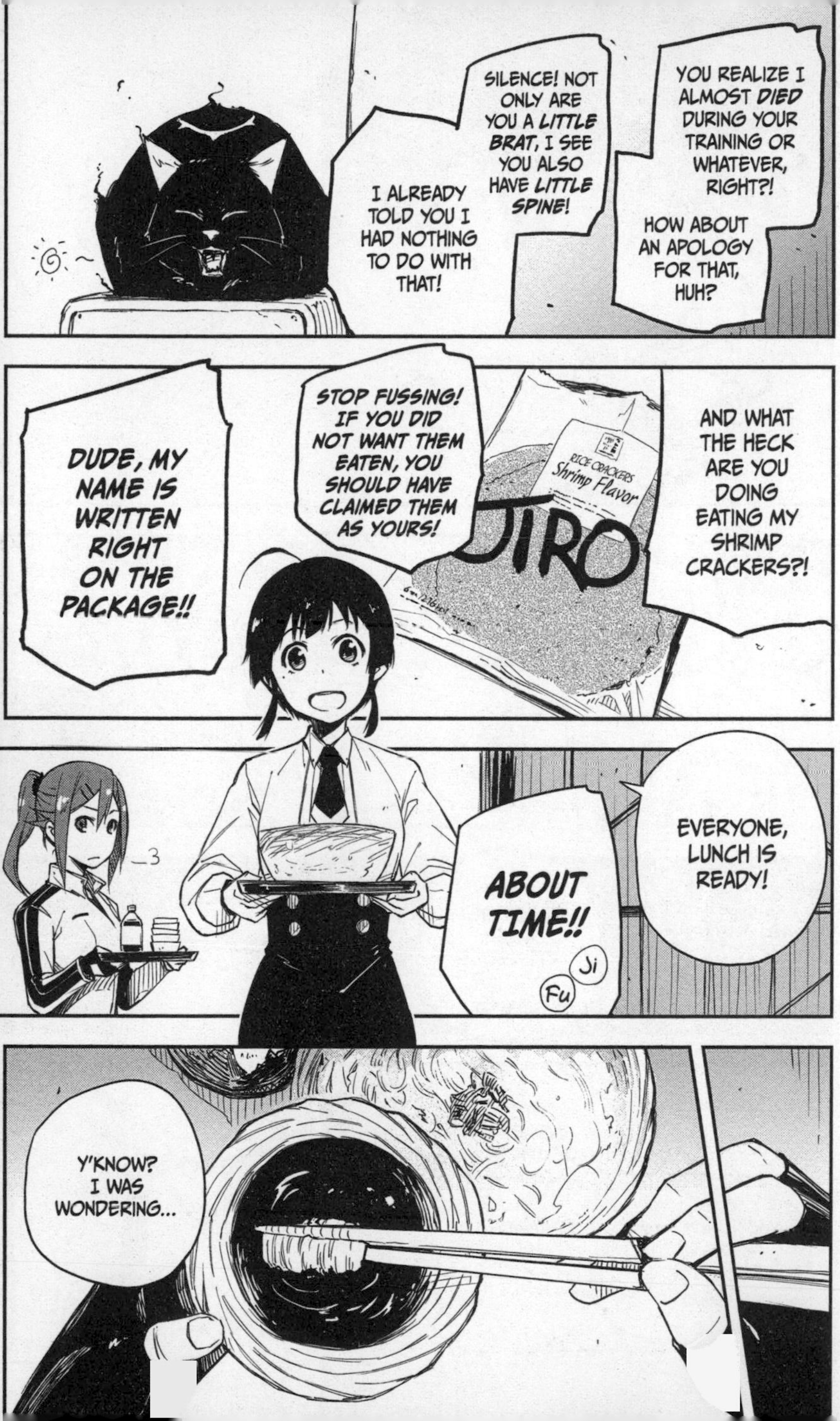
YOU REALIZE I ALMOST DIED DURING YOUR TRAINING OR WHATEVER, RIGHT?!
HOW ABOUT AN APOLOGY FOR THAT, HUH?
SILENCE! NOT ONLY ARE YOU A LITTLE BRAT, I SEE YOU ALSO HAVE LITTLE SPINE!
I ALREADY TOLD YOU I HAD NOTHING TO DO WITH THAT!
AND WHAT THE HECK ARE YOU DOING EATING MY SHRIMP CRACKERS?!
RICE CRACKERS
Shrimp Flavor
JIRO
STOP FUSSING! IF YOU DID NOT WANT THEM EATEN, YOU SHOULD HAVE CLAIMED THEM AS YOURS!
DUDE, MY NAME IS WRITTEN RIGHT ON THE PACKAGE!!
EVERYONE, LUNCH IS READY!
ABOUT TIME!!
Ji
Fu
Y'KNOW? I WAS WONDERING...

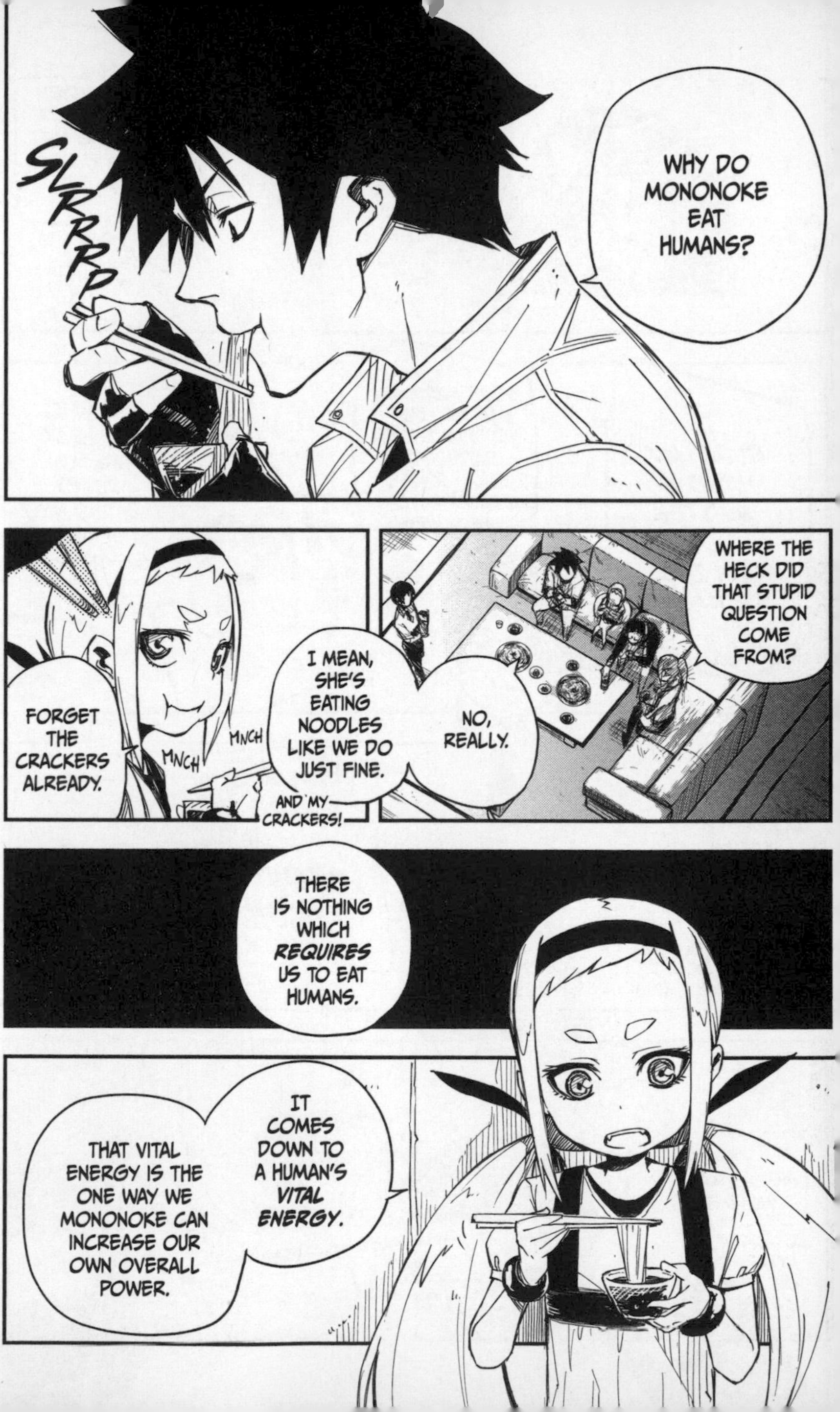
WHY DO MONONOKE EAT HUMANS?
SLRRRP
WHERE THE HECK DID THAT STUPID QUESTION COME FROM?
NO, REALLY.
I MEAN, SHE'S EATING NOODLES LIKE WE DO JUST FINE.
AND MY CRACKERS!
MNCH
MNCH
FORGET THE CRACKERS ALREADY.
THERE IS NOTHING WHICH *REQUIRES* US TO EAT HUMANS.
IT COMES DOWN TO A HUMAN'S *VITAL ENERGY*.
THAT VITAL ENERGY IS THE ONE WAY WE MONONOKE CAN INCREASE OUR OWN OVERALL POWER.

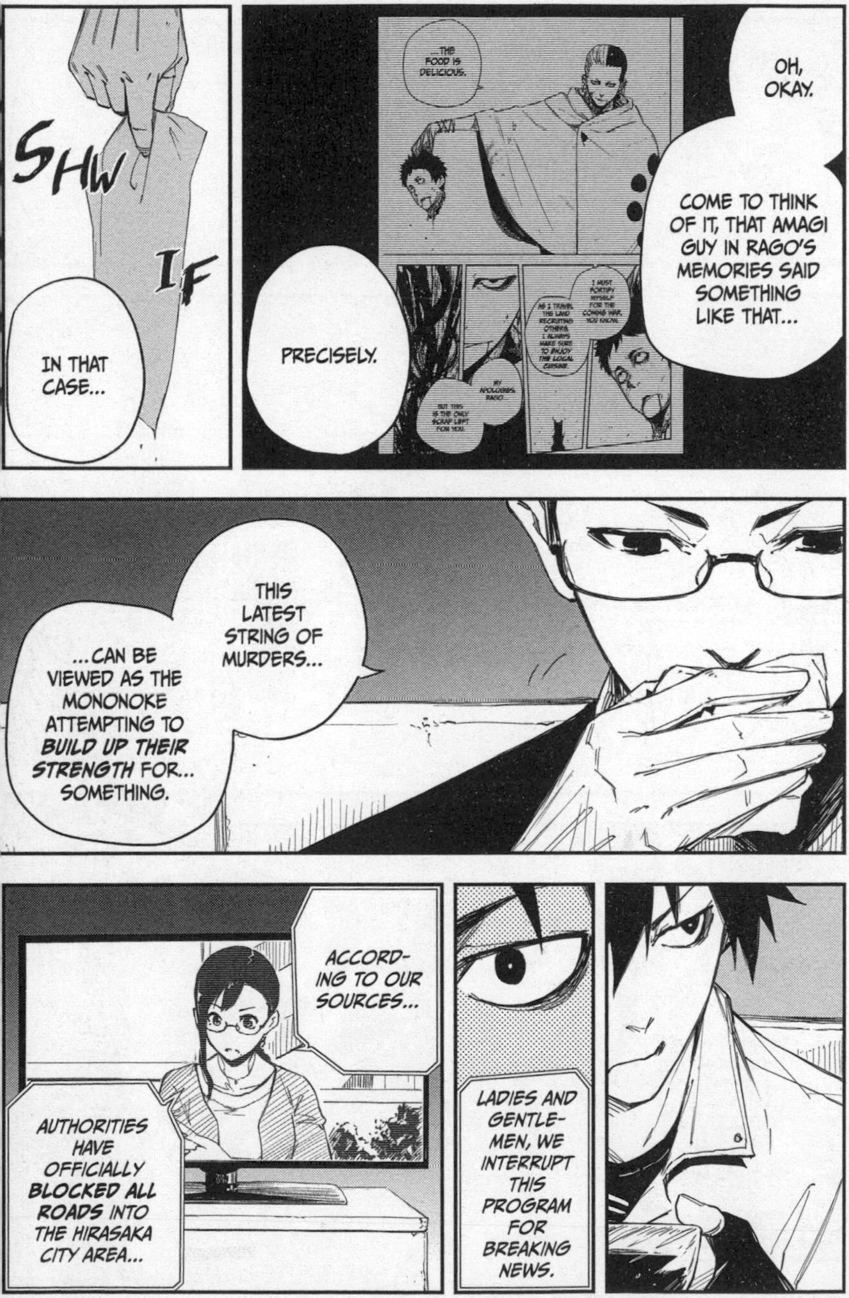
OH, OKAY.
COME TO THINK OF IT, THAT AMAGI GUY IN RAGO'S MEMORIES SAID SOMETHING LIKE THAT...
...THE FOOD IS DELICIOUS.
I MUST FORTIFY MYSELF FOR THE COMING WAR, YOU KNOW.
AS I TRAVEL THE LAND RECRUITING OTHERS, I ALWAYS MAKE SURE TO ENJOY THE LOCAL CUISINE.
MY APOLOGIES, RAGO...
BUT THIS IS THE ONLY SCRAP LEFT FOR YOU.
PRECISELY.
SHWIF
IN THAT CASE...
THIS LATEST STRING OF MURDERS...
...CAN BE VIEWED AS THE MONONOKE ATTEMPTING TO BUILD UP THEIR STRENGTH FOR... SOMETHING.
LADIES AND GENTLEMEN, WE INTERRUPT THIS PROGRAM FOR BREAKING NEWS.
ACCORDING TO OUR SOURCES...
AUTHORITIES HAVE OFFICIALLY BLOCKED ALL ROADS INTO THE HIRASAKA CITY AREA...

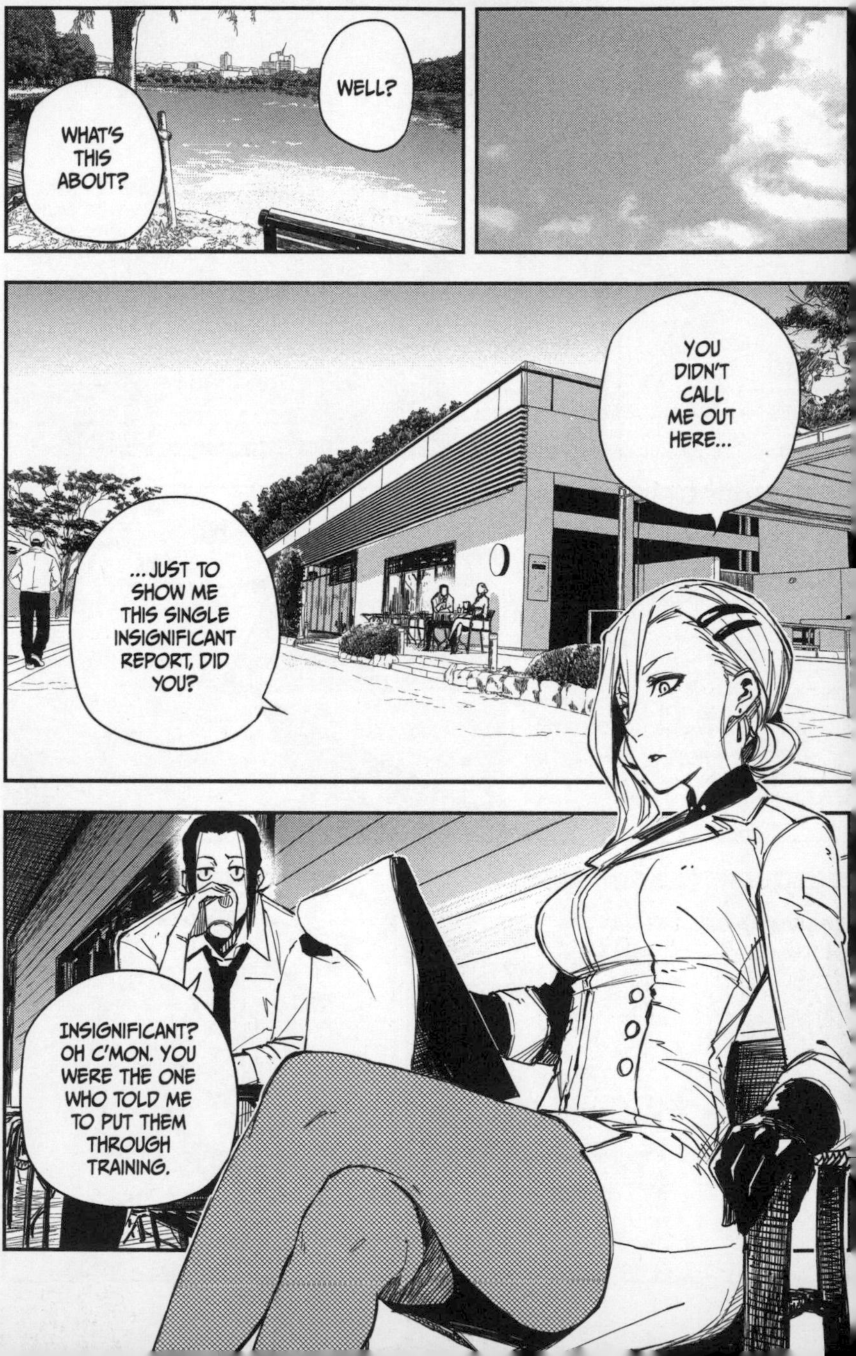
WELL?
WHAT'S THIS ABOUT?
YOU DIDN'T CALL ME OUT HERE...
...JUST TO SHOW ME THIS SINGLE INSIGNIFICANT REPORT, DID YOU?
INSIGNIFICANT? OH C'MON. YOU WERE THE ONE WHO TOLD ME TO PUT THEM THROUGH TRAINING.

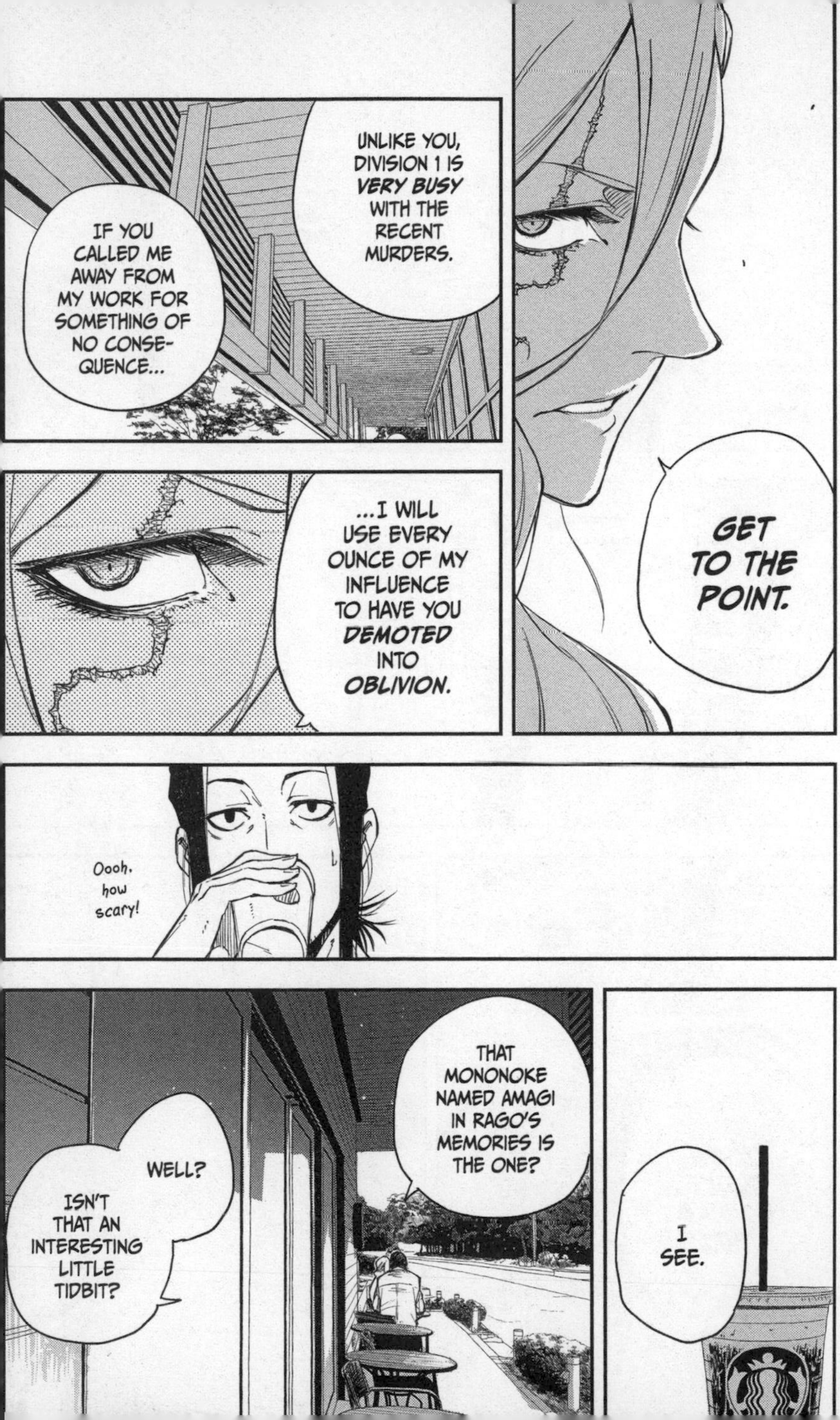
UNLIKE YOU, DIVISION 1 IS VERY BUSY WITH THE RECENT MURDERS.
IF YOU CALLED ME AWAY FROM MY WORK FOR SOMETHING OF NO CONSE-QUENCE...
...I WILL USE EVERY OUNCE OF MY INFLUENCE TO HAVE YOU DEMOTED INTO OBLIVION.
GET TO THE POINT.
Oooh. how scary!
I SEE.
THAT MONONOKE NAMED AMAGI IN RAGO'S MEMORIES IS THE ONE?
WELL?
ISN'T THAT AN INTERESTING LITTLE TIDBIT?

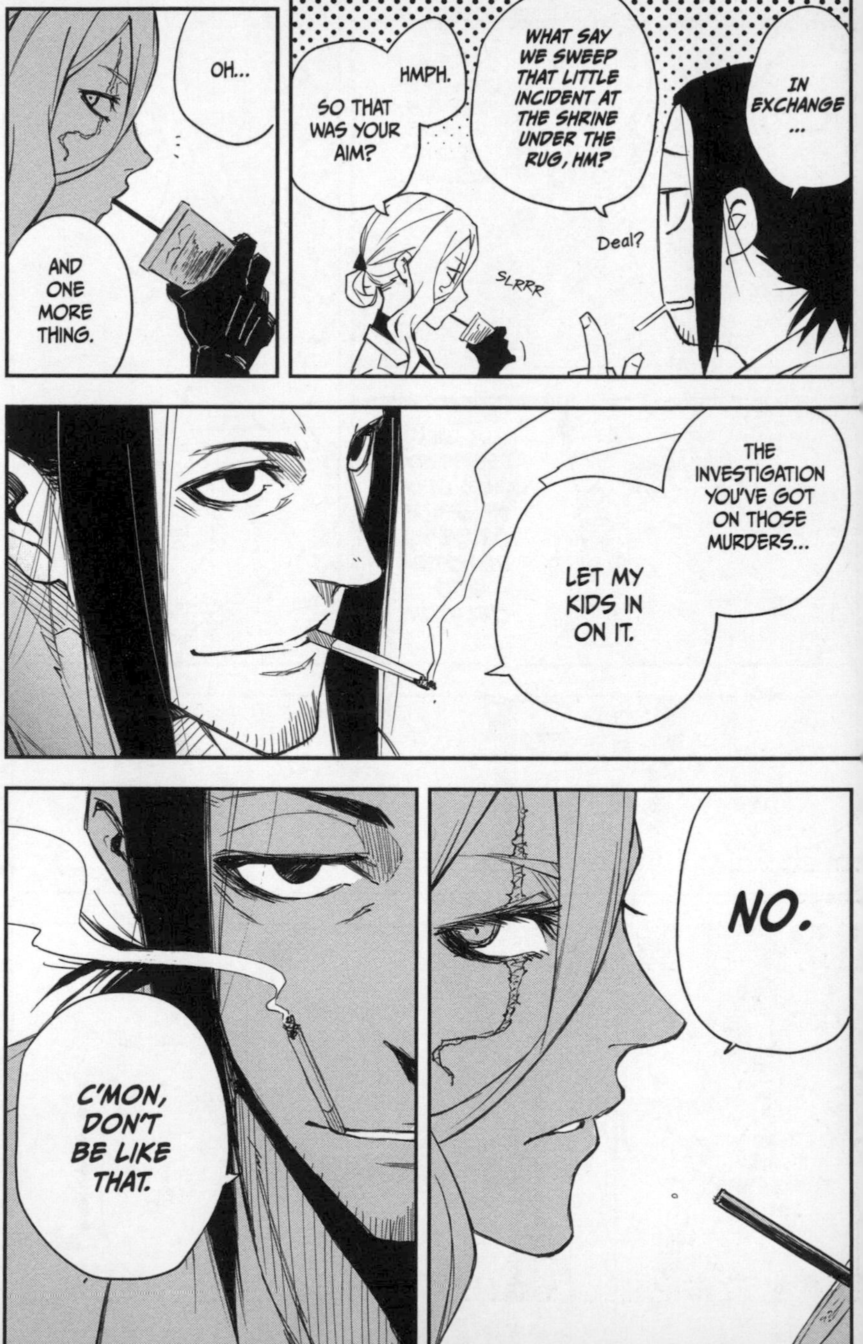
IN EXCHANGE...
WHAT SAY WE SWEEP THAT LITTLE INCIDENT AT THE SHRINE UNDER THE RUG, HM?
Deal?
HMPH.
SO THAT WAS YOUR AIM?
SLRRR
OH...
AND ONE MORE THING.
THE INVESTIGATION YOU'VE GOT ON THOSE MURDERS...
LET MY KIDS IN ON IT.
NO.
C'MON, DON'T BE LIKE THAT.

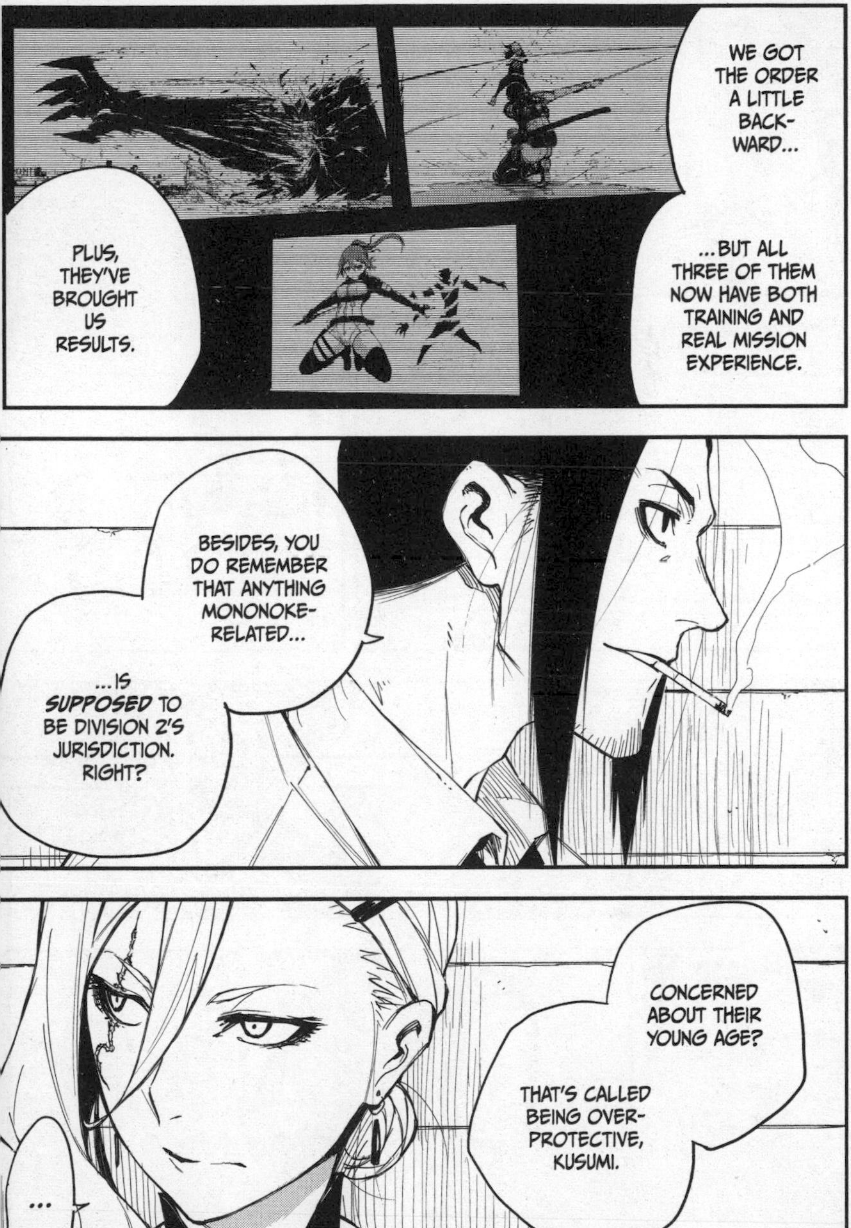
WE GOT THE ORDER A LITTLE BACK-WARD...
...BUT ALL THREE OF THEM NOW HAVE BOTH TRAINING AND REAL MISSION EXPERIENCE.
PLUS, THEY'VE BROUGHT US RESULTS.
BESIDES, YOU DO REMEMBER THAT ANYTHING MONONOKE-RELATED...
...IS *SUPPOSED* TO BE DIVISION 2'S JURISDICTION. RIGHT?
CONCERNED ABOUT THEIR YOUNG AGE?
THAT'S CALLED BEING OVER-PROTECTIVE, KUSUMI.
...

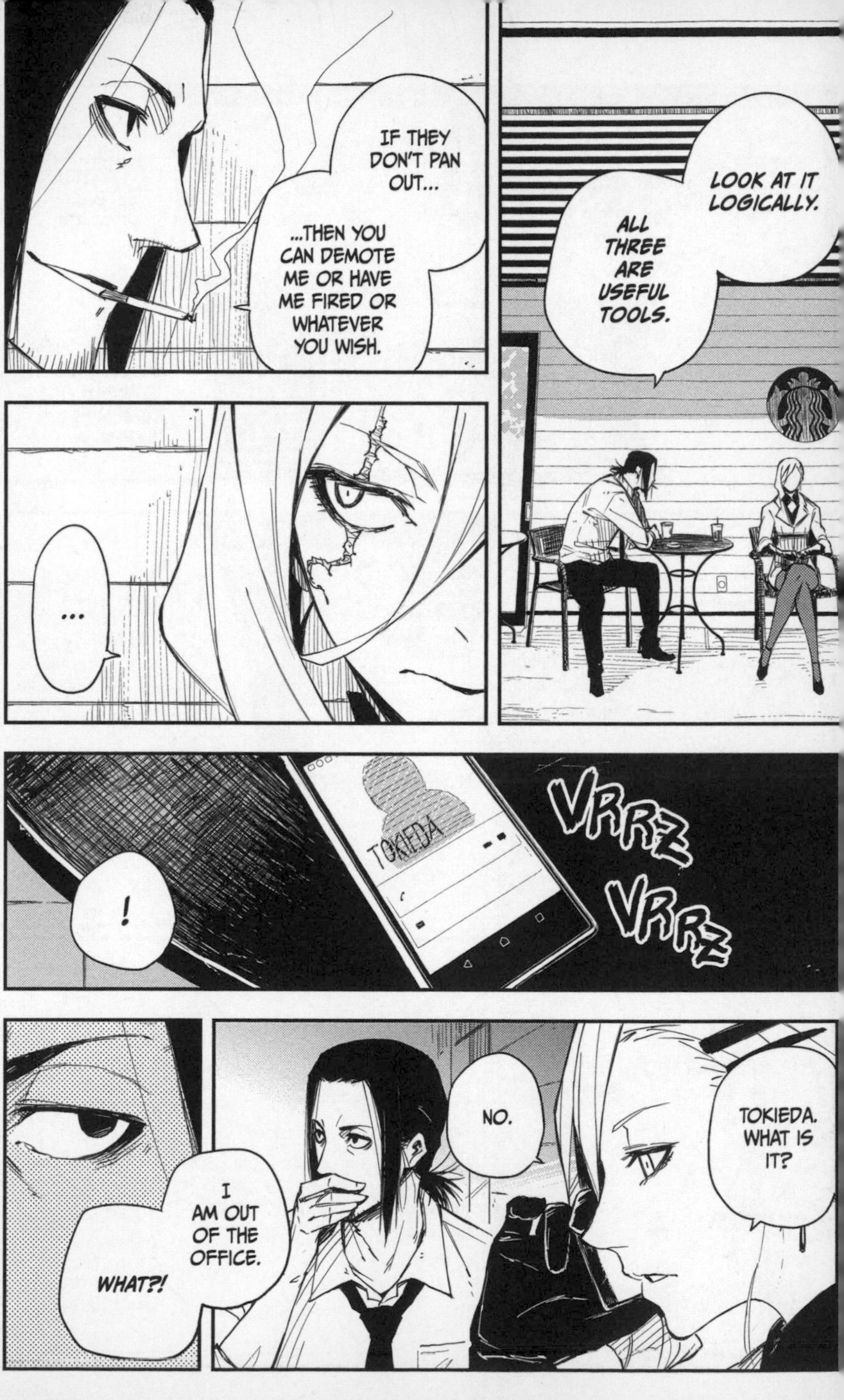
LOOK AT IT LOGICALLY.
ALL THREE ARE USEFUL TOOLS.
IF THEY DON'T PAN OUT...
...THEN YOU CAN DEMOTE ME OR HAVE ME FIRED OR WHATEVER YOU WISH.
...
VRRZ
VRRZ
TOKIEDA
!
TOKIEDA. WHAT IS IT?
NO.
I AM OUT OF THE OFFICE.
WHAT?!

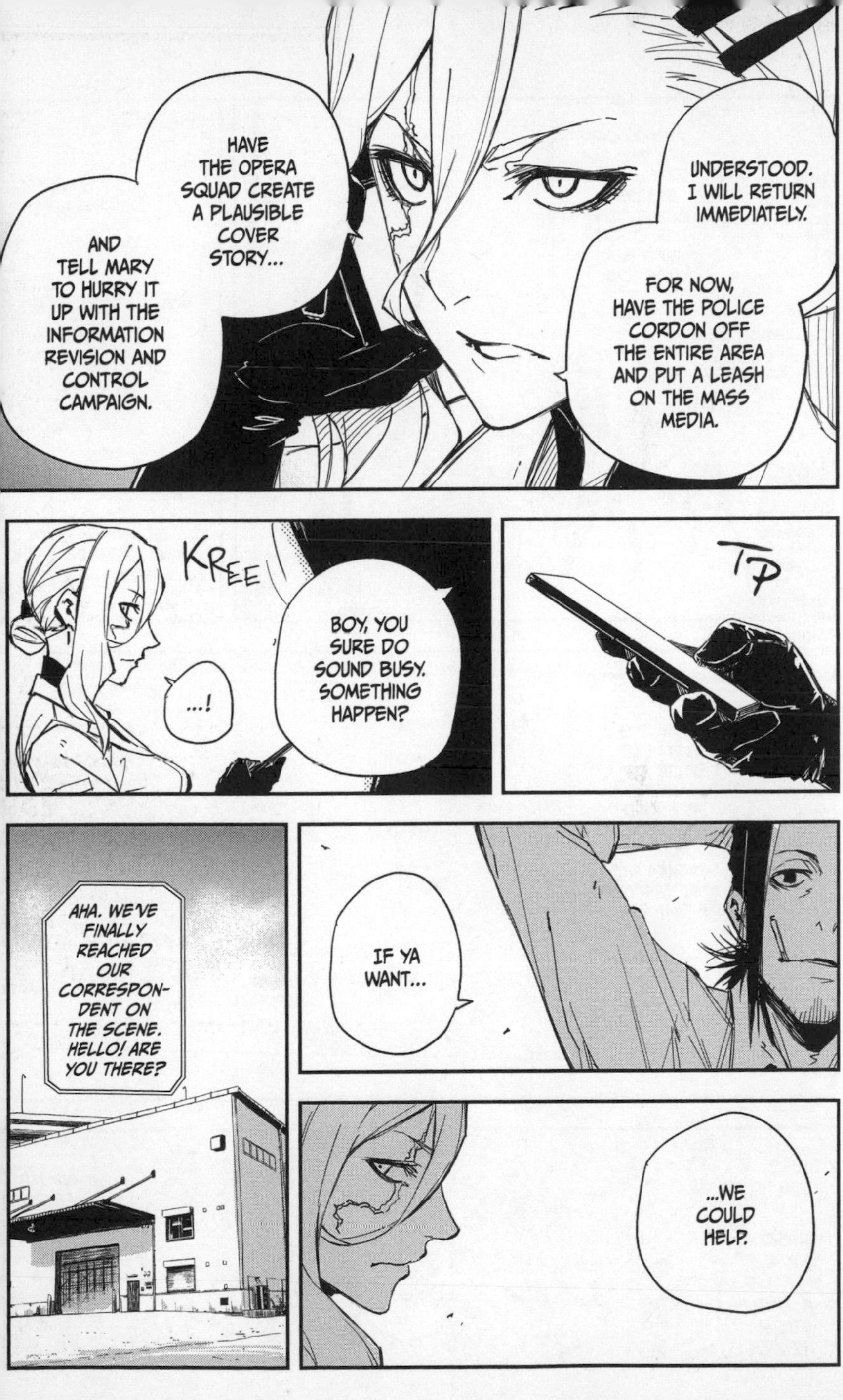
UNDERSTOOD. I WILL RETURN IMMEDIATELY.
FOR NOW, HAVE THE POLICE CORDON OFF THE ENTIRE AREA AND PUT A LEASH ON THE MASS MEDIA.
HAVE THE OPERA SQUAD CREATE A PLAUSIBLE COVER STORY...
AND TELL MARY TO HURRY IT UP WITH THE INFORMATION REVISION AND CONTROL CAMPAIGN.
TP
KREEE
BOY, YOU SURE DO SOUND BUSY. SOMETHING HAPPEN?
...!
IF YA WANT...
...WE COULD HELP.
AHA. WE'VE FINALLY REACHED OUR CORRESPONDENT ON THE SCENE. HELLO! ARE YOU THERE?

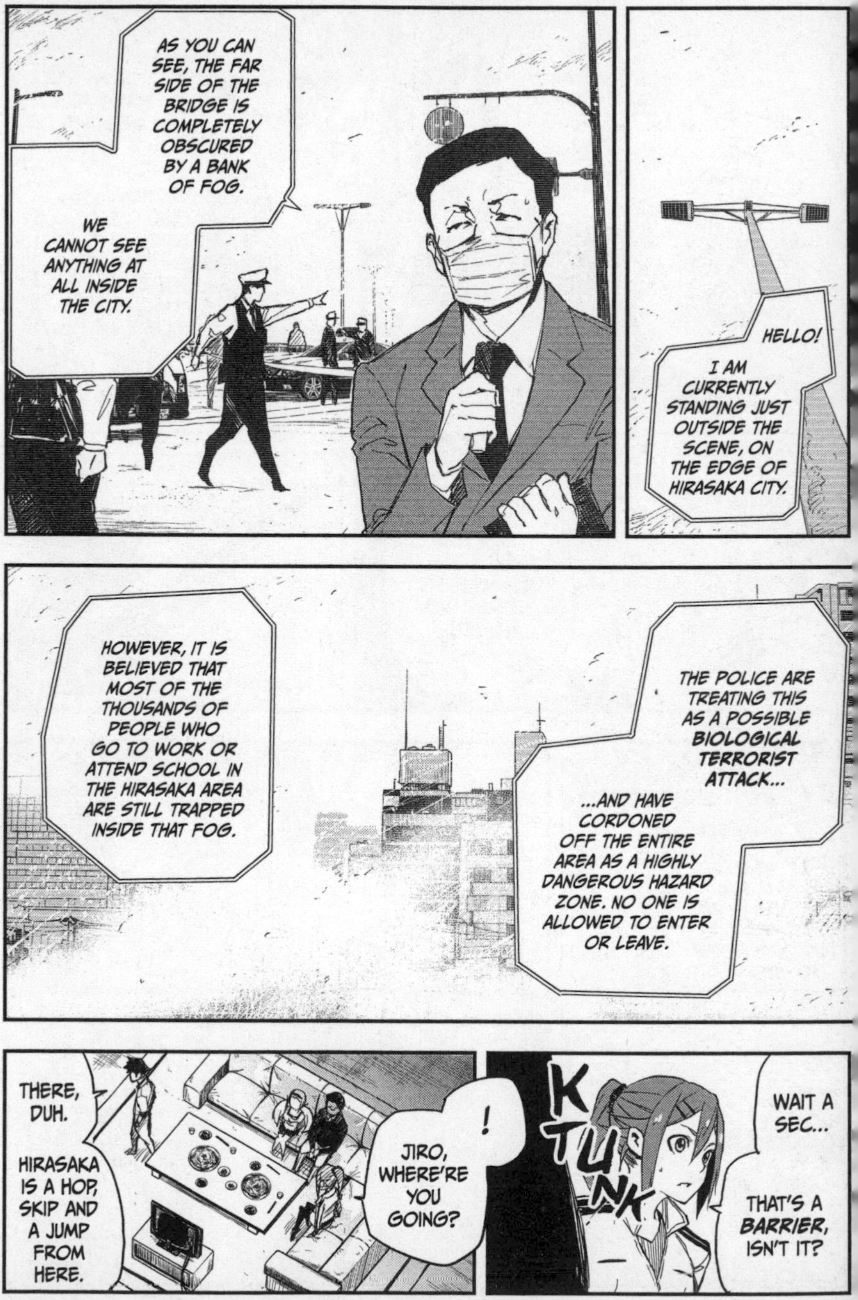
HELLO!
I AM CURRENTLY STANDING JUST OUTSIDE THE SCENE, ON THE EDGE OF HIRASAKA CITY.
AS YOU CAN SEE, THE FAR SIDE OF THE BRIDGE IS COMPLETELY OBSCURED BY A BANK OF FOG.
WE CANNOT SEE ANYTHING AT ALL INSIDE THE CITY.
HOWEVER, IT IS BELIEVED THAT MOST OF THE THOUSANDS OF PEOPLE WHO GO TO WORK OR ATTEND SCHOOL IN THE HIRASAKA AREA ARE STILL TRAPPED INSIDE THAT FOG.
THE POLICE ARE TREATING THIS AS A POSSIBLE BIOLOGICAL TERRORIST ATTACK...
...AND HAVE CORDONED OFF THE ENTIRE AREA AS A HIGHLY DANGEROUS HAZARD ZONE. NO ONE IS ALLOWED TO ENTER OR LEAVE.
WAIT A SEC...
THAT'S A BARRIER, ISN'T IT?
KTUNK
!
JIRO, WHERE'RE YOU GOING?
THERE, DUH.
HIRASAKA IS A HOP, SKIP AND A JUMP FROM HERE.

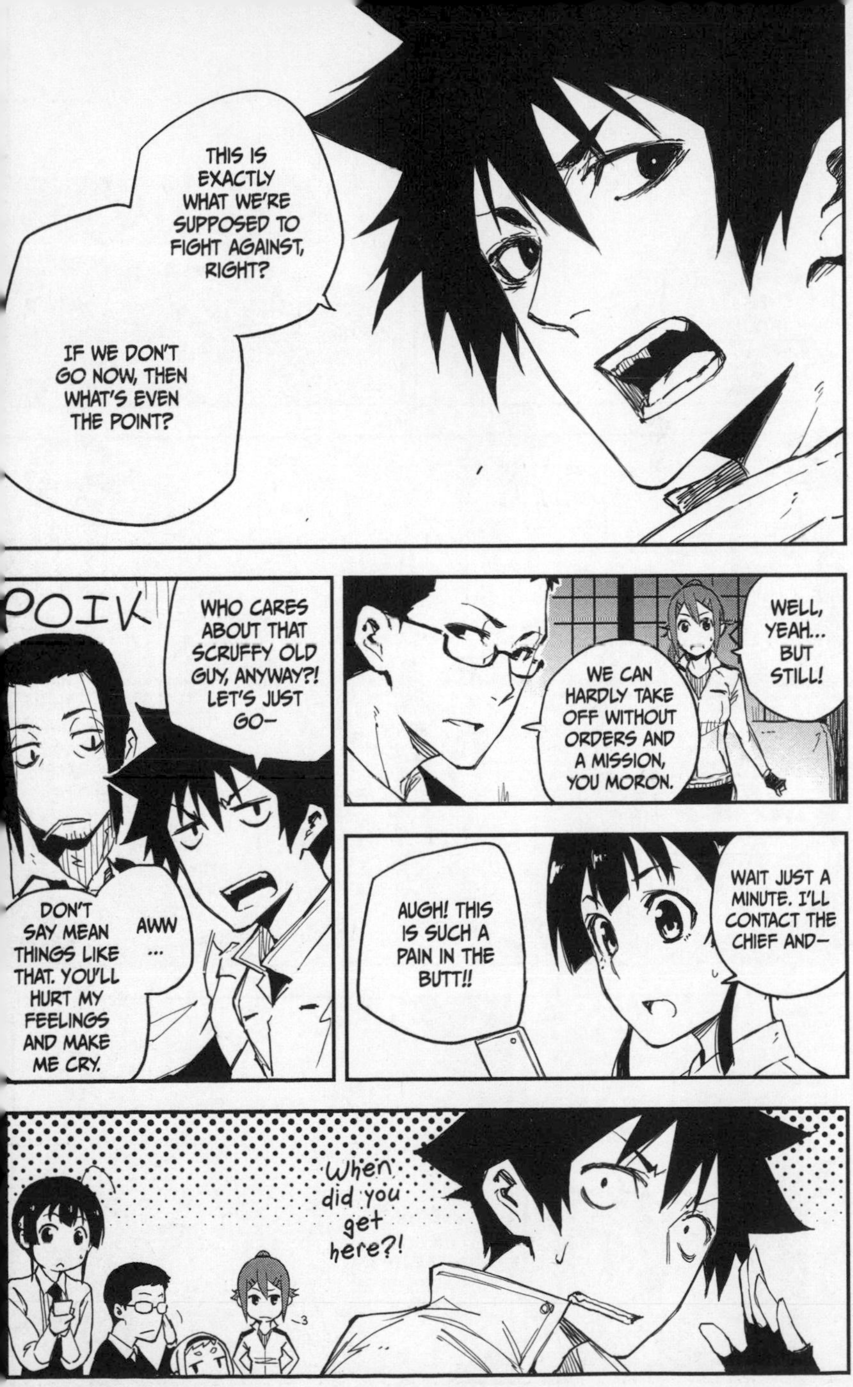
THIS IS EXACTLY WHAT WE'RE SUPPOSED TO FIGHT AGAINST, RIGHT?
IF WE DON'T GO NOW, THEN WHAT'S EVEN THE POINT?
WELL, YEAH... BUT STILL!
WE CAN HARDLY TAKE OFF WITHOUT ORDERS AND A MISSION, YOU MORON.
WAIT JUST A MINUTE. I'LL CONTACT THE CHIEF AND—
AUGH! THIS IS SUCH A PAIN IN THE BUTT!!
WHO CARES ABOUT THAT SCRUFFY OLD GUY, ANYWAY?! LET'S JUST GO—
POIK
AWW ...
DON'T SAY MEAN THINGS LIKE THAT. YOU'LL HURT MY FEELINGS AND MAKE ME CRY.
When did you get here?!

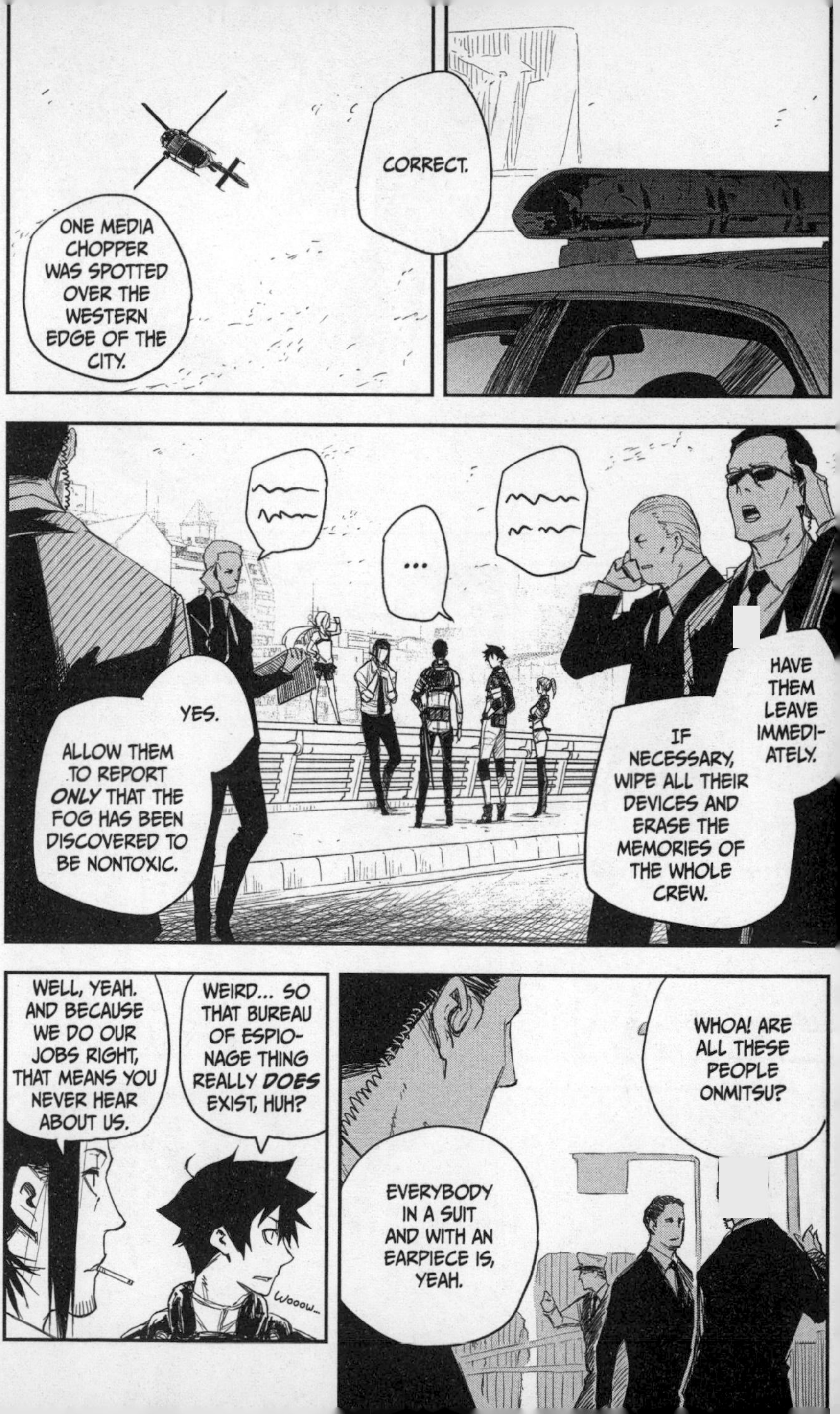
CORRECT.
ONE MEDIA CHOPPER WAS SPOTTED OVER THE WESTERN EDGE OF THE CITY.
HAVE THEM LEAVE IMMEDIATELY.
IF NECESSARY, WIPE ALL THEIR DEVICES AND ERASE THE MEMORIES OF THE WHOLE CREW.
...
YES.
ALLOW THEM TO REPORT *ONLY* THAT THE FOG HAS BEEN DISCOVERED TO BE NONTOXIC.
WHOA! ARE ALL THESE PEOPLE ONMITSU?
EVERYBODY IN A SUIT AND WITH AN EARPIECE IS, YEAH.
WEIRD... SO THAT BUREAU OF ESPIONAGE THING REALLY *DOES* EXIST, HUH?
WELL, YEAH. AND BECAUSE WE DO OUR JOBS RIGHT, THAT MEANS YOU NEVER HEAR ABOUT US.
Wooow...

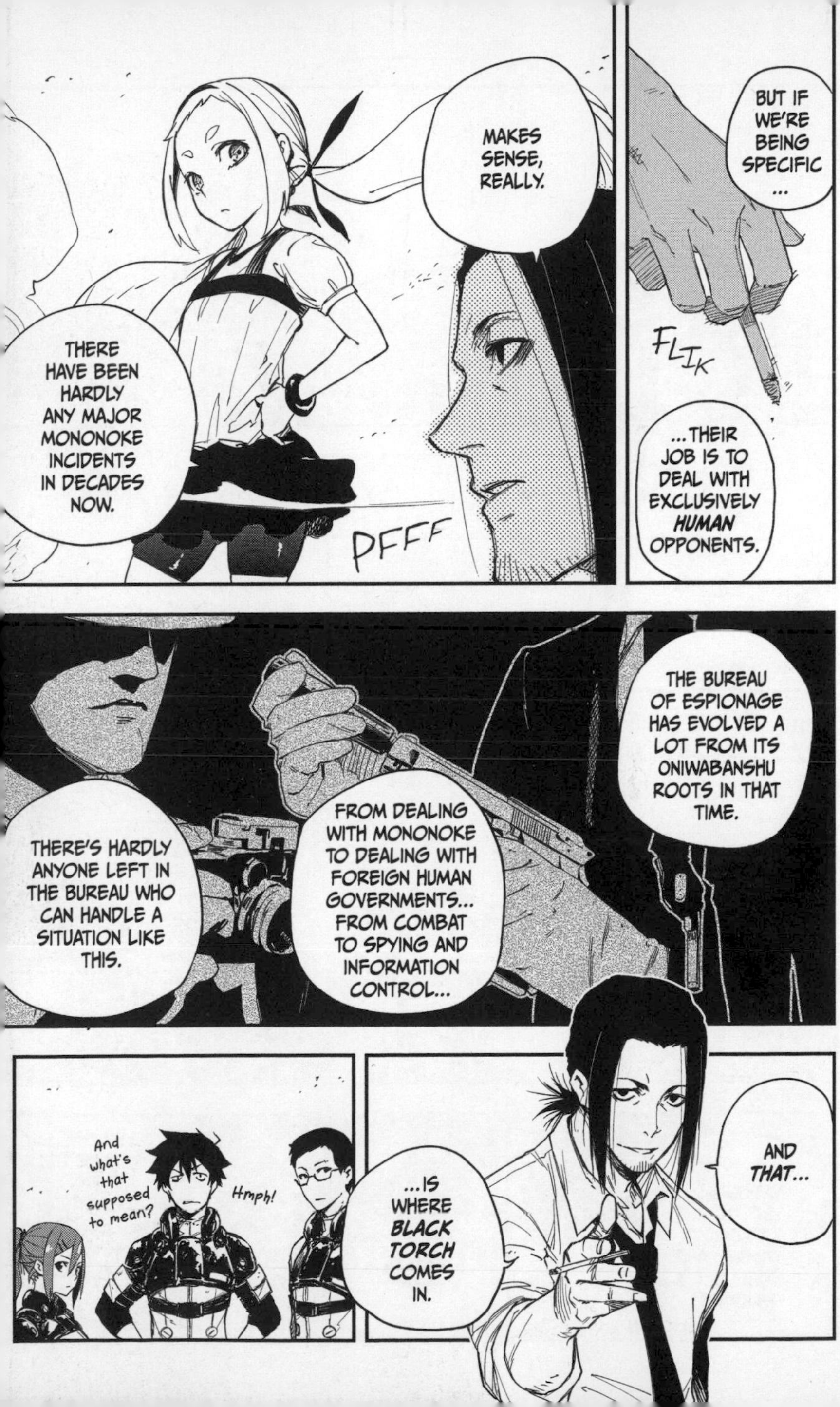
BUT IF WE'RE BEING SPECIFIC ...
FLIK
...THEIR JOB IS TO DEAL WITH EXCLUSIVELY *HUMAN* OPPONENTS.
MAKES SENSE, REALLY.
PFFF
THERE HAVE BEEN HARDLY ANY MAJOR MONONOKE INCIDENTS IN DECADES NOW.
THE BUREAU OF ESPIONAGE HAS EVOLVED A LOT FROM ITS ONIWABANSHU ROOTS IN THAT TIME.
FROM DEALING WITH MONONOKE TO DEALING WITH FOREIGN HUMAN GOVERNMENTS... FROM COMBAT TO SPYING AND INFORMATION CONTROL...
THERE'S HARDLY ANYONE LEFT IN THE BUREAU WHO CAN HANDLE A SITUATION LIKE THIS.
AND *THAT*...
...IS WHERE *BLACK TORCH* COMES IN.
Hmph!
And what's that supposed to mean?

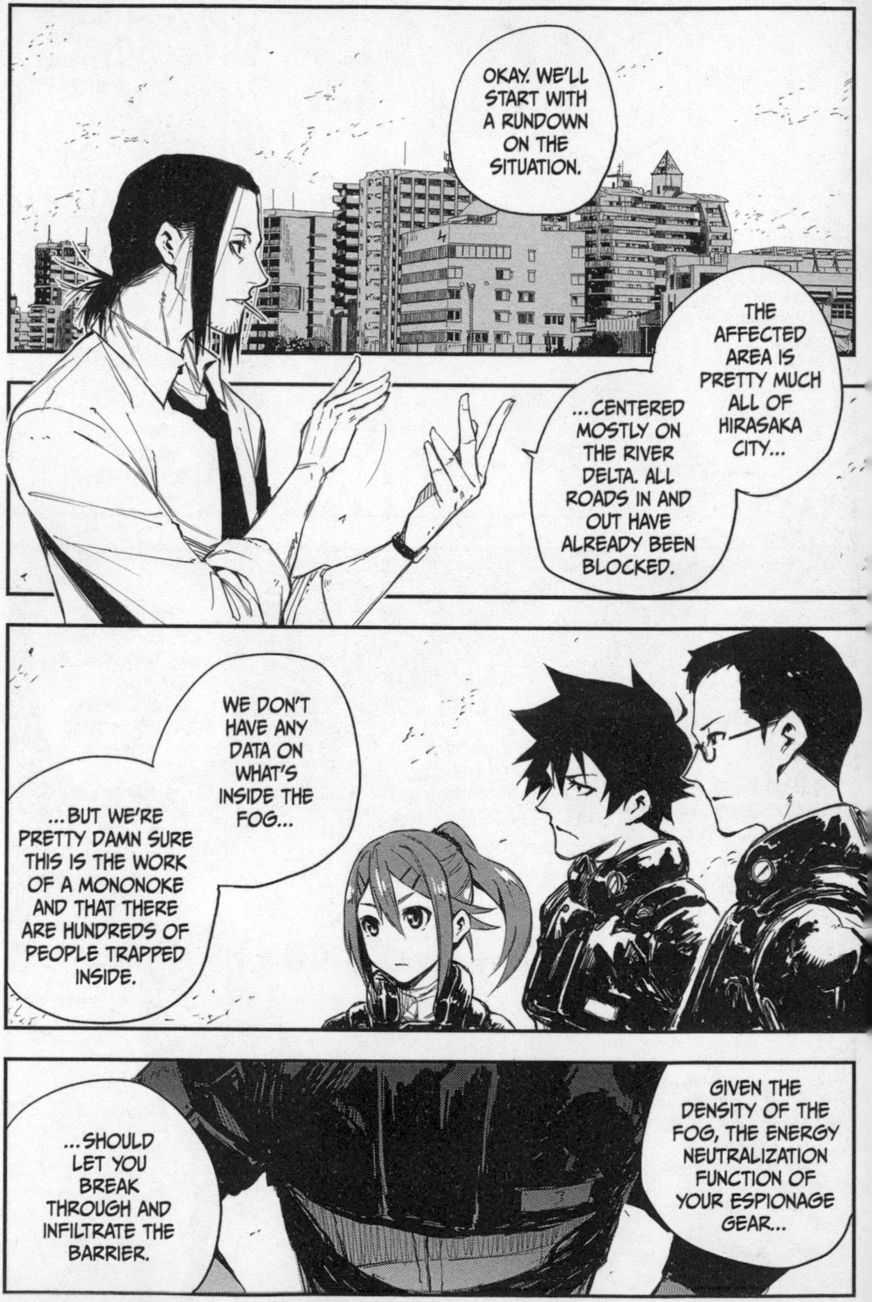
OKAY. WE'LL START WITH A RUNDOWN ON THE SITUATION.
THE AFFECTED AREA IS PRETTY MUCH ALL OF HIRASAKA CITY...
...CENTERED MOSTLY ON THE RIVER DELTA. ALL ROADS IN AND OUT HAVE ALREADY BEEN BLOCKED.
WE DON'T HAVE ANY DATA ON WHAT'S INSIDE THE FOG...
...BUT WE'RE PRETTY DAMN SURE THIS IS THE WORK OF A MONONOKE AND THAT THERE ARE HUNDREDS OF PEOPLE TRAPPED INSIDE.
GIVEN THE DENSITY OF THE FOG, THE ENERGY NEUTRALIZATION FUNCTION OF YOUR ESPIONAGE GEAR...
...SHOULD LET YOU BREAK THROUGH AND INFILTRATE THE BARRIER.

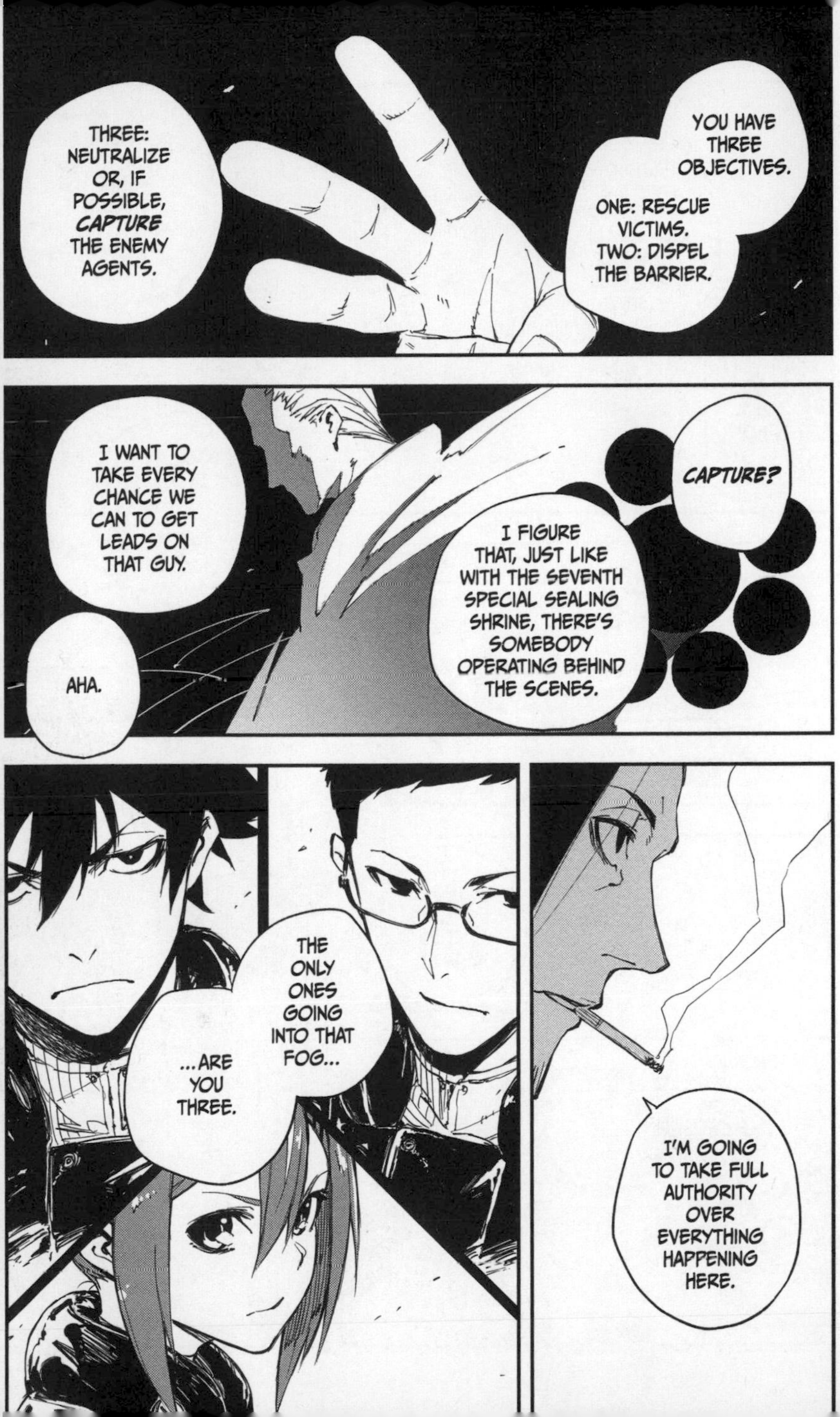
YOU HAVE THREE OBJECTIVES.
ONE: RESCUE VICTIMS. TWO: DISPEL THE BARRIER.
THREE: NEUTRALIZE OR, IF POSSIBLE, *CAPTURE* THE ENEMY AGENTS.
CAPTURE?
I FIGURE THAT, JUST LIKE WITH THE SEVENTH SPECIAL SEALING SHRINE, THERE'S SOMEBODY OPERATING BEHIND THE SCENES.
I WANT TO TAKE EVERY CHANCE WE CAN TO GET LEADS ON THAT GUY.
AHA.
I'M GOING TO TAKE FULL AUTHORITY OVER EVERYTHING HAPPENING HERE.
THE ONLY ONES GOING INTO THAT FOG...
...ARE YOU THREE.

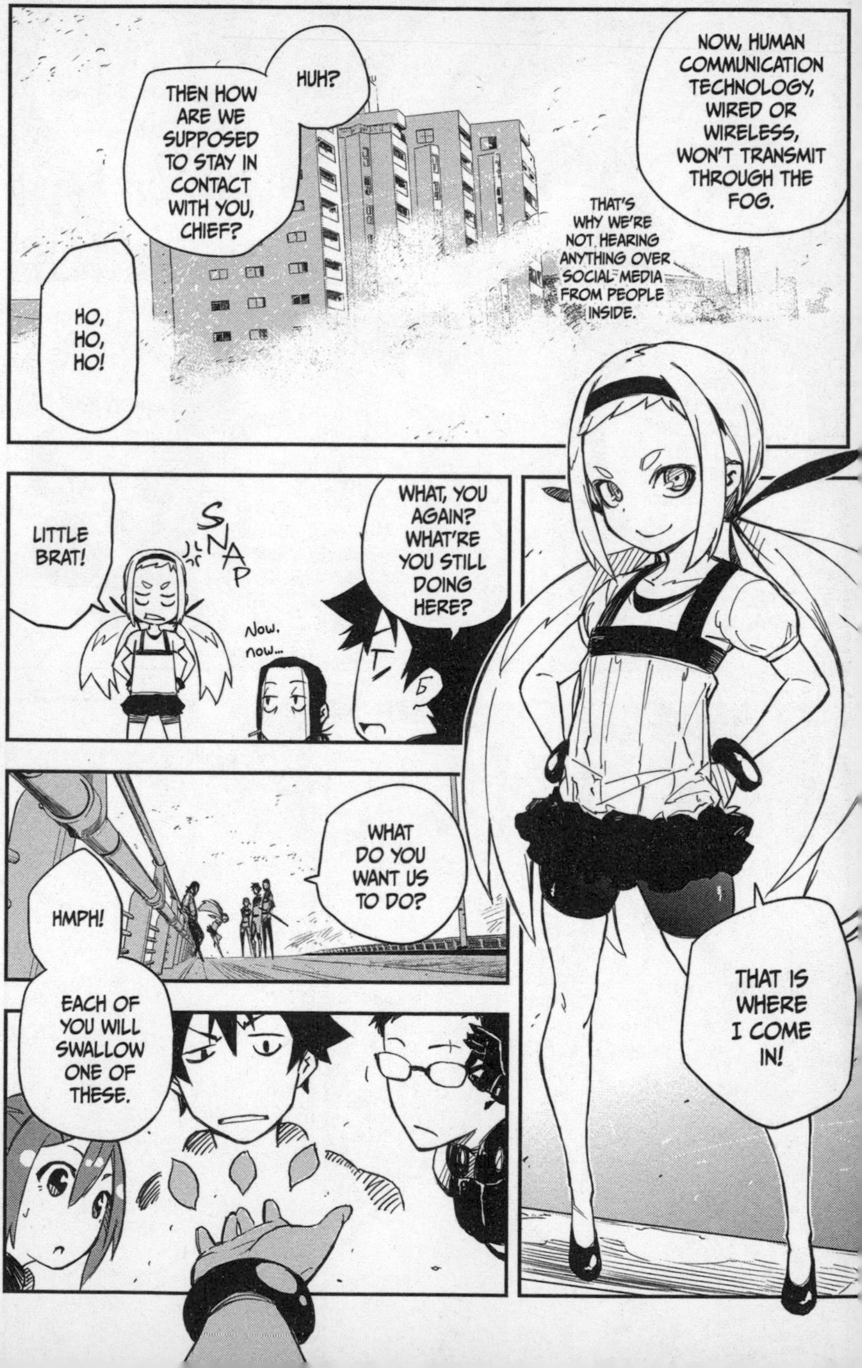
NOW, HUMAN COMMUNICATION TECHNOLOGY, WIRED OR WIRELESS, WON'T TRANSMIT THROUGH THE FOG.
THAT'S WHY WE'RE NOT HEARING ANYTHING OVER SOCIAL MEDIA FROM PEOPLE INSIDE.
HUH?
THEN HOW ARE WE SUPPOSED TO STAY IN CONTACT WITH YOU, CHIEF?
HO, HO, HO!
THAT IS WHERE I COME IN!
WHAT, YOU AGAIN? WHAT'RE YOU STILL DOING HERE?
SNAP
LITTLE BRAT!
Now, now...
WHAT DO YOU WANT US TO DO?
HMPH!
EACH OF YOU WILL SWALLOW ONE OF THESE.

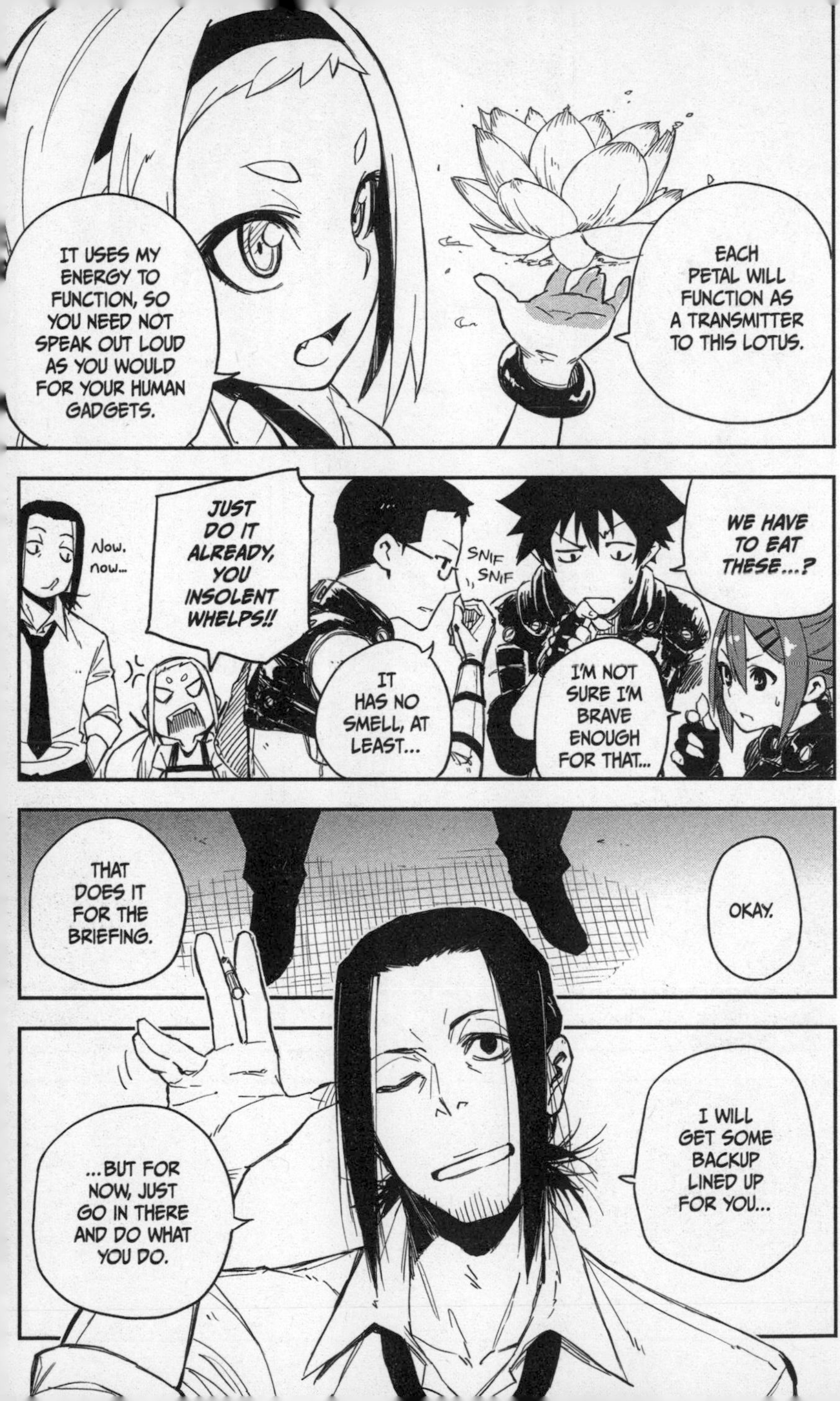
EACH PETAL WILL FUNCTION AS A TRANSMITTER TO THIS LOTUS.
IT USES MY ENERGY TO FUNCTION, SO YOU NEED NOT SPEAK OUT LOUD AS YOU WOULD FOR YOUR HUMAN GADGETS.
WE HAVE TO EAT THESE...?
SNIF SNIF
I'M NOT SURE I'M BRAVE ENOUGH FOR THAT...
IT HAS NO SMELL, AT LEAST...
JUST DO IT ALREADY, YOU INSOLENT WHELPS!!
Now, now...
OKAY.
THAT DOES IT FOR THE BRIEFING.
I WILL GET SOME BACKUP LINED UP FOR YOU...
...BUT FOR NOW, JUST GO IN THERE AND DO WHAT YOU DO.

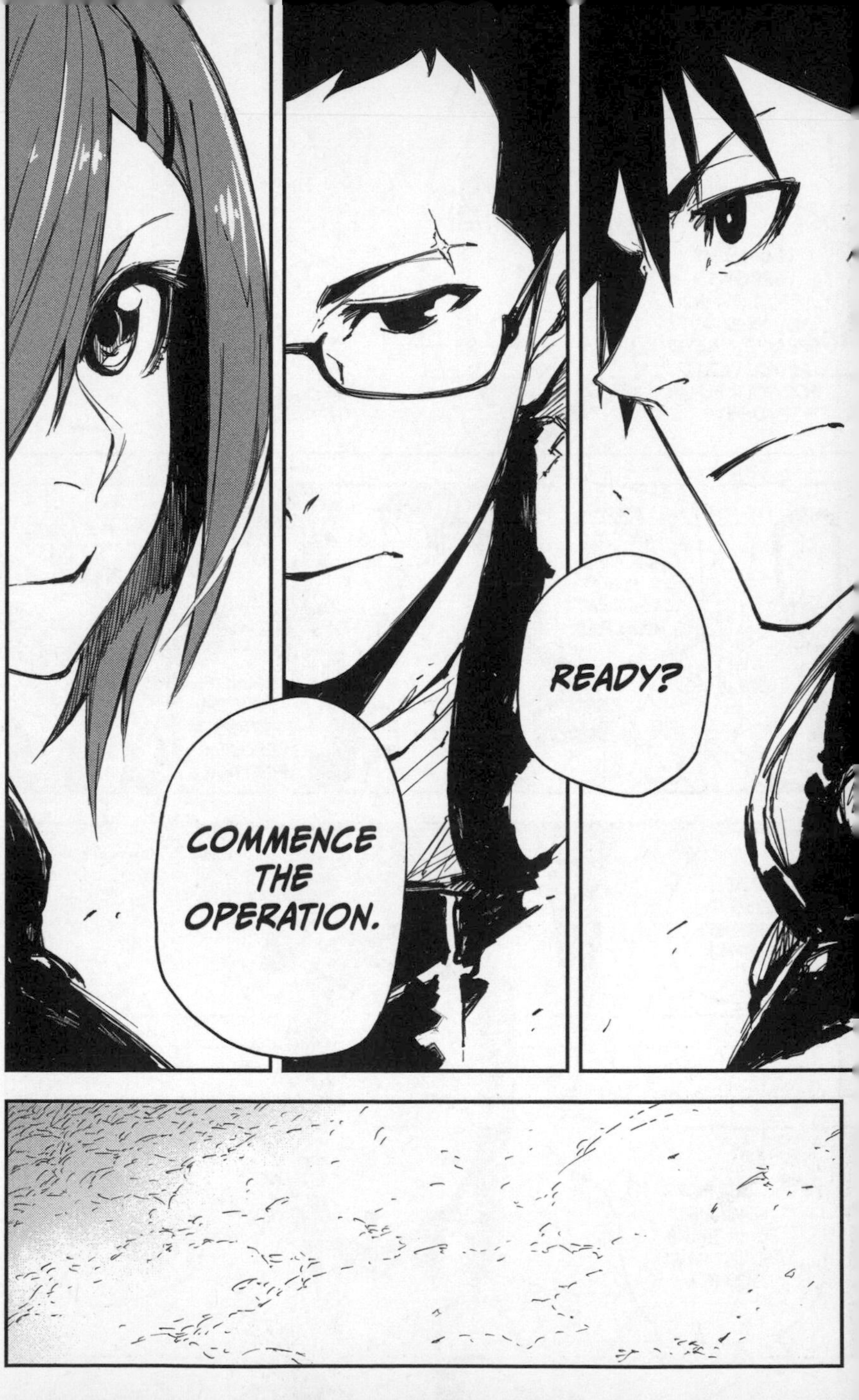
READY?
COMMENCE THE OPERATION.

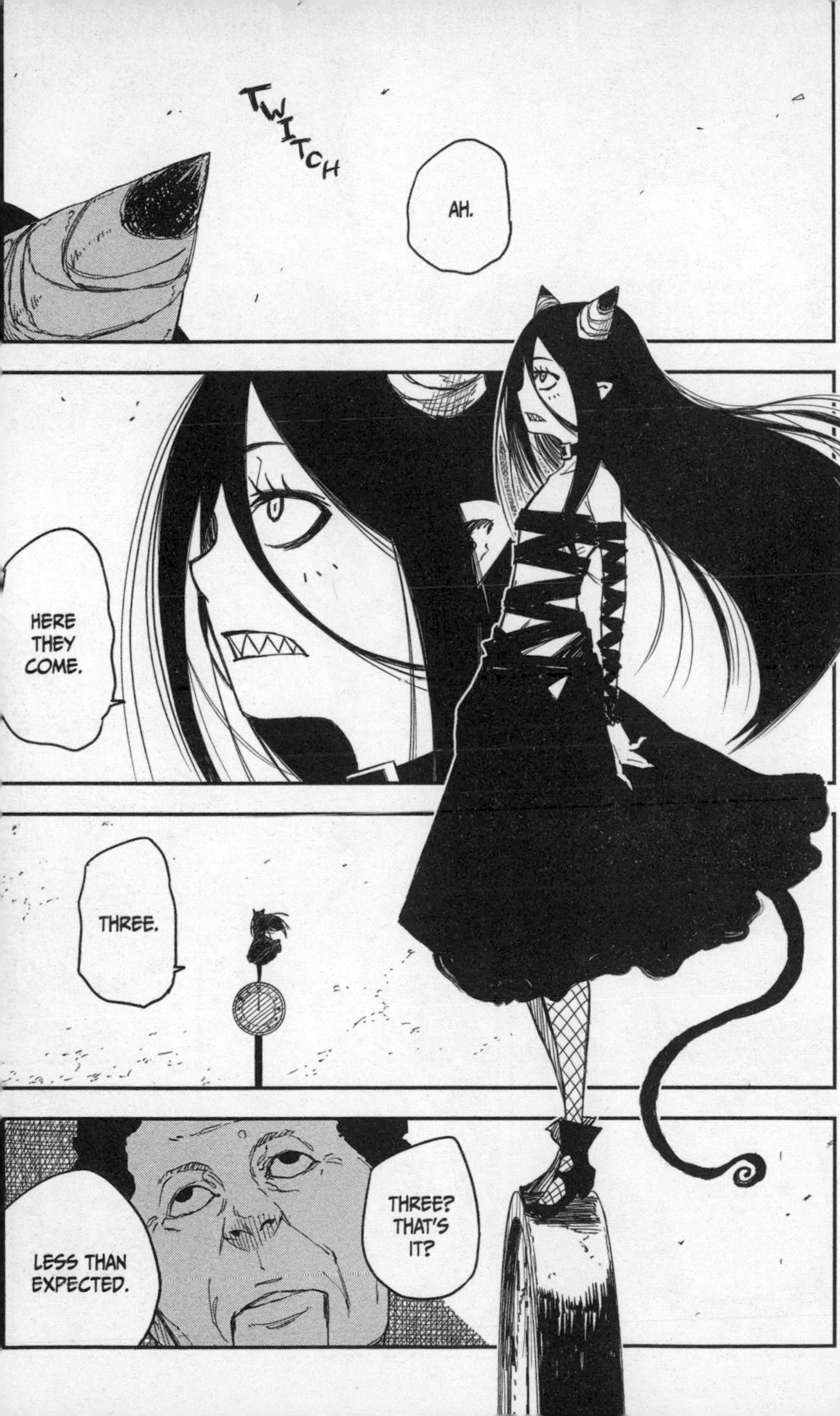
TWITCH
AH.
HERE THEY COME.
THREE.
THREE? THAT'S IT?
LESS THAN EXPECTED.

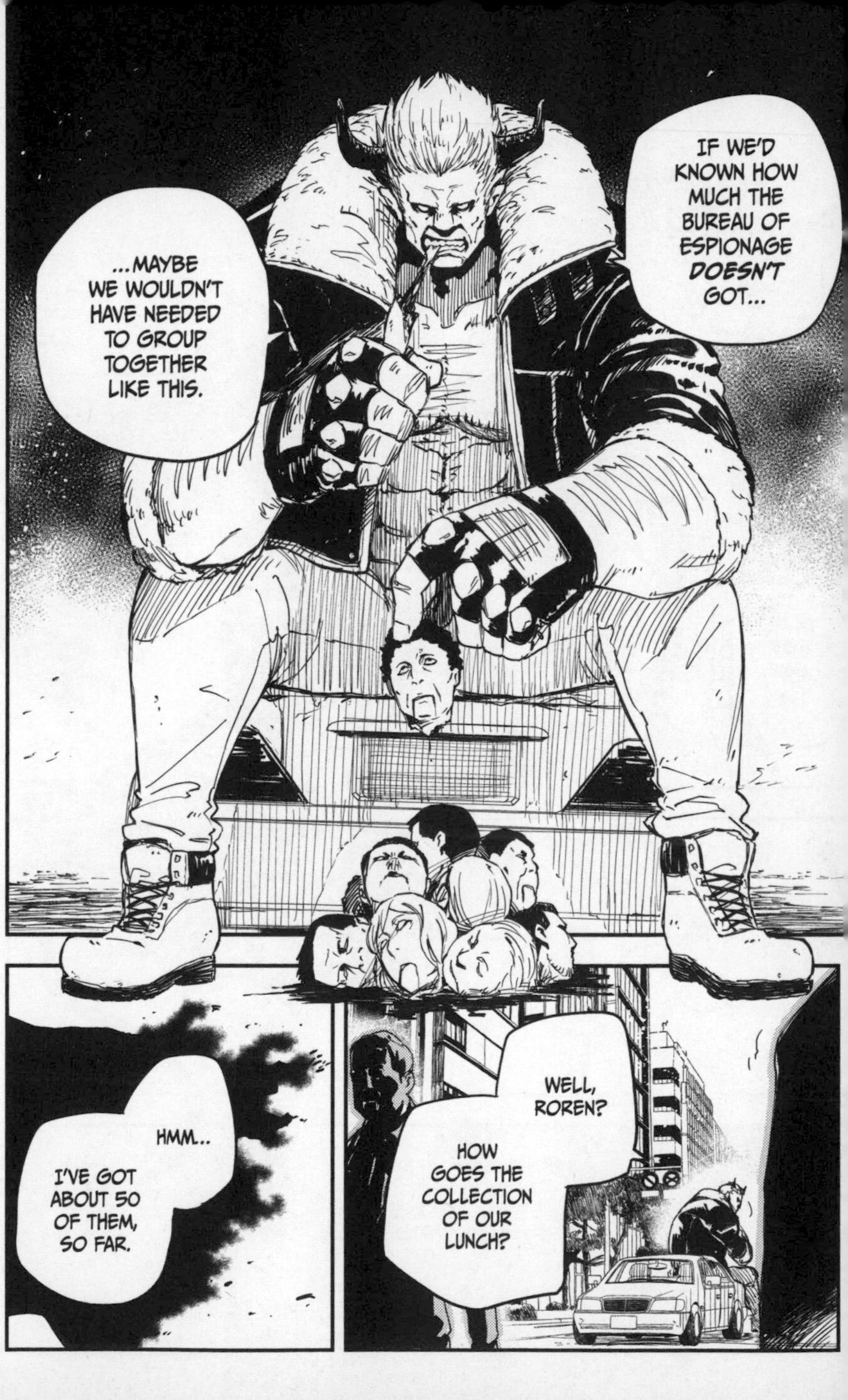
IF WE'D KNOWN HOW MUCH THE BUREAU OF ESPIONAGE *DOESN'T* GOT...
...MAYBE WE WOULDN'T HAVE NEEDED TO GROUP TOGETHER LIKE THIS.
WELL, ROREN?
HOW GOES THE COLLECTION OF OUR LUNCH?
HMM..
I'VE GOT ABOUT 50 OF THEM, SO FAR.

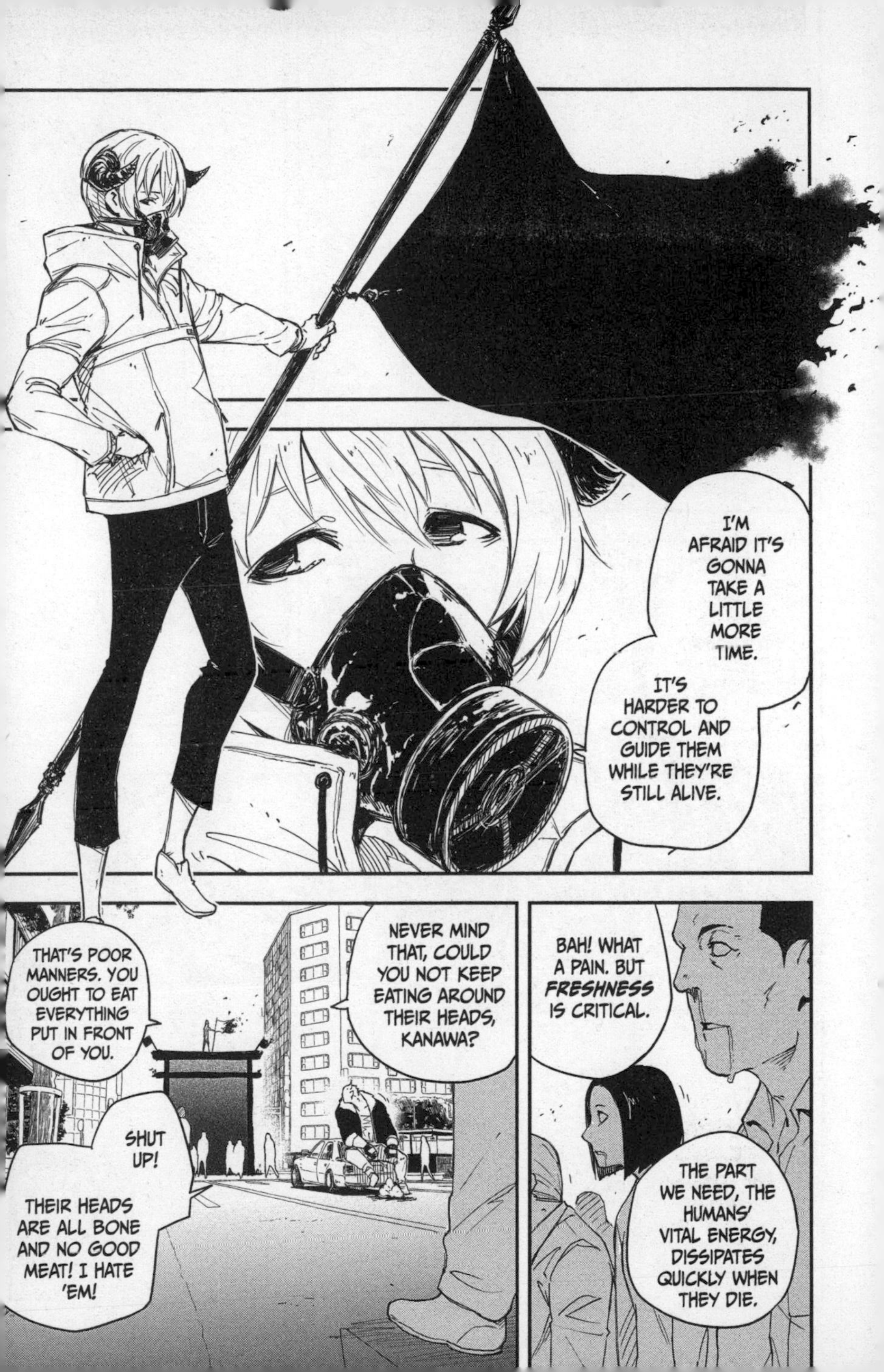
I'M AFRAID IT'S GONNA TAKE A LITTLE MORE TIME.
IT'S HARDER TO CONTROL AND GUIDE THEM WHILE THEY'RE STILL ALIVE.
BAH! WHAT A PAIN. BUT *FRESHNESS* IS CRITICAL.
THE PART WE NEED, THE HUMANS' VITAL ENERGY, DISSIPATES QUICKLY WHEN THEY DIE.
NEVER MIND THAT, COULD YOU NOT KEEP EATING AROUND THEIR HEADS, KANAWA?
THAT'S POOR MANNERS. YOU OUGHT TO EAT EVERYTHING PUT IN FRONT OF YOU.
SHUT UP!
THEIR HEADS ARE ALL BONE AND NO GOOD MEAT! I HATE 'EM!

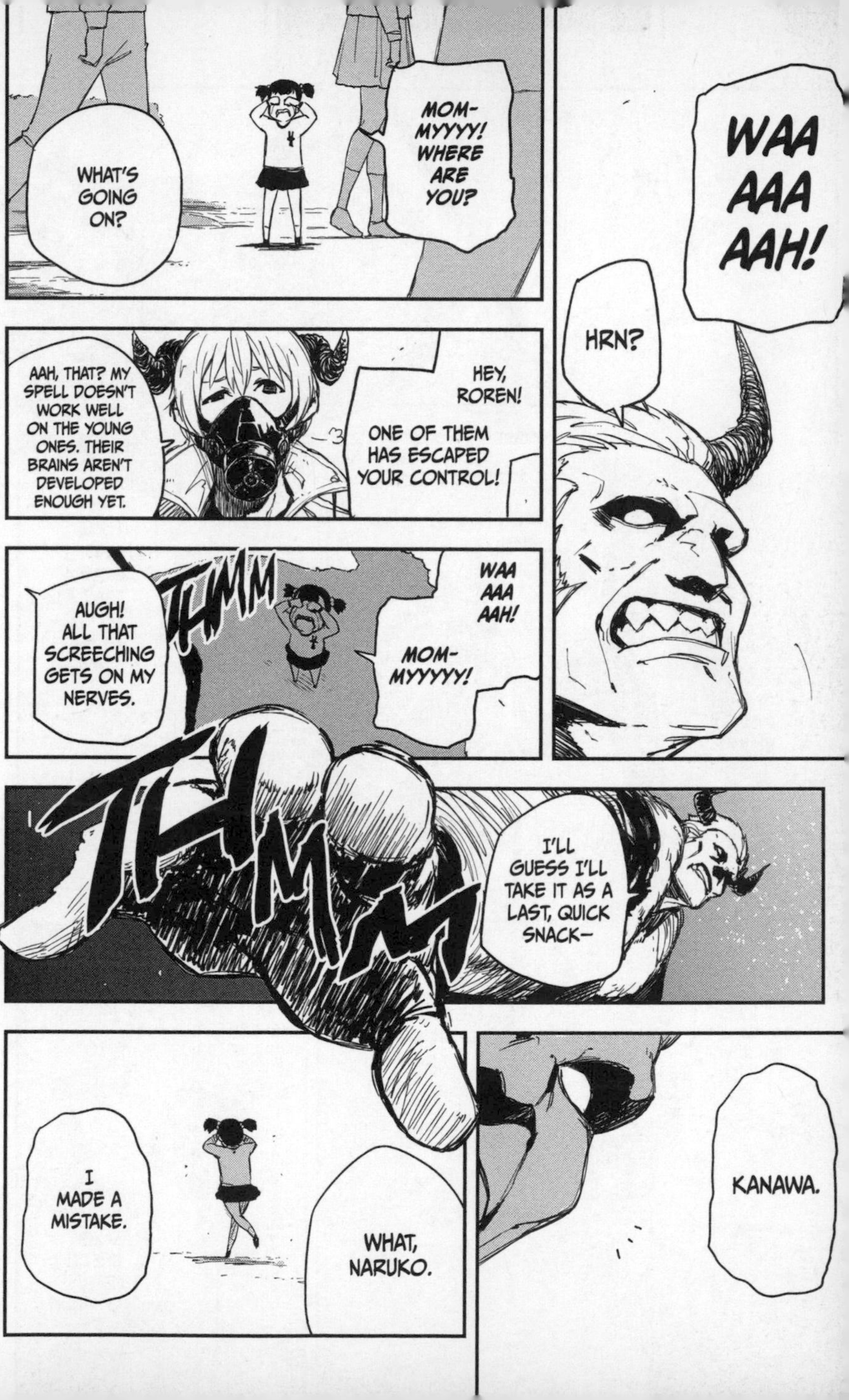
WAA AAA AAH!
HRN?
MOM-MYYYY! WHERE ARE YOU?
WHAT'S GOING ON?
HEY, ROREN!
ONE OF THEM HAS ESCAPED YOUR CONTROL!
AAH, THAT? MY SPELL DOESN'T WORK WELL ON THE YOUNG ONES. THEIR BRAINS AREN'T DEVELOPED ENOUGH YET.
WAA AAA AAH!
MOM-MYYYYY!
THMM
AUGH! ALL THAT SCREECHING GETS ON MY NERVES.
I'LL GUESS I'LL TAKE IT AS A LAST, QUICK SNACK—
THMMMM
KANAWA.
WHAT, NARUKO.
I MADE A MISTAKE.

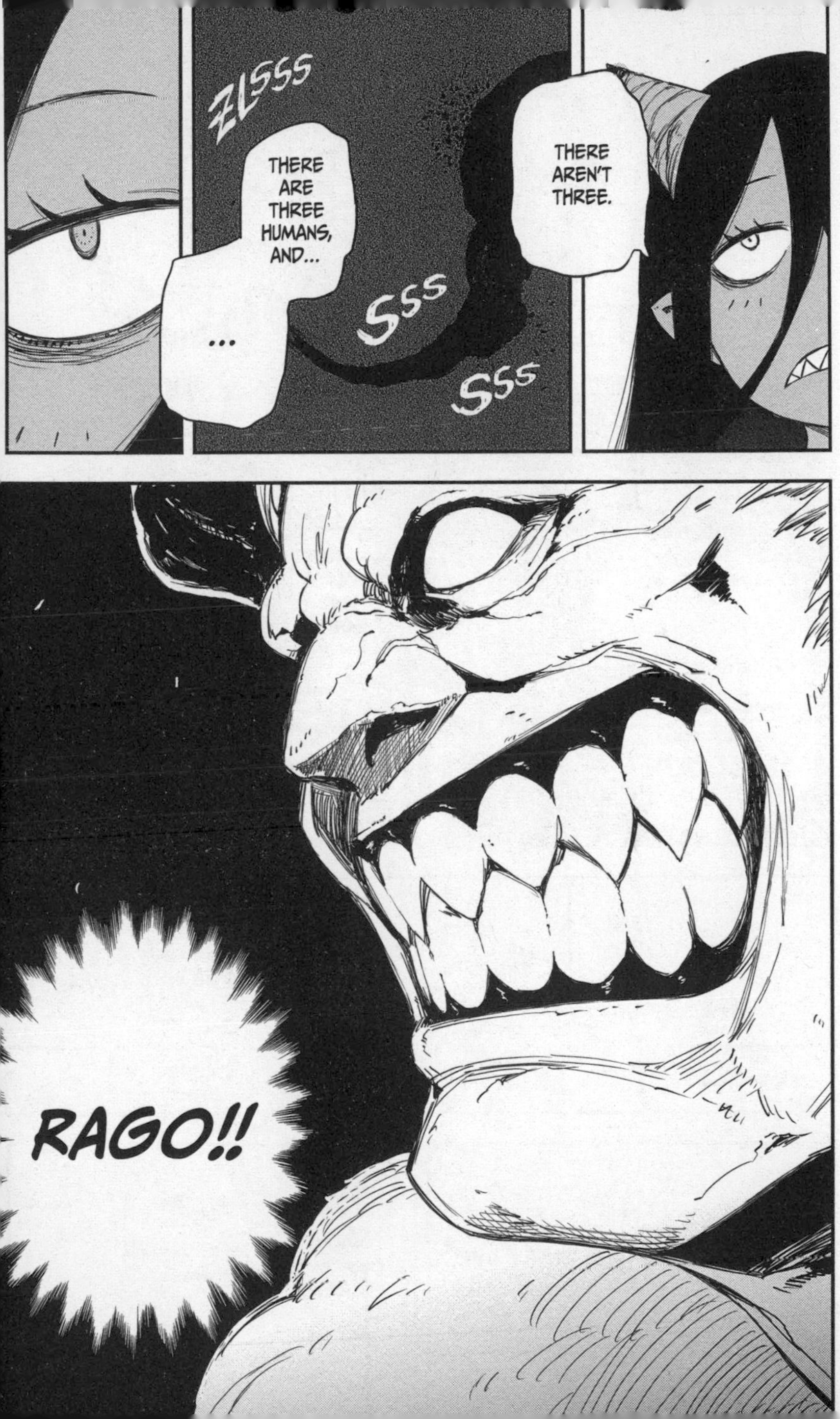
THERE AREN'T THREE.
ZLSSS
THERE ARE THREE HUMANS, AND...
SSS
SSS
...
RAGO!!

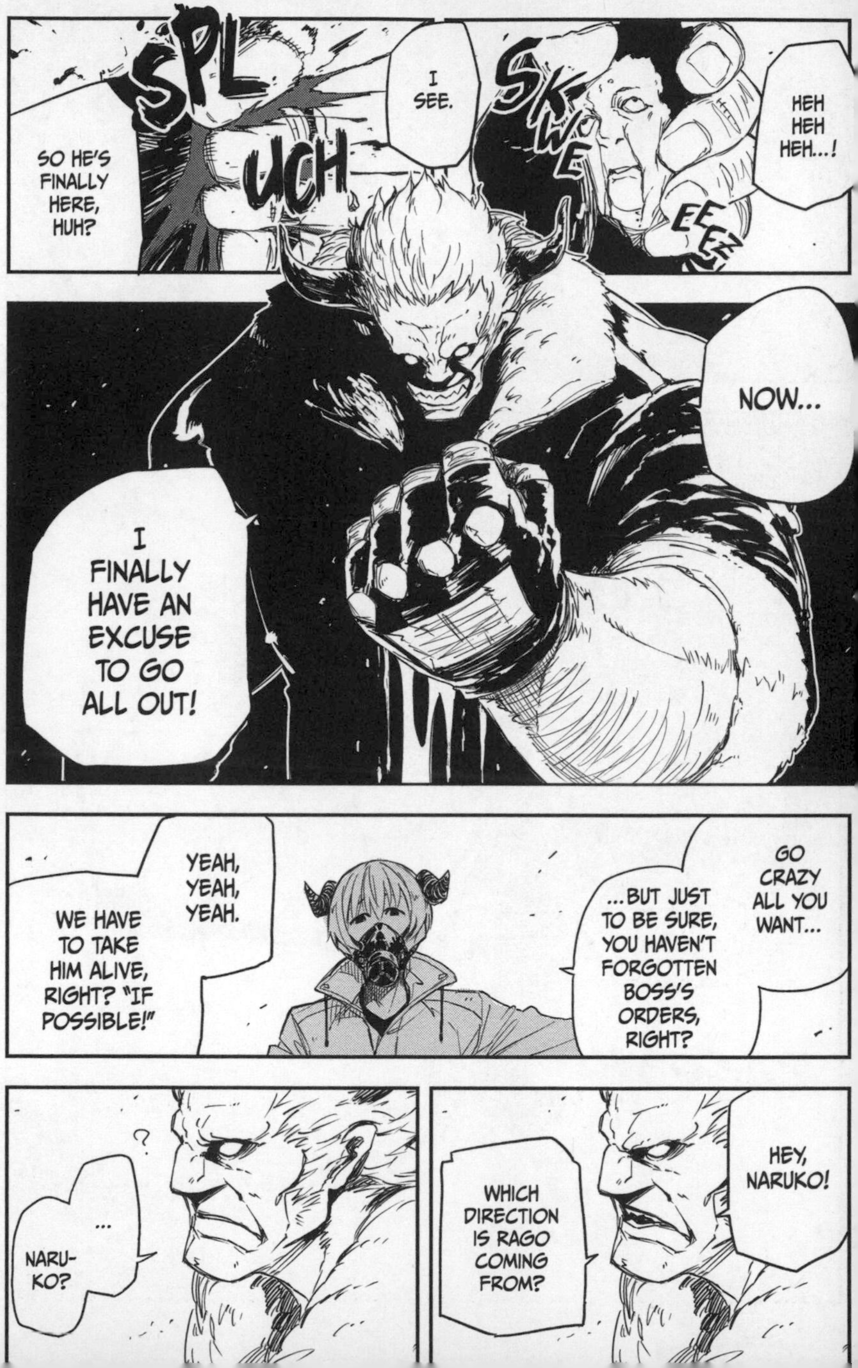
HEH HEH HEH...!
SKWEEEZ
I SEE.
SPLUCH
SO HE'S FINALLY HERE, HUH?
NOW...
I FINALLY HAVE AN EXCUSE TO GO ALL OUT!
GO CRAZY ALL YOU WANT...
...BUT JUST TO BE SURE, YOU HAVEN'T FORGOTTEN BOSS'S ORDERS, RIGHT?
YEAH, YEAH, YEAH.
WE HAVE TO TAKE HIM ALIVE, RIGHT? "IF POSSIBLE!"
HEY, NARUKO!
WHICH DIRECTION IS RAGO COMING FROM?
?
...
NARU-KO?

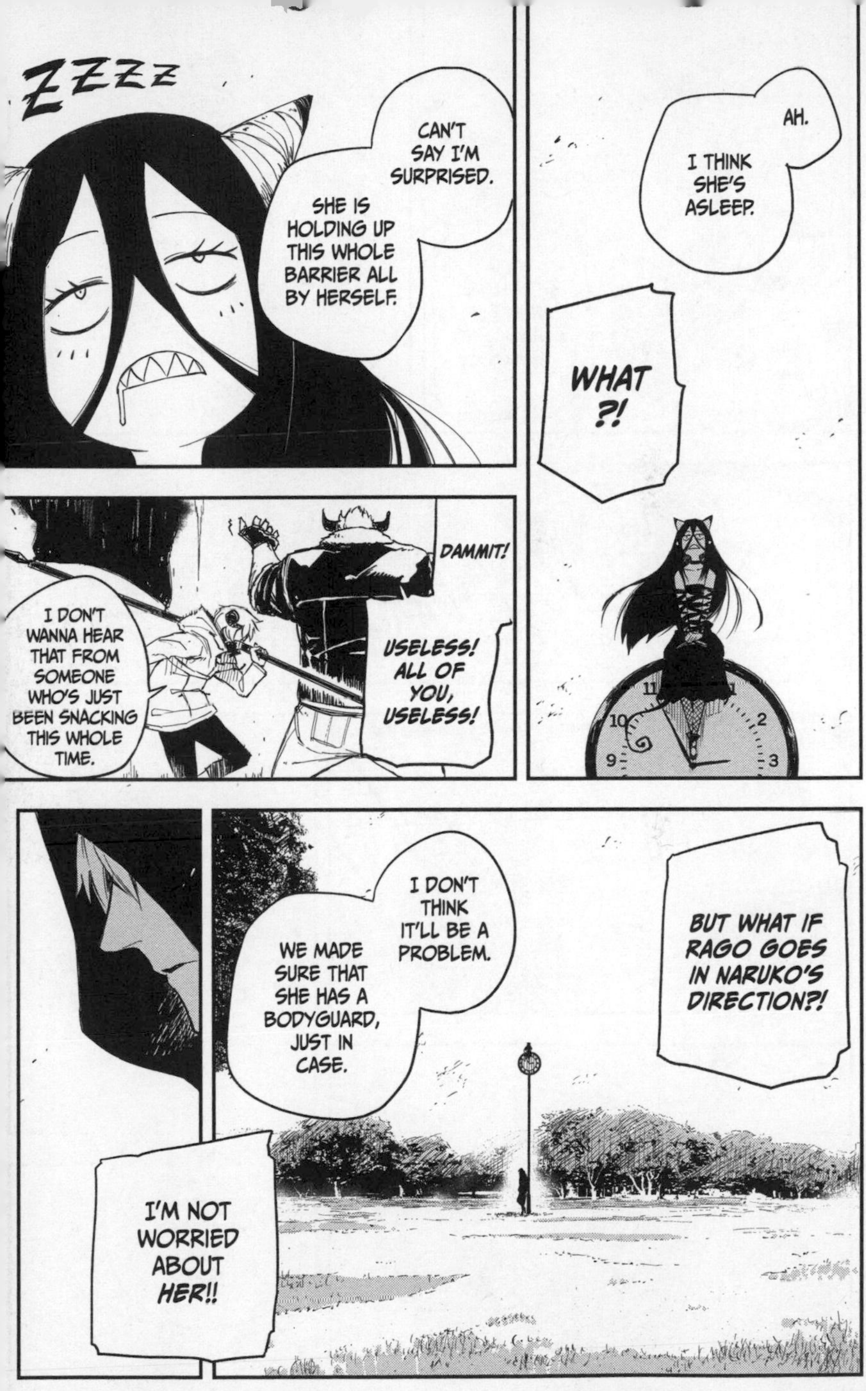
AH.
I THINK SHE'S ASLEEP.
WHAT?!
ZZZZ
CAN'T SAY I'M SURPRISED.
SHE IS HOLDING UP THIS WHOLE BARRIER ALL BY HERSELF.
DAMMIT!
USELESS! ALL OF YOU, USELESS!
I DON'T WANNA HEAR THAT FROM SOMEONE WHO'S JUST BEEN SNACKING THIS WHOLE TIME.
BUT WHAT IF RAGO GOES IN NARUKO'S DIRECTION?!
I DON'T THINK IT'LL BE A PROBLEM.
WE MADE SURE THAT SHE HAS A BODYGUARD, JUST IN CASE.
I'M NOT WORRIED ABOUT HER!!

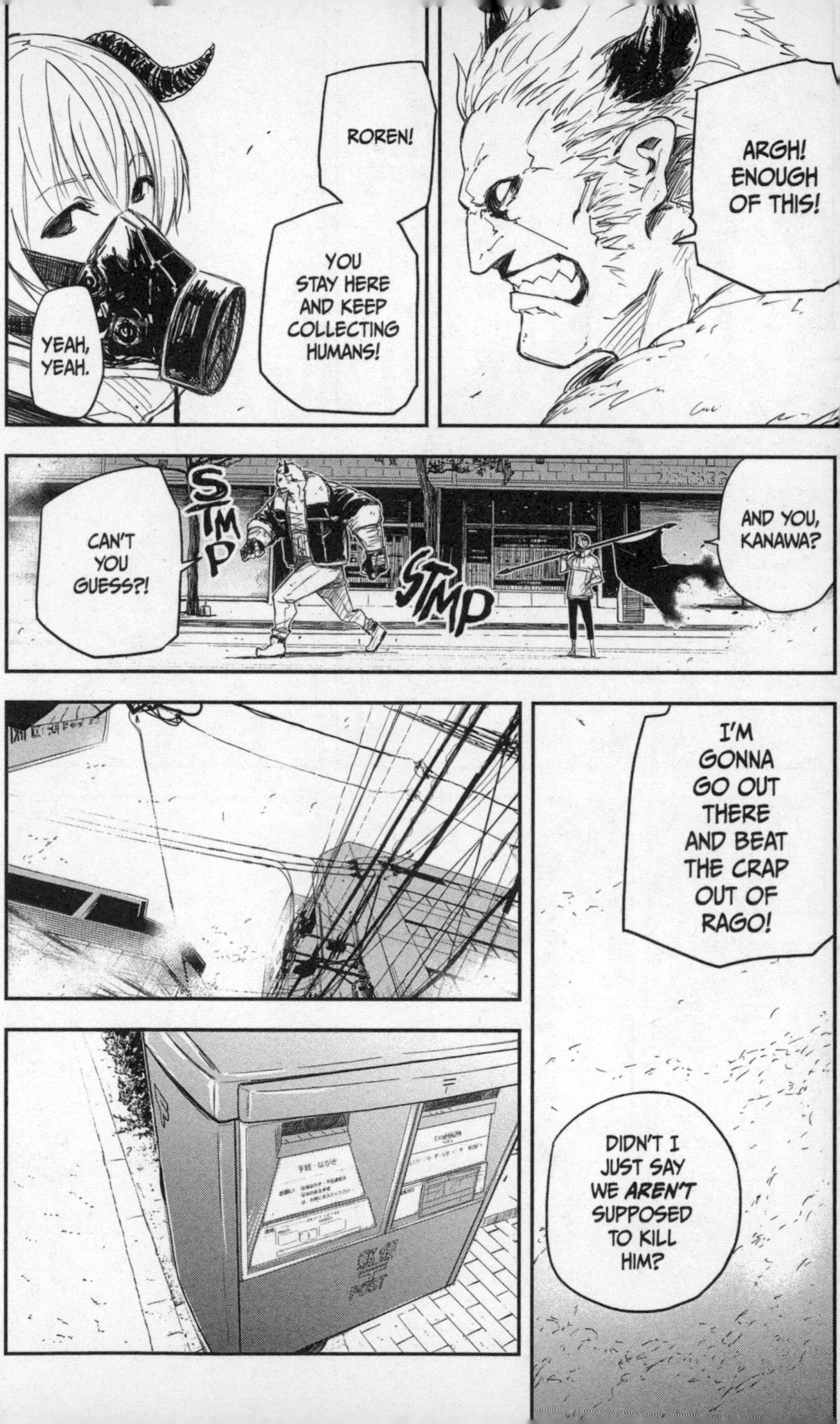
ARGH! ENOUGH OF THIS!
RORENI!
YOU STAY HERE AND KEEP COLLECTING HUMANS!
YEAH, YEAH.
AND YOU, KANAWA?
STMP
STMP
CAN'T YOU GUESS?!
I'M GONNA GO OUT THERE AND BEAT THE CRAP OUT OF RAGO!
DIDN'T I JUST SAY WE *AREN'T* SUPPOSED TO KILL HIM?
POST

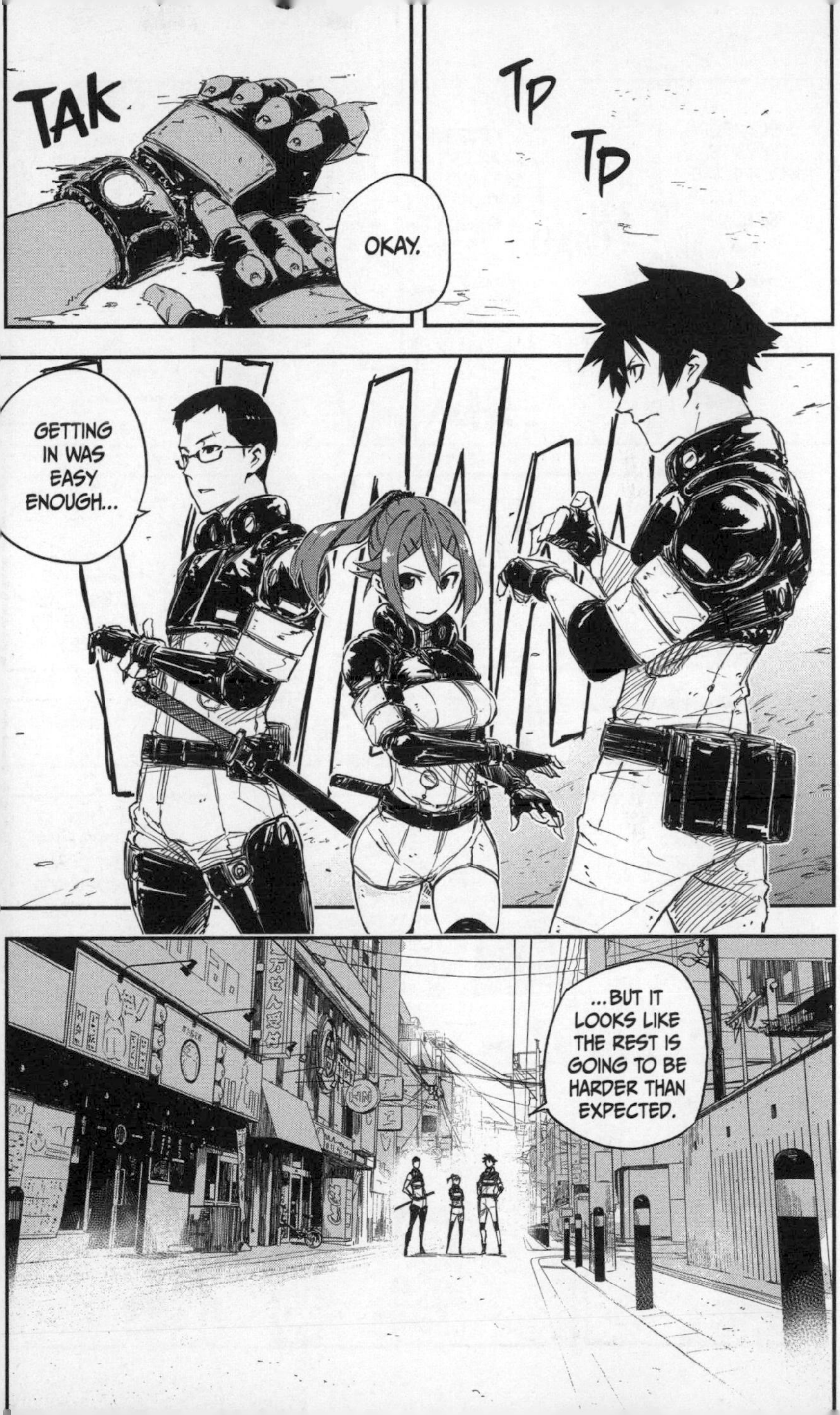
Tp
Tp
TAK
OKAY.
GETTING IN WAS EASY ENOUGH...
...BUT IT LOOKS LIKE THE REST IS GOING TO BE HARDER THAN EXPECTED.

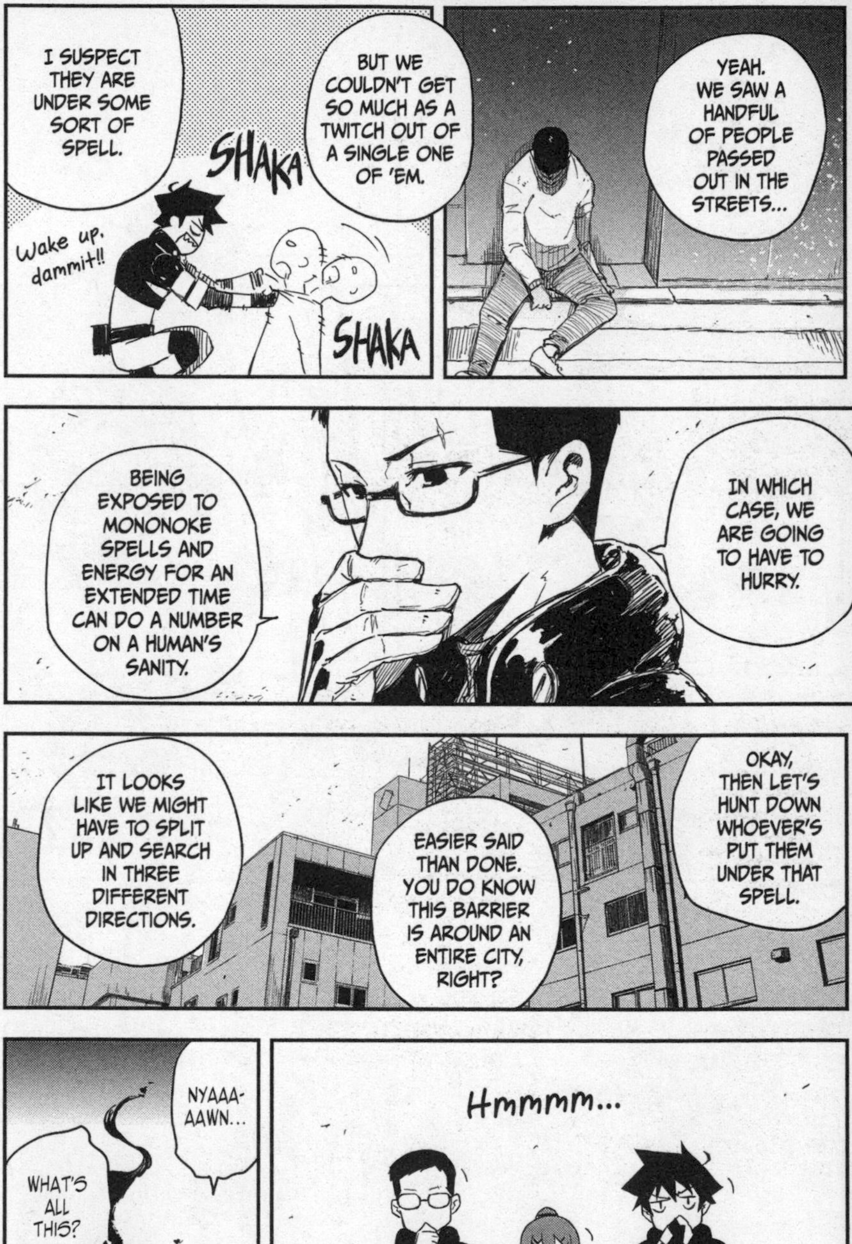
YEAH. WE SAW A HANDFUL OF PEOPLE PASSED OUT IN THE STREETS...
BUT WE COULDN'T GET SO MUCH AS A TWITCH OUT OF A SINGLE ONE OF 'EM.
I SUSPECT THEY ARE UNDER SOME SORT OF SPELL.
SHAKA
Wake up, dammit!!
SHAKA
IN WHICH CASE, WE ARE GOING TO HAVE TO HURRY.
BEING EXPOSED TO MONONOKE SPELLS AND ENERGY FOR AN EXTENDED TIME CAN DO A NUMBER ON A HUMAN'S SANITY.
OKAY, THEN LET'S HUNT DOWN WHOEVER'S PUT THEM UNDER THAT SPELL.
EASIER SAID THAN DONE. YOU DO KNOW THIS BARRIER IS AROUND AN ENTIRE CITY, RIGHT?
IT LOOKS LIKE WE MIGHT HAVE TO SPLIT UP AND SEARCH IN THREE DIFFERENT DIRECTIONS.
Hmmmm...
NYAAA-AAWN...
WHAT'S ALL THIS?

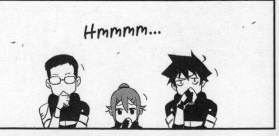

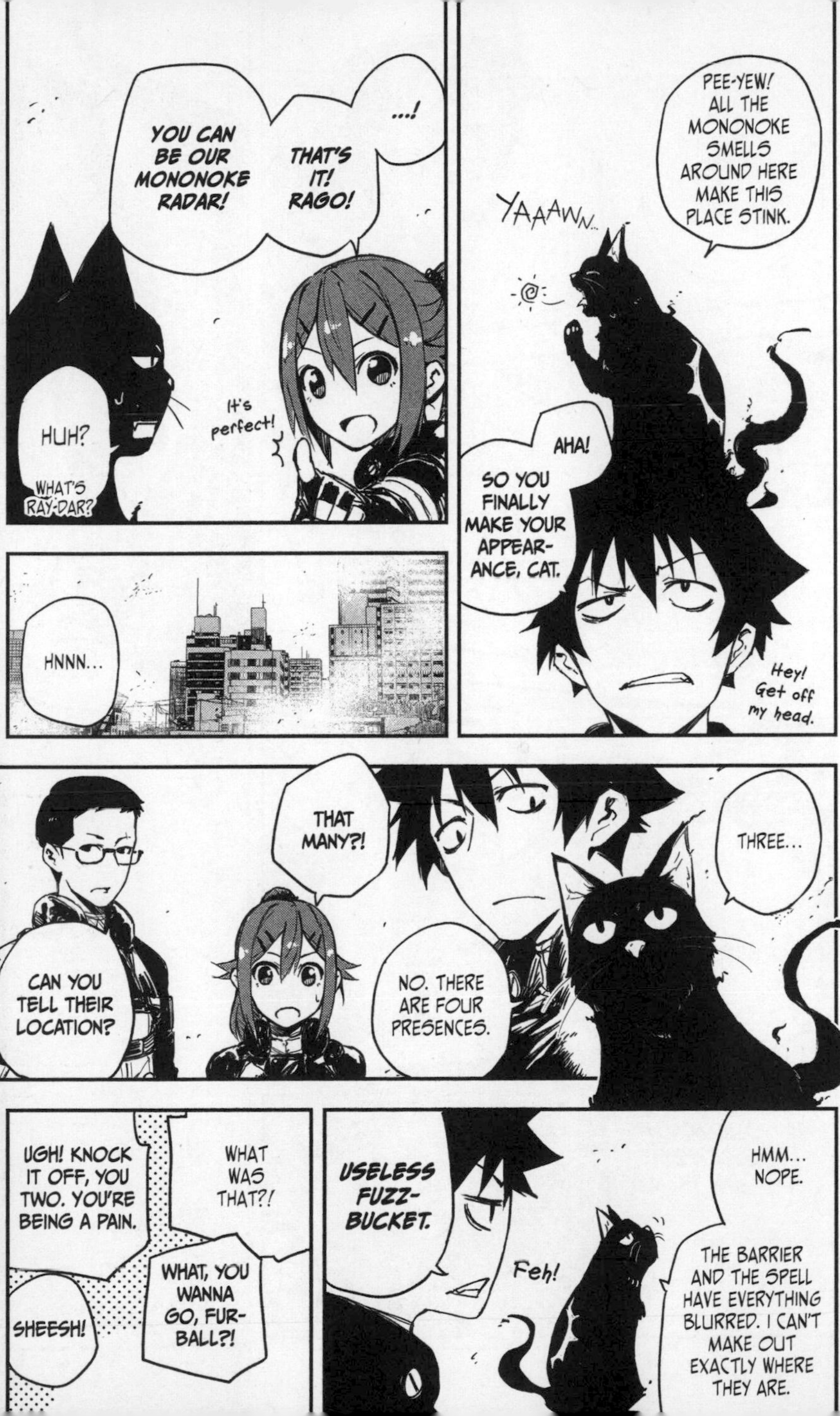
YAAAWN...
PEE-YEW! ALL THE MONONOKE SMELLS AROUND HERE MAKE THIS PLACE STINK.
AHA!
SO YOU FINALLY MAKE YOUR APPEARANCE, CAT.
Hey! Get off my head.
...!
THAT'S IT! RAGO!
YOU CAN BE OUR MONONOKE RADAR!
It's perfect!
HUH?
WHAT'S RAY-DAR?
HNNN...
THREE...
THAT MANY?!
NO. THERE ARE FOUR PRESENCES.
CAN YOU TELL THEIR LOCATION?
HMM... NOPE.
THE BARRIER AND THE SPELL HAVE EVERYTHING BLURRED. I CAN'T MAKE OUT EXACTLY WHERE THEY ARE.
USELESS FUZZ-BUCKET.
Feh!
WHAT WAS THAT?!
UGH! KNOCK IT OFF, YOU TWO. YOU'RE BEING A PAIN.
WHAT, YOU WANNA GO, FUR-BALL?!
SHEESH!

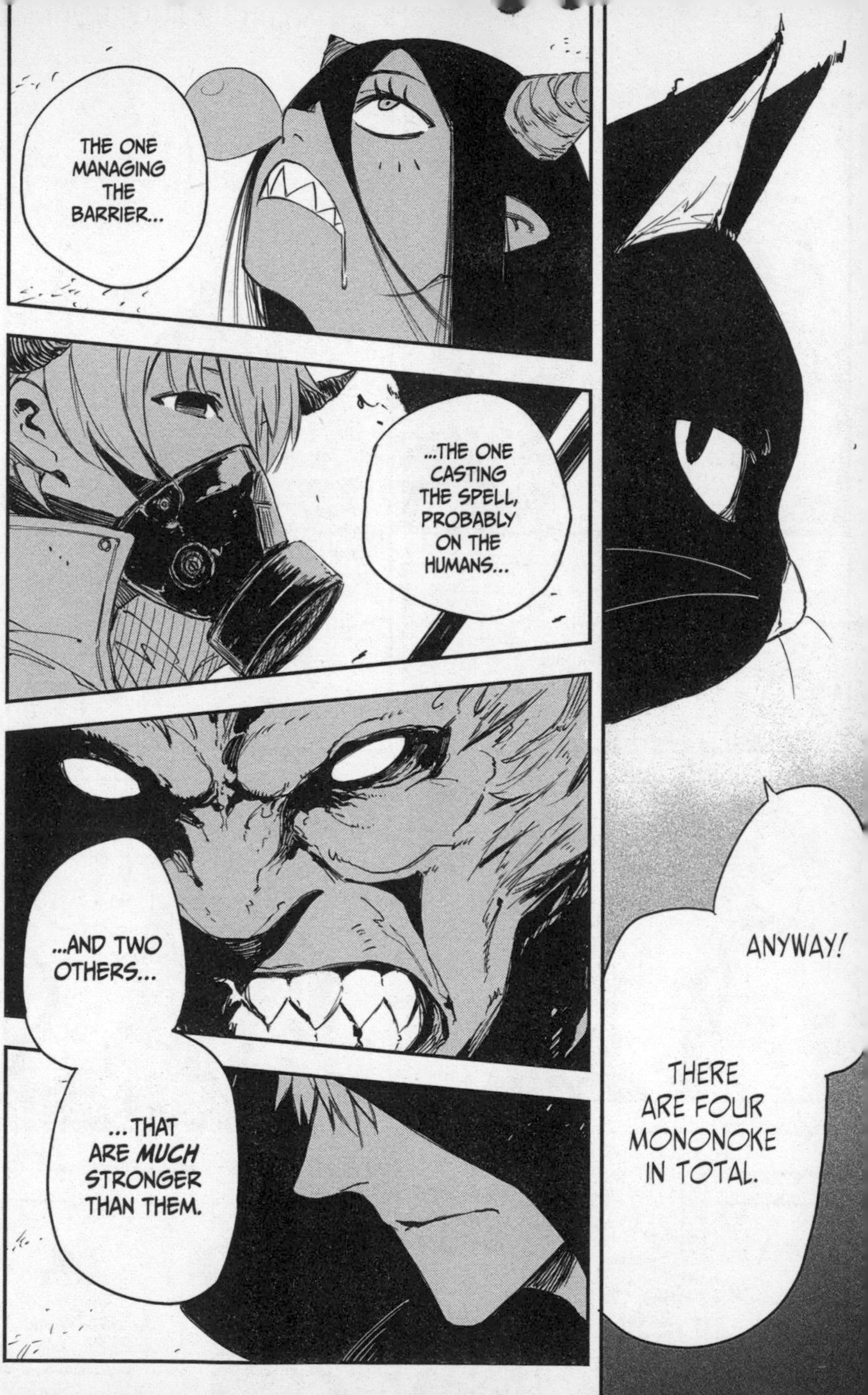
ANYWAY!
THERE ARE FOUR MONONOKE IN TOTAL.
THE ONE MANAGING THE BARRIER...
...THE ONE CASTING THE SPELL, PROBABLY ON THE HUMANS...
...AND TWO OTHERS...
...THAT ARE *MUCH* STRONGER THAN THEM.

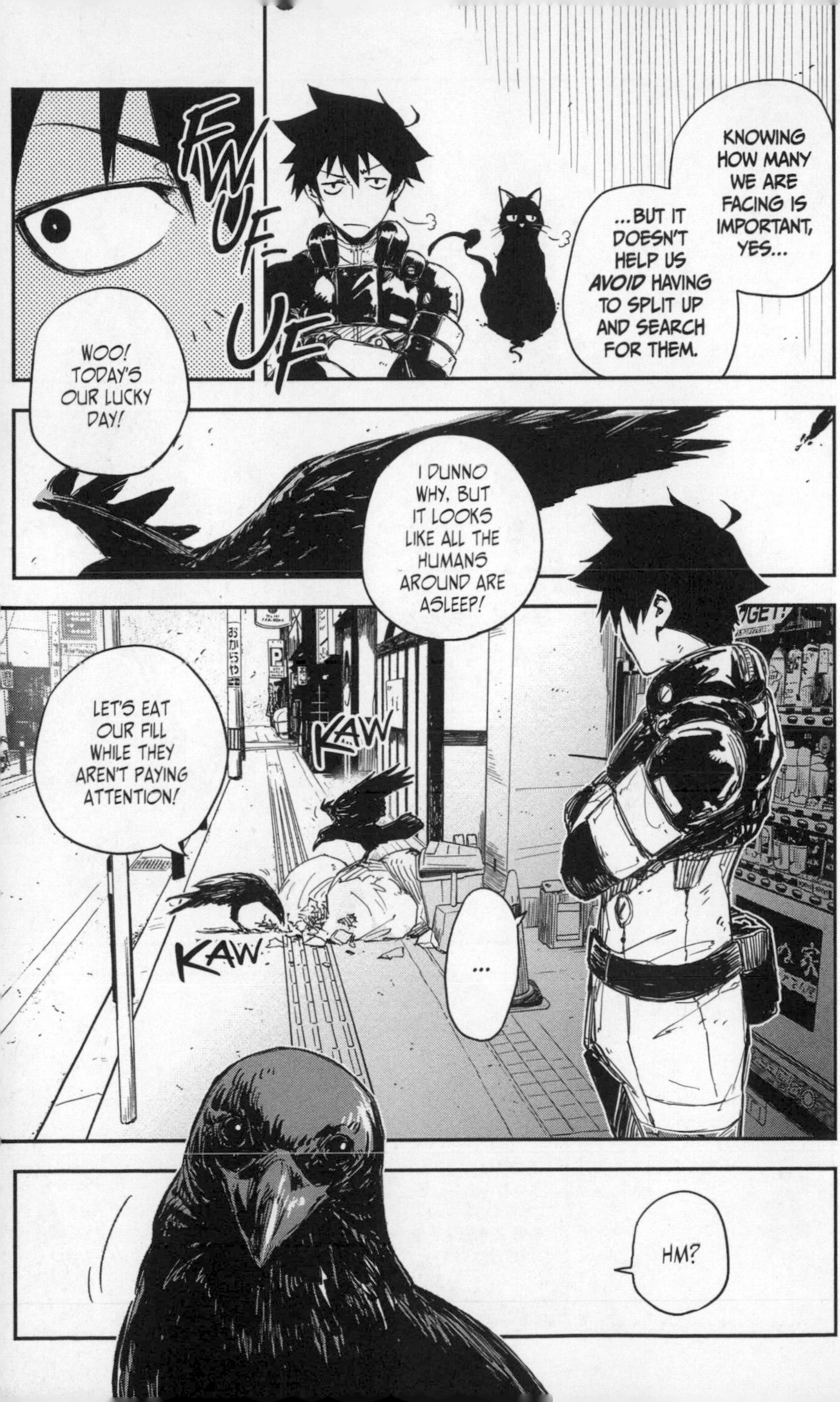
KNOWING HOW MANY WE ARE FACING IS IMPORTANT, YES...
...BUT IT DOESN'T HELP US AVOID HAVING TO SPLIT UP AND SEARCH FOR THEM.
FWUF
WOO! TODAY'S OUR LUCKY DAY!
I DUNNO WHY, BUT IT LOOKS LIKE ALL THE HUMANS AROUND ARE ASLEEP!
...
KAW
LET'S EAT OUR FILL WHILE THEY AREN'T PAYING ATTENTION!
KAW
HM?

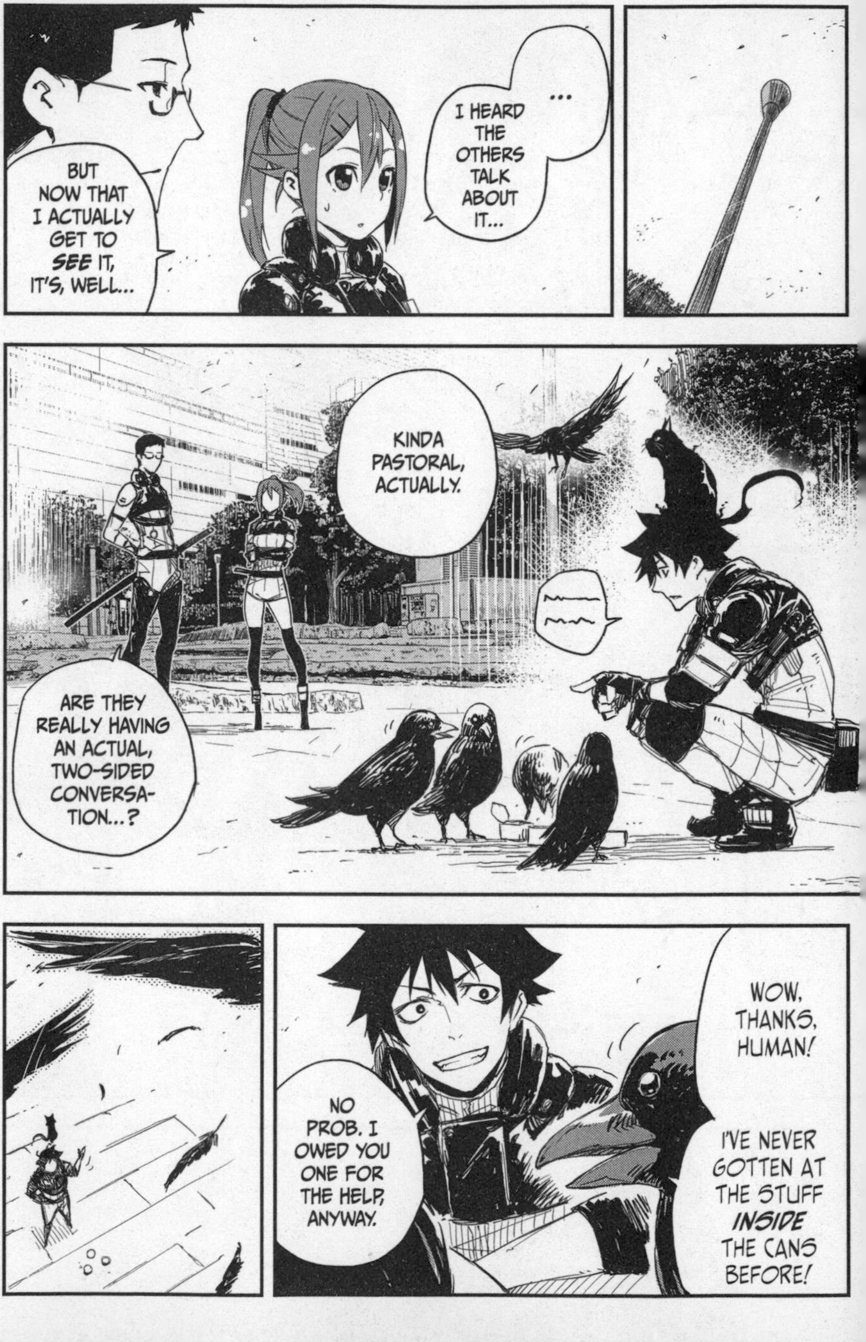

... I HEARD THE OTHERS TALK ABOUT IT...
BUT NOW THAT I ACTUALLY GET TO *SEE* IT, IT'S, WELL...
KINDA PASTORAL, ACTUALLY.
ARE THEY REALLY HAVING AN ACTUAL, TWO-SIDED CONVERSATION...?
WOW, THANKS, HUMAN!
I'VE NEVER GOTTEN AT THE STUFF *INSIDE* THE CANS BEFORE!
NO PROB. I OWED YOU ONE FOR THE HELP, ANYWAY.

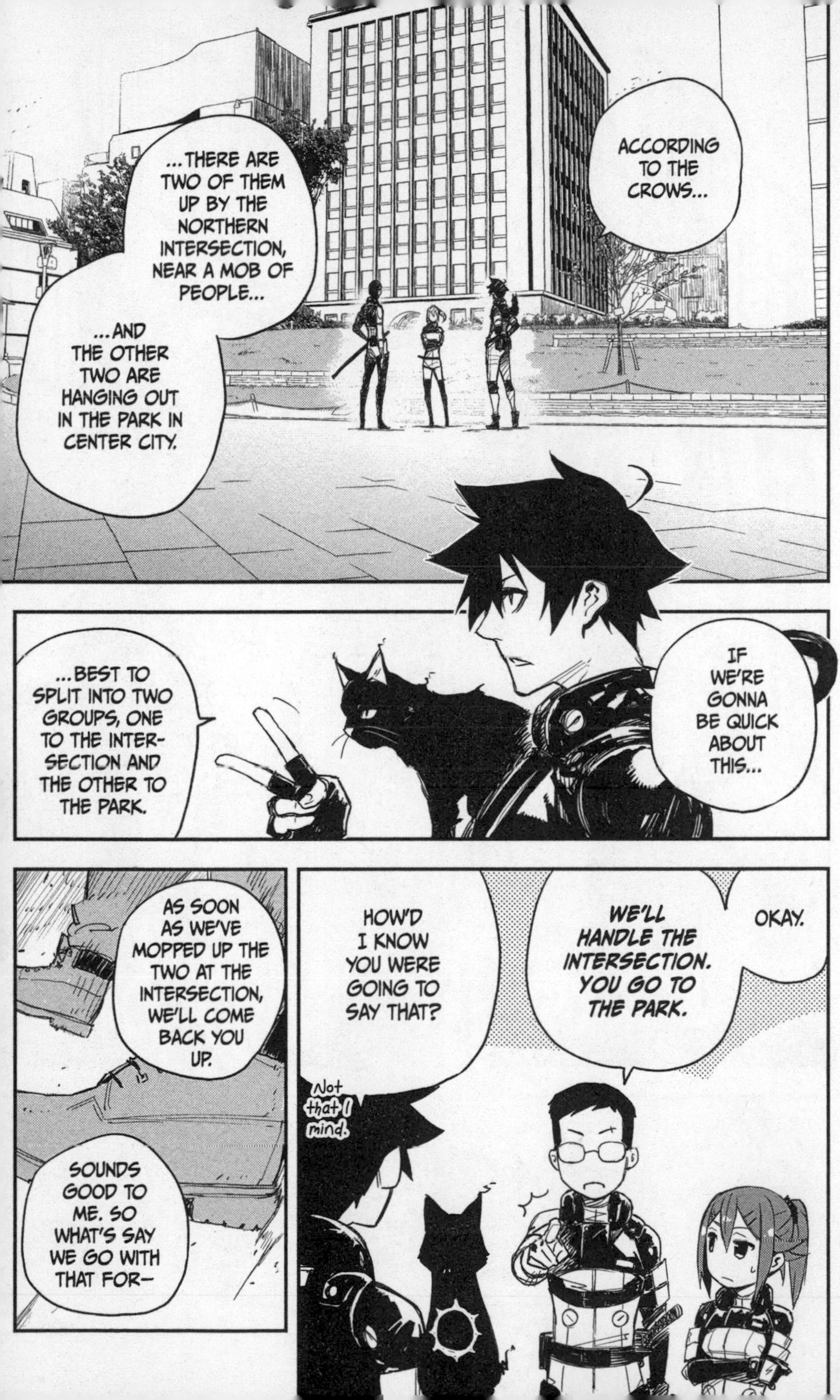
ACCORDING TO THE CROWS...
...THERE ARE TWO OF THEM UP BY THE NORTHERN INTERSECTION, NEAR A MOB OF PEOPLE...
...AND THE OTHER TWO ARE HANGING OUT IN THE PARK IN CENTER CITY.
IF WE'RE GONNA BE QUICK ABOUT THIS...
...BEST TO SPLIT INTO TWO GROUPS, ONE TO THE INTER-SECTION AND THE OTHER TO THE PARK.
OKAY.
WE'LL HANDLE THE INTERSECTION. YOU GO TO THE PARK.
HOW'D I KNOW YOU WERE GOING TO SAY THAT?
Not that I mind.
AS SOON AS WE'VE MOPPED UP THE TWO AT THE INTERSECTION, WE'LL COME BACK YOU UP.
SOUNDS GOOD TO ME. SO WHAT'S SAY WE GO WITH THAT FOR—

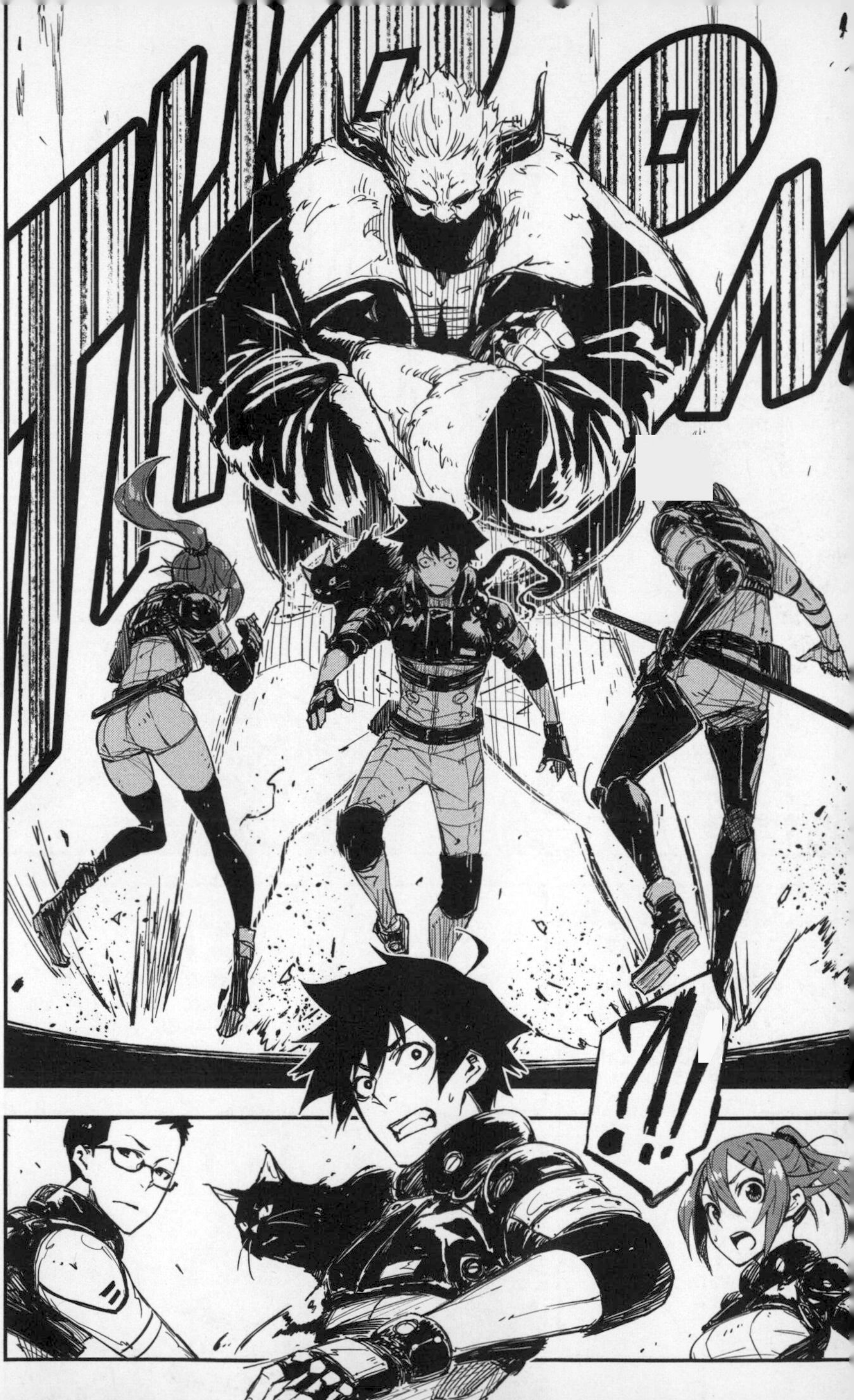
?!!

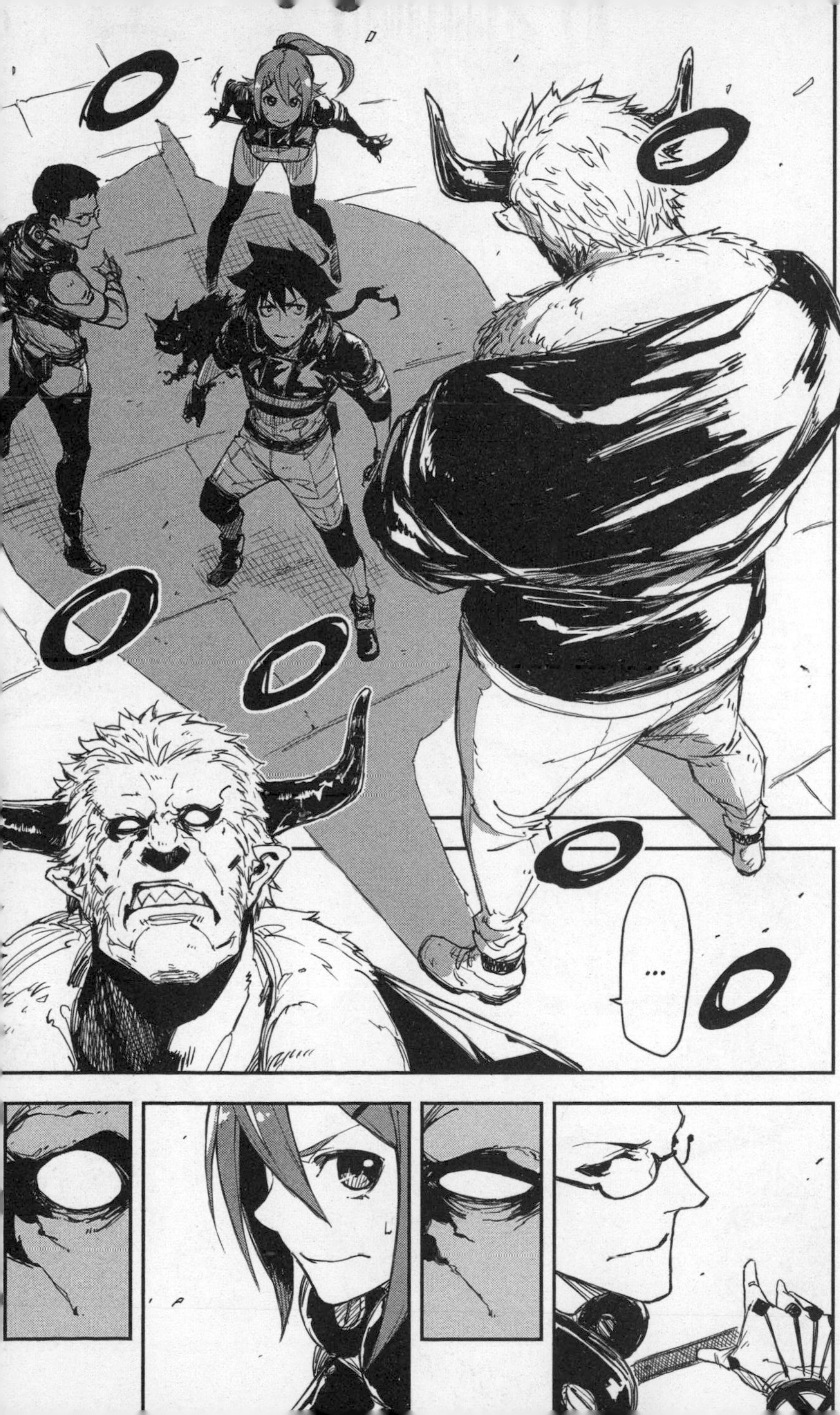
...

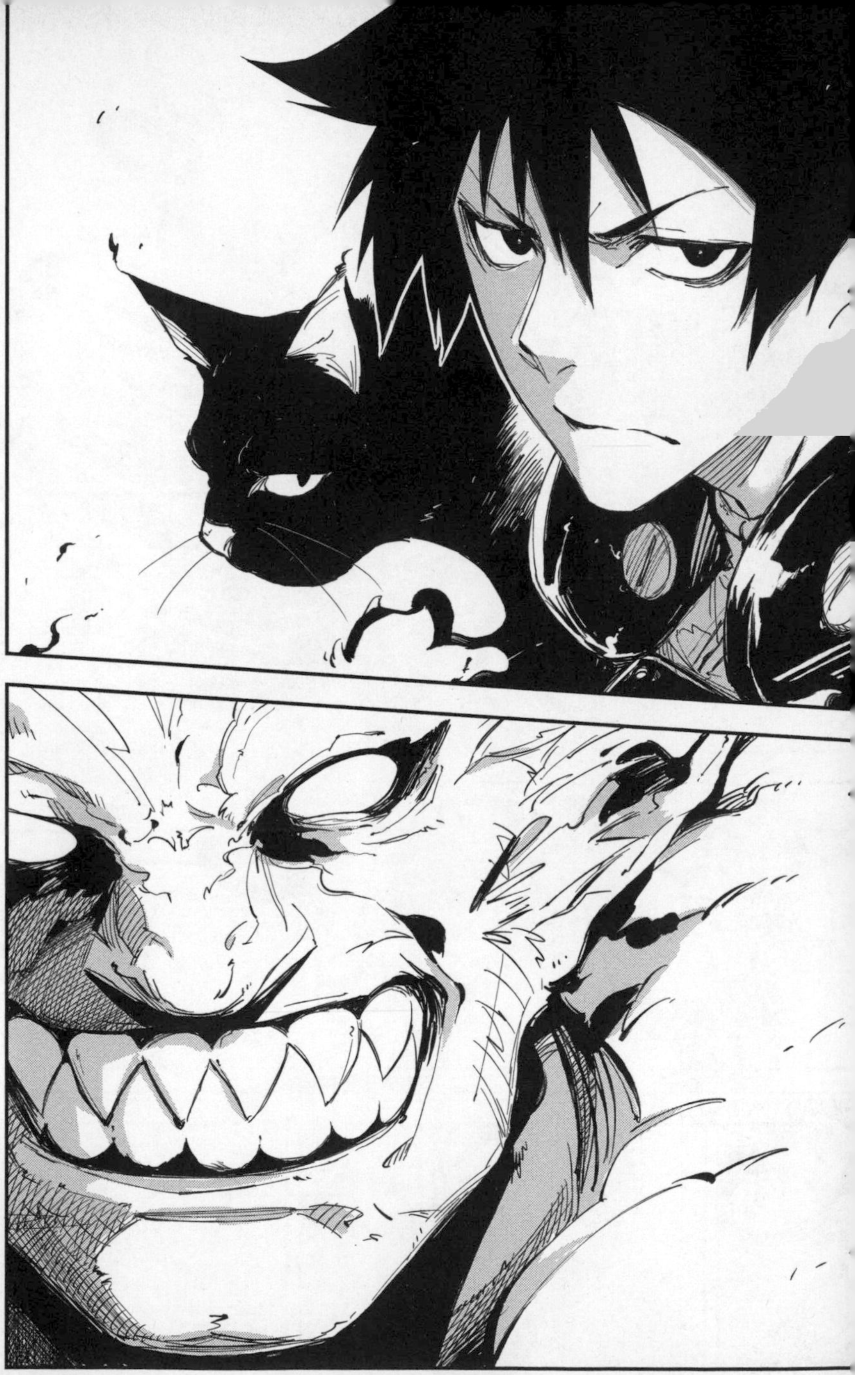

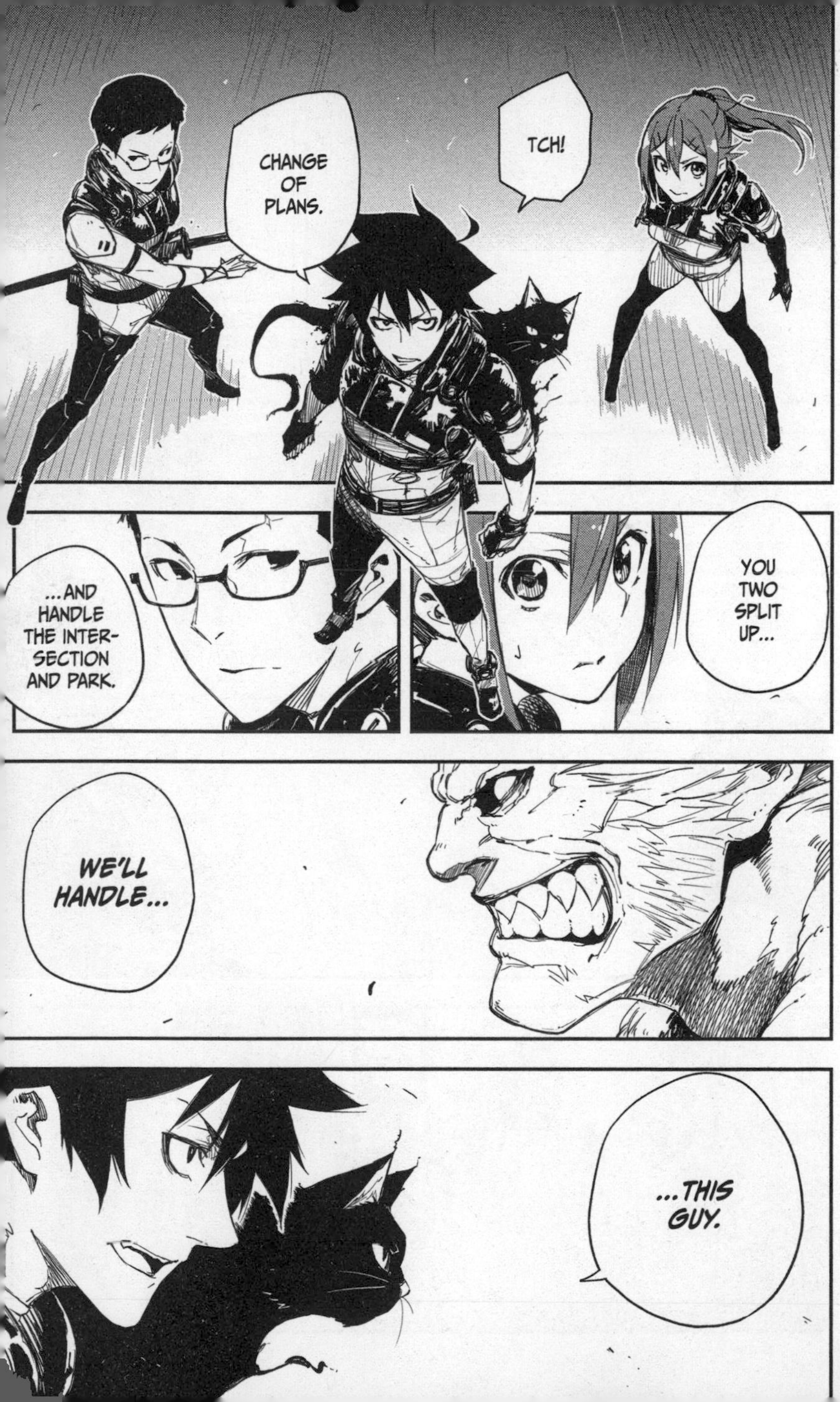
TCH!
CHANGE OF PLANS.
YOU TWO SPLIT UP...
...AND HANDLE THE INTER-SECTION AND PARK.
WE'LL HANDLE...
...THIS GUY.

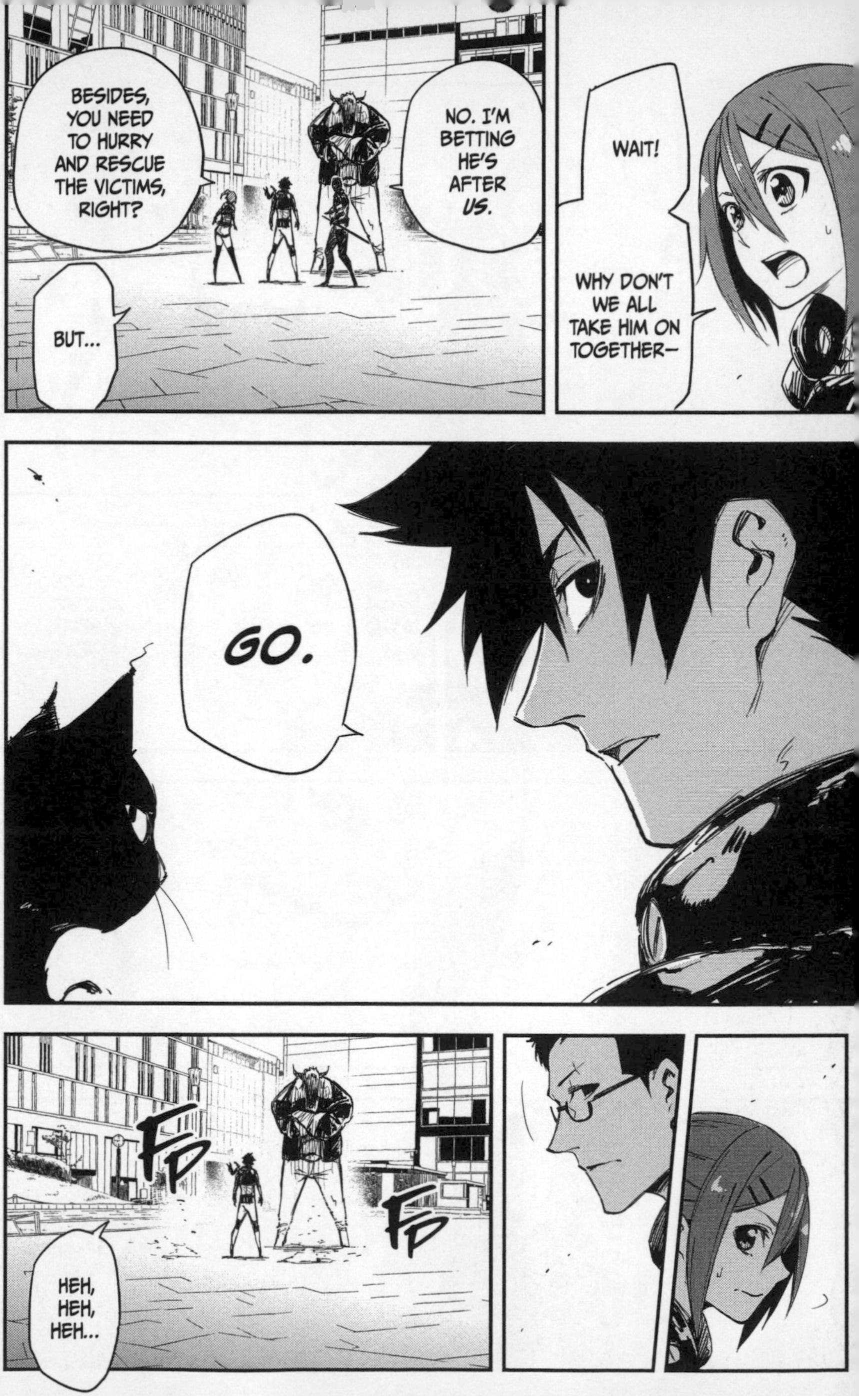
WAIT!
WHY DON'T WE ALL TAKE HIM ON TOGETHER—
NO. I'M BETTING HE'S AFTER *US.*
BESIDES, YOU NEED TO HURRY AND RESCUE THE VICTIMS, RIGHT?
BUT...
GO.
FP
FP
HEH, HEH, HEH...

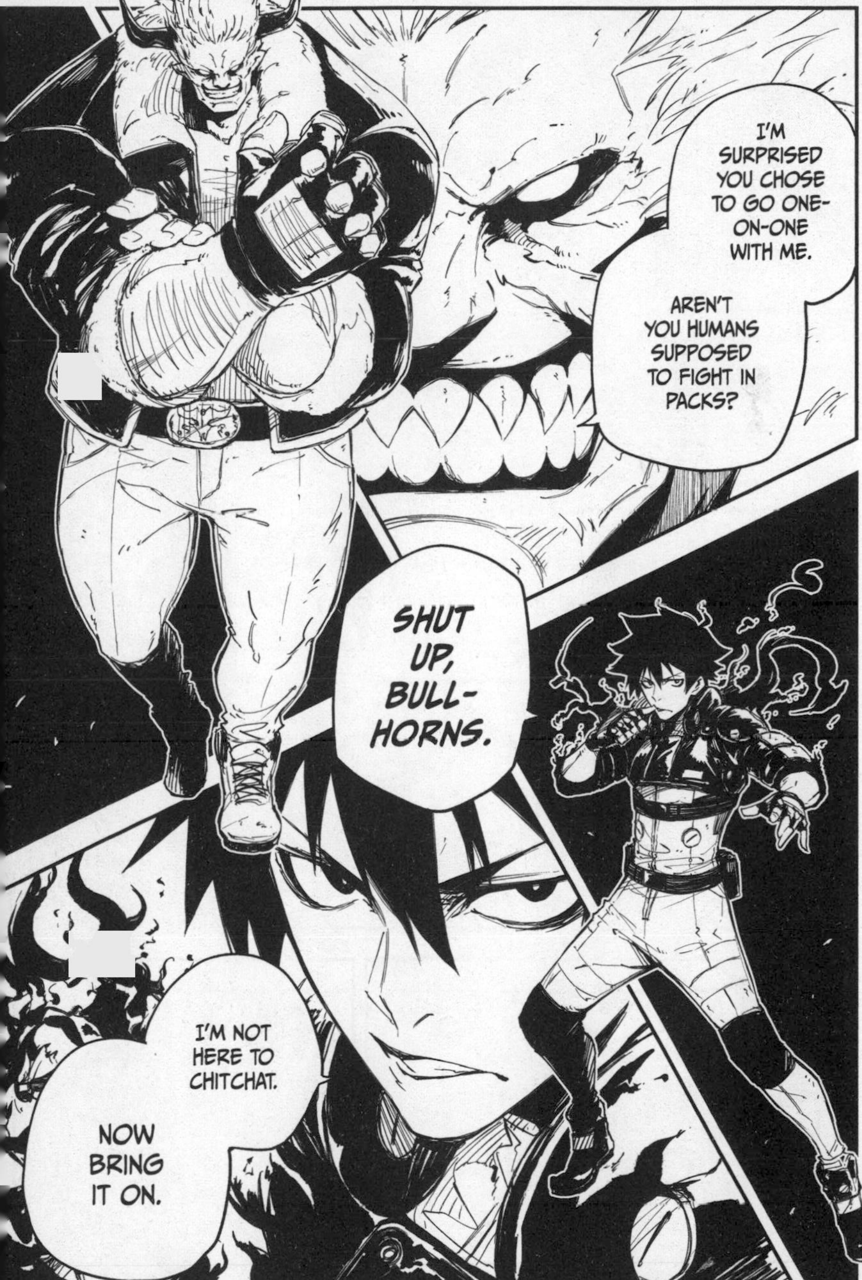
I'M SURPRISED YOU CHOSE TO GO ONE-ON-ONE WITH ME.
AREN'T YOU HUMANS SUPPOSED TO FIGHT IN PACKS?
SHUT UP, BULL-HORNS.
I'M NOT HERE TO CHITCHAT.
NOW BRING IT ON.

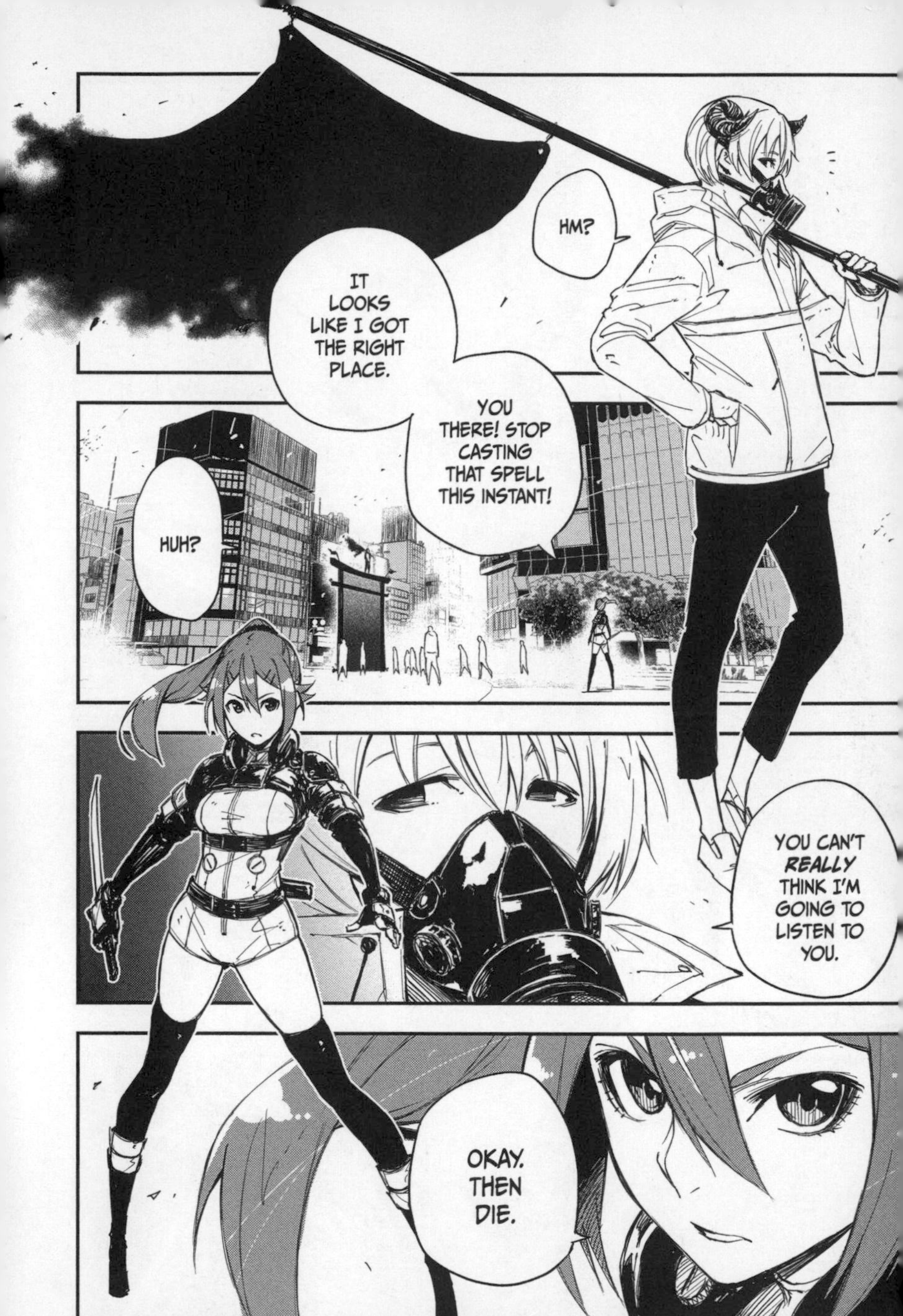
HM?
IT LOOKS LIKE I GOT THE RIGHT PLACE.
YOU THERE! STOP CASTING THAT SPELL THIS INSTANT!
HUH?
YOU CAN'T *REALLY* THINK I'M GOING TO LISTEN TO YOU.
OKAY. THEN DIE.

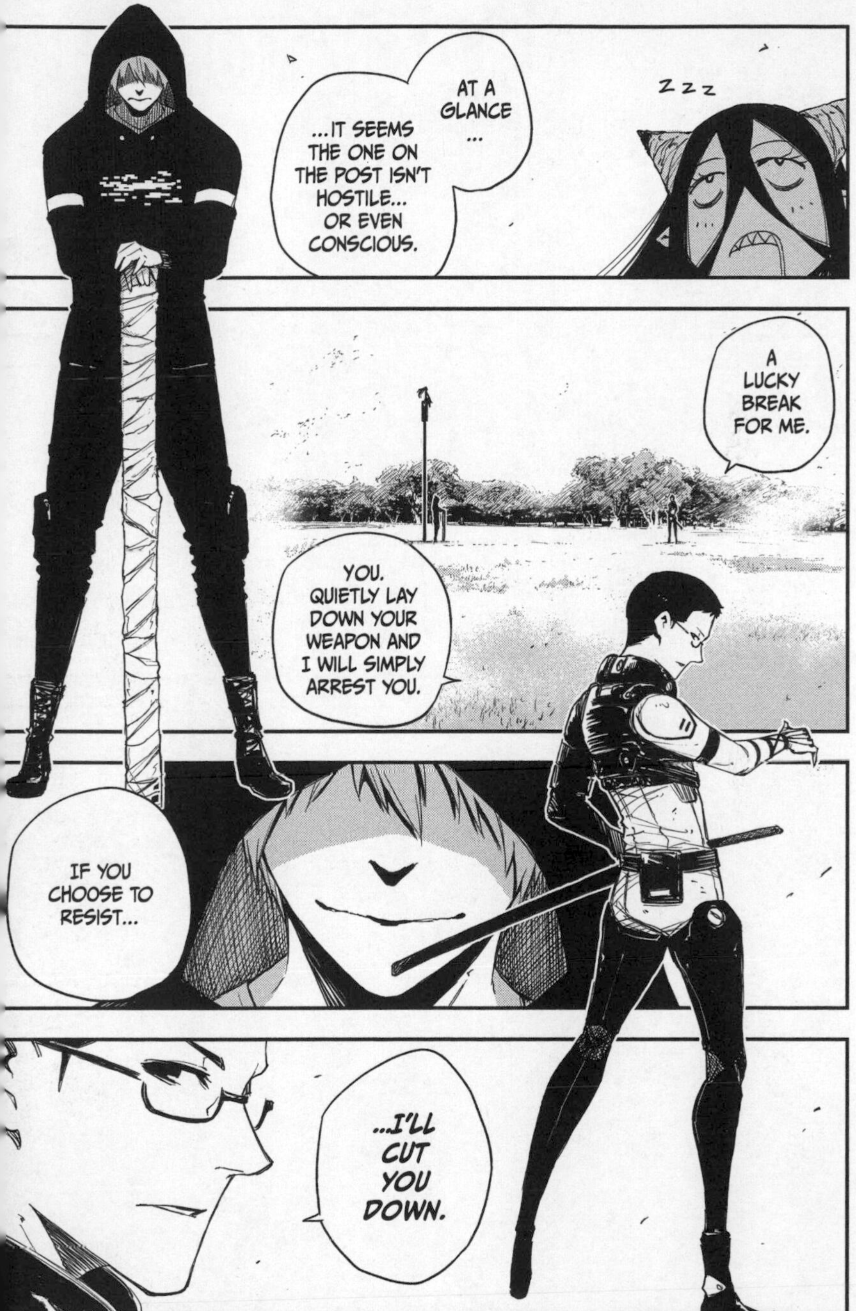
Z Z Z
AT A GLANCE ...
...IT SEEMS THE ONE ON THE POST ISN'T HOSTILE... OR EVEN CONSCIOUS.
A LUCKY BREAK FOR ME.
YOU. QUIETLY LAY DOWN YOUR WEAPON AND I WILL SIMPLY ARREST YOU.
IF YOU CHOOSE TO RESIST...
...I'LL CUT YOU DOWN.

BLACK TORCH

#10 3 ON THREE

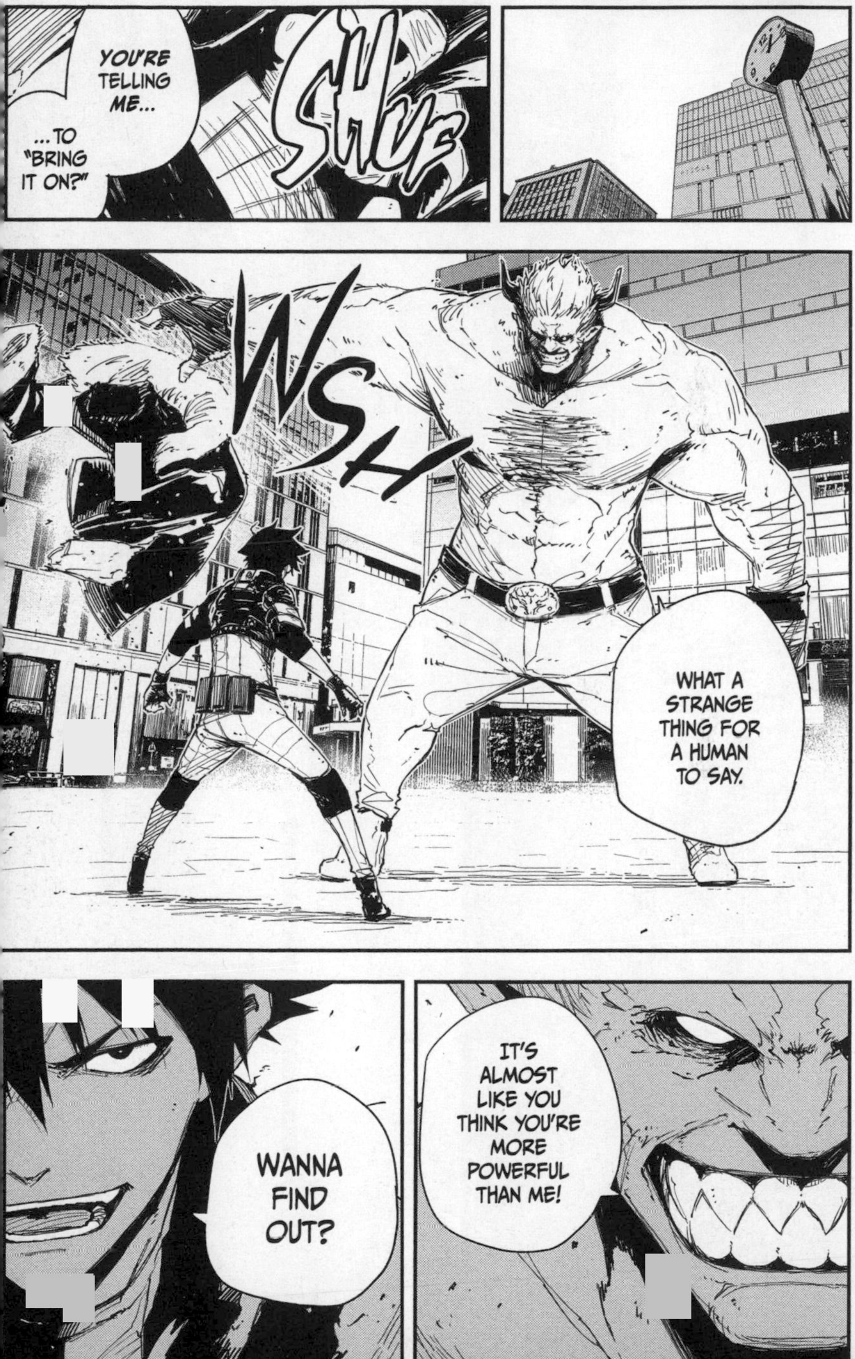
SHUF
YOU'RE TELLING ME...
...TO "BRING IT ON?"
WSH
WHAT A STRANGE THING FOR A HUMAN TO SAY.
IT'S ALMOST LIKE YOU THINK YOU'RE MORE POWERFUL THAN ME!
WANNA FIND OUT?

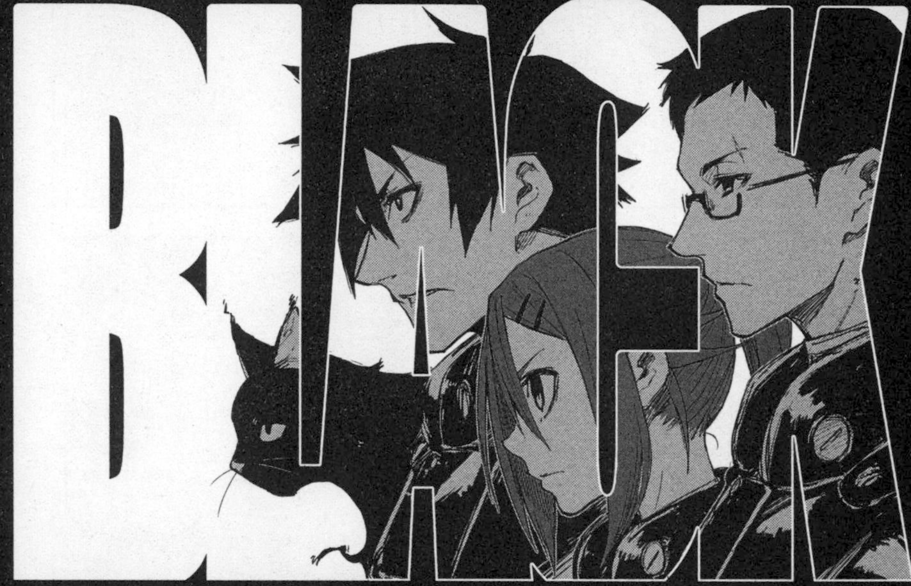
BLACK

#10 3 ON THREE

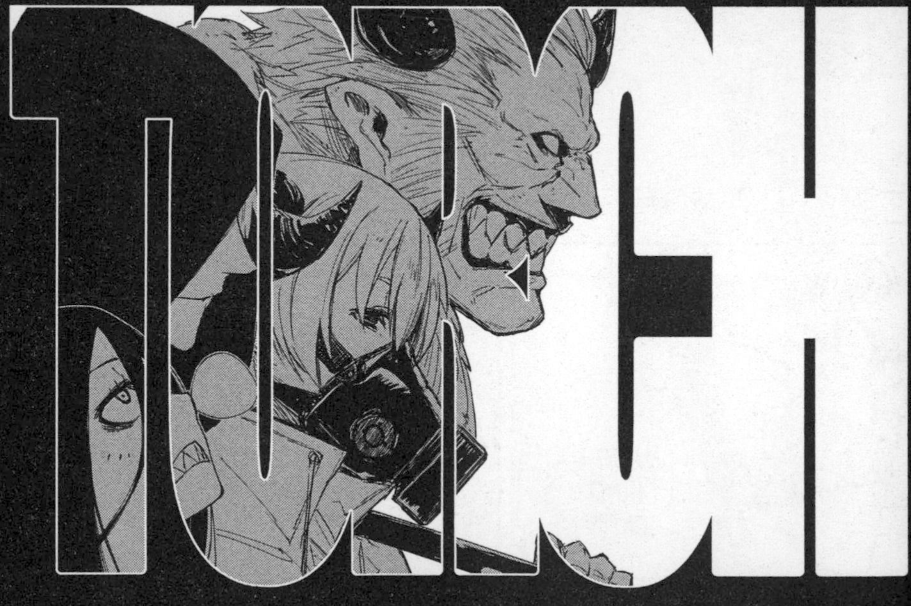
TORCH

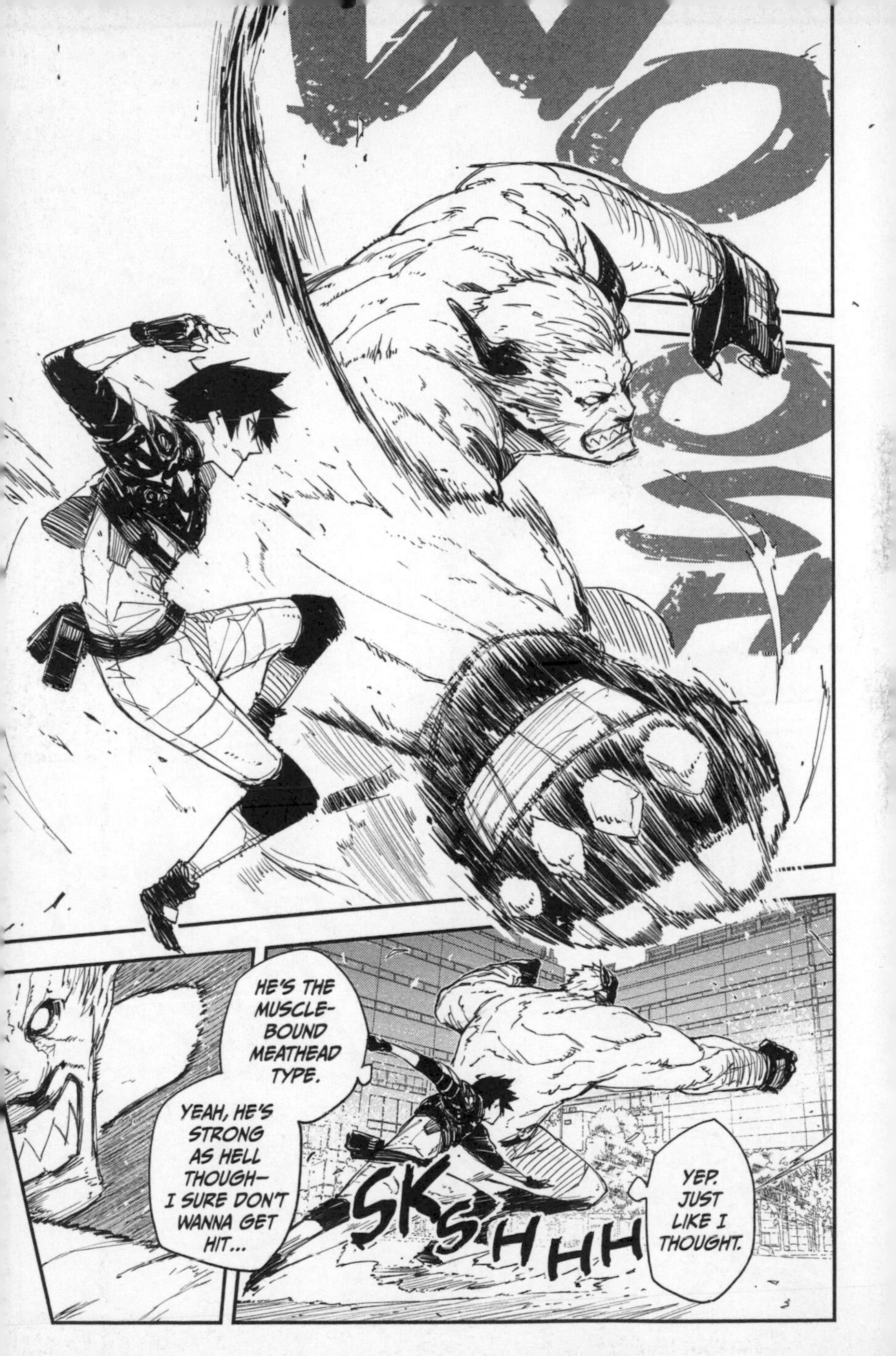
YEP. JUST LIKE I THOUGHT.
SKSHHHH
HE'S THE MUSCLE-BOUND MEATHEAD TYPE.
YEAH, HE'S STRONG AS HELL THOUGH— I SURE DON'T WANNA GET HIT...

...BUT HIS ATTACKS ARE SIMPLE AND STRAIGHT-FORWARD.

ZW IP

AND HE'S LEFT WIDE OPEN!

DODGE 'EM AT THE LAST SECOND...

WOOSH

ZISSS

SORRY, BULL-HORNS.

OHO!

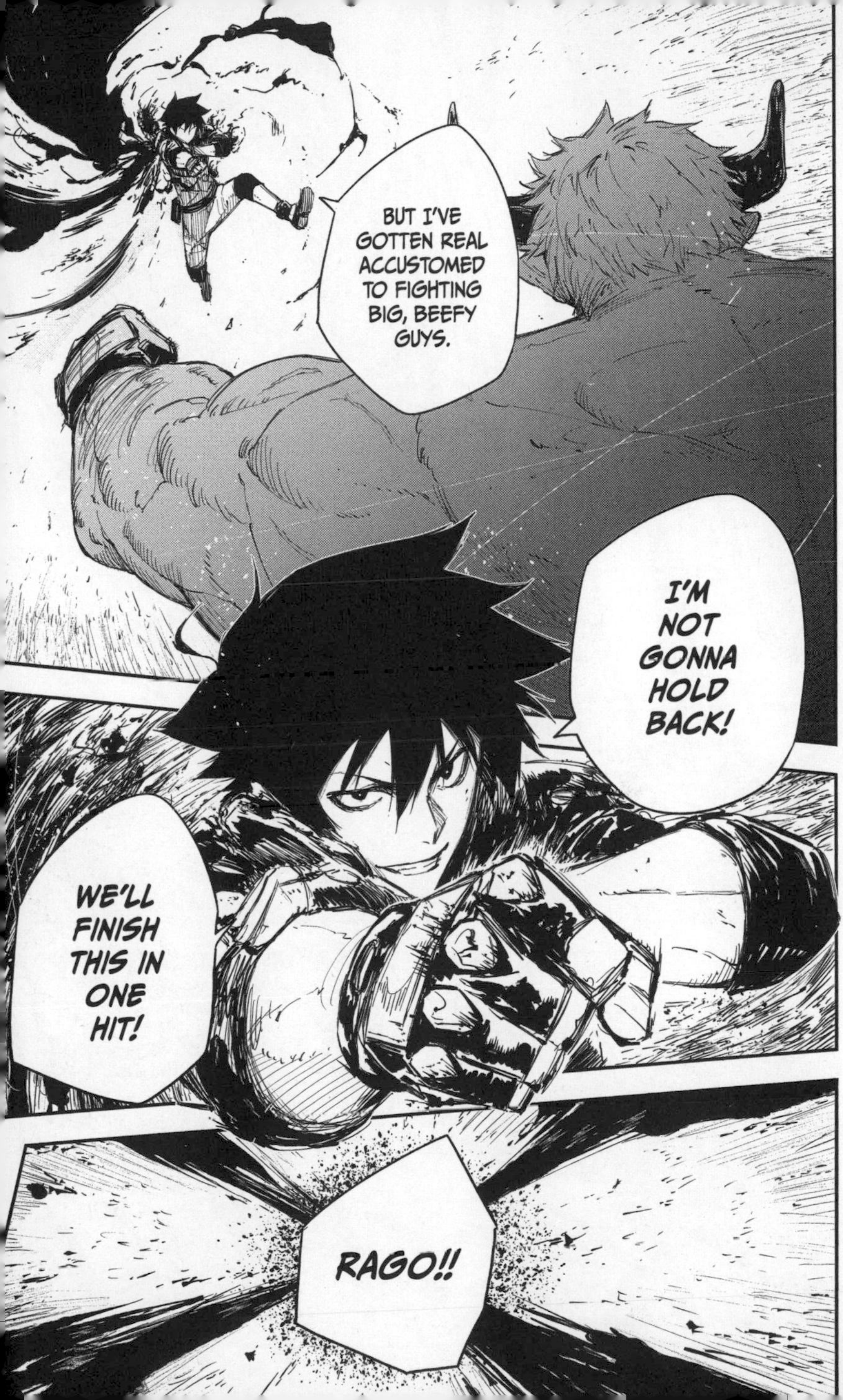
BUT I'VE GOTTEN REAL ACCUSTOMED TO FIGHTING BIG, BEEFY GUYS.
I'M NOT GONNA HOLD BACK!
WE'LL FINISH THIS IN ONE HIT!
RAGO!!

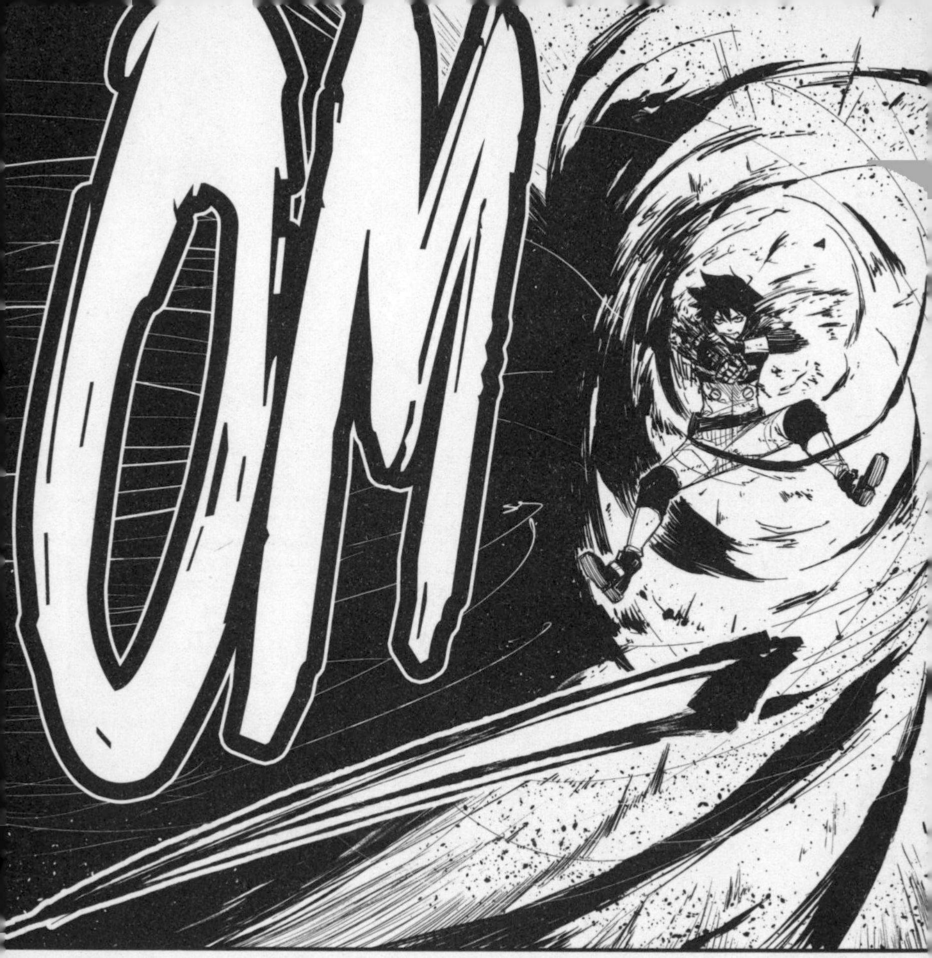
OM
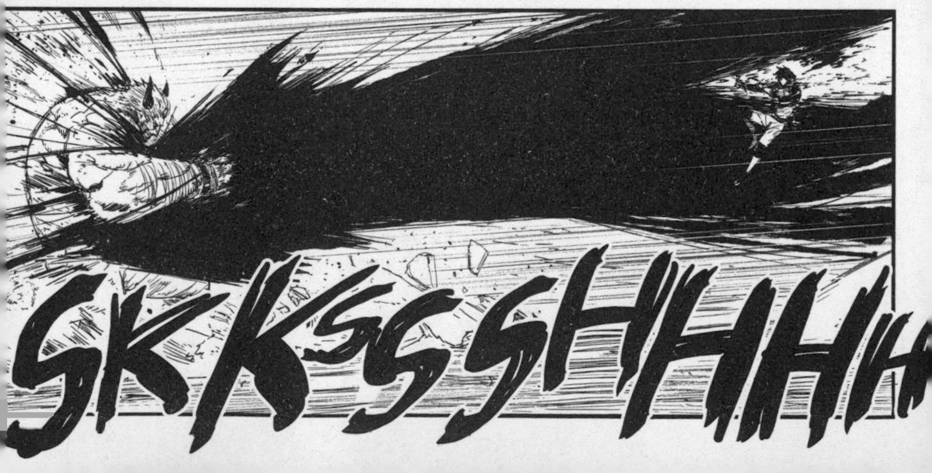
SKSSSHHHH

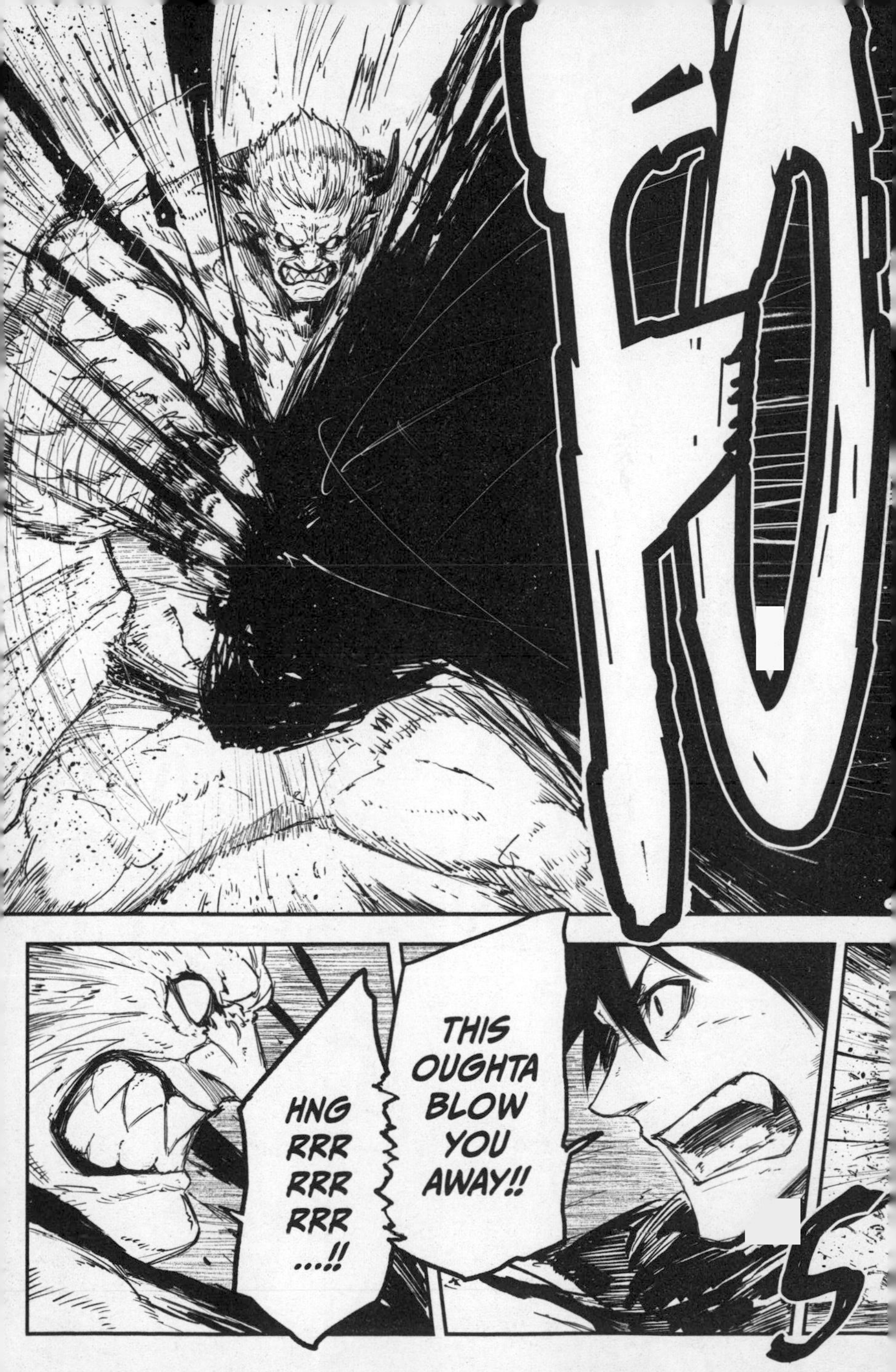
THIS OUGHTA BLOW YOU AWAY!!
HNG RRR RRR RRR ...!!

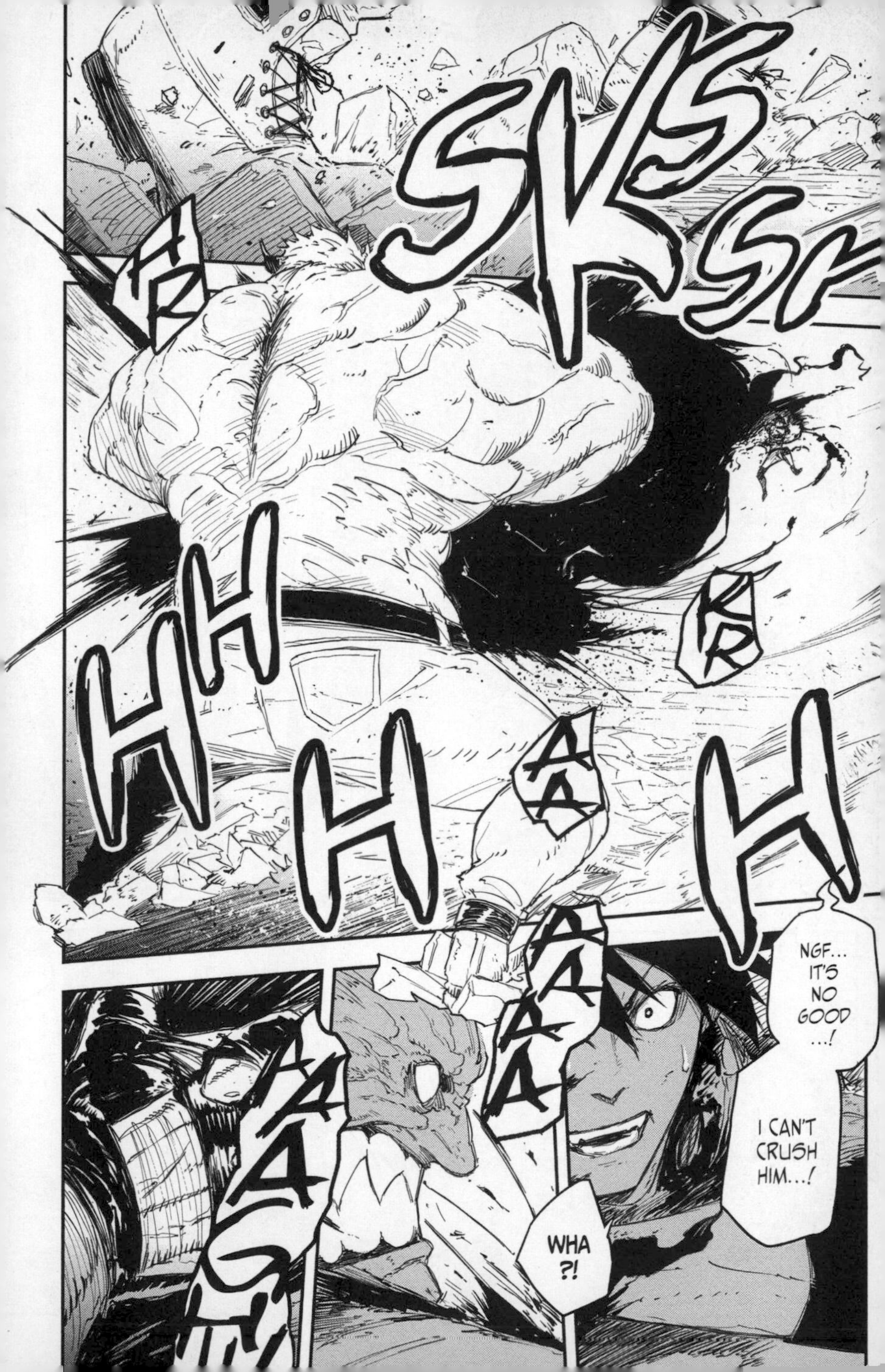
NGF... IT'S NO GOOD ...!
I CAN'T CRUSH HIM...!
WHA ?!

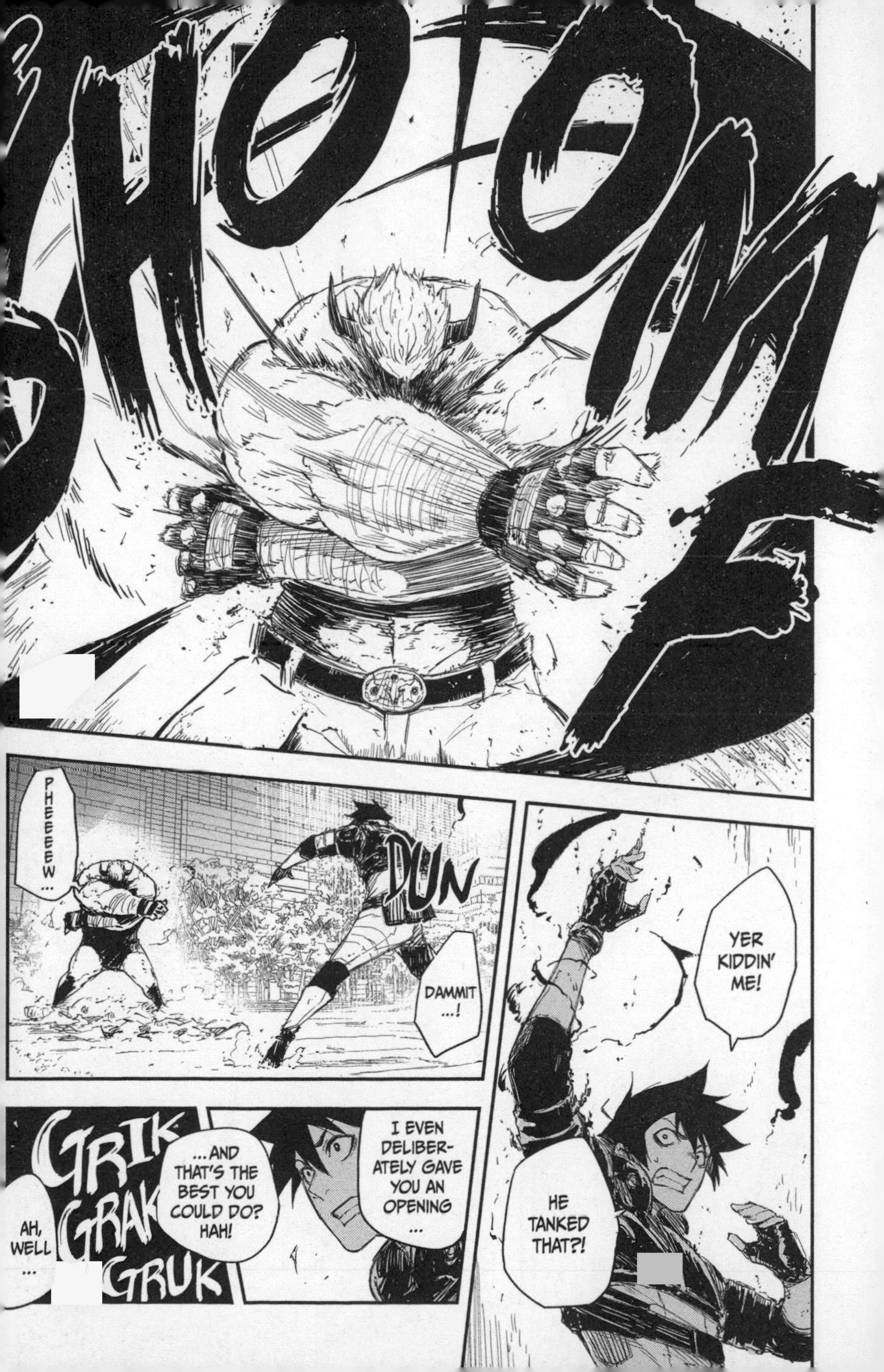
YER KIDDIN' ME!
HE TANKED THAT?!
DUN
PHEEEEEW ...
DAMMIT ...!
I EVEN DELIBER-ATELY GAVE YOU AN OPENING ...
...AND THAT'S THE BEST YOU COULD DO? HAH!
GRIK GRAK GRUK
AH, WELL ...

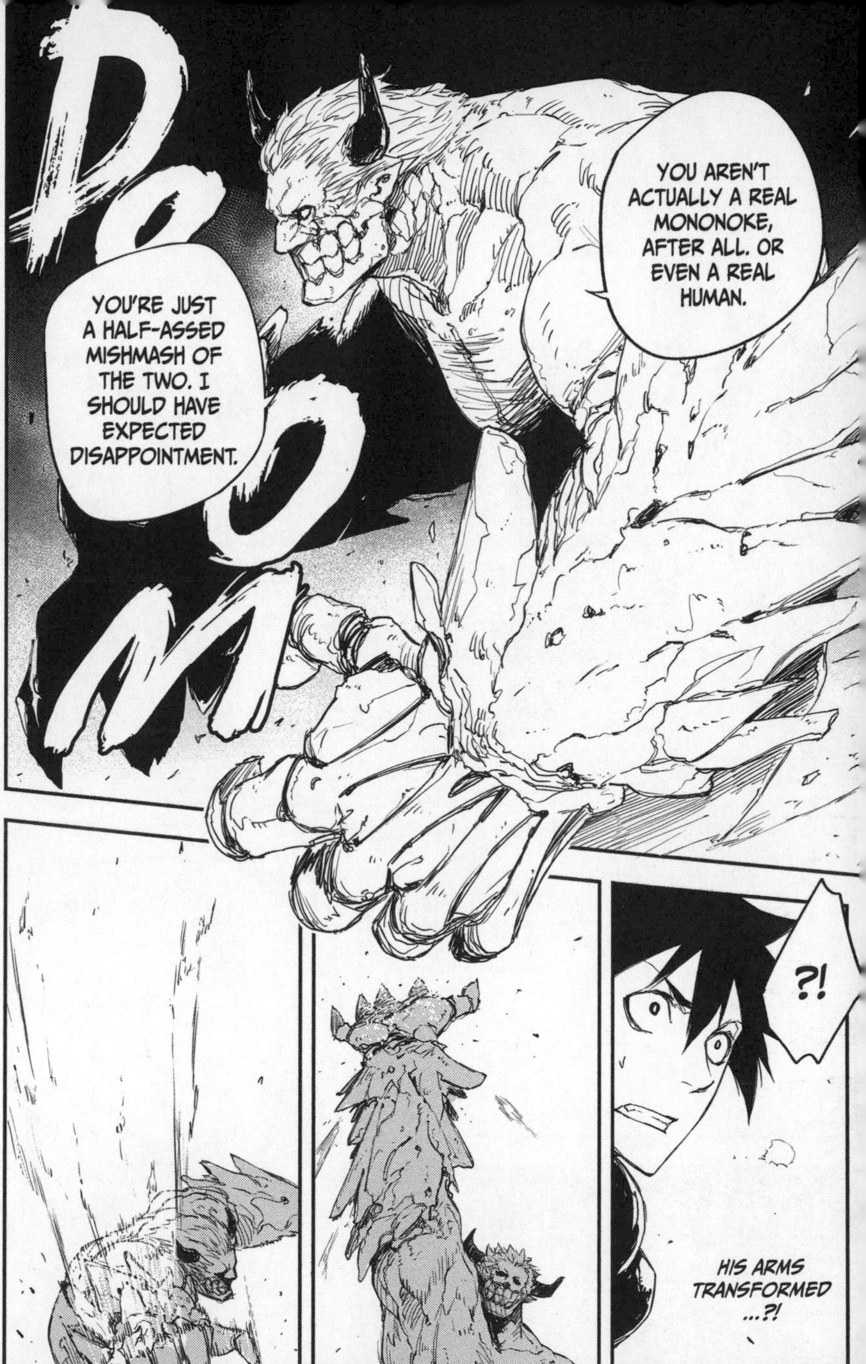
YOU AREN'T ACTUALLY A REAL MONONOKE, AFTER ALL. OR EVEN A REAL HUMAN.
YOU'RE JUST A HALF-ASSED MISHMASH OF THE TWO. I SHOULD HAVE EXPECTED DISAPPOINTMENT.
DOOM
?!
HIS ARMS TRANSFORMED ...?!

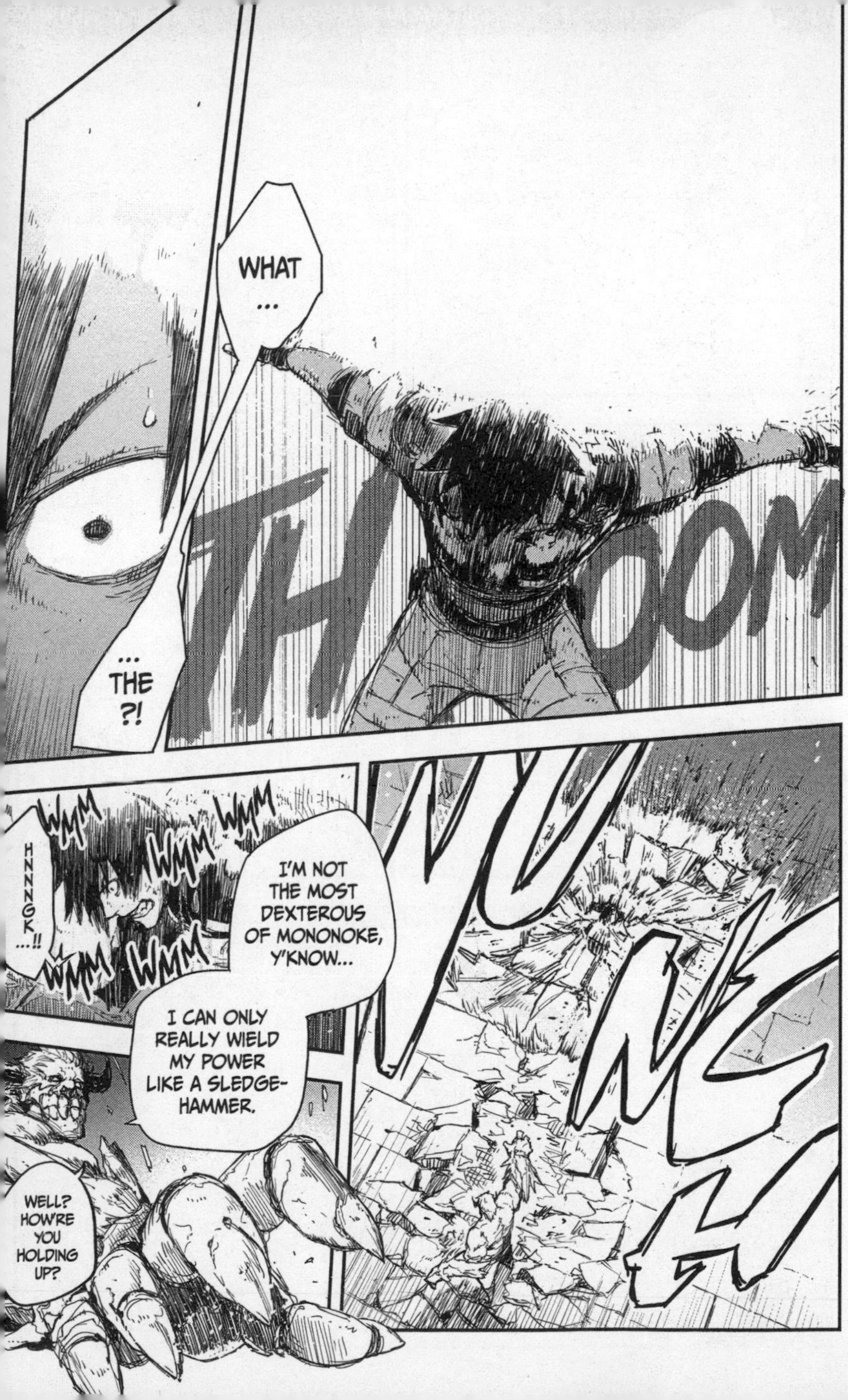
WHAT ...
THOOM
... THE ?!
I'M NOT THE MOST DEXTEROUS OF MONONOKE, Y'KNOW...
WMM WMM WMM WMM WMM WMM
HNNNGK ...!!
I CAN ONLY REALLY WIELD MY POWER LIKE A SLEDGE-HAMMER.
WELL? HOW'RE YOU HOLDING UP?

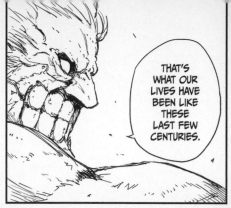

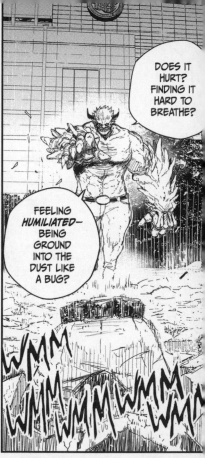

DOES IT HURT? FINDING IT HARD TO BREATHE?
FEELING *HUMILIATED*—BEING GROUND INTO THE DUST LIKE A BUG?
WMM WMM WMM WMM WMM WMM
THAT'S WHAT OUR LIVES HAVE BEEN LIKE THESE LAST FEW CENTURIES.
OPPRESSED AND *HUNTED* BY YOU ONMITSU.
ME...
I WAS ONCE THE GOD OF A MOUNTAIN FOREST.
YOU HUMANS FEARED AND REVERED ME AS AN OGRE LORD.

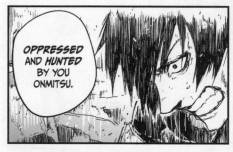

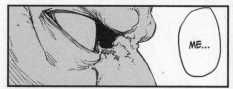

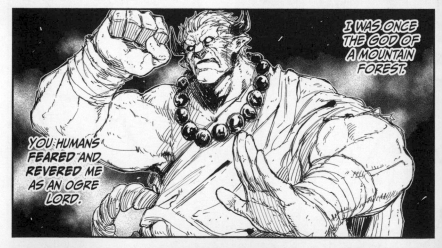

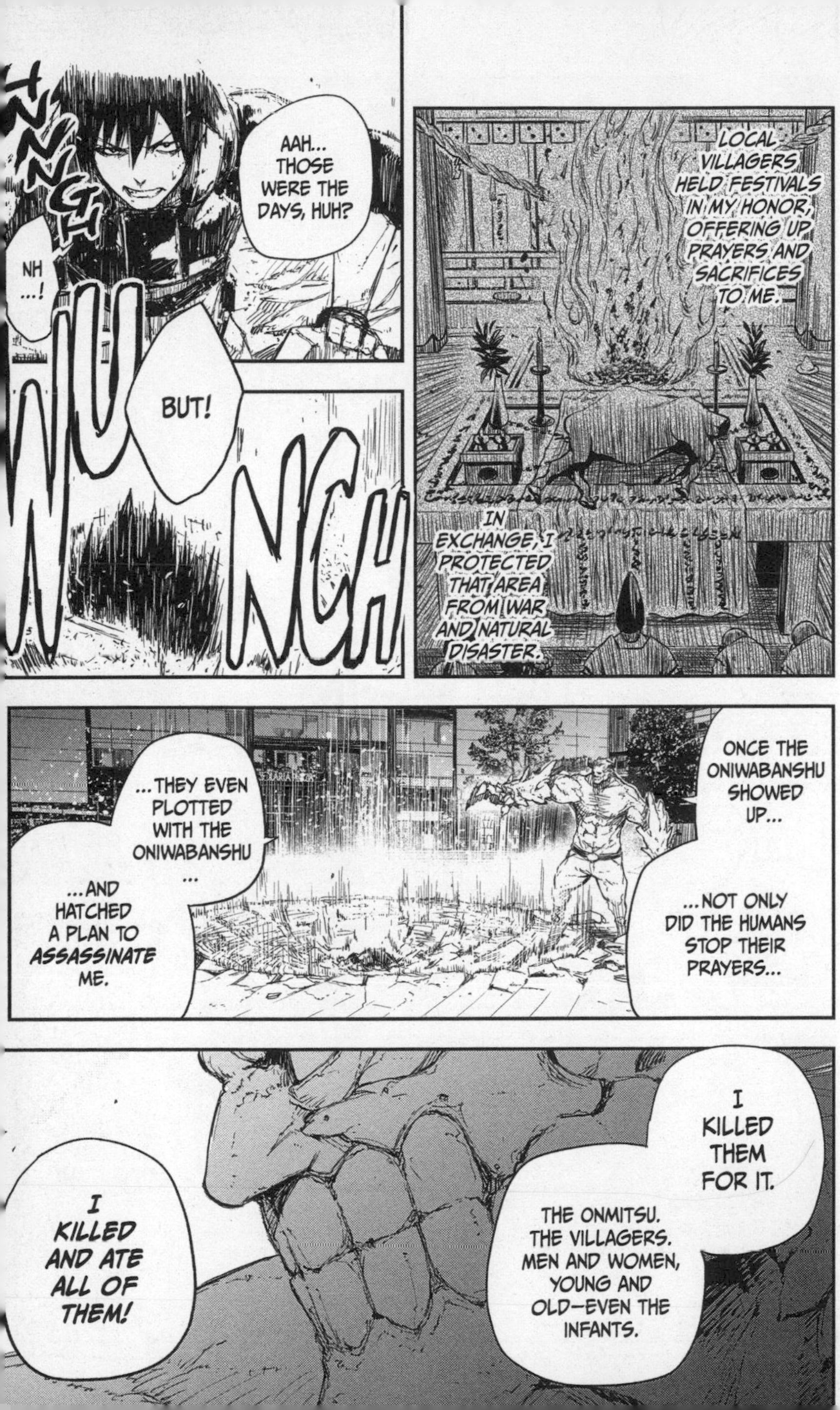
LOCAL VILLAGERS HELD FESTIVALS IN MY HONOR, OFFERING UP PRAYERS AND SACRIFICES TO ME.
IN EXCHANGE, I PROTECTED THAT AREA FROM WAR AND NATURAL DISASTER.
AAH... THOSE WERE THE DAYS, HUH?
TNNGH
NH ...!
BUT!
WUNCH
ONCE THE ONIWABANSHU SHOWED UP...
...NOT ONLY DID THE HUMANS STOP THEIR PRAYERS...
...THEY EVEN PLOTTED WITH THE ONIWABANSHU ...
...AND HATCHED A PLAN TO ASSASSINATE ME.
I KILLED THEM FOR IT.
THE ONMITSU. THE VILLAGERS. MEN AND WOMEN, YOUNG AND OLD—EVEN THE INFANTS.
I KILLED AND ATE ALL OF THEM!

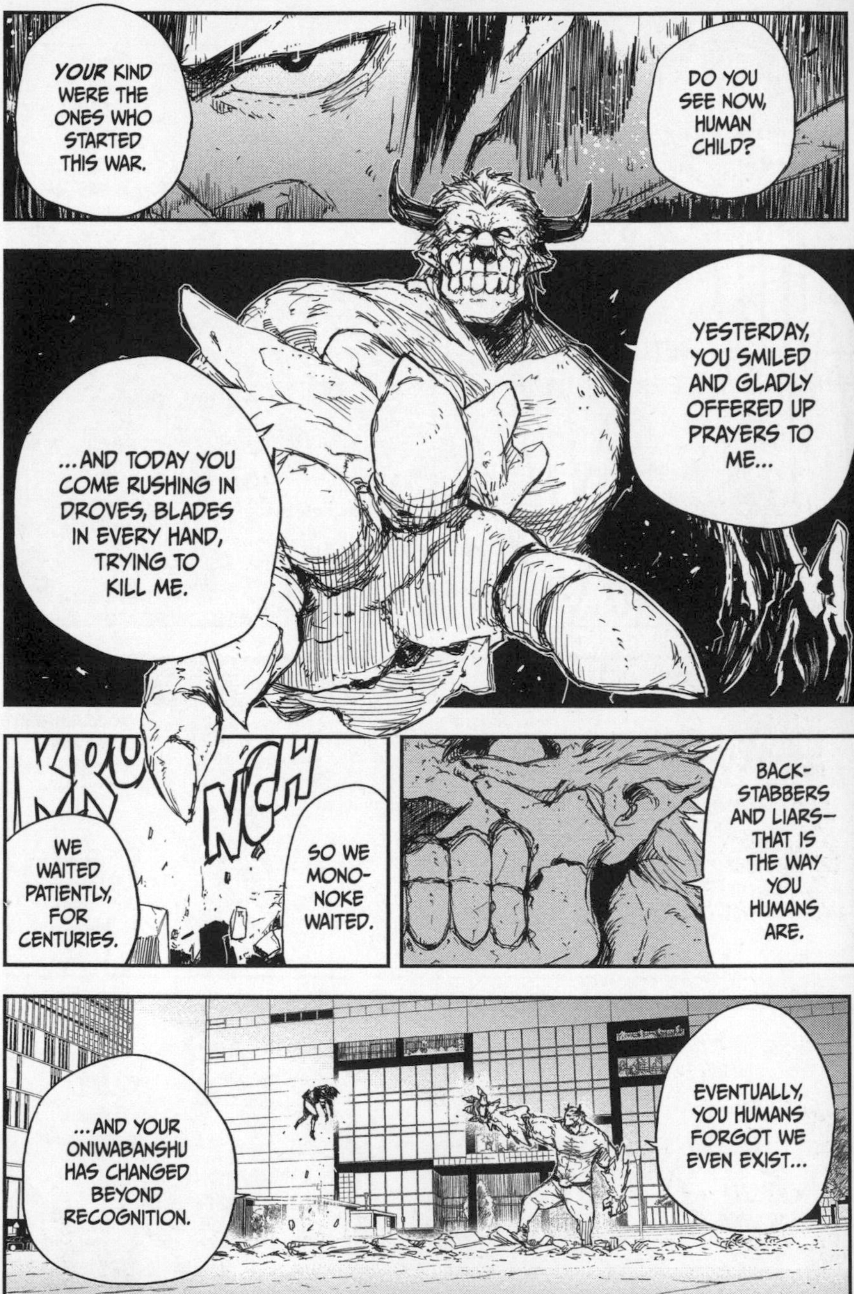
DO YOU SEE NOW, HUMAN CHILD?
YOUR KIND WERE THE ONES WHO STARTED THIS WAR.
YESTERDAY, YOU SMILED AND GLADLY OFFERED UP PRAYERS TO ME...
...AND TODAY YOU COME RUSHING IN DROVES, BLADES IN EVERY HAND, TRYING TO KILL ME.
BACK-STABBERS AND LIARS—THAT IS THE WAY YOU HUMANS ARE.
KRUNCH
SO WE MONONOKE WAITED.
WE WAITED PATIENTLY, FOR CENTURIES.
EVENTUALLY, YOU HUMANS FORGOT WE EVEN EXIST...
...AND YOUR ONIWABANSHU HAS CHANGED BEYOND RECOGNITION.

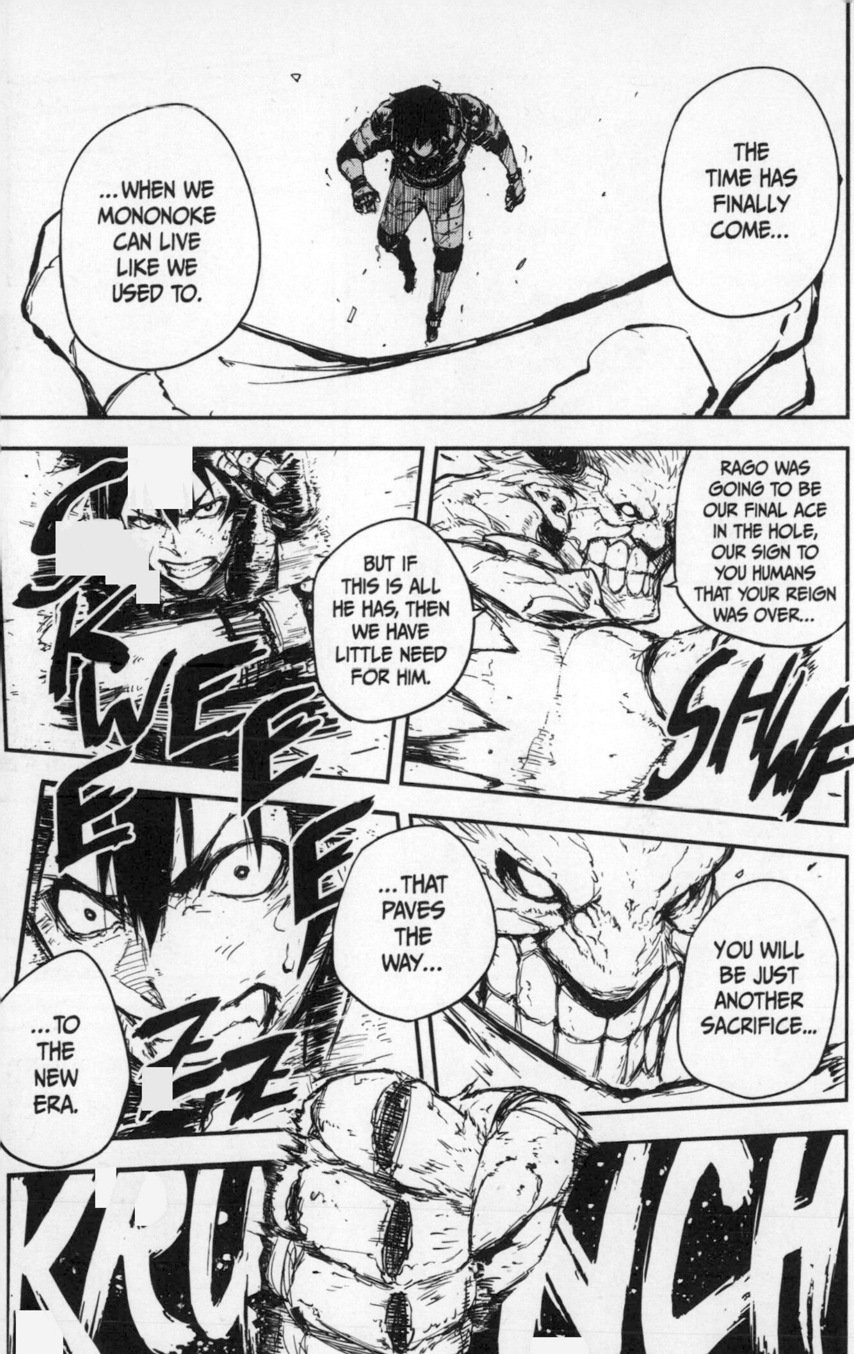
THE TIME HAS FINALLY COME...
...WHEN WE MONONOKE CAN LIVE LIKE WE USED TO.
RAGO WAS GOING TO BE OUR FINAL ACE IN THE HOLE, OUR SIGN TO YOU HUMANS THAT YOUR REIGN WAS OVER...
BUT IF THIS IS ALL HE HAS, THEN WE HAVE LITTLE NEED FOR HIM.
SHWF
KWEEEE
YOU WILL BE JUST ANOTHER SACRIFICE...
...THAT PAVES THE WAY...
...TO THE NEW ERA.
KRU NCH

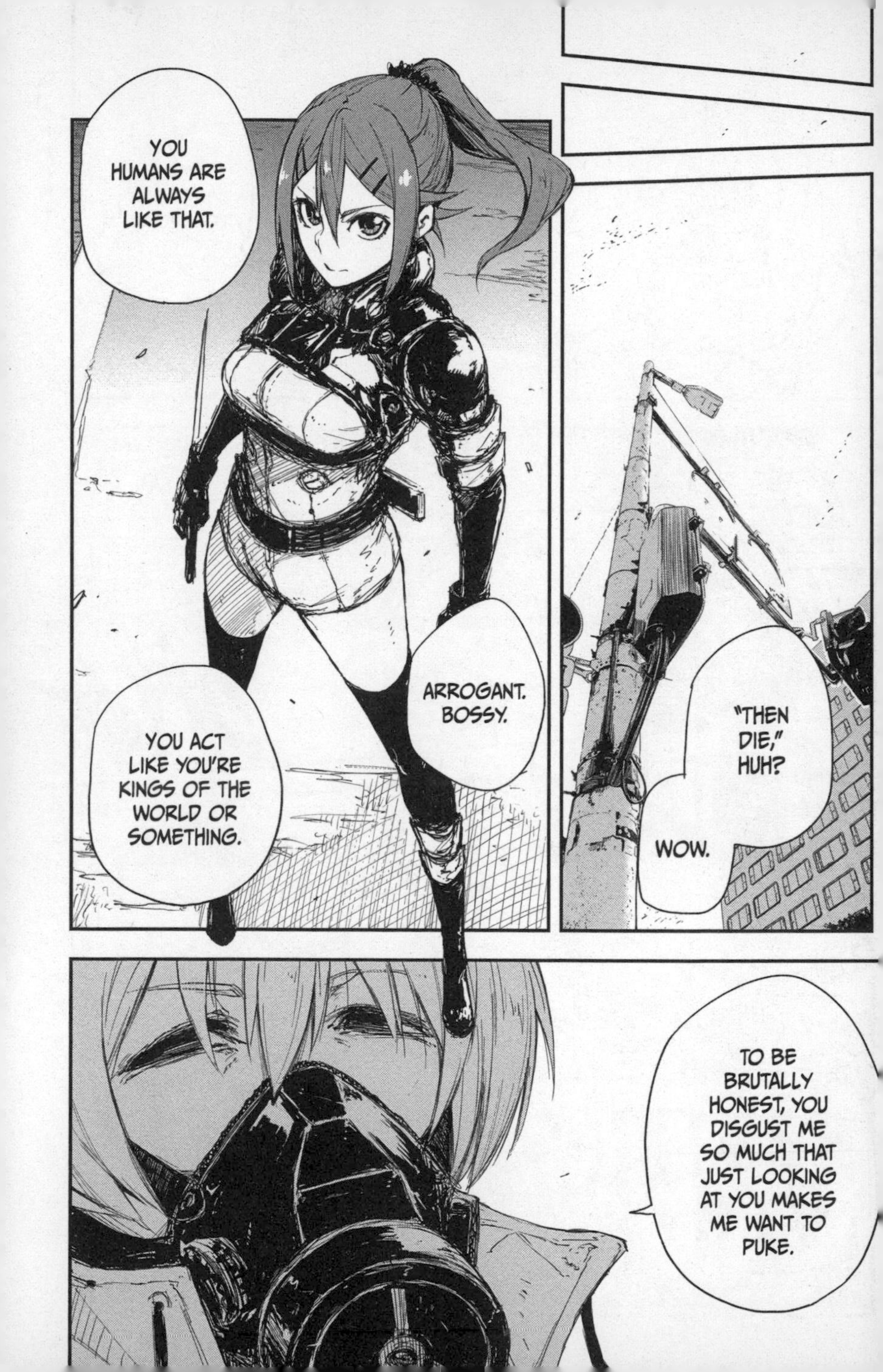
"THEN DIE," HUH?
WOW.
YOU HUMANS ARE ALWAYS LIKE THAT.
ARROGANT. BOSSY.
YOU ACT LIKE YOU'RE KINGS OF THE WORLD OR SOMETHING.
TO BE BRUTALLY HONEST, YOU DISGUST ME SO MUCH THAT JUST LOOKING AT YOU MAKES ME WANT TO PUKE.

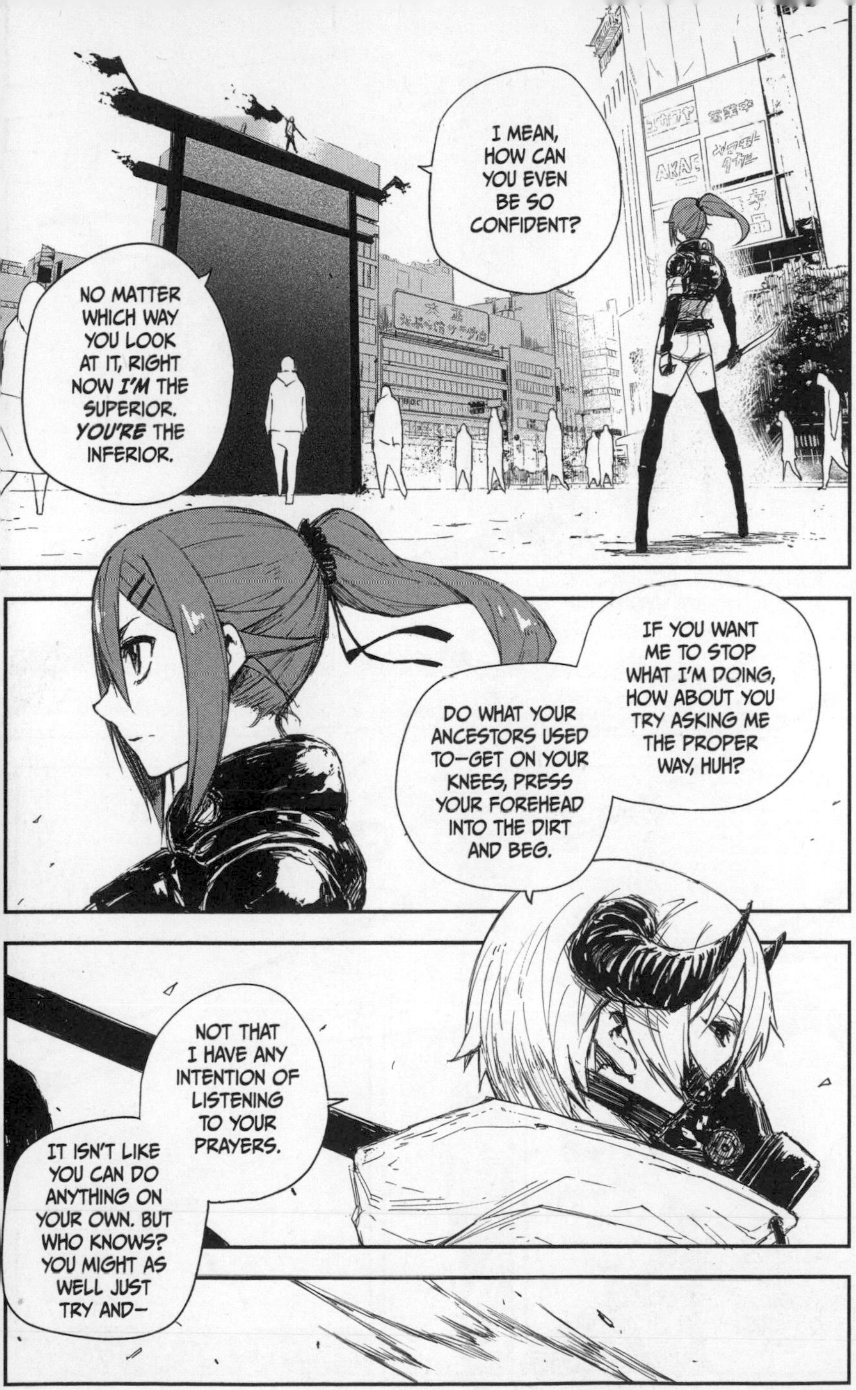
I MEAN, HOW CAN YOU EVEN BE SO CONFIDENT?
NO MATTER WHICH WAY YOU LOOK AT IT, RIGHT NOW *I'M* THE SUPERIOR. ***YOU'RE*** THE INFERIOR.
IF YOU WANT ME TO STOP WHAT I'M DOING, HOW ABOUT YOU TRY ASKING ME THE PROPER WAY, HUH?
DO WHAT YOUR ANCESTORS USED TO—GET ON YOUR KNEES, PRESS YOUR FOREHEAD INTO THE DIRT AND BEG.
NOT THAT I HAVE ANY INTENTION OF LISTENING TO YOUR PRAYERS.
IT ISN'T LIKE YOU CAN DO ANYTHING ON YOUR OWN. BUT WHO KNOWS? YOU MIGHT AS WELL JUST TRY AND—

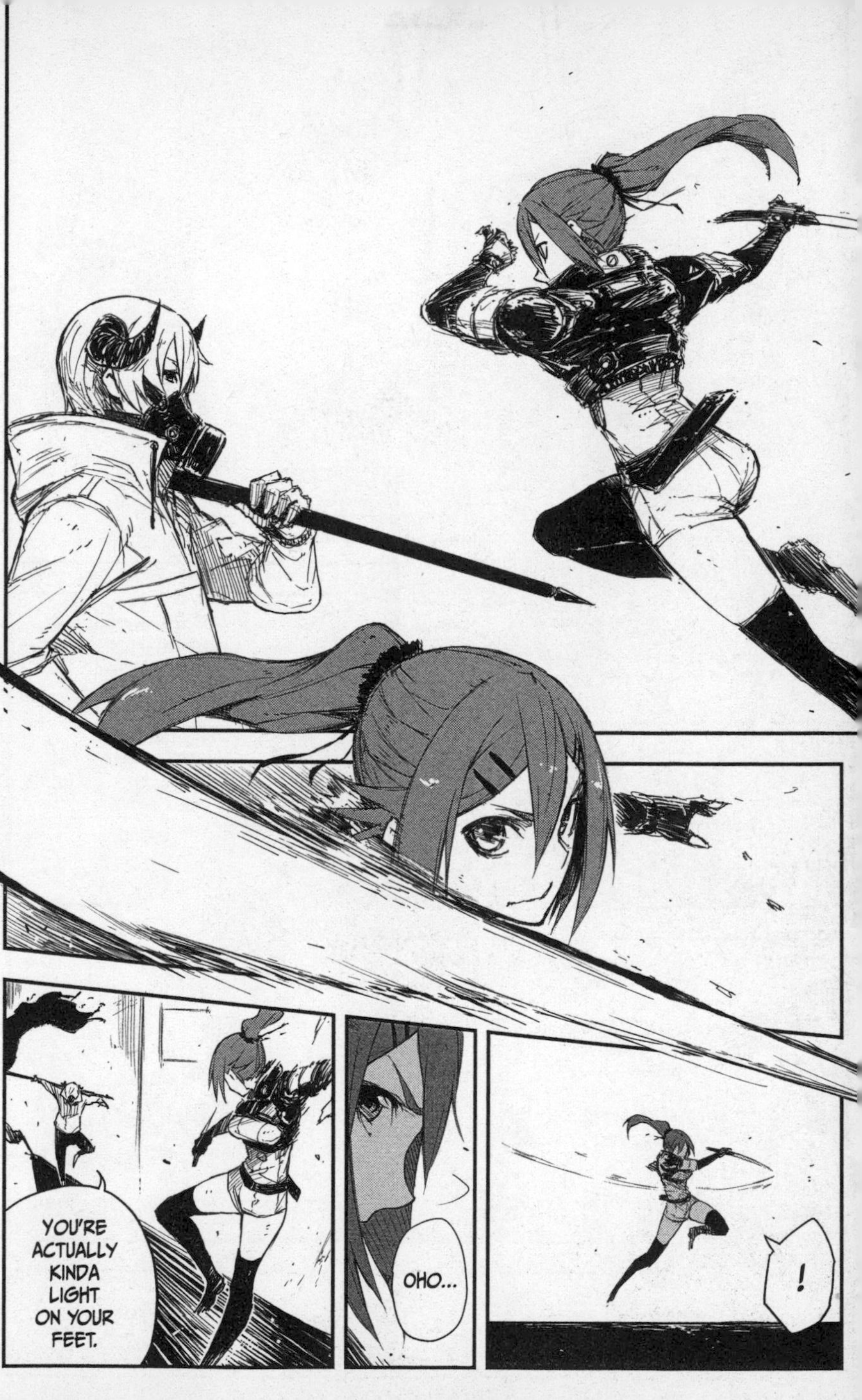
!
OHO...
YOU'RE ACTUALLY KINDA LIGHT ON YOUR FEET.

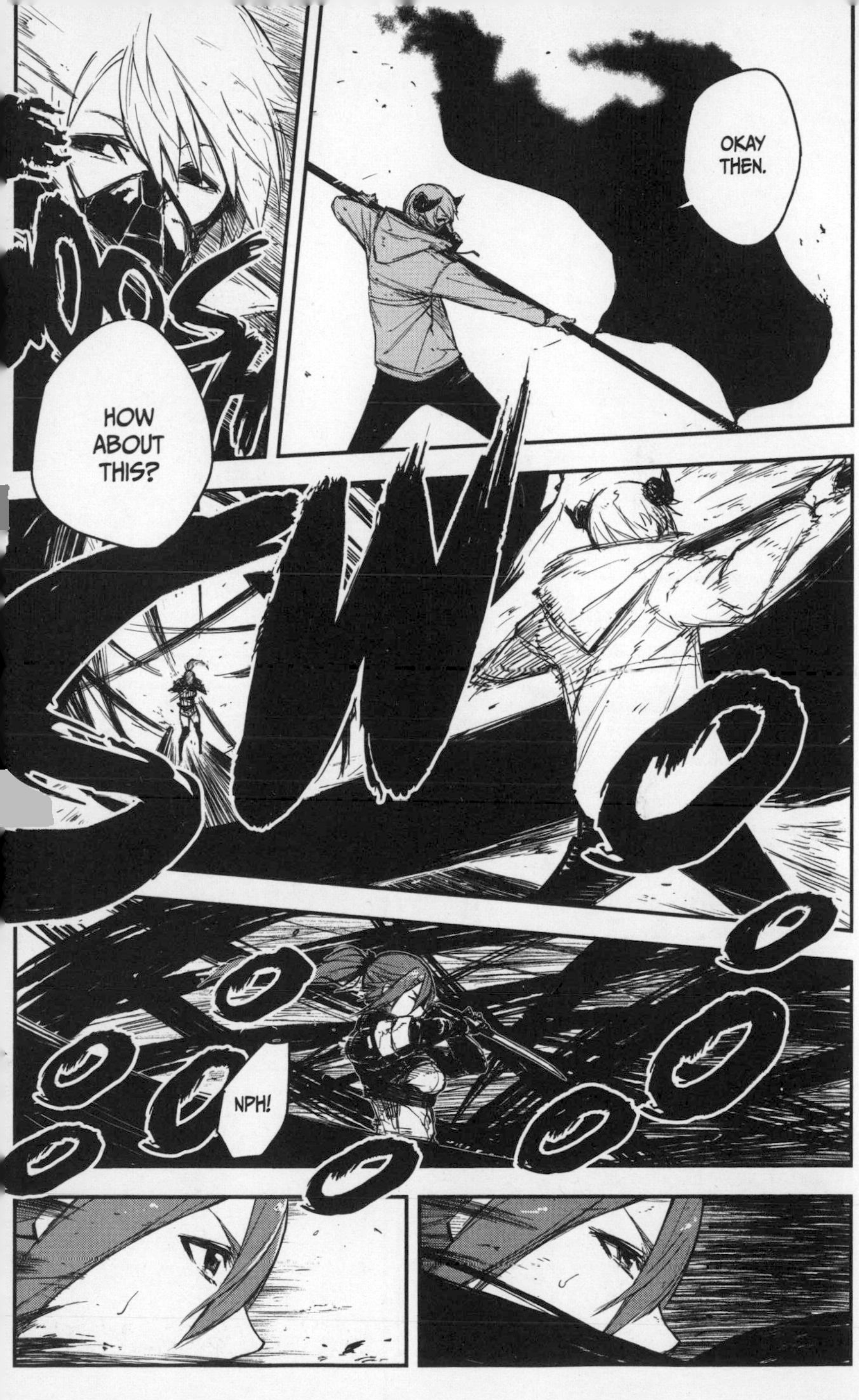
OKAY THEN.
HOW ABOUT THIS?
NPH!

FWII ISH

?!

WELL? WHAT DO YOU THINK OF MY ILLUSION?

NOT EVEN THAT VEE-ARR THING COMES CLOSE TO THIS!

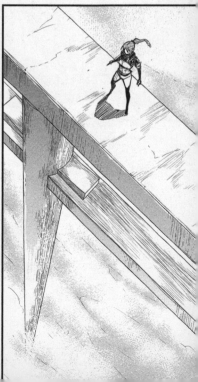

OH, BUT JUST SO YOU KNOW...FALL OFF AND YOU REALLY WILL DIE.

SEE, MY SPELL ISN'T JUST AFFECTING YOUR EYES. IT AFFECTS YOUR ENTIRE NERVOUS SYSTEM.

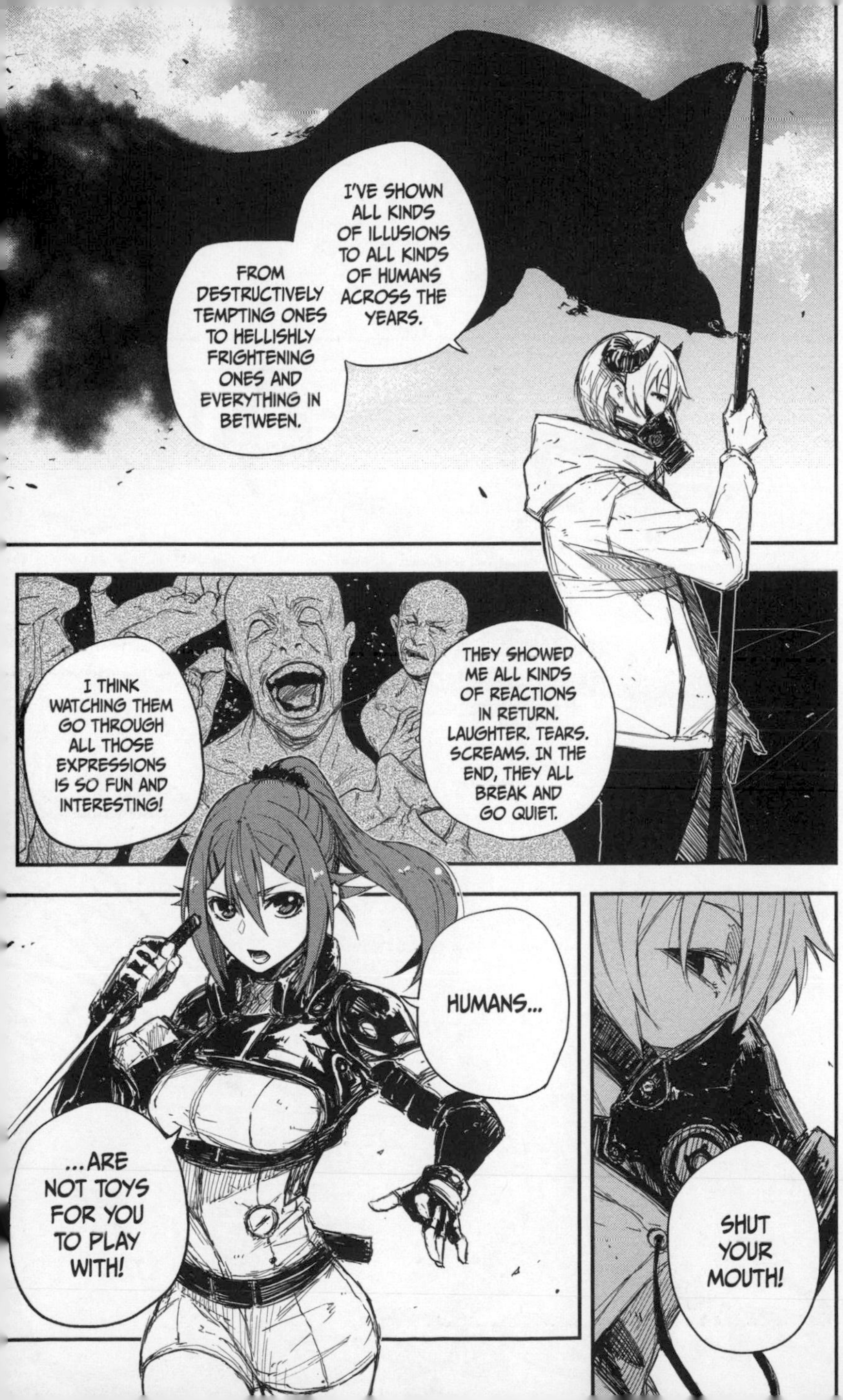
I'VE SHOWN ALL KINDS OF ILLUSIONS TO ALL KINDS OF HUMANS ACROSS THE YEARS.
FROM DESTRUCTIVELY TEMPTING ONES TO HELLISHLY FRIGHTENING ONES AND EVERYTHING IN BETWEEN.
THEY SHOWED ME ALL KINDS OF REACTIONS IN RETURN. LAUGHTER. TEARS. SCREAMS. IN THE END, THEY ALL BREAK AND GO QUIET.
I THINK WATCHING THEM GO THROUGH ALL THOSE EXPRESSIONS IS SO FUN AND INTERESTING!
SHUT YOUR MOUTH!
HUMANS...
...ARE NOT TOYS FOR YOU TO PLAY WITH!

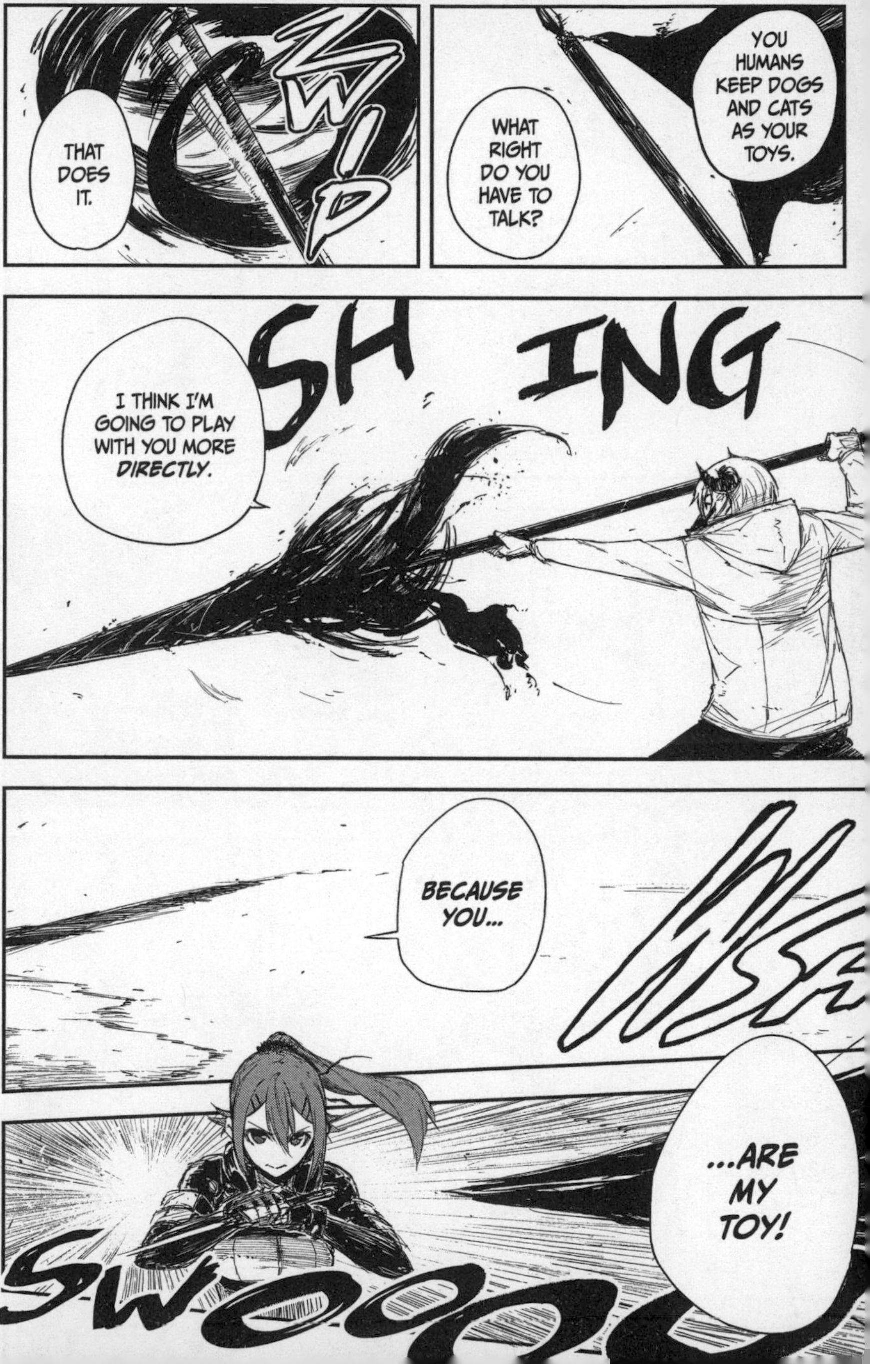
YOU HUMANS KEEP DOGS AND CATS AS YOUR TOYS.
WHAT RIGHT DO YOU HAVE TO TALK?
ZWID
THAT DOES IT.
SHING
I THINK I'M GOING TO PLAY WITH YOU MORE *DIRECTLY*.
BECAUSE YOU...
...ARE MY TOY!
SWOOO

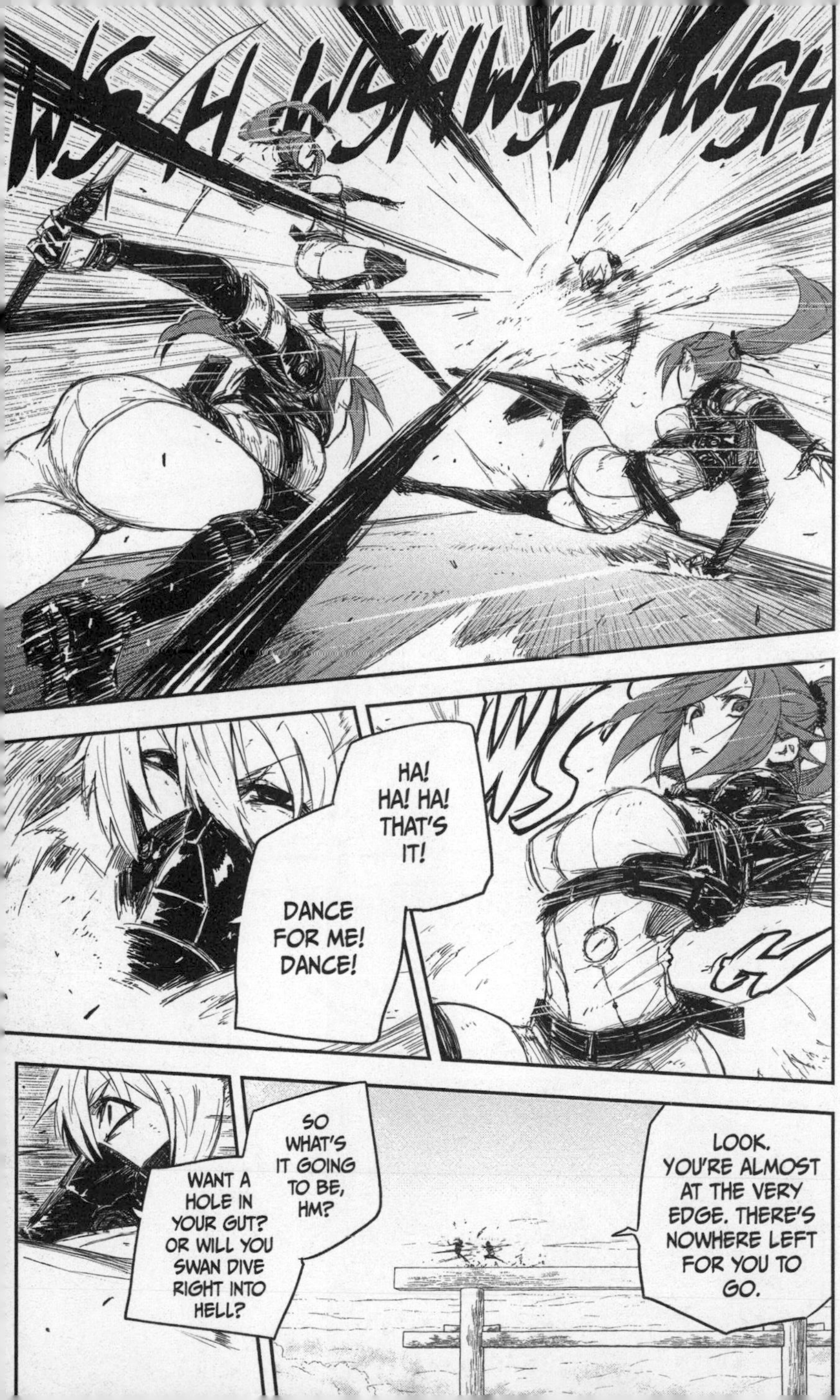
HA! HA! HA! THAT'S IT!
DANCE FOR ME! DANCE!
LOOK. YOU'RE ALMOST AT THE VERY EDGE. THERE'S NOWHERE LEFT FOR YOU TO GO.
SO WHAT'S IT GOING TO BE, HM?
WANT A HOLE IN YOUR GUT? OR WILL YOU SWAN DIVE RIGHT INTO HELL?

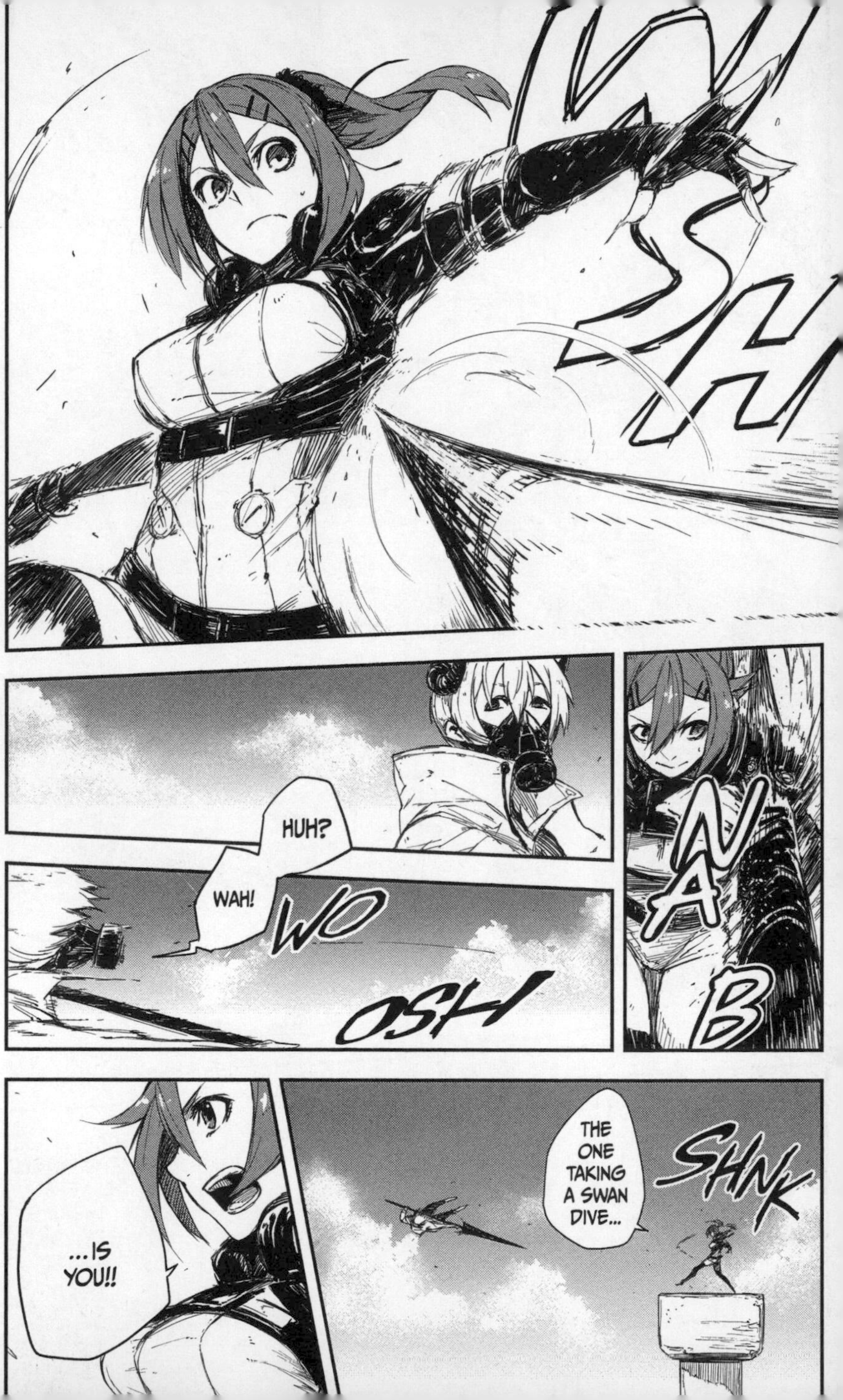
WHSH
NAB
HUH?
WAH!
WOOSH
THE ONE TAKING A SWAN DIVE...
SHNK
...IS YOU!!

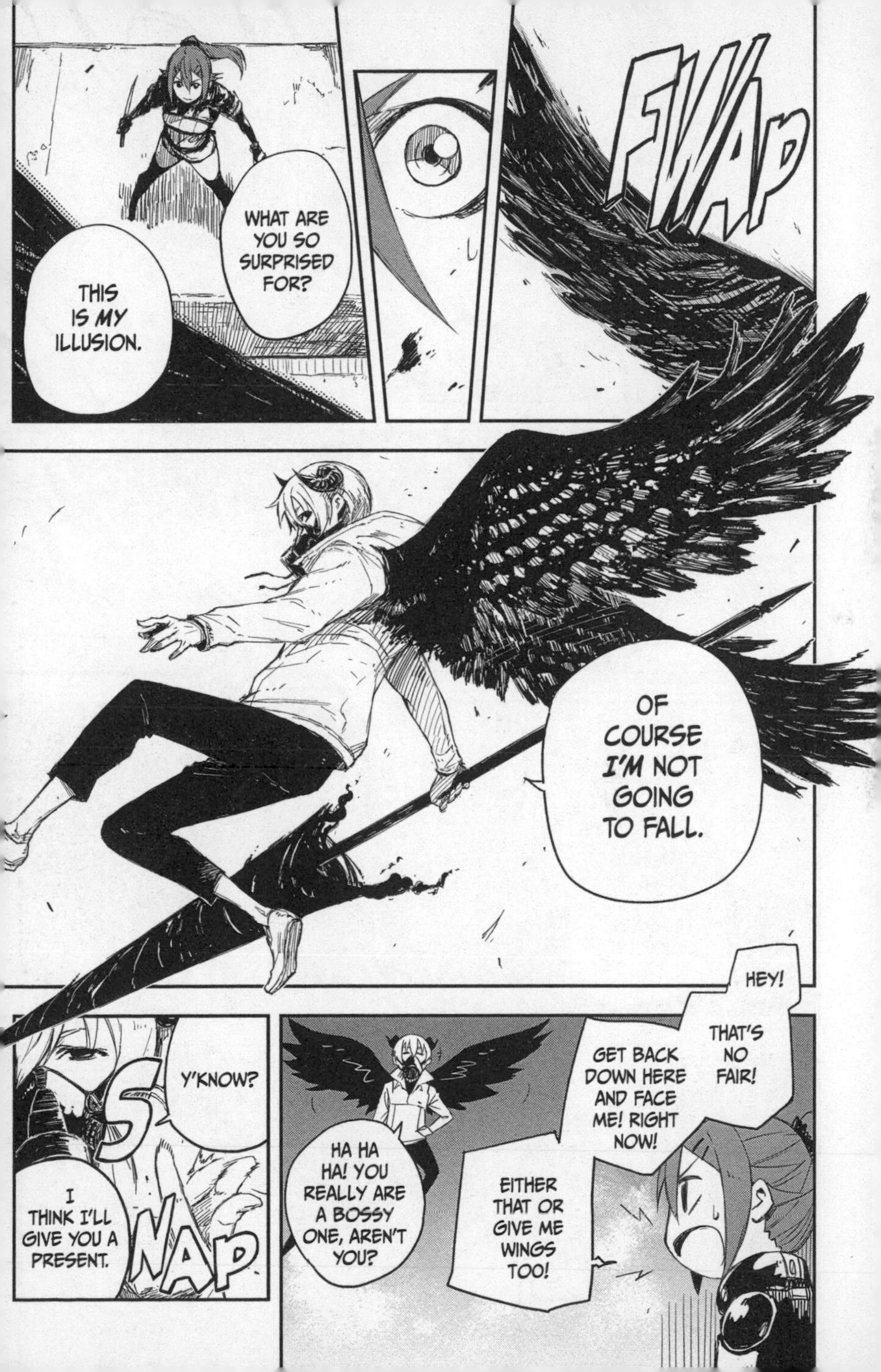
FWAP
WHAT ARE YOU SO SURPRISED FOR?
THIS IS MY ILLUSION.
OF COURSE I'M NOT GOING TO FALL.
HEY!
THAT'S NO FAIR!
GET BACK DOWN HERE AND FACE ME! RIGHT NOW!
EITHER THAT OR GIVE ME WINGS TOO!
HA HA HA! YOU REALLY ARE A BOSSY ONE, AREN'T YOU?
Y'KNOW?
SNAP
I THINK I'LL GIVE YOU A PRESENT.

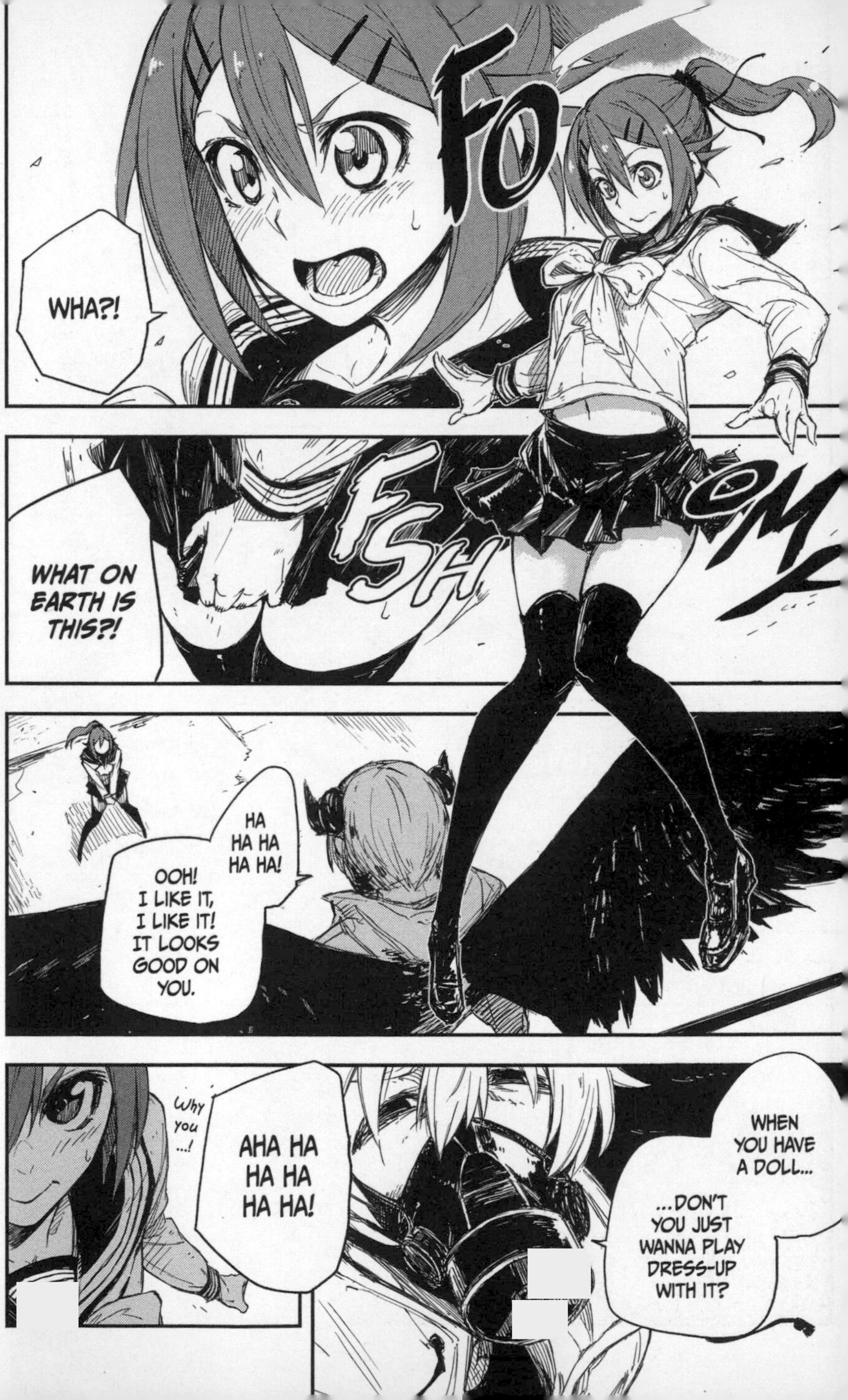
FO
WHA?!
FSH
OM
WHAT ON EARTH IS THIS?!
HA HA HA HA HA!
OOH! I LIKE IT, I LIKE IT! IT LOOKS GOOD ON YOU.
WHEN YOU HAVE A DOLL...
...DON'T YOU JUST WANNA PLAY DRESS-UP WITH IT?
AHA HA HA HA HA HA!
Why you ...!

HE SEES ME AS SO INFERIOR HE CAN JUST TOY WITH ME.

AND THAT'S A WEAKNESS I CAN EXPLOIT.

THIS IS JUST AN ILLUSION.

I STILL HAVE MY ESPIONAGE GEAR ON. I'M STILL HOLDING MY DAGGER.

I HAVE TO CALM DOWN.

LOSING MY COOL IS PLAYING RIGHT INTO HIS HANDS.

ALL I'LL GET...

...IS ONE CHANCE!

SORRY, BUT I SAY NO TO BOTH.

OH?

SO WHAT SHOULD I PUT YOU IN NEXT?

A MAID OUTFIT? MAYBE A NURSE'S UNIFORM.

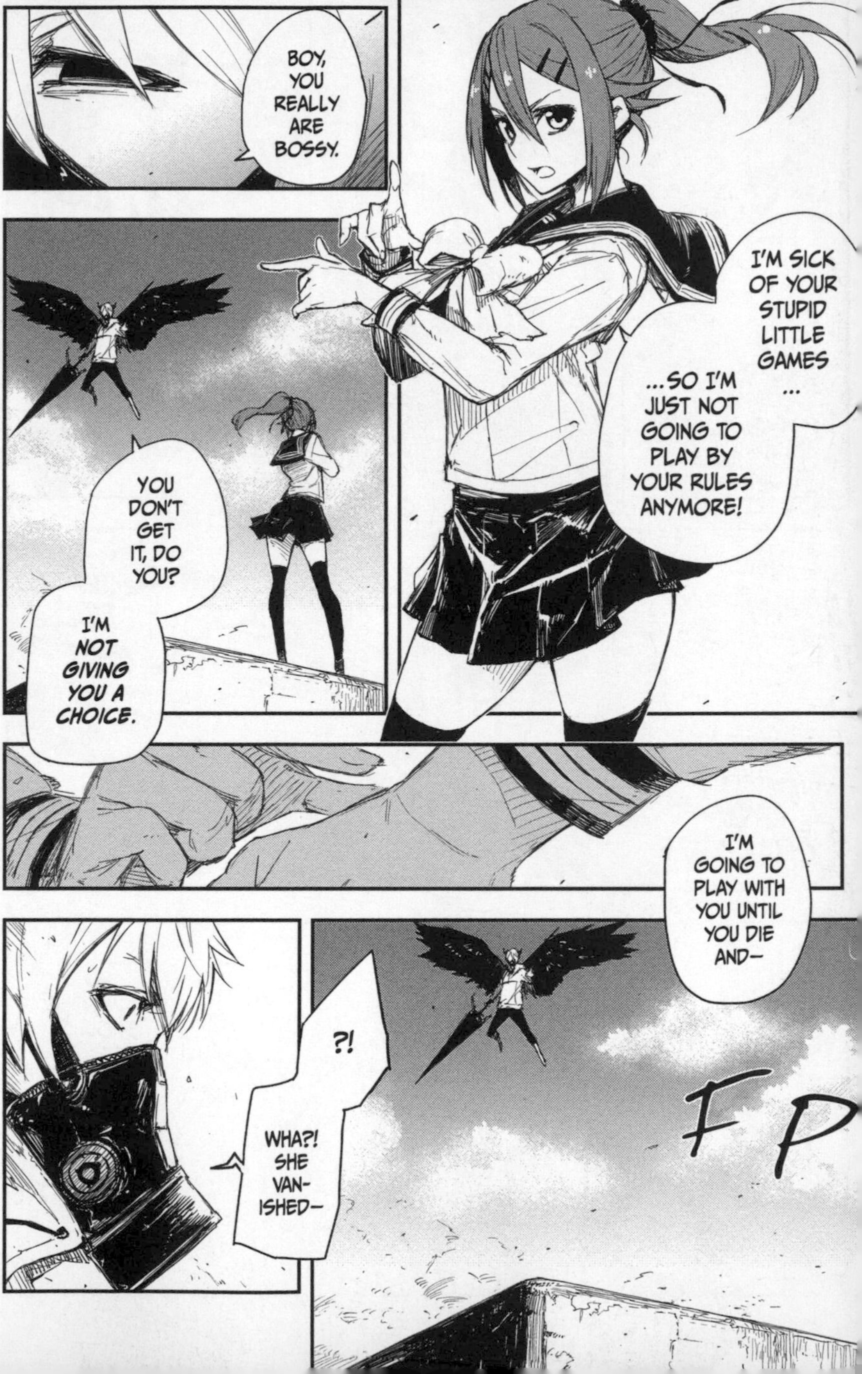
I'M SICK OF YOUR STUPID LITTLE GAMES...
...SO I'M JUST NOT GOING TO PLAY BY YOUR RULES ANYMORE!
BOY, YOU REALLY ARE BOSSY.
YOU DON'T GET IT, DO YOU?
I'M NOT GIVING YOU A CHOICE.
I'M GOING TO PLAY WITH YOU UNTIL YOU DIE AND–
FP
?!
WHA?! SHE VAN-ISHED–

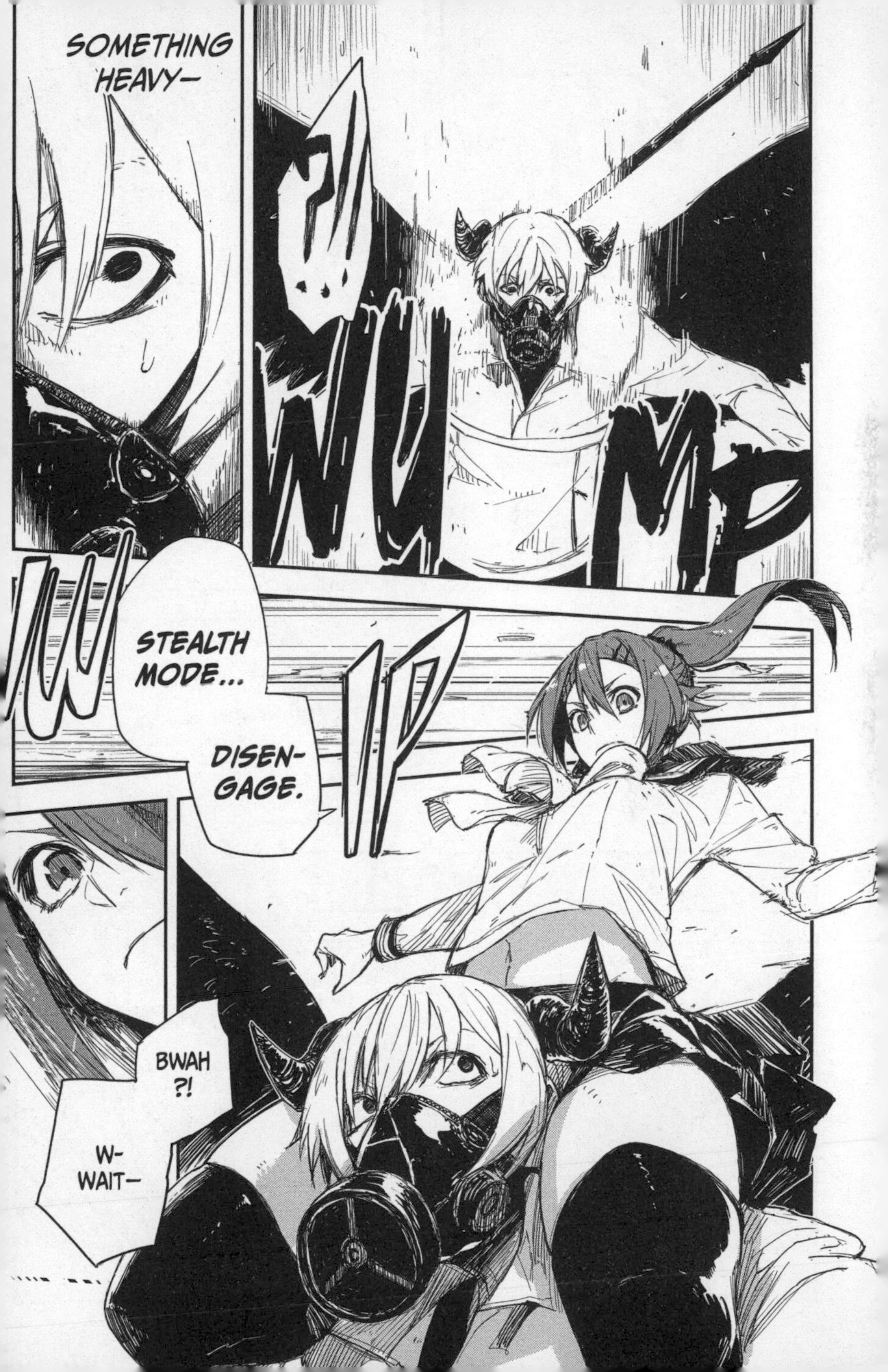
?!
WUMP
SOMETHING HEAVY—
STEALTH MODE...
DISENGAGE.
BWAH ?!
W- WAIT—

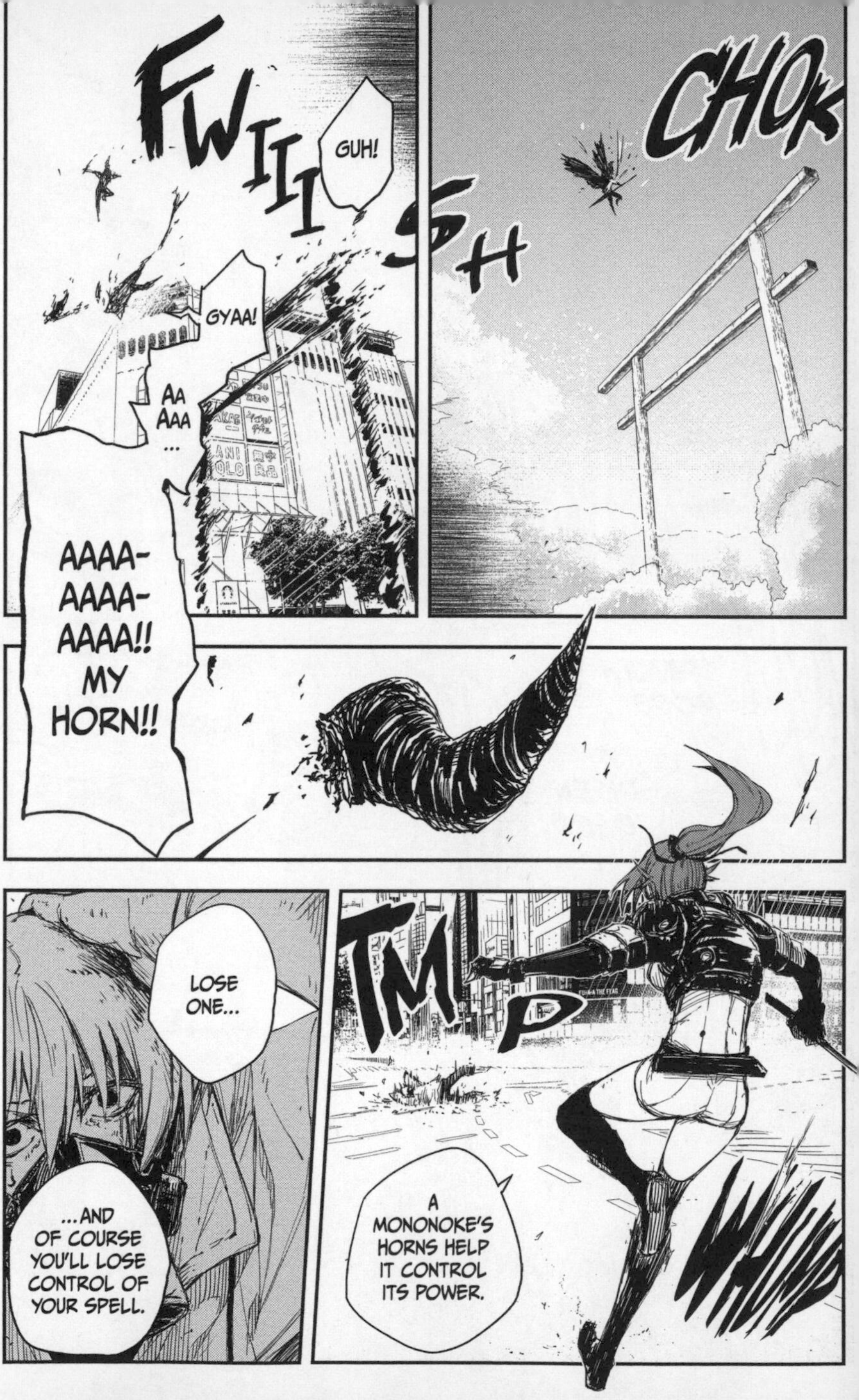
CHOK
FWIIISH
GUH!
GYAA!
AA AAA...
AAAA-AAAA-AAAA!! MY HORN!!
TMP
A MONONOKE'S HORNS HELP IT CONTROL ITS POWER.
LOSE ONE...
...AND OF COURSE YOU'LL LOSE CONTROL OF YOUR SPELL.

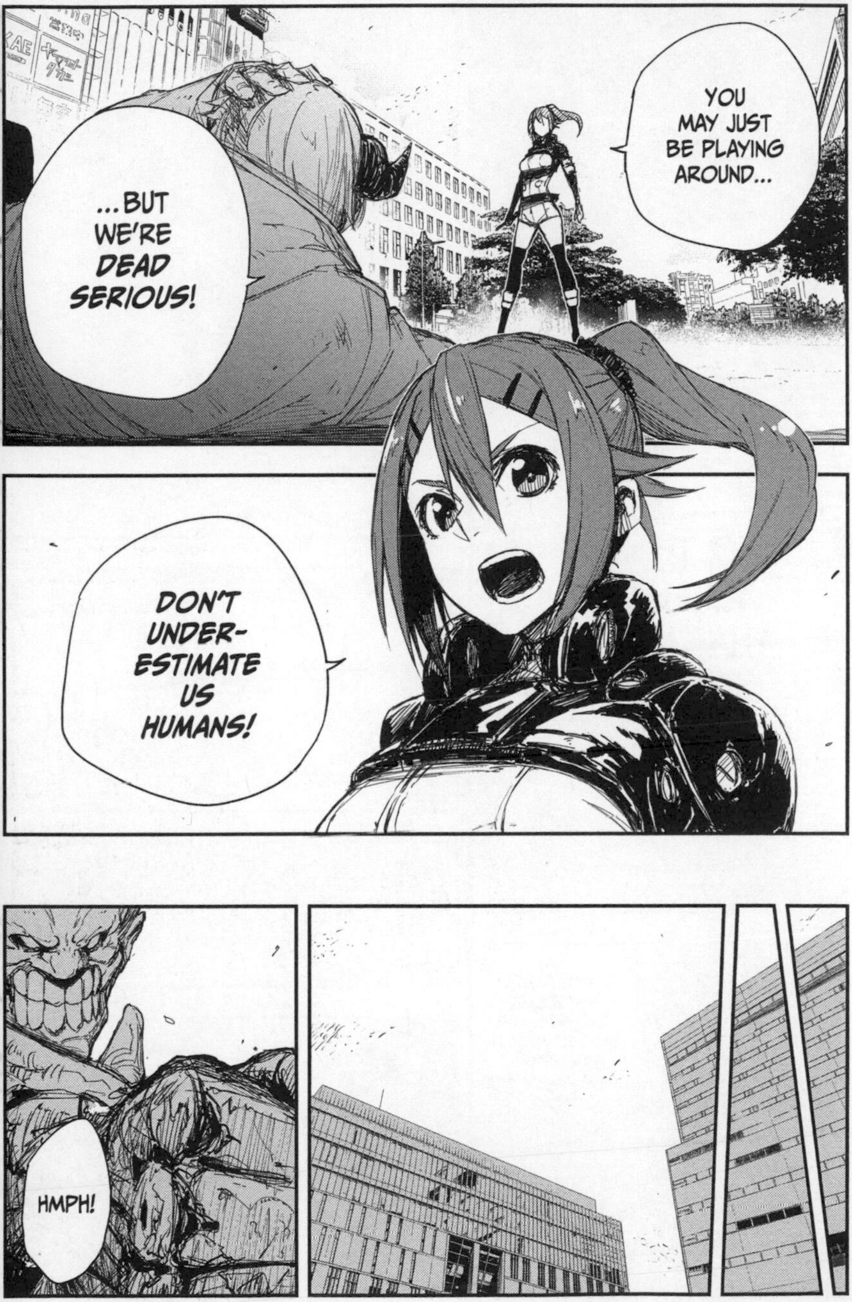
YOU MAY JUST BE PLAYING AROUND...
...BUT WE'RE DEAD SERIOUS!
DON'T UNDER-ESTIMATE US HUMANS!
HMPH!

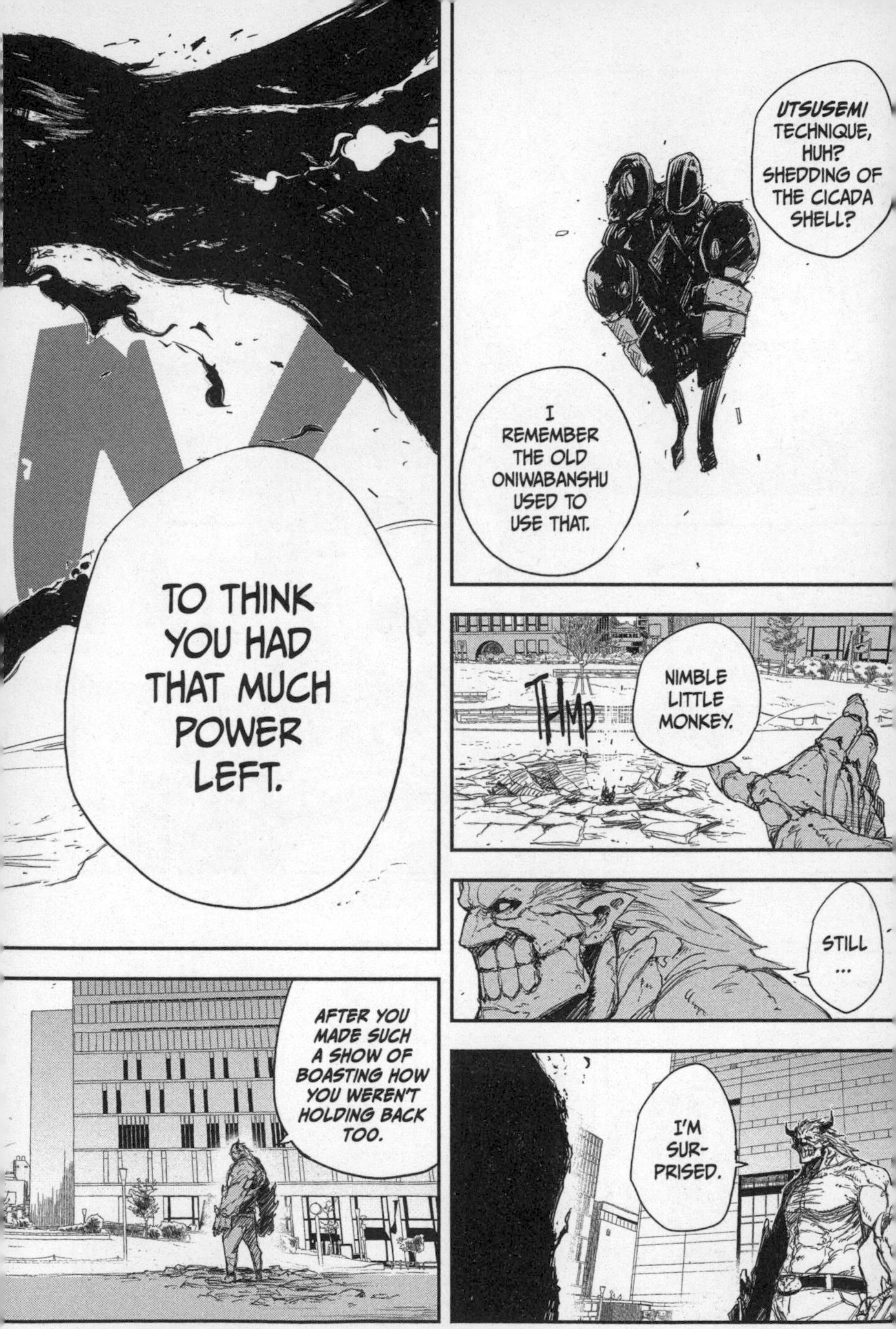
UTSUSEMI TECHNIQUE, HUH? SHEDDING OF THE CICADA SHELL?
I REMEMBER THE OLD ONIWABANSHU USED TO USE THAT.
NIMBLE LITTLE MONKEY.
THMP
STILL ...
TO THINK YOU HAD THAT MUCH POWER LEFT.
I'M SUR-PRISED.
AFTER YOU MADE SUCH A SHOW OF BOASTING HOW YOU WEREN'T HOLDING BACK TOO.

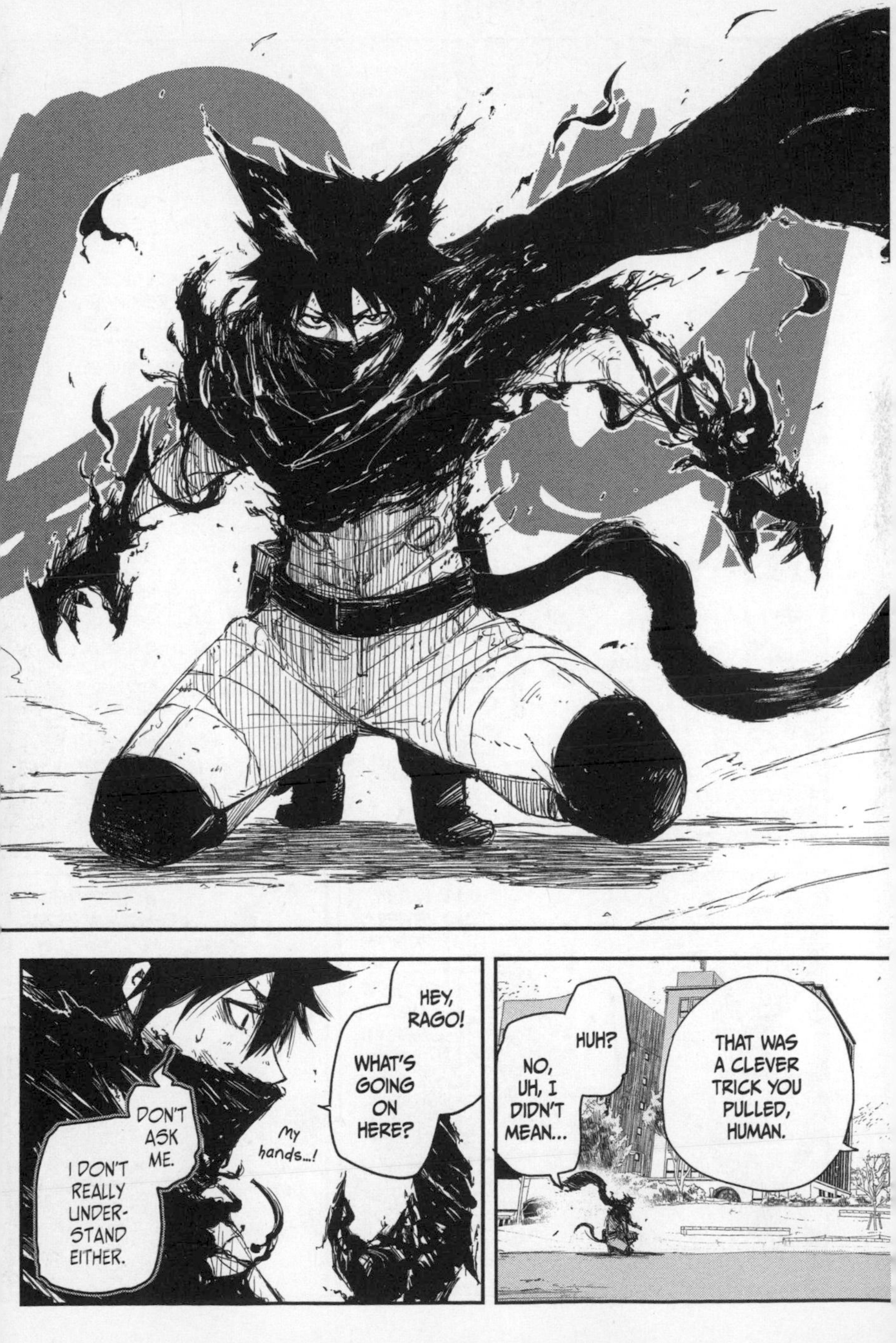
THAT WAS A CLEVER TRICK YOU PULLED, HUMAN.
HUH?
NO, UH, I DIDN'T MEAN...
HEY, RAGO!
WHAT'S GOING ON HERE?
My hands...!
DON'T ASK ME.
I DON'T REALLY UNDER-STAND EITHER.

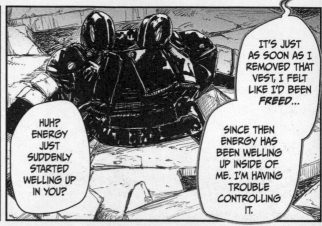

IT'S JUST AS SOON AS I REMOVED THAT VEST, I FELT LIKE I'D BEEN *FREED*...
SINCE THEN ENERGY HAS BEEN WELLING UP INSIDE OF ME. I'M HAVING TROUBLE CONTROLLING IT.
HUH? ENERGY JUST SUDDENLY STARTED WELLING UP IN YOU?
WAIT A MINUTE. WHAT DID SHIBA SAY BEFORE WE STARTED THIS MISSION AGAIN?
"GIVEN THE DENSITY OF THE FOG, THE ENERGY NEUTRALIZATION FUNCTION OF YOUR ESPIONAGE GEAR..."
"...SHOULD LET YOU BREAK THROUGH AND INFILTRATE THE
RIER."
YEAH. THERE WAS SOMETHING ABOUT AN ENERGY NEUTRALIZATION FUNCTION.
COULD THAT FUNCTION WORK NOT JUST ON THE AMBIENT ENERGY IN THE AIR...
...BUT ALSO ON THE ENERGY RAGO HAS IN ME...?
I'VE WORN THAT STUPID VEST PRETTY MUCH ALL THE TIME OUTSIDE OF SHOWERING AND SLEEPING, SO I DIDN'T REALLY NOTICE.
BUT MAYBE, SINCE IT GOT SUDDENLY STRIPPED OFF ME IN THE MIDDLE OF A TENSE FIGHT—
...!!
JIRO!
!

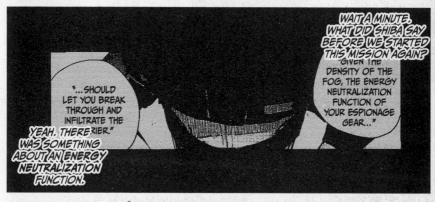

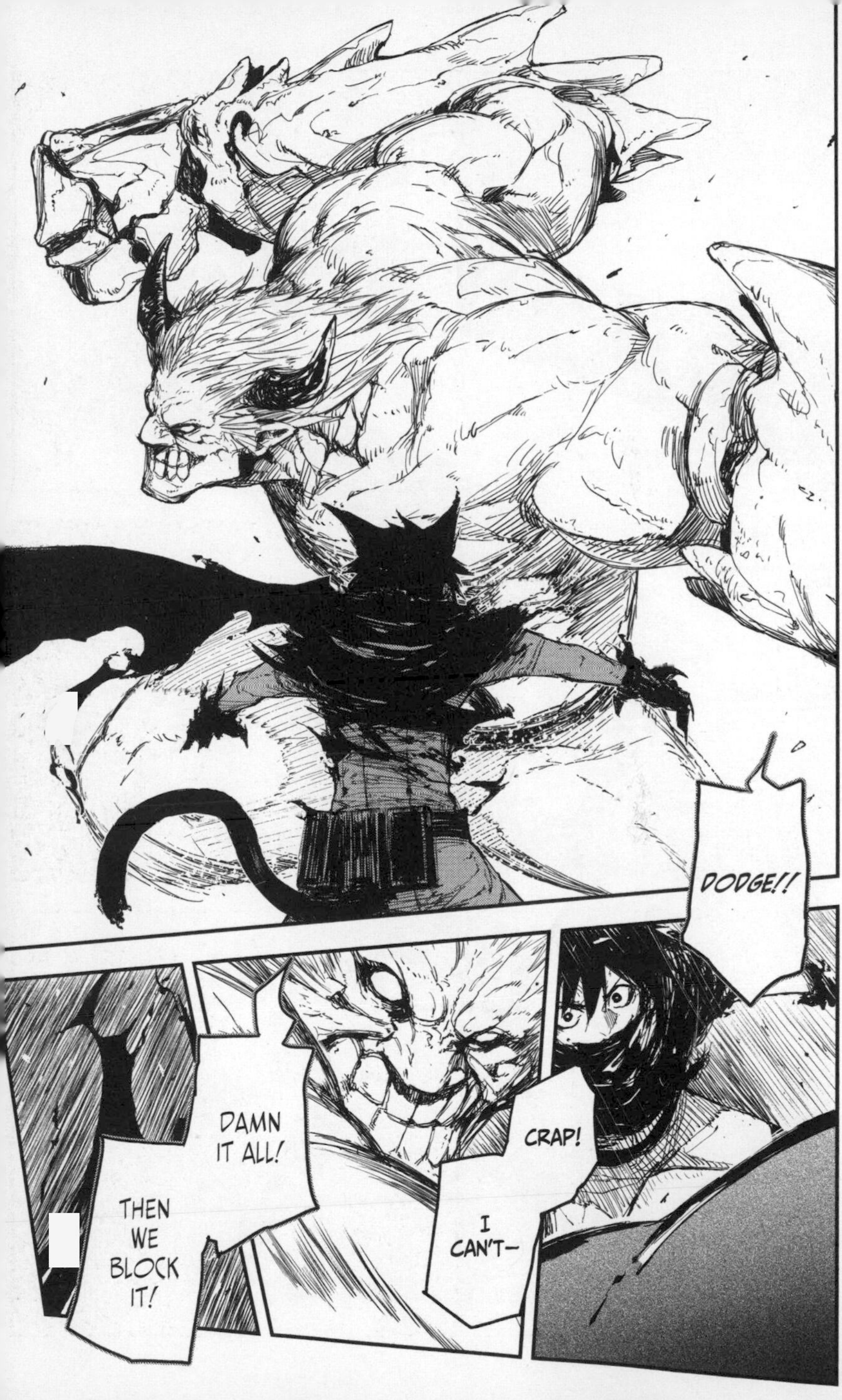
DODGE!!
CRAP!
I CAN'T—
DAMN IT ALL!
THEN WE BLOCK IT!

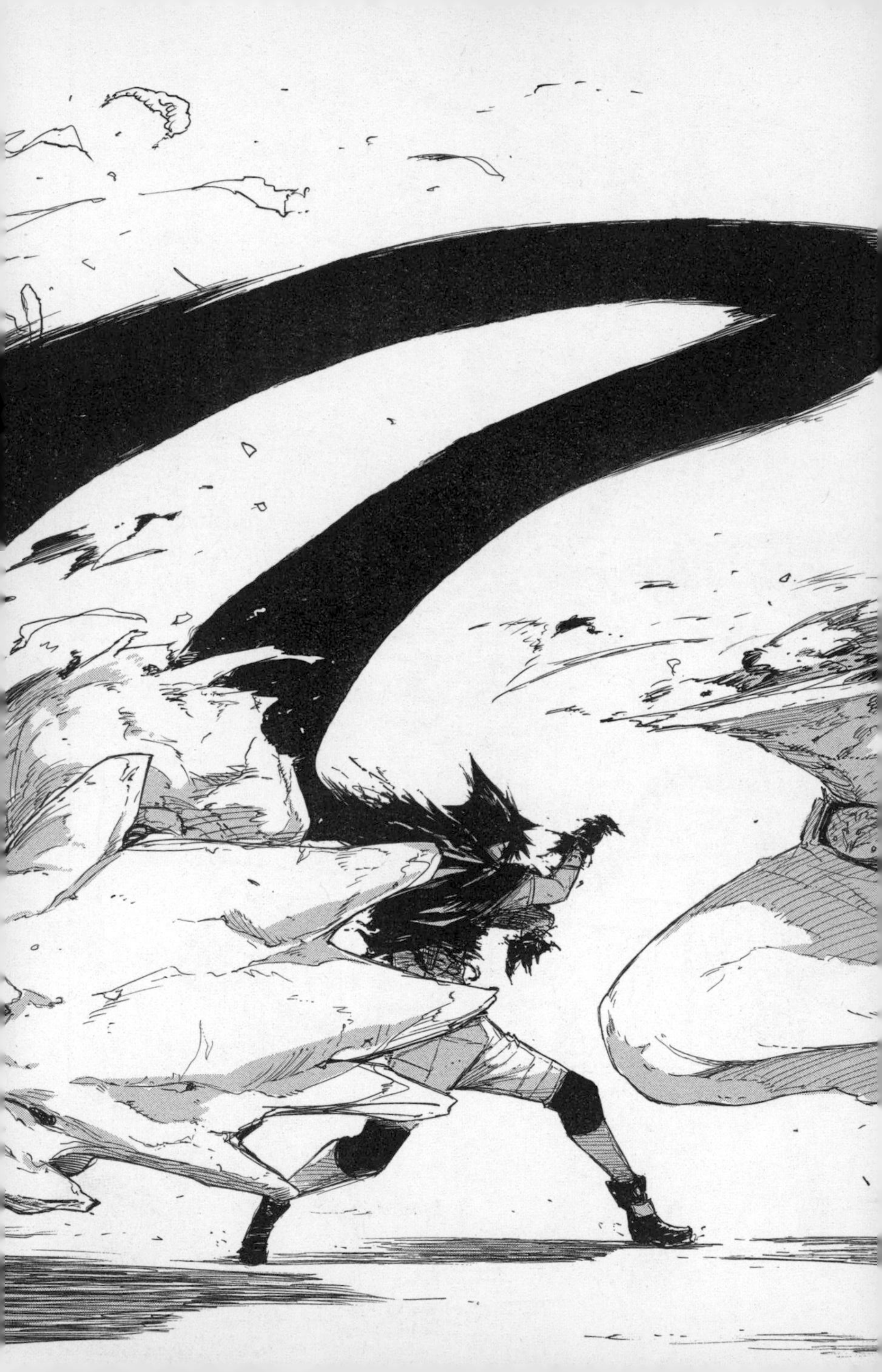

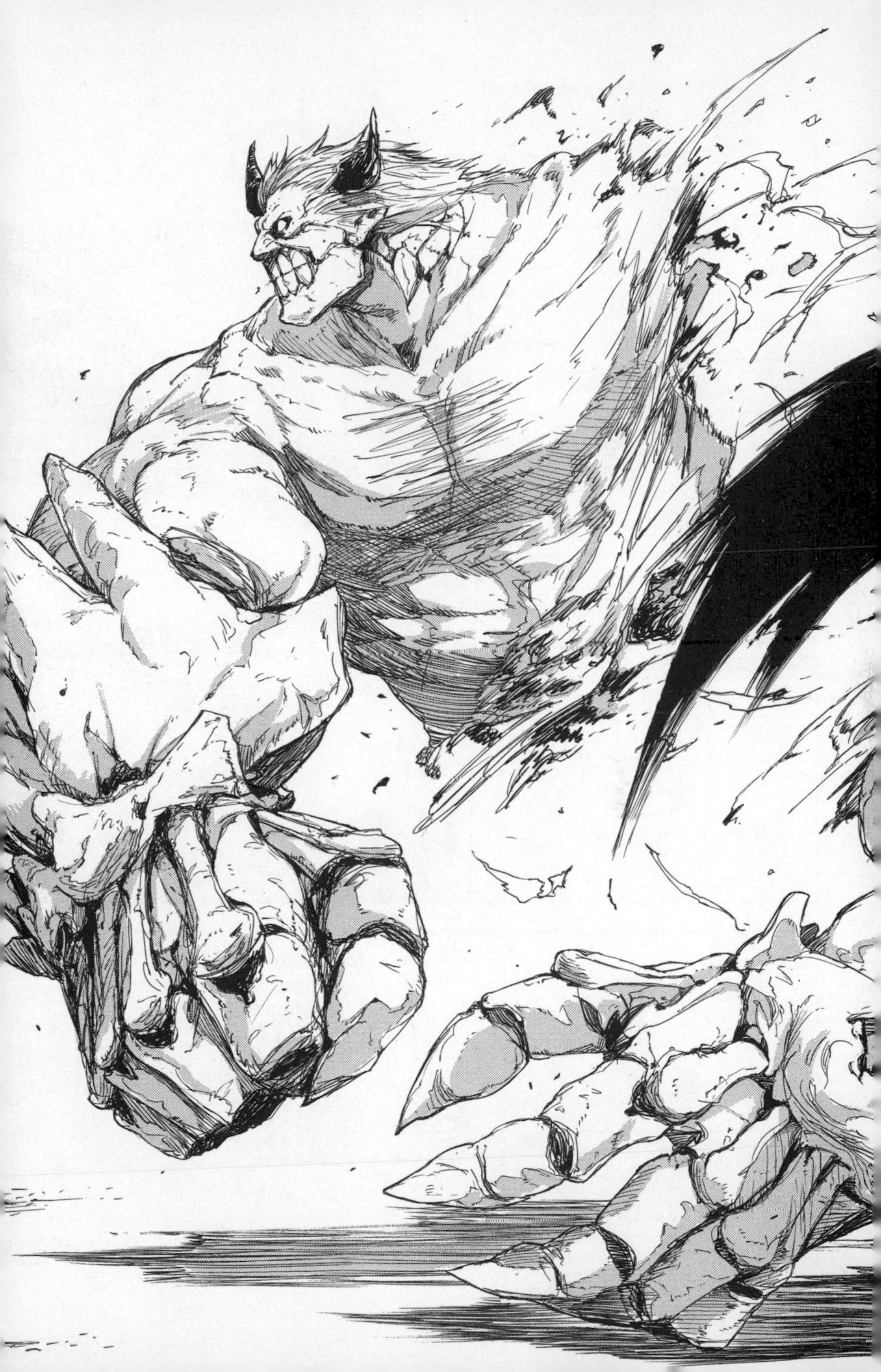

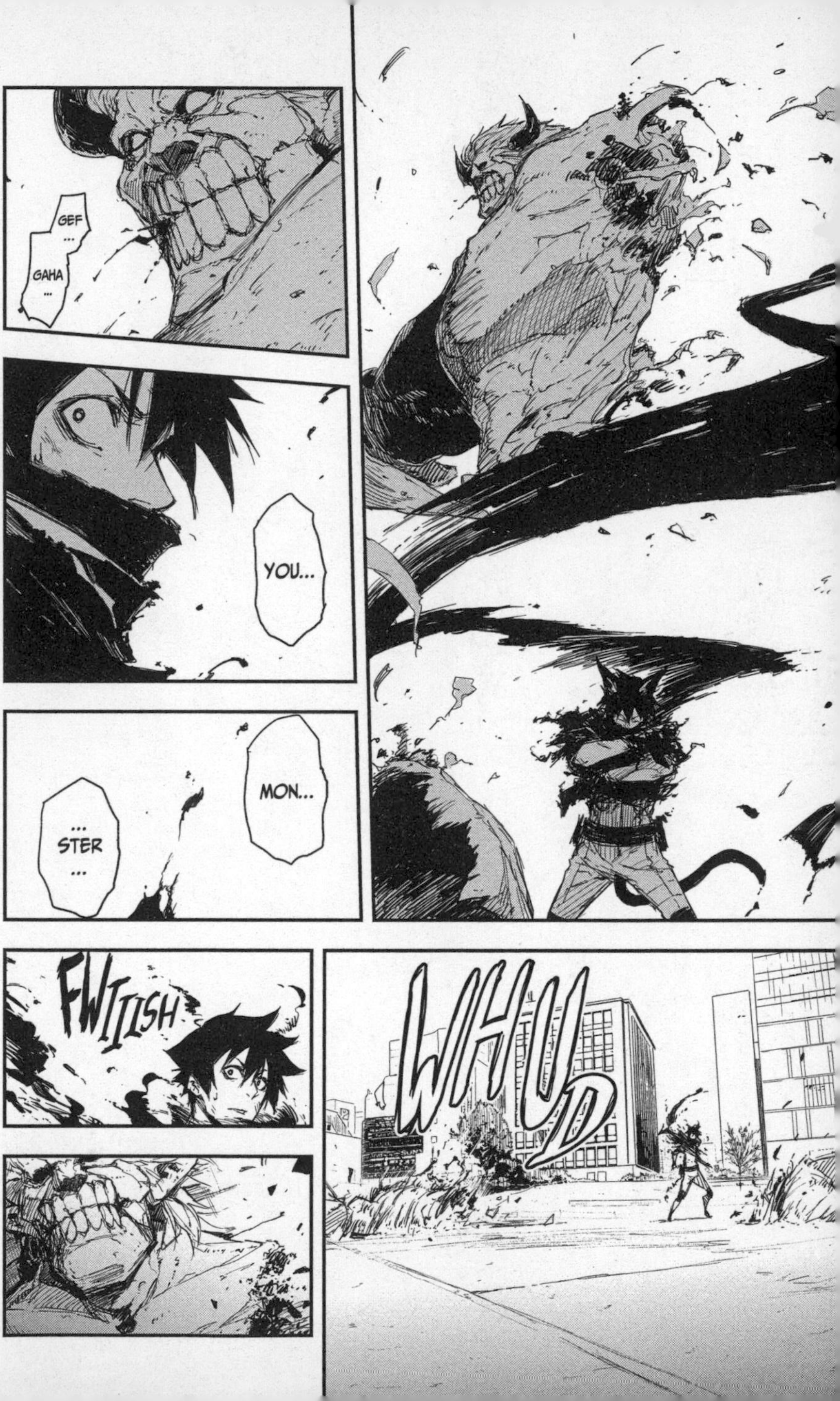
GEF ... GAHA ...
YOU...
MON...
... STER ...
WHUD
FWIIISH

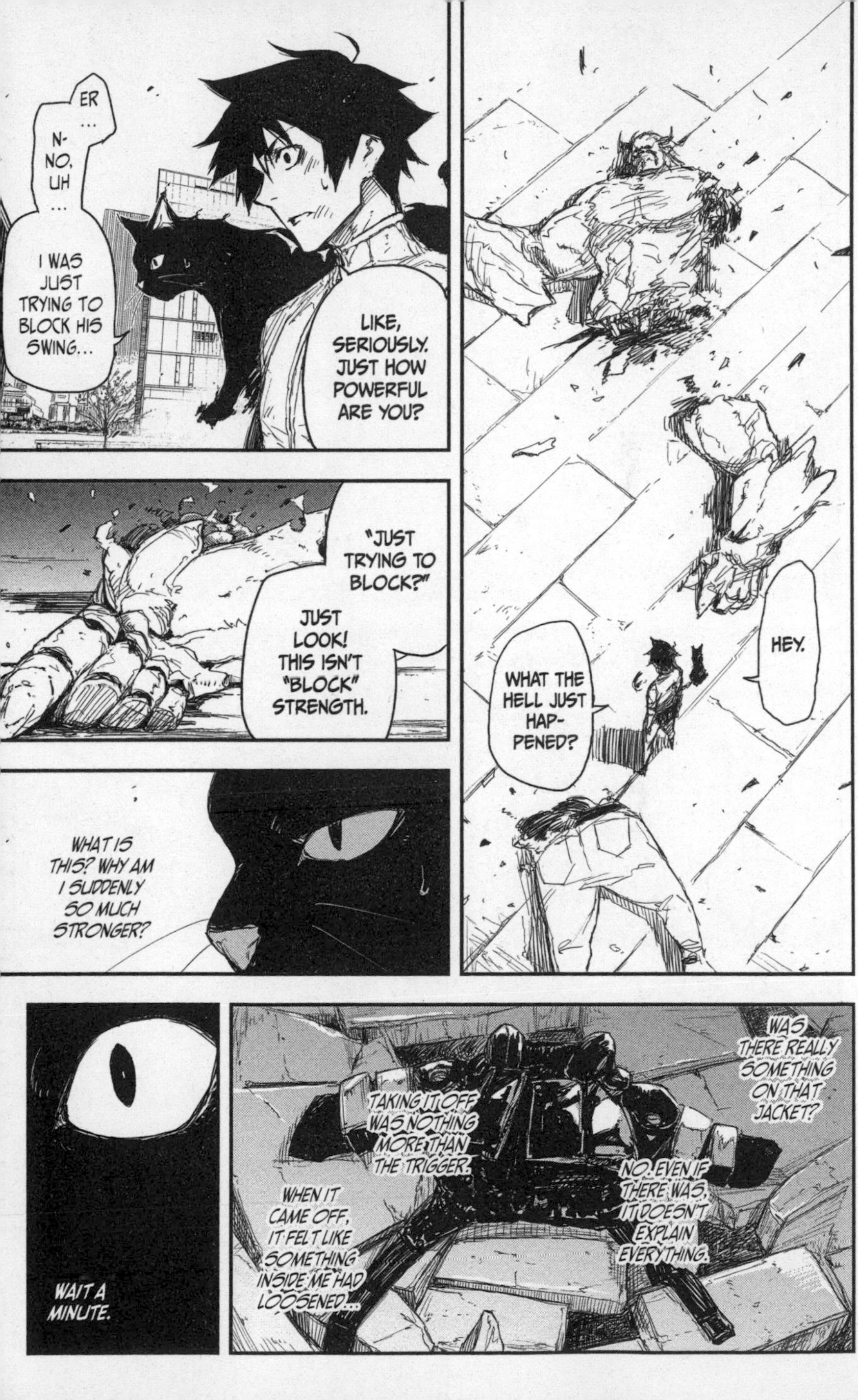
HEY.
WHAT THE HELL JUST HAP-PENED?
LIKE, SERIOUSLY. JUST HOW POWERFUL ARE YOU?
ER ... N-NO, UH ...
I WAS JUST TRYING TO BLOCK HIS SWING...
"JUST TRYING TO BLOCK?"
JUST LOOK! THIS ISN'T "BLOCK" STRENGTH.
WHAT IS THIS? WHY AM I SUDDENLY SO MUCH STRONGER?
WAS THERE REALLY SOMETHING ON THAT JACKET?
NO, EVEN IF THERE WAS, IT DOESN'T EXPLAIN EVERYTHING.
TAKING IT OFF WAS NOTHING MORE THAN THE TRIGGER.
WHEN IT CAME OFF, IT FELT LIKE SOMETHING INSIDE ME HAD LOOSENED...
WAIT A MINUTE.

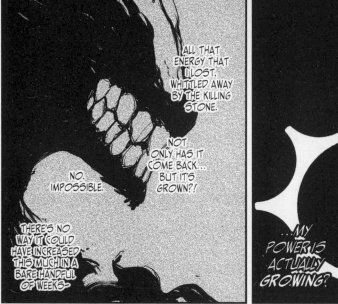

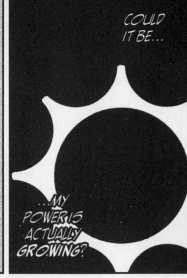

COULD IT BE...
...MY POWER IS ACTUALLY GROWING?
ALL THAT ENERGY THAT I LOST, WHITTLED AWAY BY THE KILLING STONE.
NOT ONLY HAS IT COME BACK... BUT IT'S GROWN?!
NO. IMPOSSIBLE.
THERE'S NO WAY IT COULD HAVE INCREASED THIS MUCH IN A BARE HANDFUL OF WEEKS-
"You haven't eaten anything in years, right?"
"HUMAN VITAL ENERGY..."
"Once you're full and your powers return..."
"...IS THE ONE WAY WE MONONOKE CAN INCREASE OUR OWN OVERALL POWER."
OH...!

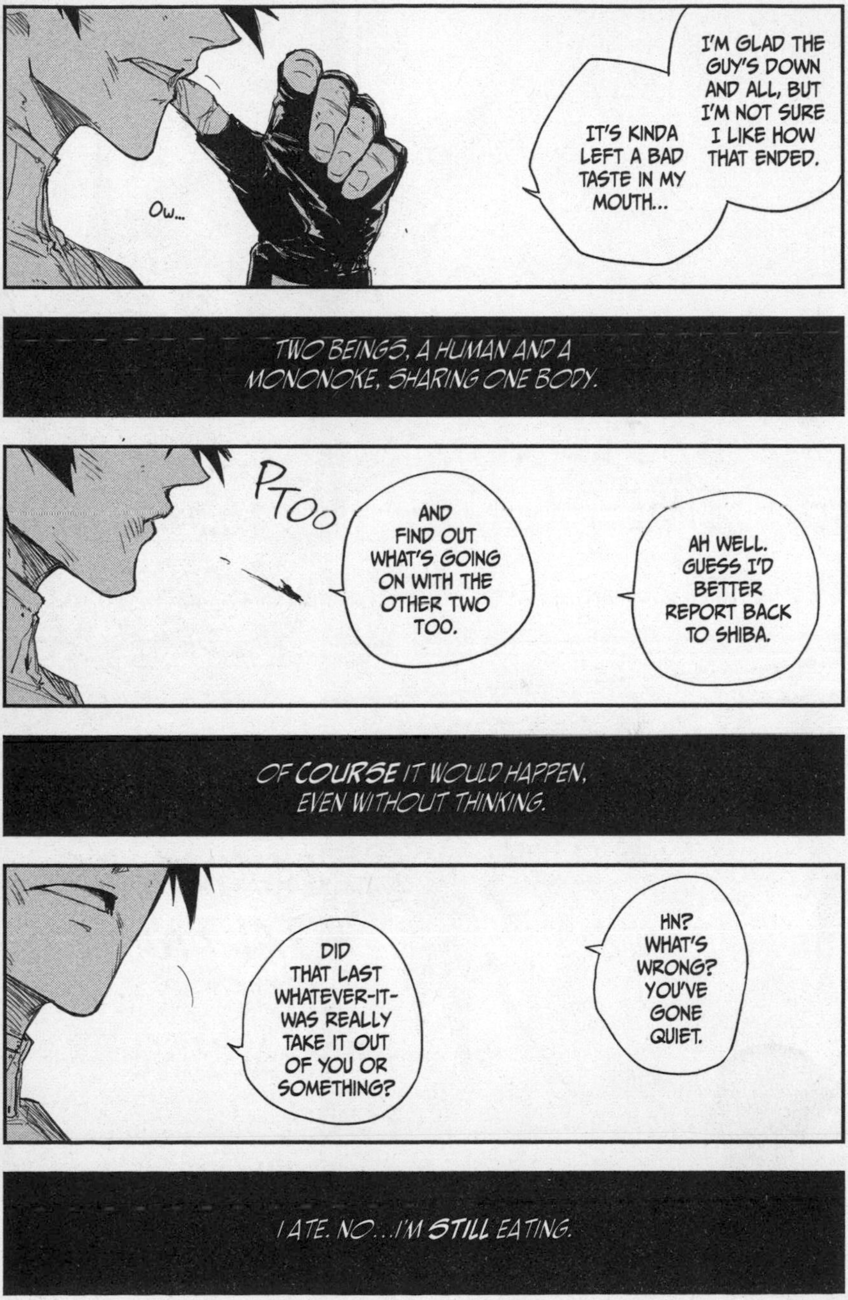
I'M GLAD THE GUY'S DOWN AND ALL, BUT I'M NOT SURE I LIKE HOW THAT ENDED.
IT'S KINDA LEFT A BAD TASTE IN MY MOUTH...
Ow...
TWO BEINGS, A HUMAN AND A MONONOKE, SHARING ONE BODY.
AH WELL. GUESS I'D BETTER REPORT BACK TO SHIBA.
AND FIND OUT WHAT'S GOING ON WITH THE OTHER TWO TOO.
PTOO
OF COURSE IT WOULD HAPPEN, EVEN WITHOUT THINKING.
HN? WHAT'S WRONG? YOU'VE GONE QUIET.
DID THAT LAST WHATEVER-IT-WAS REALLY TAKE IT OUT OF YOU OR SOMETHING?
I ATE. NO...I'M STILL EATING.

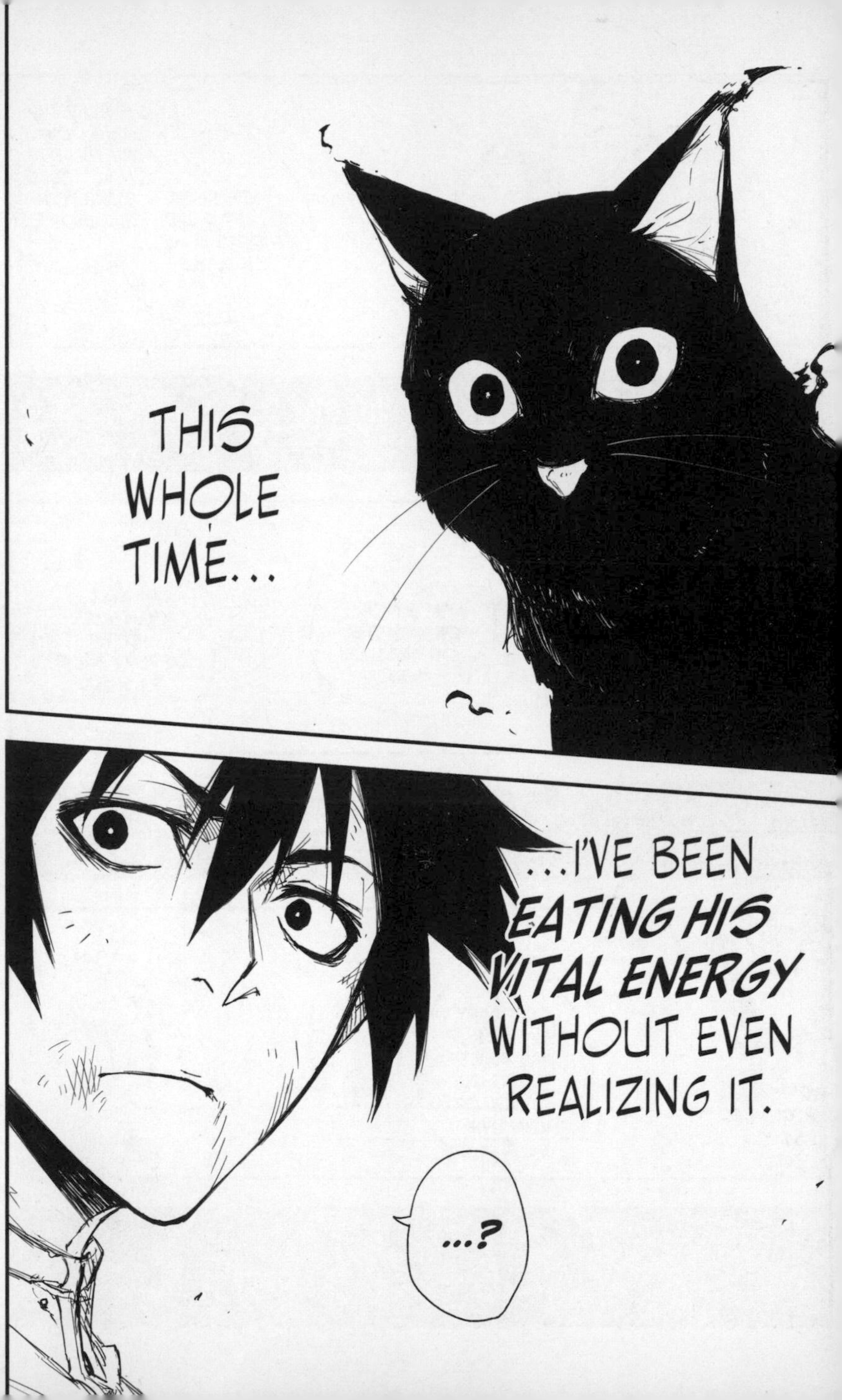
THIS WHOLE TIME...
...I'VE BEEN EATING HIS VITAL ENERGY WITHOUT EVEN REALIZING IT.
...?

FWIII

SH

DON'T MOVE.

LOWER YOUR WEAPON AND SURRENDER QUIETLY.

IF YOU REFUSE...

I WILL SAY IT ONLY ONE MORE TIME. *THIS IS A WARNING.*

LOWER YOUR WEAPON AND SUR-RENDER.

REFUSE, AND I SHALL HAVE NO CHOICE BUT TO USE FORCE.

SHWIF

SHWIF

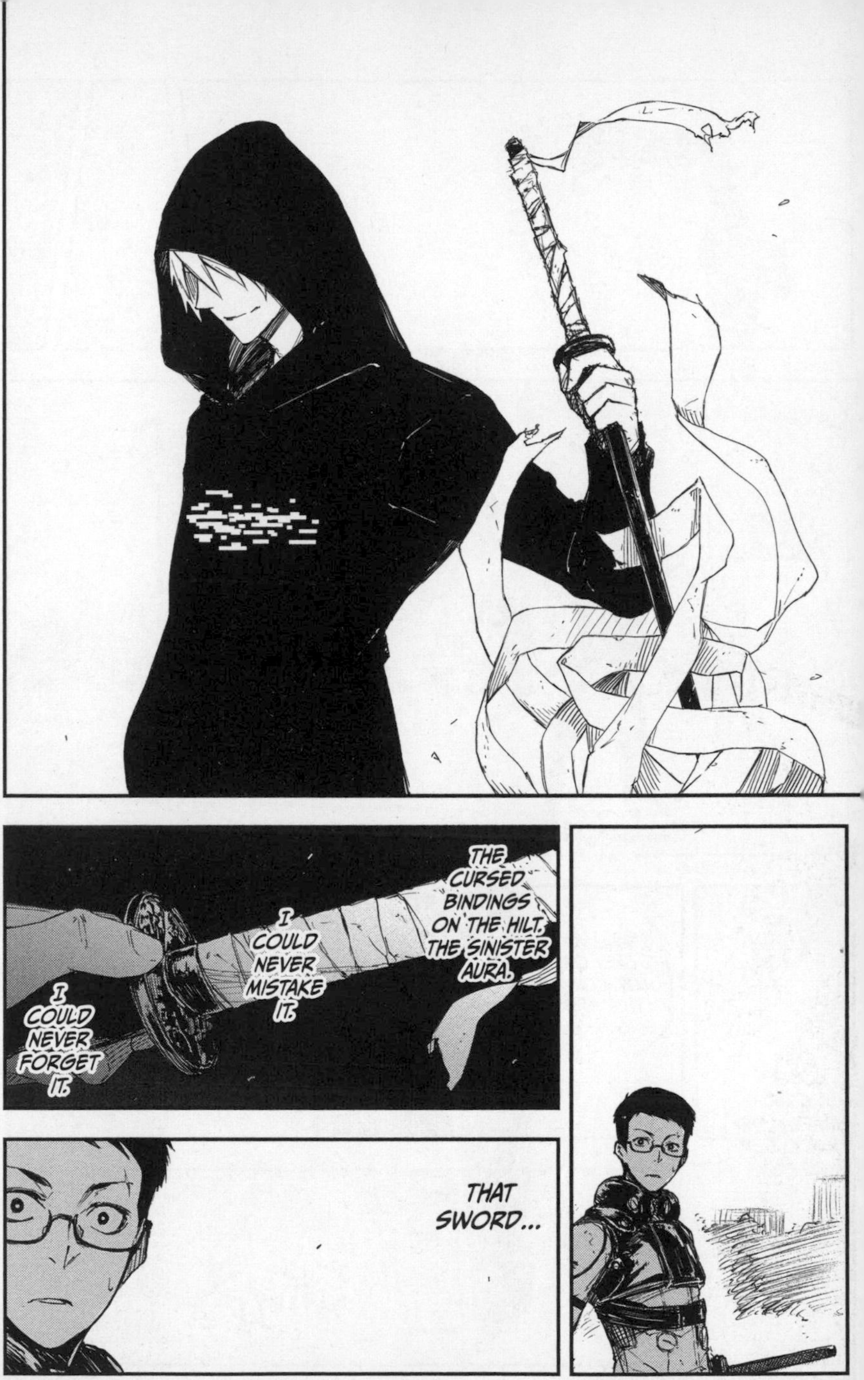
THE CURSED BINDINGS ON THE HILT. THE SINISTER AURA.
I COULD NEVER MISTAKE IT.
I COULD NEVER FORGET IT.
THAT SWORD...

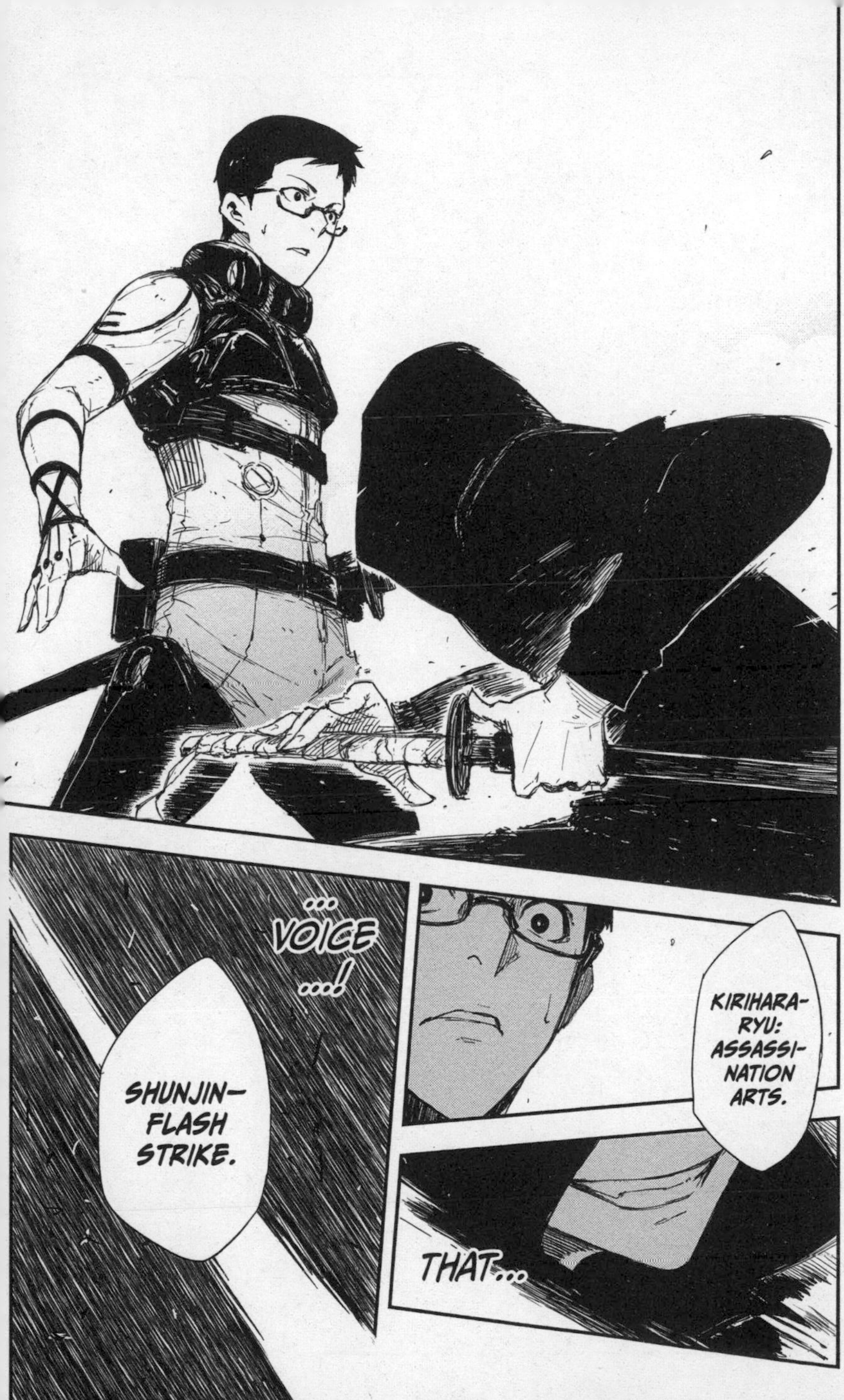
KIRIHARA-RYU: ASSASSI-NATION ARTS.
THAT...
...VOICE ...!
SHUNJIN—FLASH STRIKE.

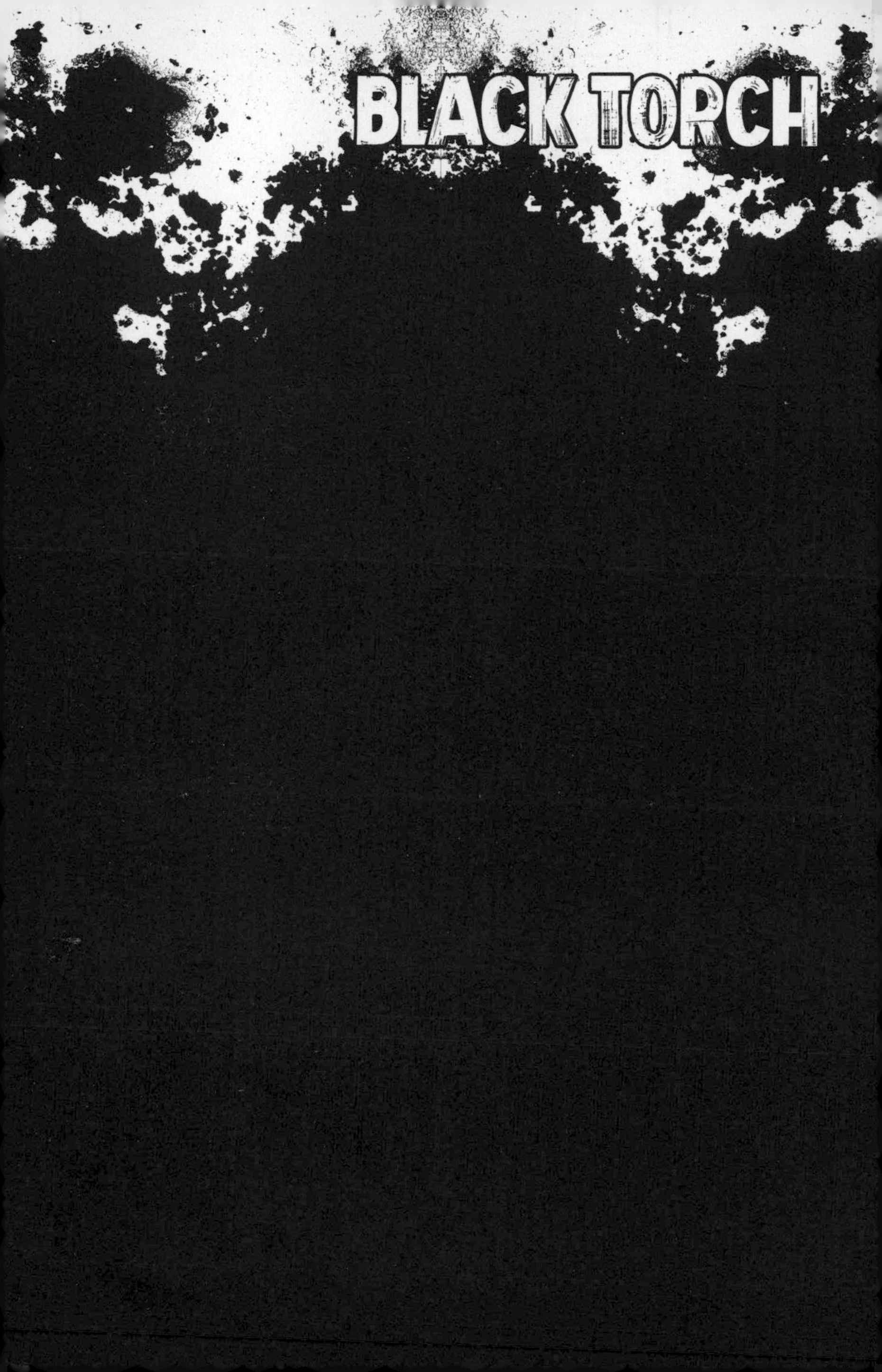
BLACK TORCH

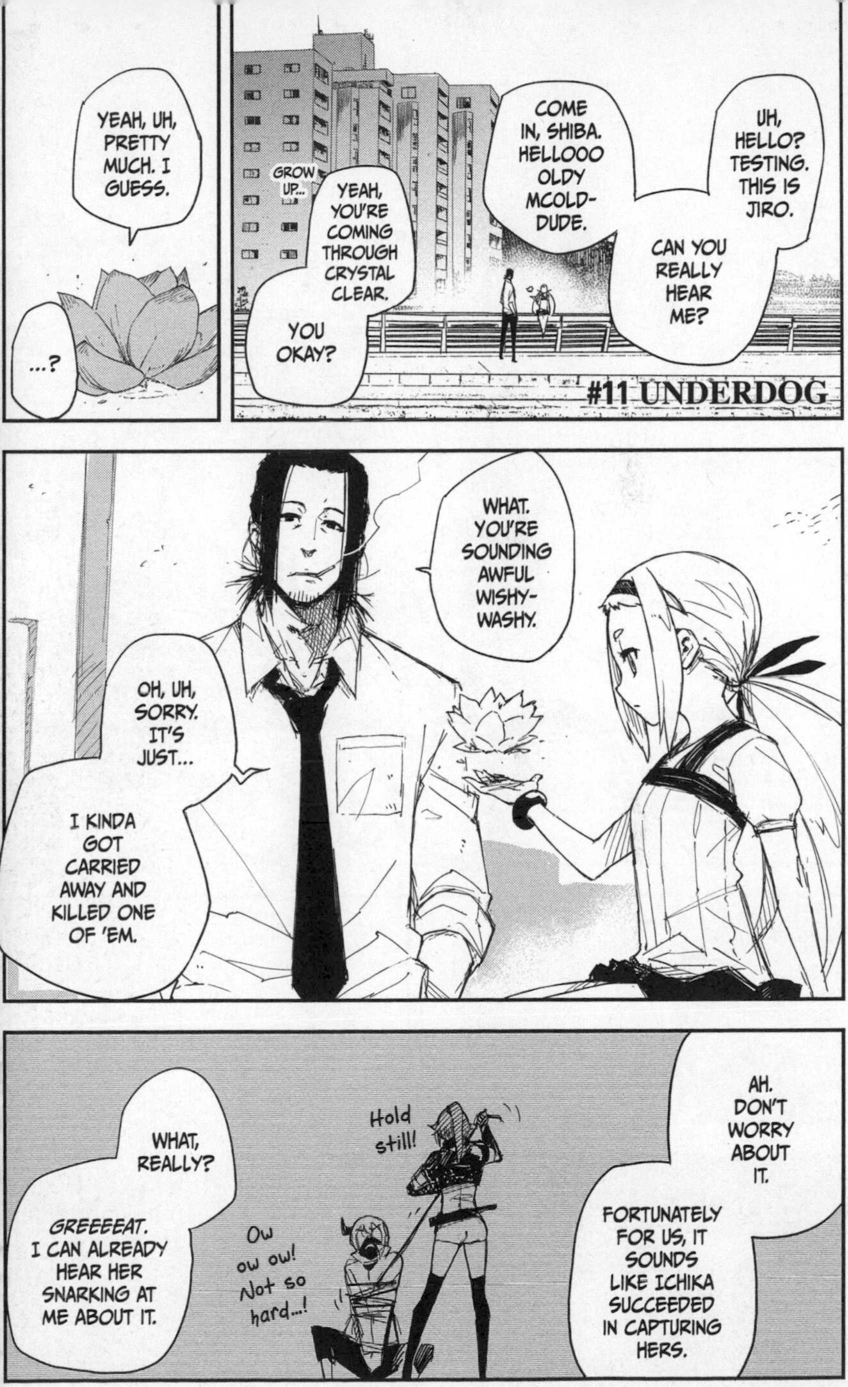
UH, HELLO? TESTING. THIS IS JIRO.
CAN YOU REALLY HEAR ME?
COME IN, SHIBA. HELLOOO OLDY MCOLD-DUDE.
#11 UNDERDOG
YEAH, YOU'RE COMING THROUGH CRYSTAL CLEAR.
GROW UP...
YOU OKAY?
YEAH, UH, PRETTY MUCH. I GUESS.
...?
WHAT. YOU'RE SOUNDING AWFUL WISHY-WASHY.
OH, UH, SORRY. IT'S JUST...
I KINDA GOT CARRIED AWAY AND KILLED ONE OF 'EM.
AH. DON'T WORRY ABOUT IT.
FORTUNATELY FOR US, IT SOUNDS LIKE ICHIKA SUCCEEDED IN CAPTURING HERS.
Hold still!
WHAT, REALLY?
Ow ow ow! Not so hard...!
GREEEEAT. I CAN ALREADY HEAR HER SNARKING AT ME ABOUT IT.

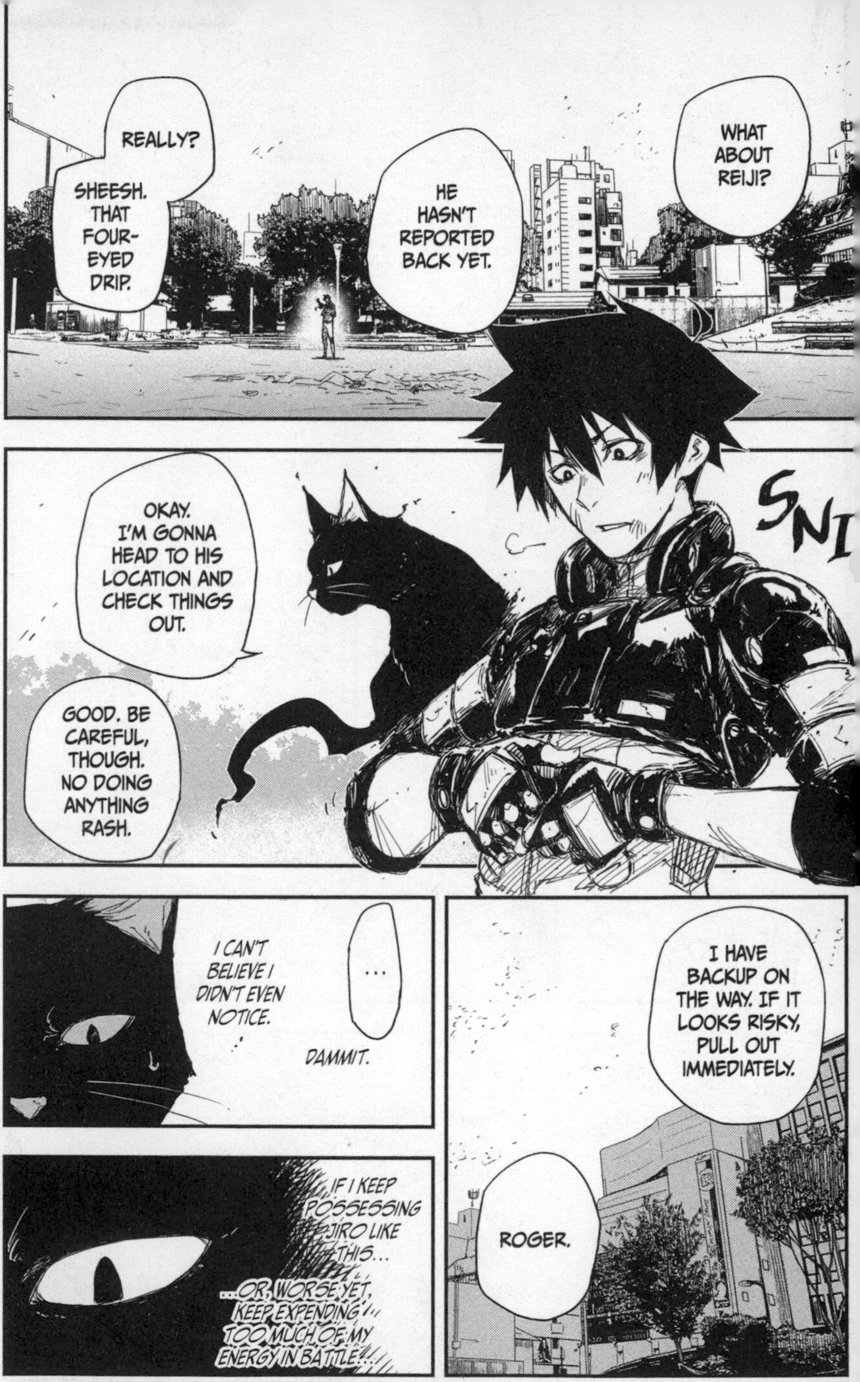
WHAT ABOUT REIJI?
HE HASN'T REPORTED BACK YET.
REALLY?
SHEESH. THAT FOUR-EYED DRIP.
SNI
OKAY. I'M GONNA HEAD TO HIS LOCATION AND CHECK THINGS OUT.
GOOD. BE CAREFUL, THOUGH. NO DOING ANYTHING RASH.
I HAVE BACKUP ON THE WAY. IF IT LOOKS RISKY, PULL OUT IMMEDIATELY.
ROGER.
...
I CAN'T BELIEVE I DIDN'T EVEN NOTICE.
DAMMIT.
IF I KEEP POSSESSING JIRO LIKE THIS...
...OR, WORSE YET, KEEP EXPENDING TOO MUCH OF MY ENERGY IN BATTLE...

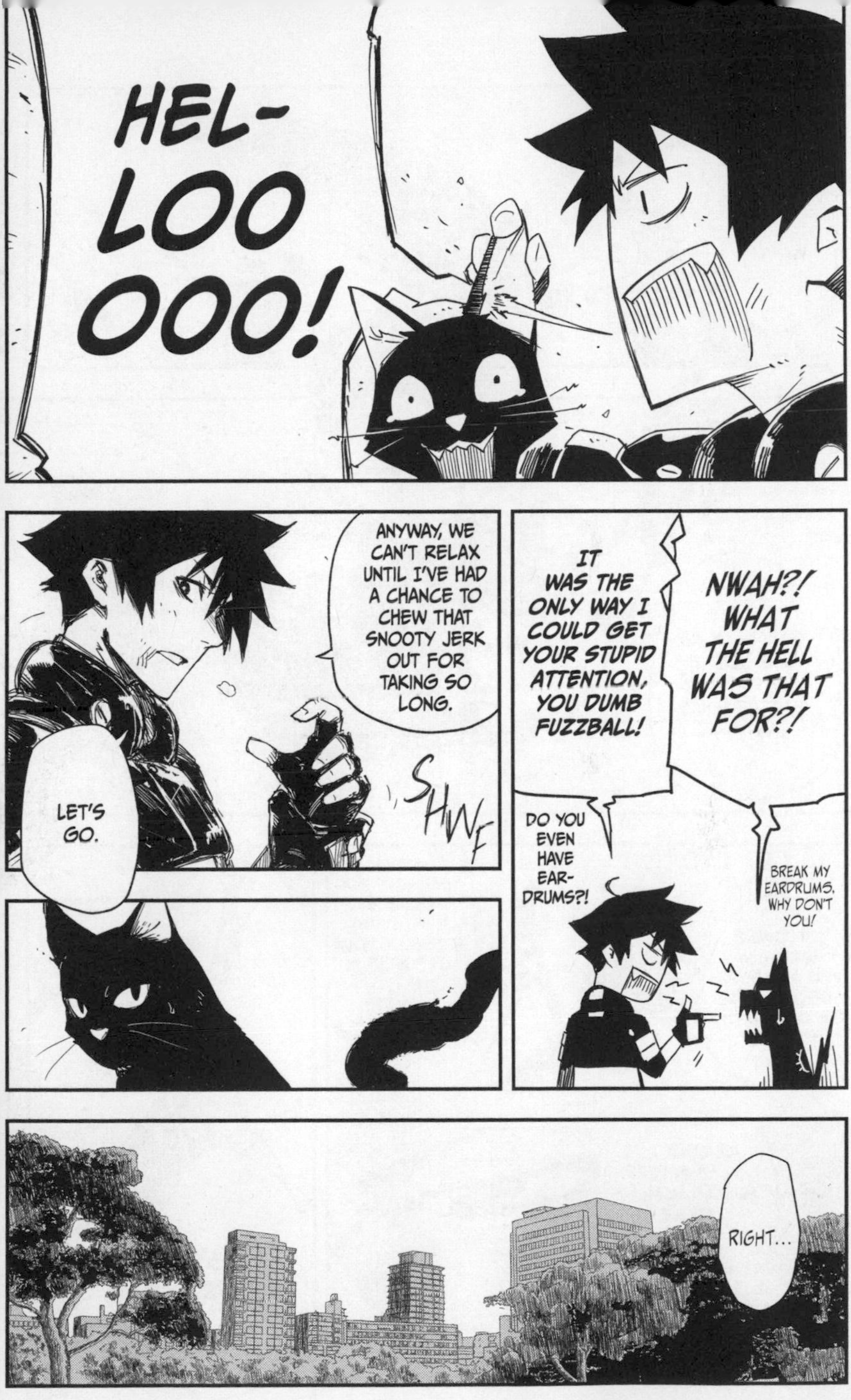
HEL-LOOOOO!
NWAH?! WHAT THE HELL WAS THAT FOR?!
IT WAS THE ONLY WAY I COULD GET YOUR STUPID ATTENTION, YOU DUMB FUZZBALL!
BREAK MY EARDRUMS, WHY DON'T YOU!
DO YOU EVEN HAVE EAR-DRUMS?!
ANYWAY, WE CAN'T RELAX UNTIL I'VE HAD A CHANCE TO CHEW THAT SNOOTY JERK OUT FOR TAKING SO LONG.
SHWF
LET'S GO.
RIGHT...

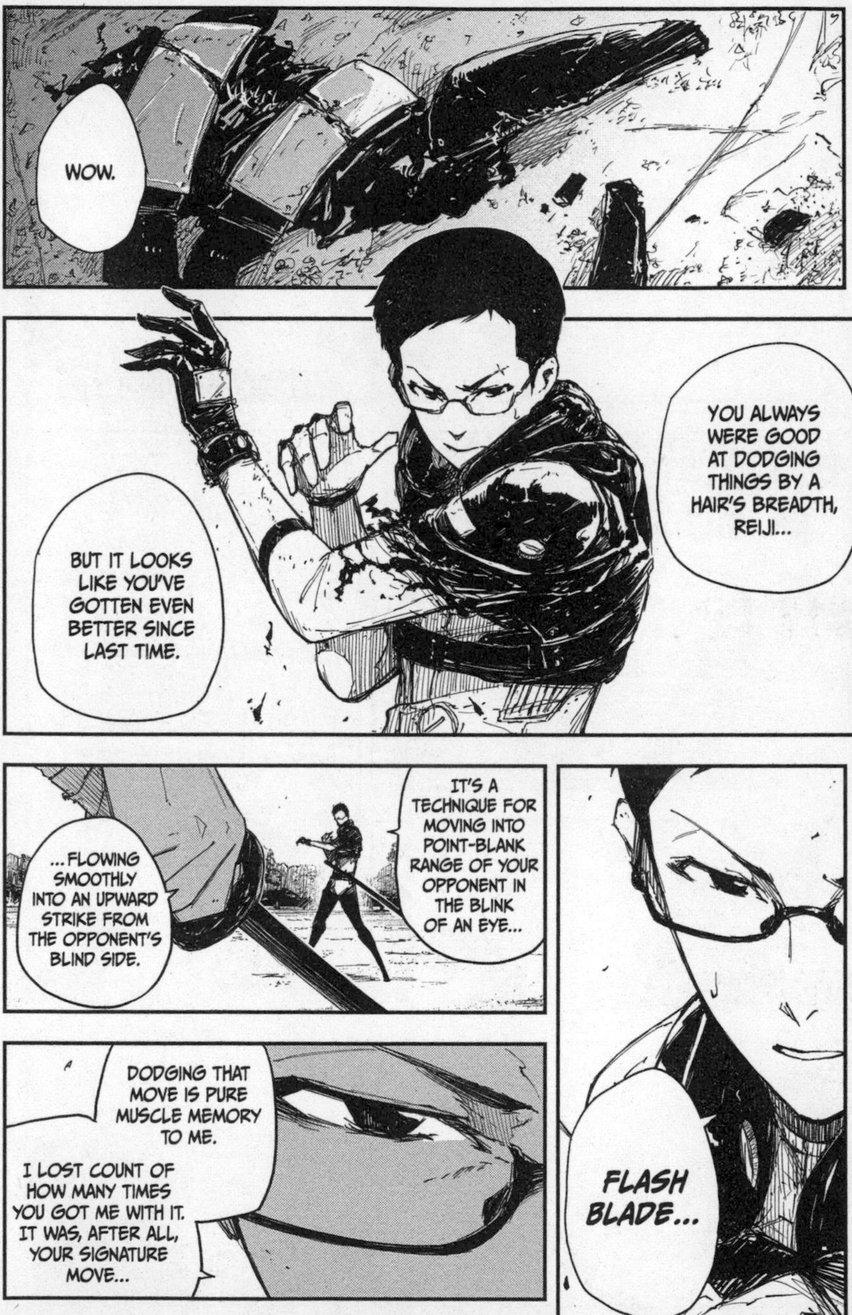
WOW.
YOU ALWAYS WERE GOOD AT DODGING THINGS BY A HAIR'S BREADTH, REIJI...
BUT IT LOOKS LIKE YOU'VE GOTTEN EVEN BETTER SINCE LAST TIME.
FLASH BLADE...
IT'S A TECHNIQUE FOR MOVING INTO POINT-BLANK RANGE OF YOUR OPPONENT IN THE BLINK OF AN EYE...
...FLOWING SMOOTHLY INTO AN UPWARD STRIKE FROM THE OPPONENT'S BLIND SIDE.
DODGING THAT MOVE IS PURE MUSCLE MEMORY TO ME.
I LOST COUNT OF HOW MANY TIMES YOU GOT ME WITH IT. IT WAS, AFTER ALL, YOUR SIGNATURE MOVE...

#11 UNDERDOG

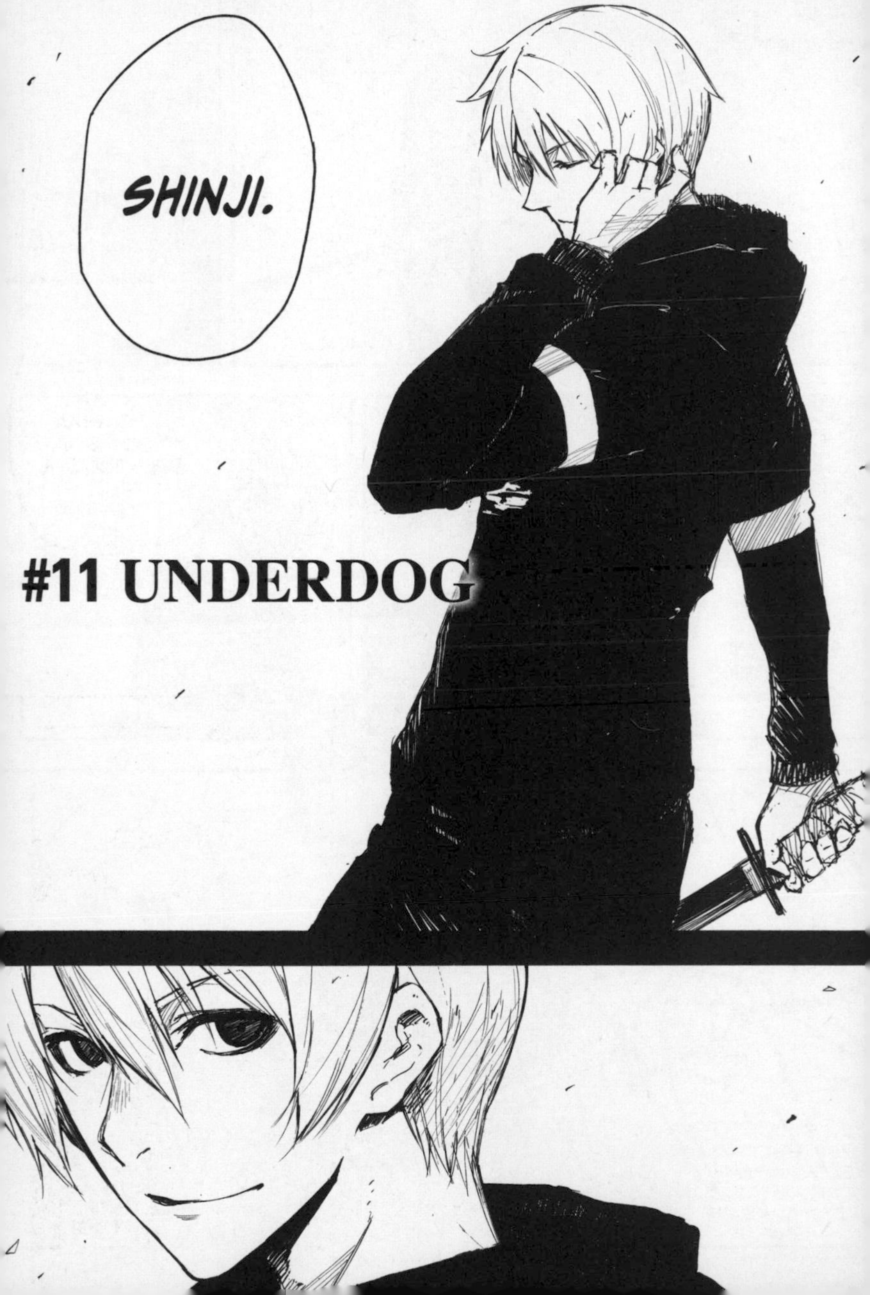
SHINJI.

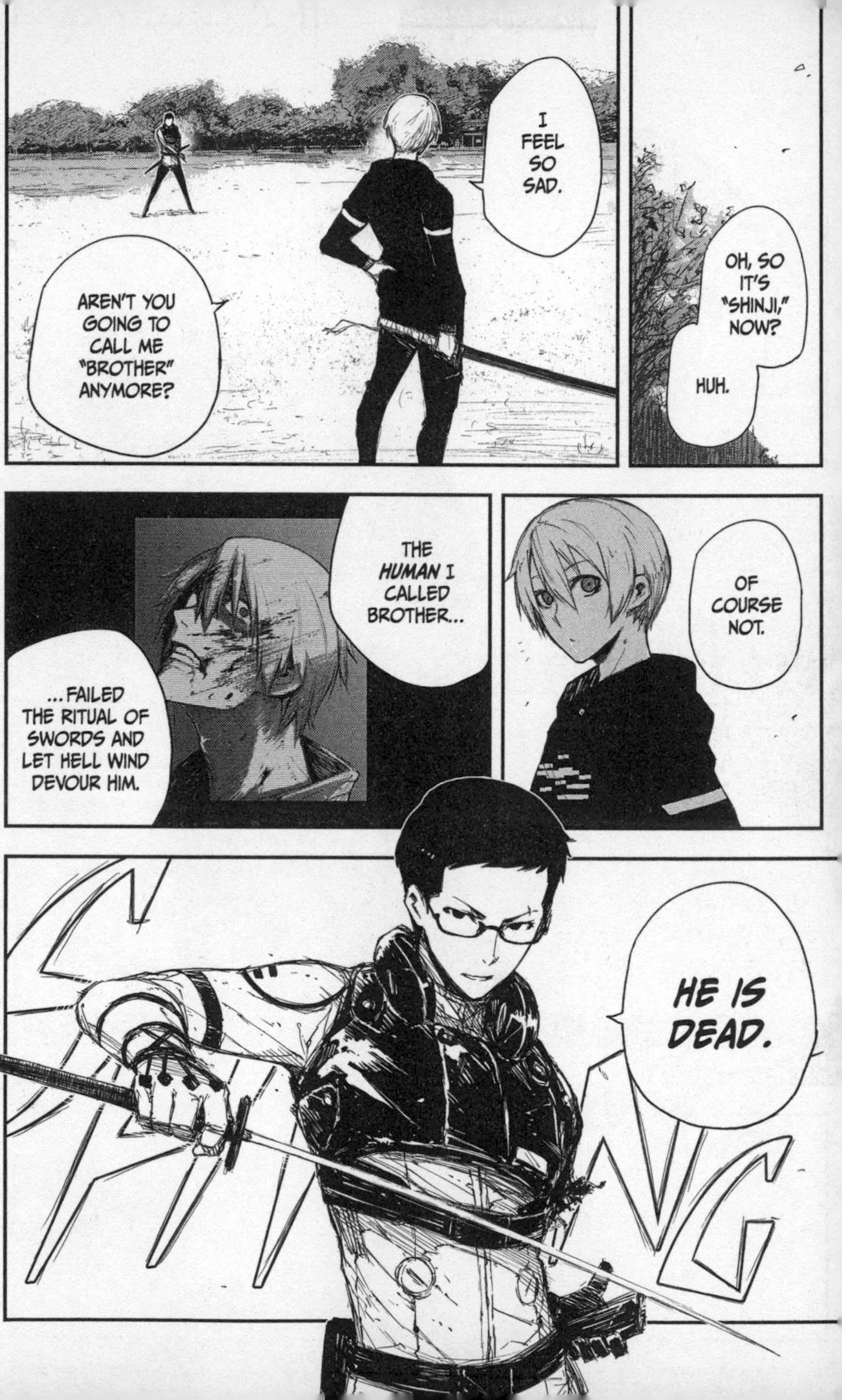
OH, SO IT'S "SHINJI," NOW?
HUH.
I FEEL SO SAD.
AREN'T YOU GOING TO CALL ME "BROTHER" ANYMORE?
OF COURSE NOT.
THE *HUMAN* I CALLED BROTHER...
...FAILED THE RITUAL OF SWORDS AND LET HELL WIND DEVOUR HIM.
HE IS DEAD.

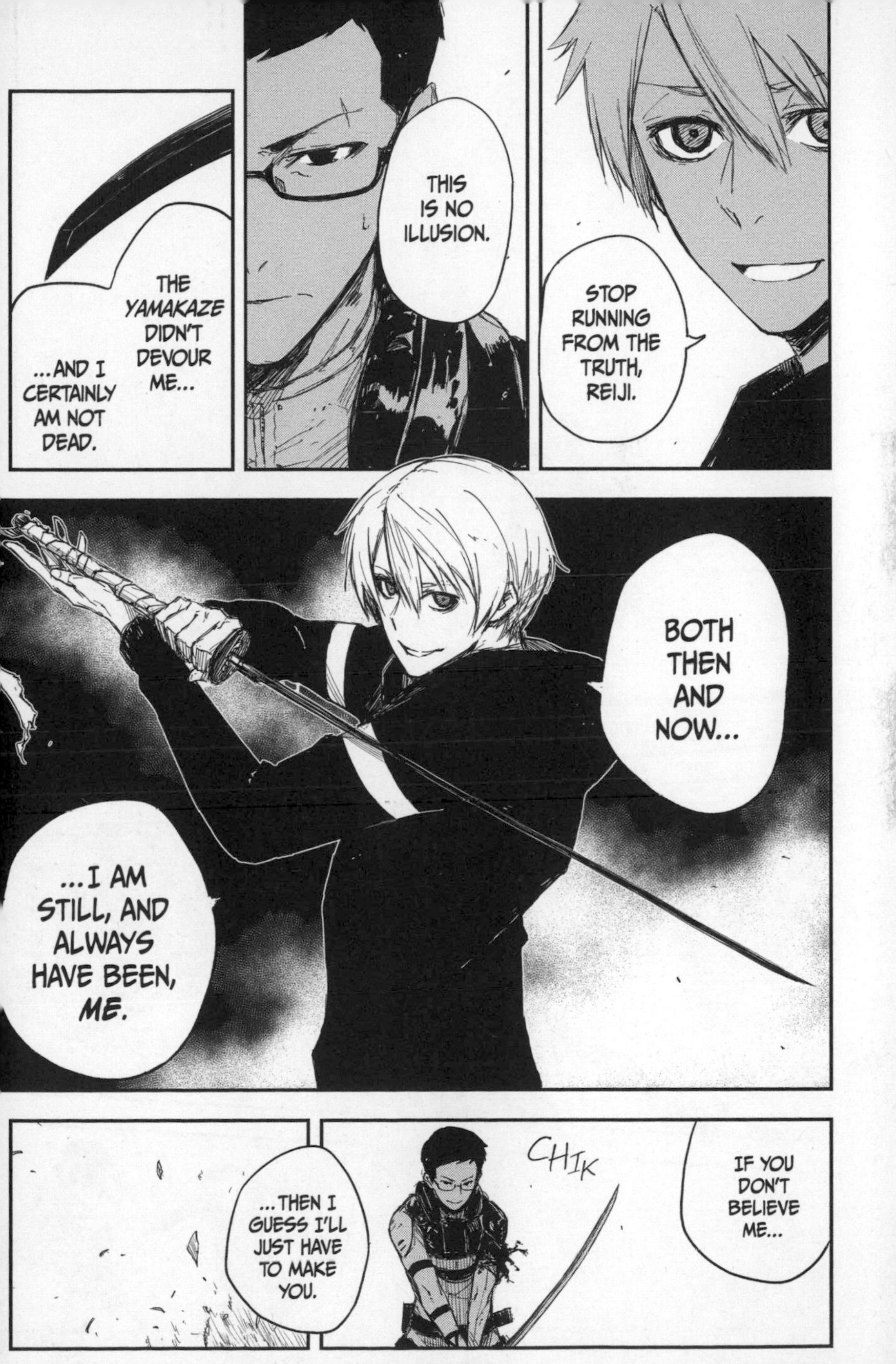
STOP RUNNING FROM THE TRUTH, REIJI.
THIS IS NO ILLUSION.
THE YAMAKAZE DIDN'T DEVOUR ME...
...AND I CERTAINLY AM NOT DEAD.
BOTH THEN AND NOW...
...I AM STILL, AND ALWAYS HAVE BEEN, *ME*.
IF YOU DON'T BELIEVE ME...
CHIK
...THEN I GUESS I'LL JUST HAVE TO MAKE YOU.

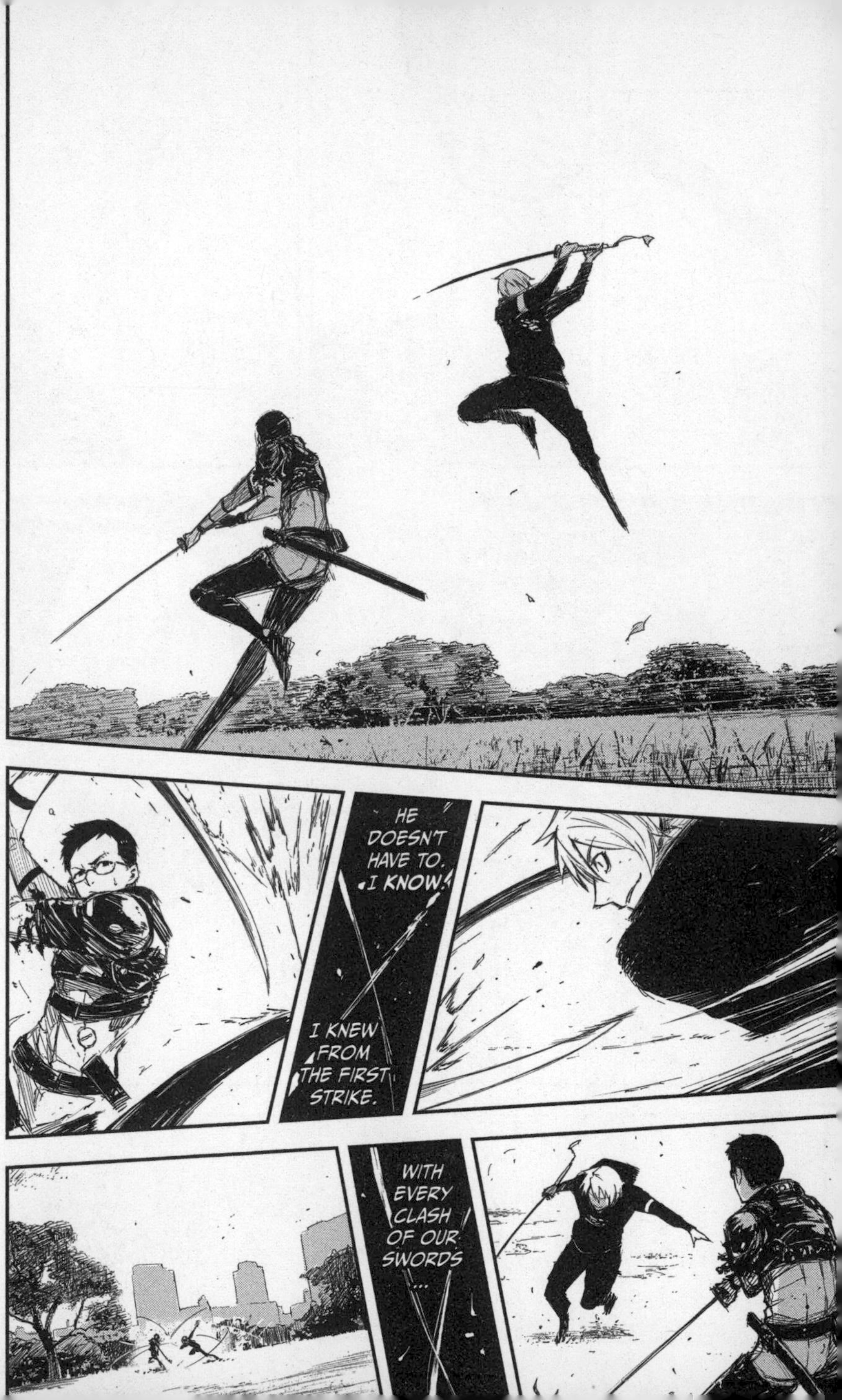
HE DOESN'T HAVE TO. I KNOW!
I KNEW FROM THE FIRST STRIKE.
WITH EVERY CLASH OF OUR SWORDS ...

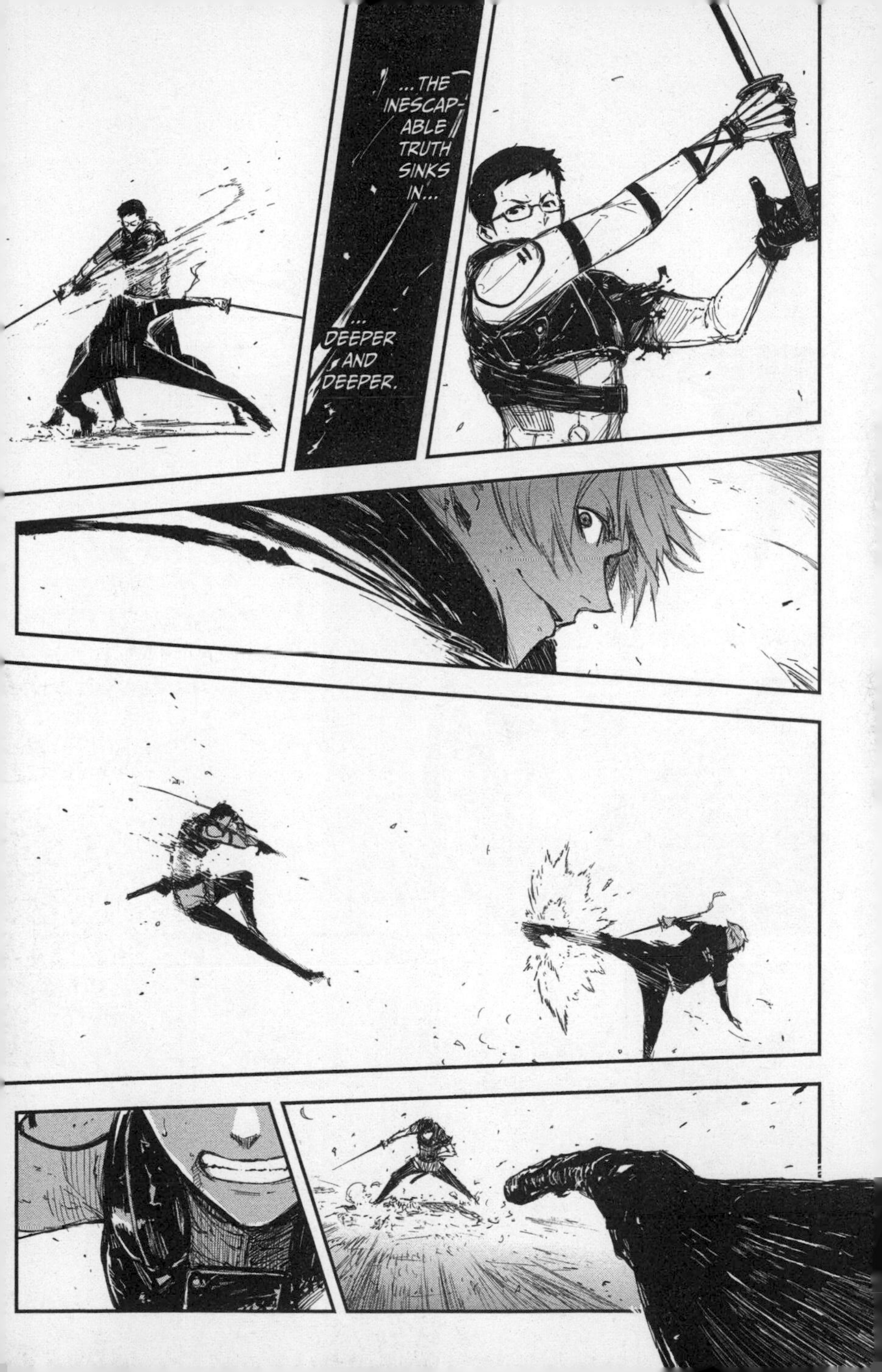
...THE INESCAPABLE TRUTH SINKS IN...
...DEEPER AND DEEPER.

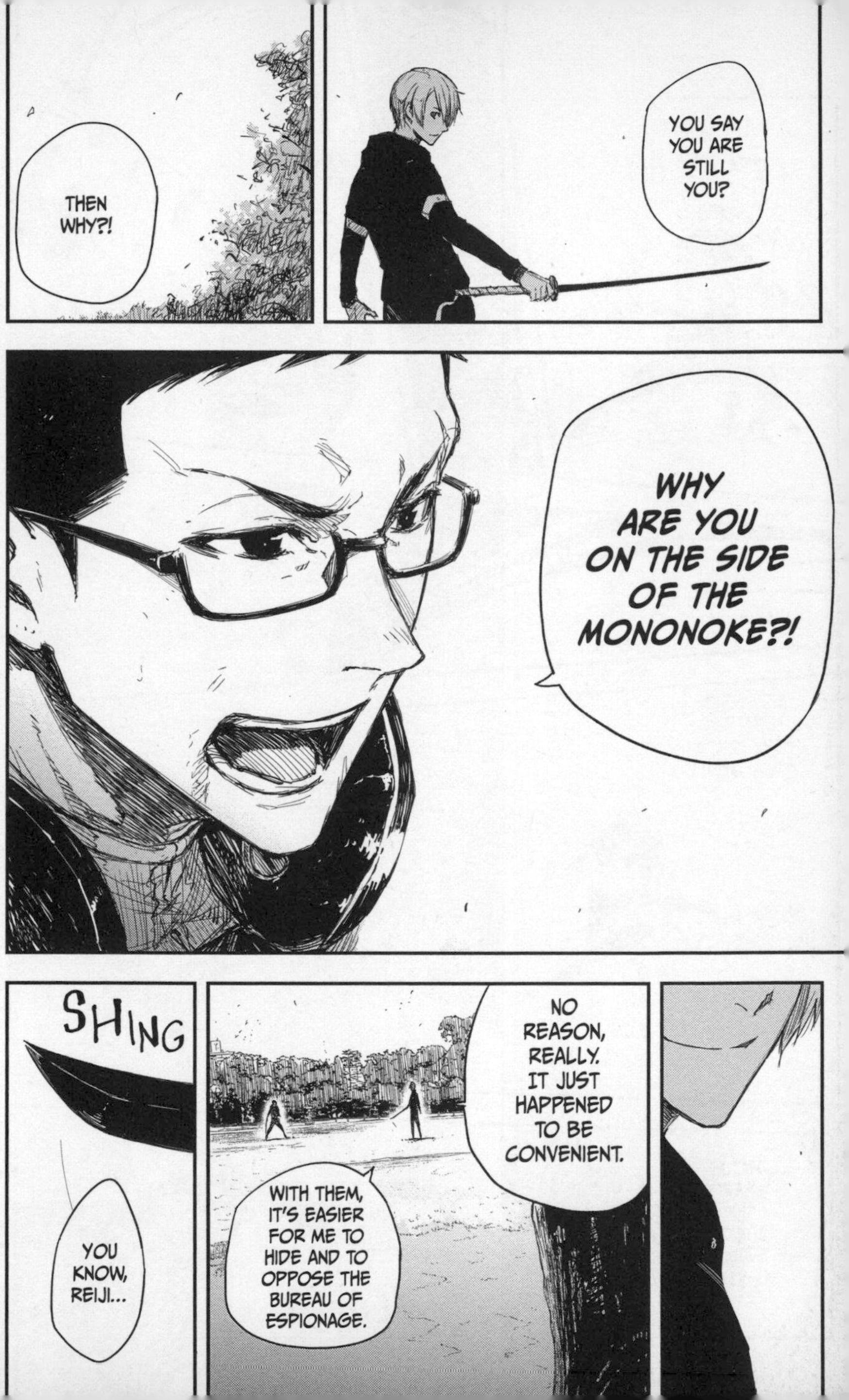
YOU SAY YOU ARE STILL YOU?
THEN WHY?!
WHY ARE YOU ON THE SIDE OF THE MONONOKE?!
NO REASON, REALLY. IT JUST HAPPENED TO BE CONVENIENT.
WITH THEM, IT'S EASIER FOR ME TO HIDE AND TO OPPOSE THE BUREAU OF ESPIONAGE.
SHING
YOU KNOW, REIJI...

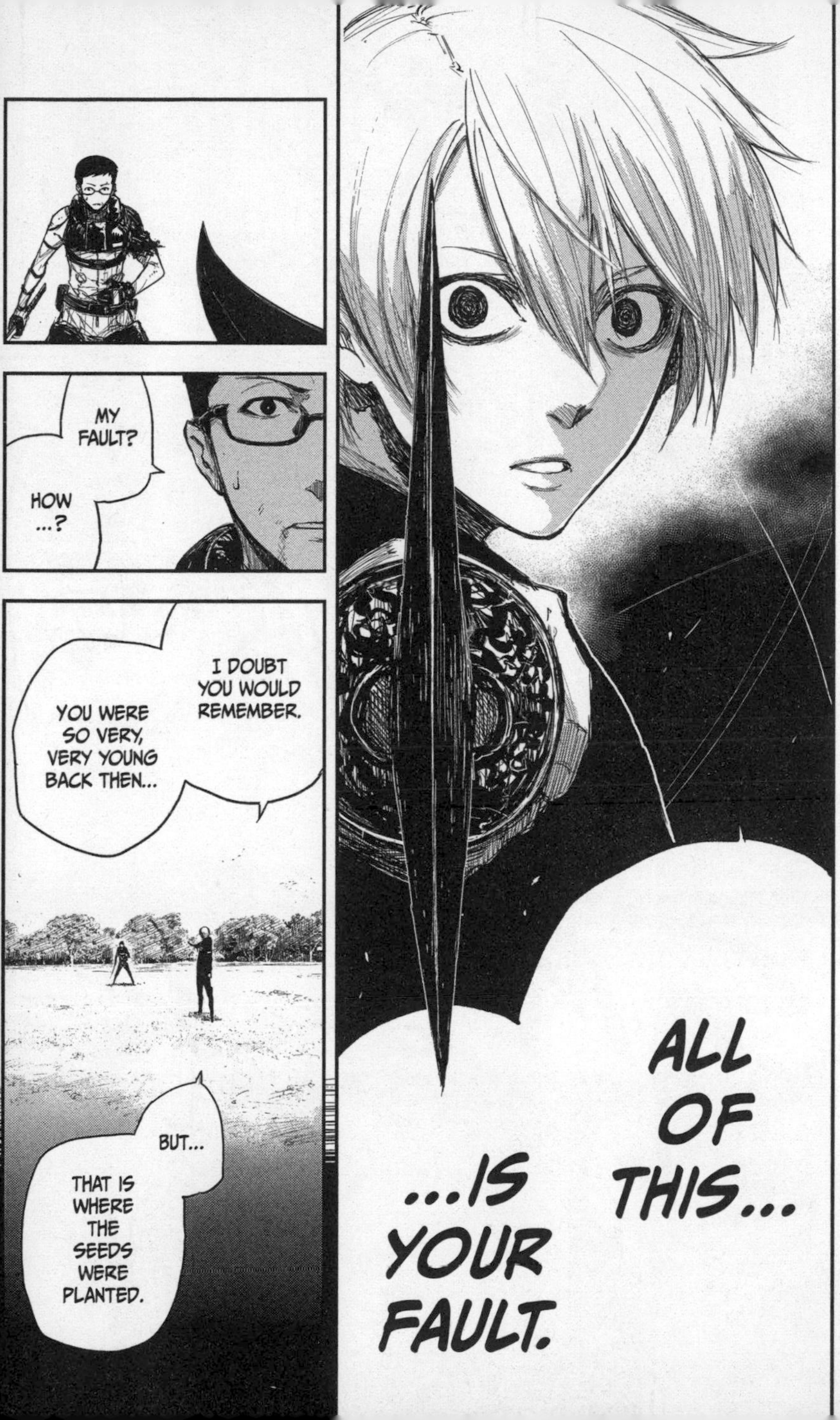
ALL OF THIS...
...IS YOUR FAULT.
MY FAULT?
HOW ...?
I DOUBT YOU WOULD REMEMBER.
YOU WERE SO VERY, VERY YOUNG BACK THEN...
BUT...
THAT IS WHERE THE SEEDS WERE PLANTED.

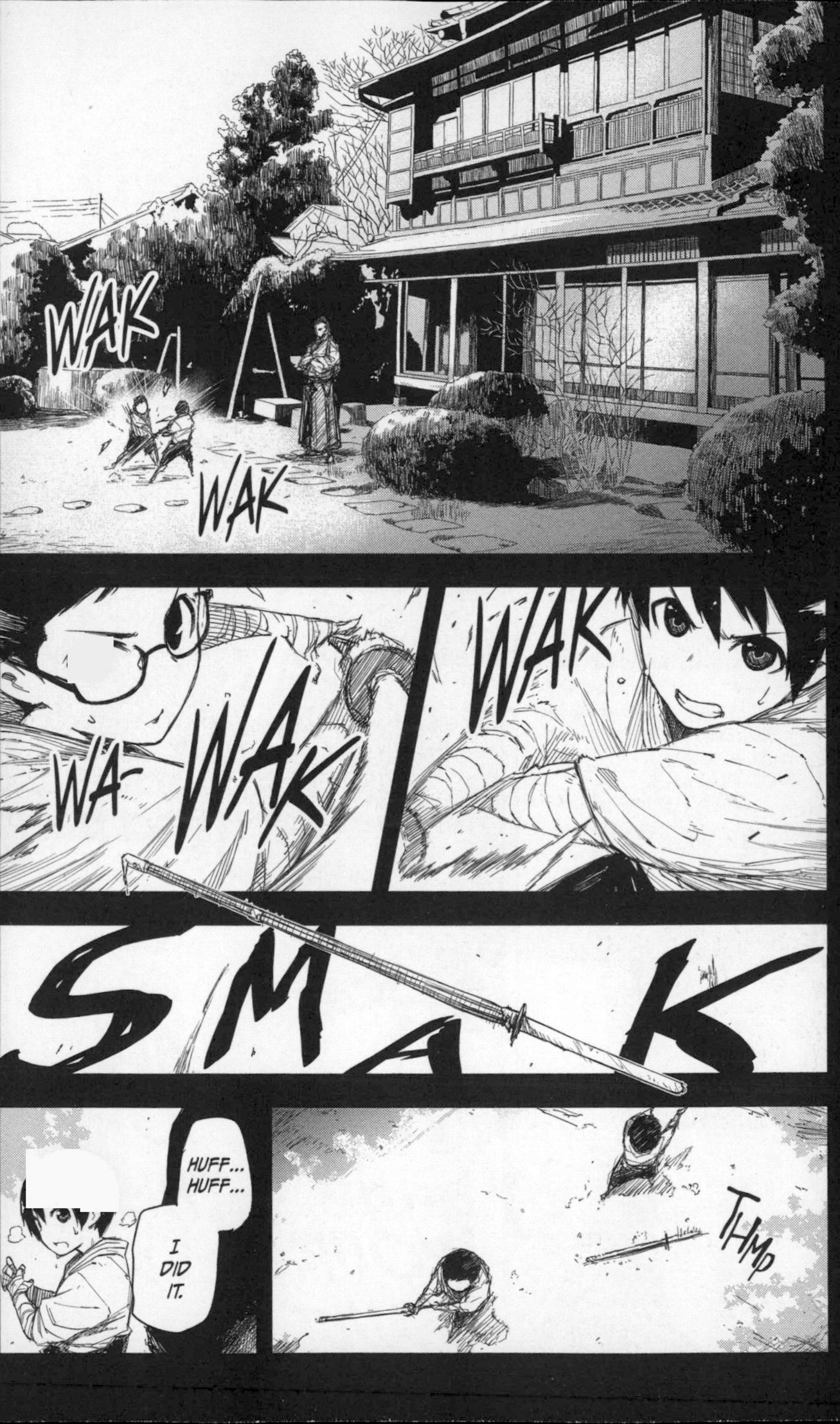
WAK
WAK
WAK
WA-WAK
SMAK
THMP
HUFF... HUFF...
I DID IT.

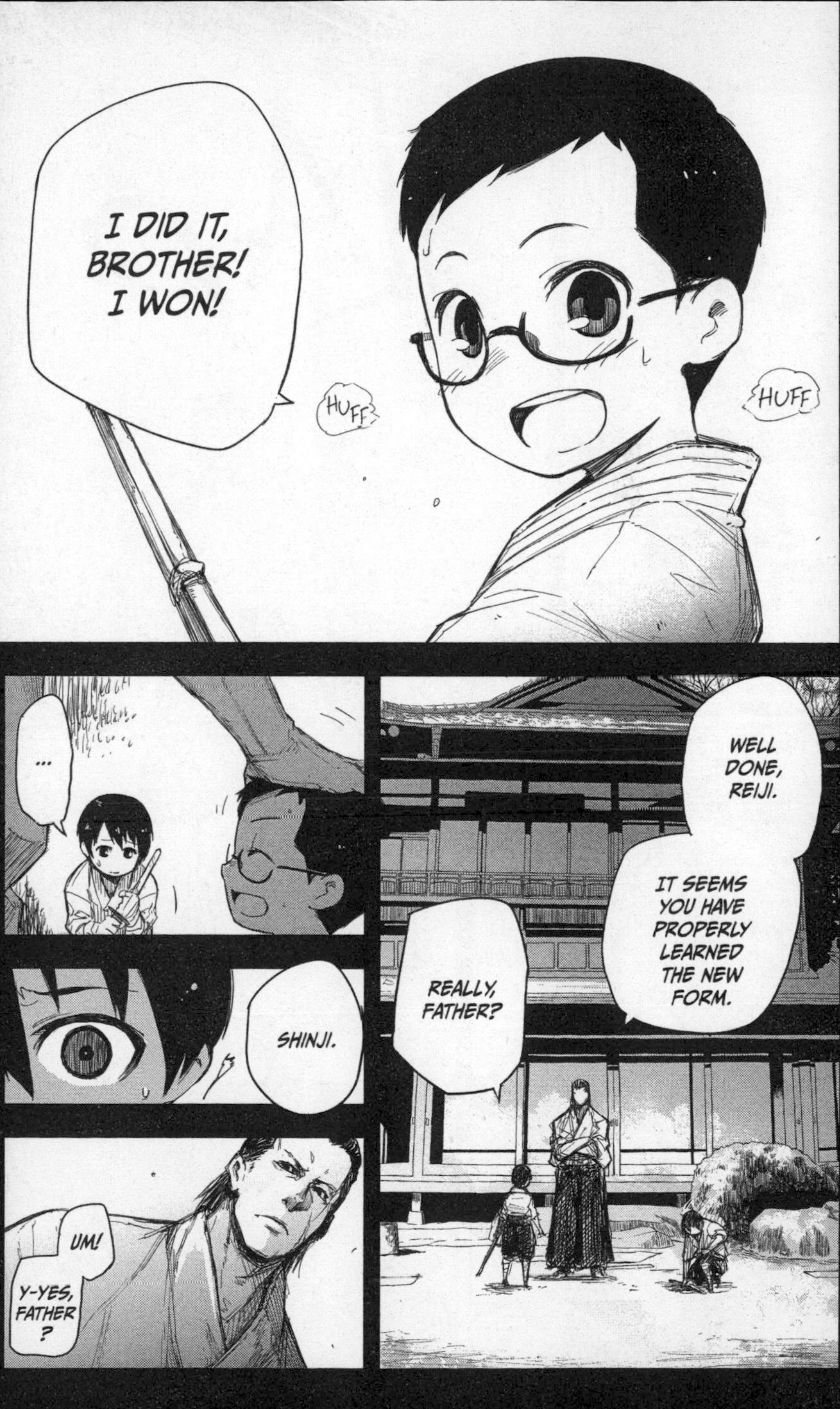
I DID IT, BROTHER! I WON!
HUFF
HUFF
WELL DONE, REIJI.
IT SEEMS YOU HAVE PROPERLY LEARNED THE NEW FORM.
REALLY, FATHER?
...
SHINJI.
UM!
Y-YES, FATHER ?

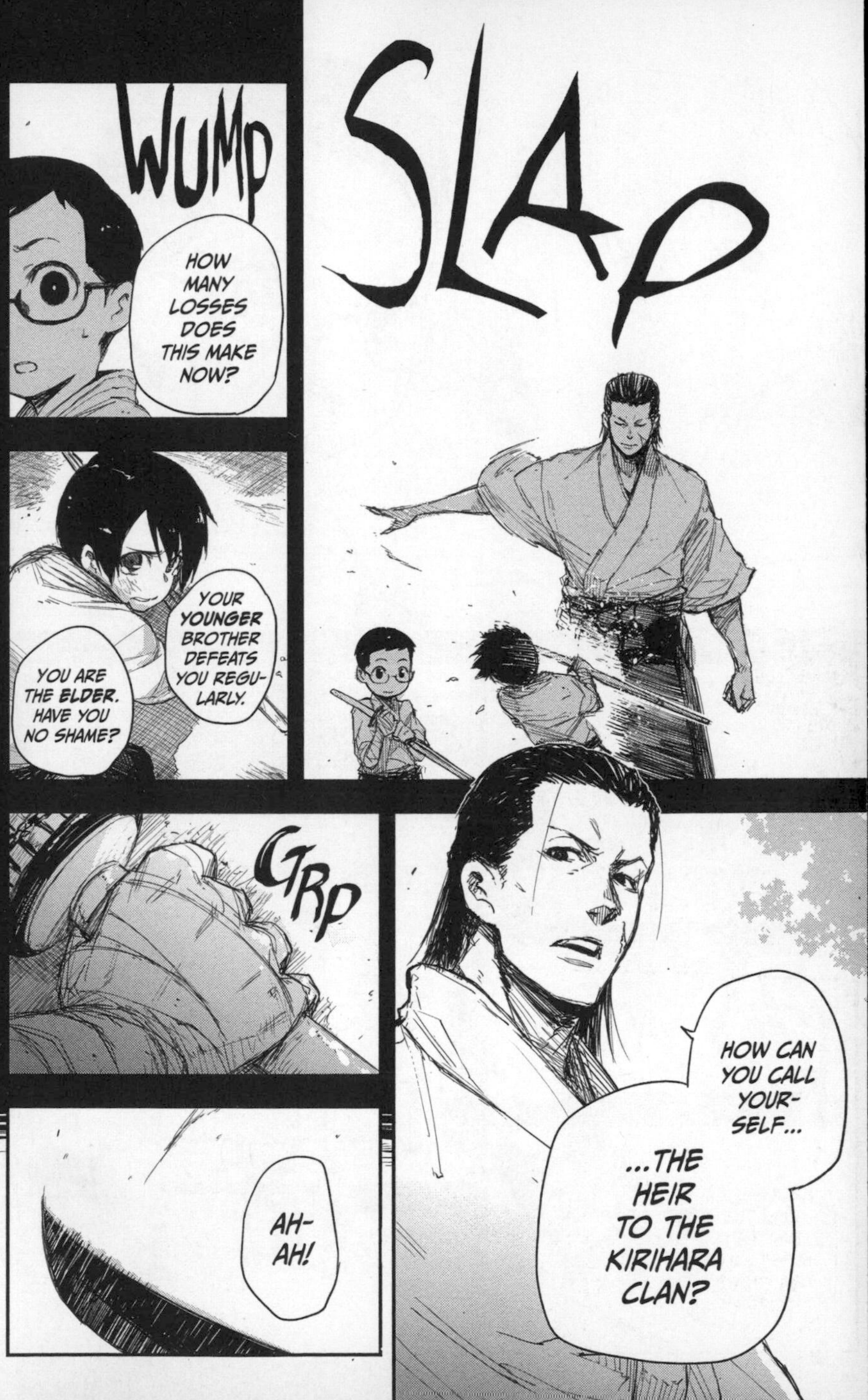
SLAP
WUMP
HOW MANY LOSSES DOES THIS MAKE NOW?
YOUR YOUNGER BROTHER DEFEATS YOU REGU-LARLY.
YOU ARE THE ELDER. HAVE YOU NO SHAME?
HOW CAN YOU CALL YOUR-SELF...
...THE HEIR TO THE KIRIHARA CLAN?
GRP
AH-AH!

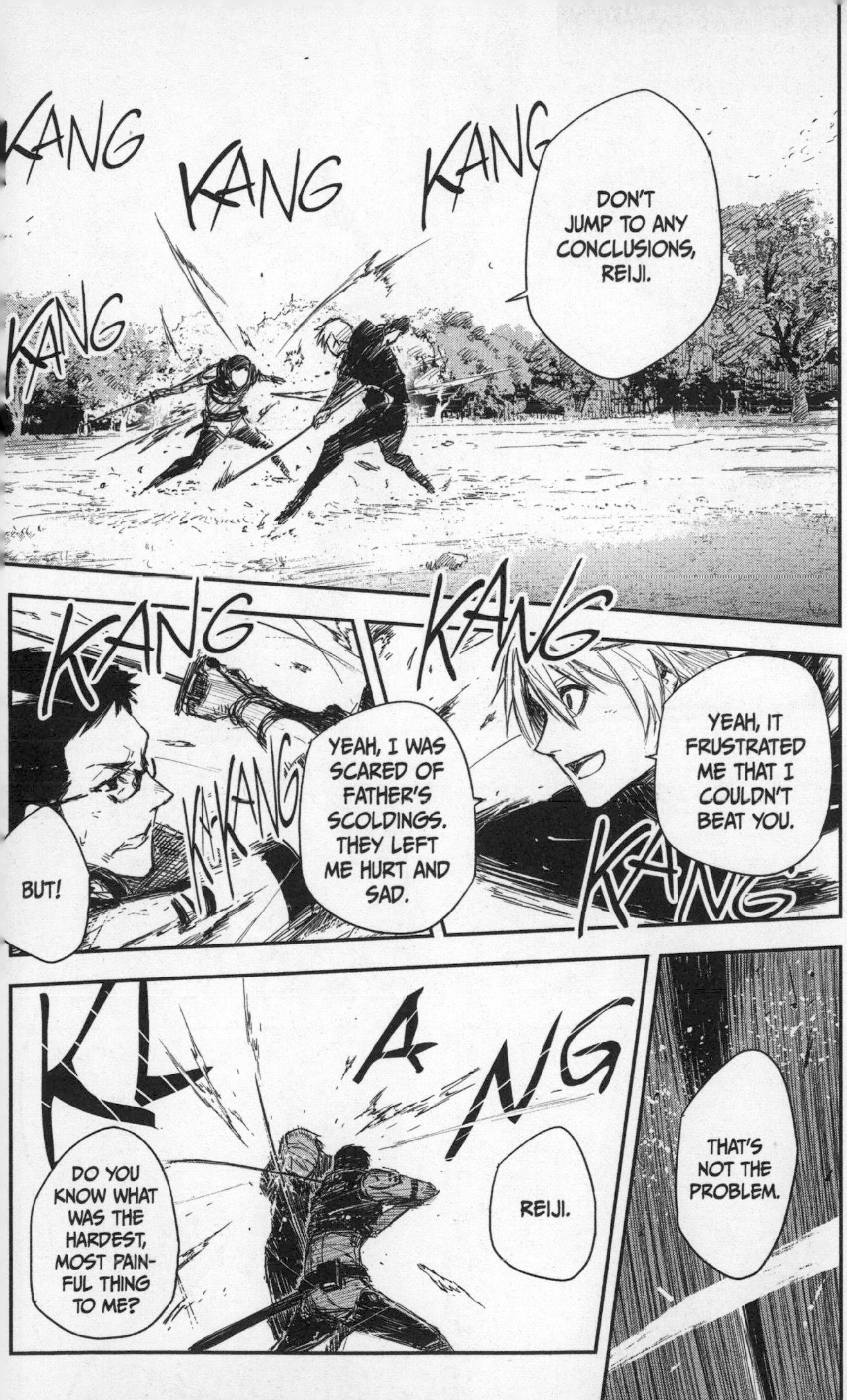
KANG
KANG
KANG
KANG
DON'T JUMP TO ANY CONCLUSIONS, REIJI.
KANG
YEAH, IT FRUSTRATED ME THAT I COULDN'T BEAT YOU.
KANG
KANG
YEAH, I WAS SCARED OF FATHER'S SCOLDINGS. THEY LEFT ME HURT AND SAD.
KA-KANG
BUT!
THAT'S NOT THE PROBLEM.
KL A NG
REIJI.
DO YOU KNOW WHAT WAS THE HARDEST, MOST PAIN-FUL THING TO ME?

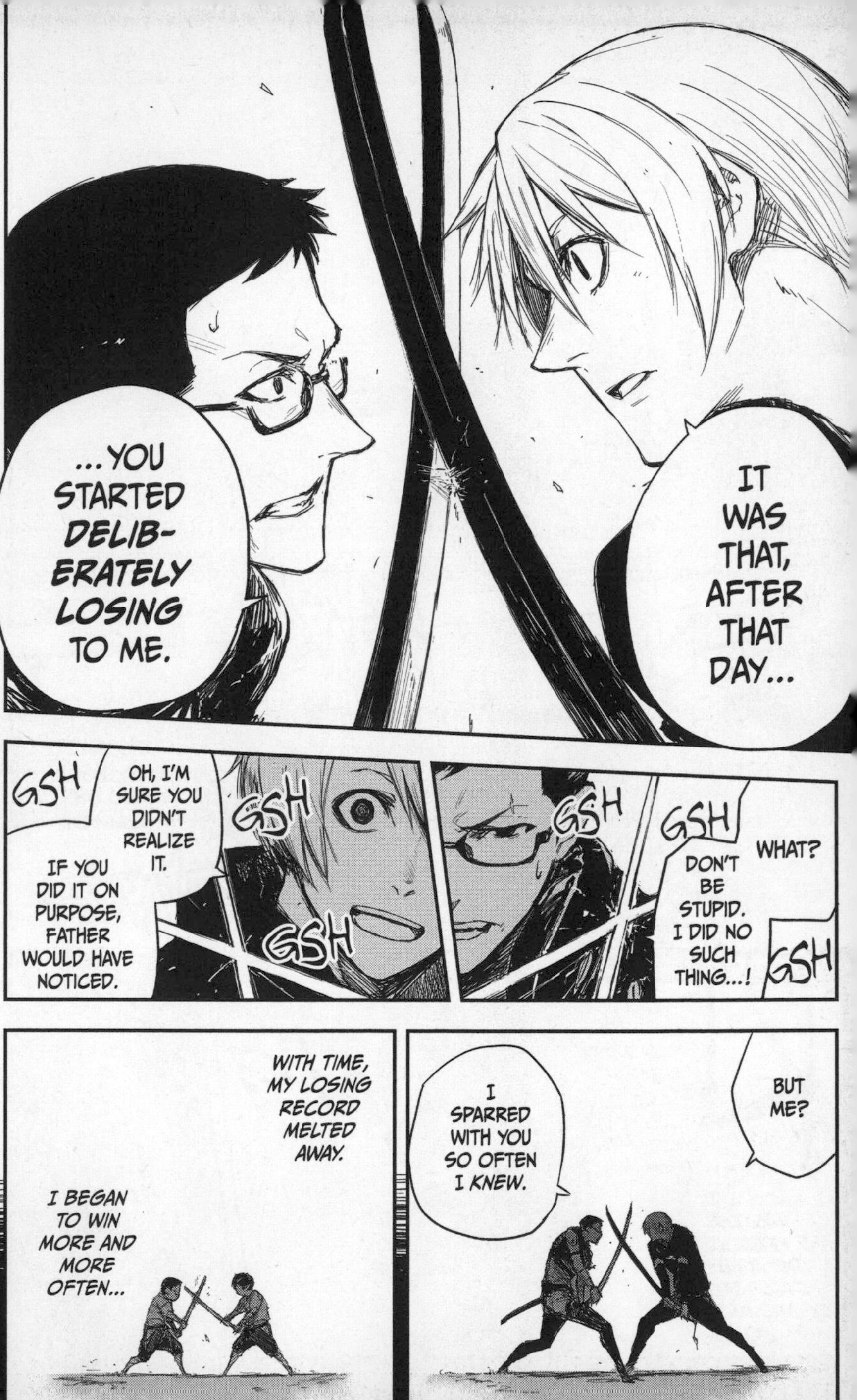
IT WAS THAT, AFTER THAT DAY...
...YOU STARTED DELIBERATELY LOSING TO ME.
WHAT?
GSH
DON'T BE STUPID. I DID NO SUCH THING...!
GSH
GSH
GSH
GSH
OH, I'M SURE YOU DIDN'T REALIZE IT.
GSH
IF YOU DID IT ON PURPOSE, FATHER WOULD HAVE NOTICED.
BUT ME?
I SPARRED WITH YOU SO OFTEN I KNEW.
WITH TIME, MY LOSING RECORD MELTED AWAY.
I BEGAN TO WIN MORE AND MORE OFTEN...

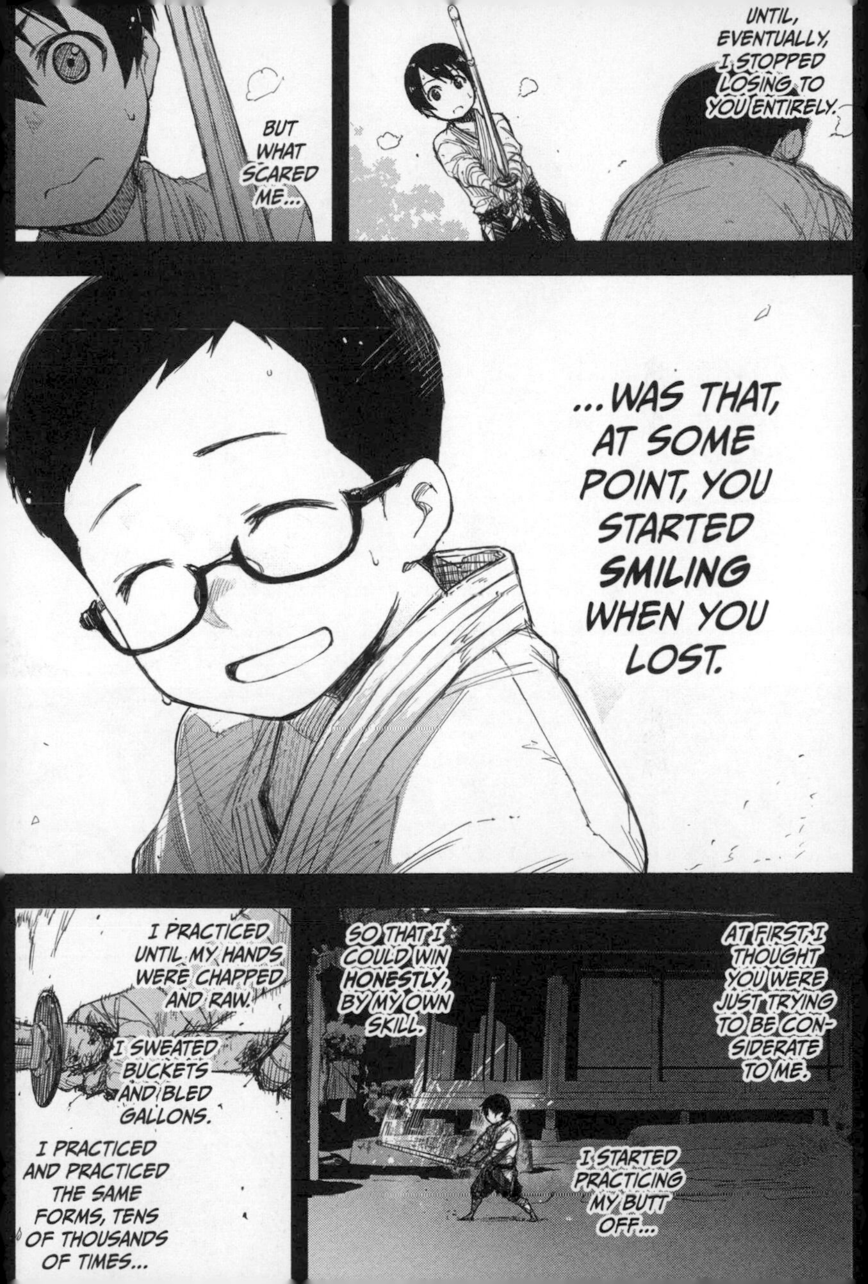
UNTIL, EVENTUALLY, I STOPPED LOSING TO YOU ENTIRELY.
BUT WHAT SCARED ME...
...WAS THAT, AT SOME POINT, YOU STARTED SMILING WHEN YOU LOST.
AT FIRST, I THOUGHT YOU WERE JUST TRYING TO BE CON-SIDERATE TO ME.
SO THAT I COULD WIN HONESTLY, BY MY OWN SKILL,
I STARTED PRACTICING MY BUTT OFF...
I PRACTICED UNTIL MY HANDS WERE CHAPPED AND RAW.
I SWEATED BUCKETS AND BLED GALLONS.
I PRACTICED AND PRACTICED THE SAME FORMS, TENS OF THOUSANDS OF TIMES...

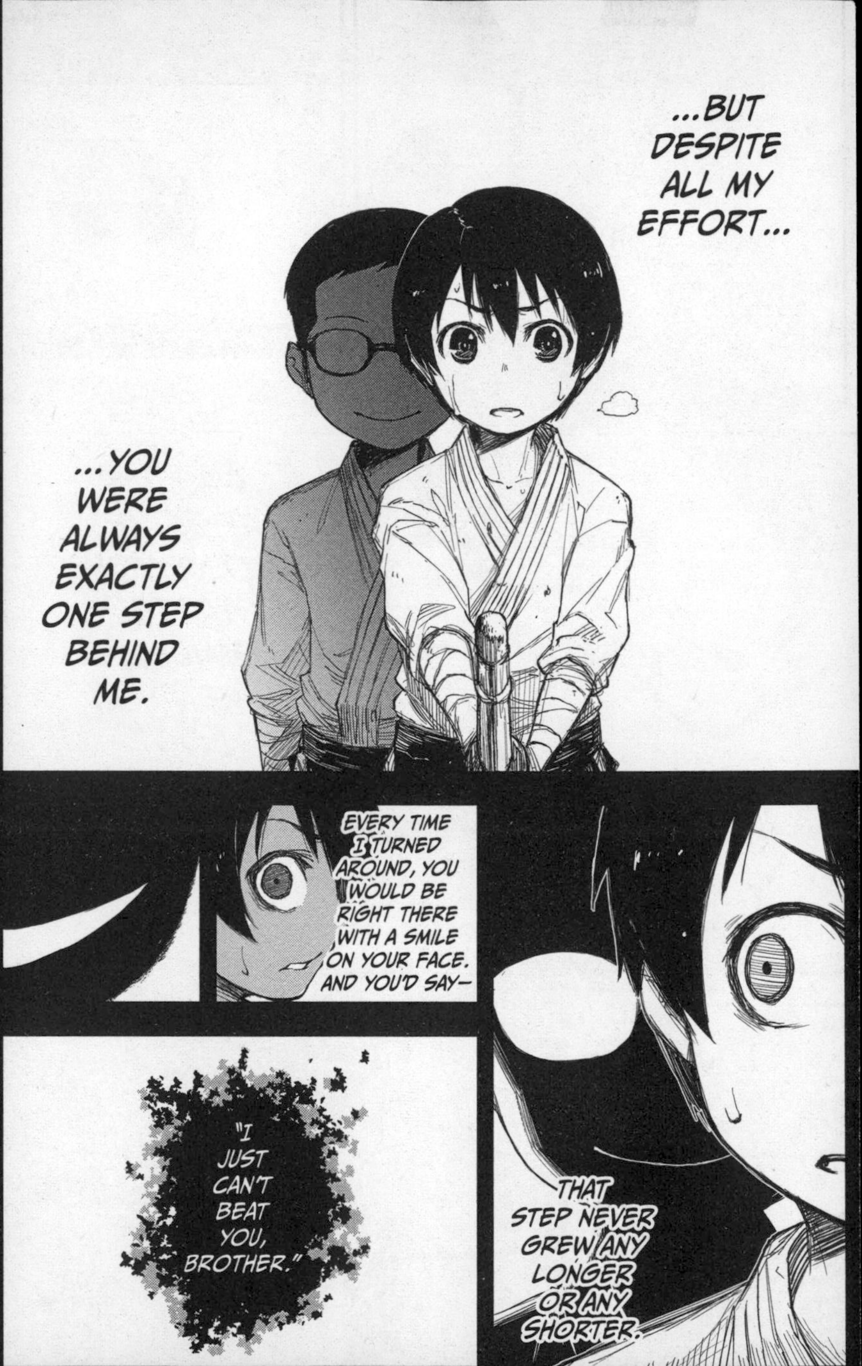
...BUT DESPITE ALL MY EFFORT...
...YOU WERE ALWAYS EXACTLY ONE STEP BEHIND ME.
EVERY TIME I TURNED AROUND, YOU WOULD BE RIGHT THERE WITH A SMILE ON YOUR FACE. AND YOU'D SAY—
"I JUST CAN'T BEAT YOU, BROTHER."
THAT STEP NEVER GREW ANY LONGER OR ANY SHORTER.

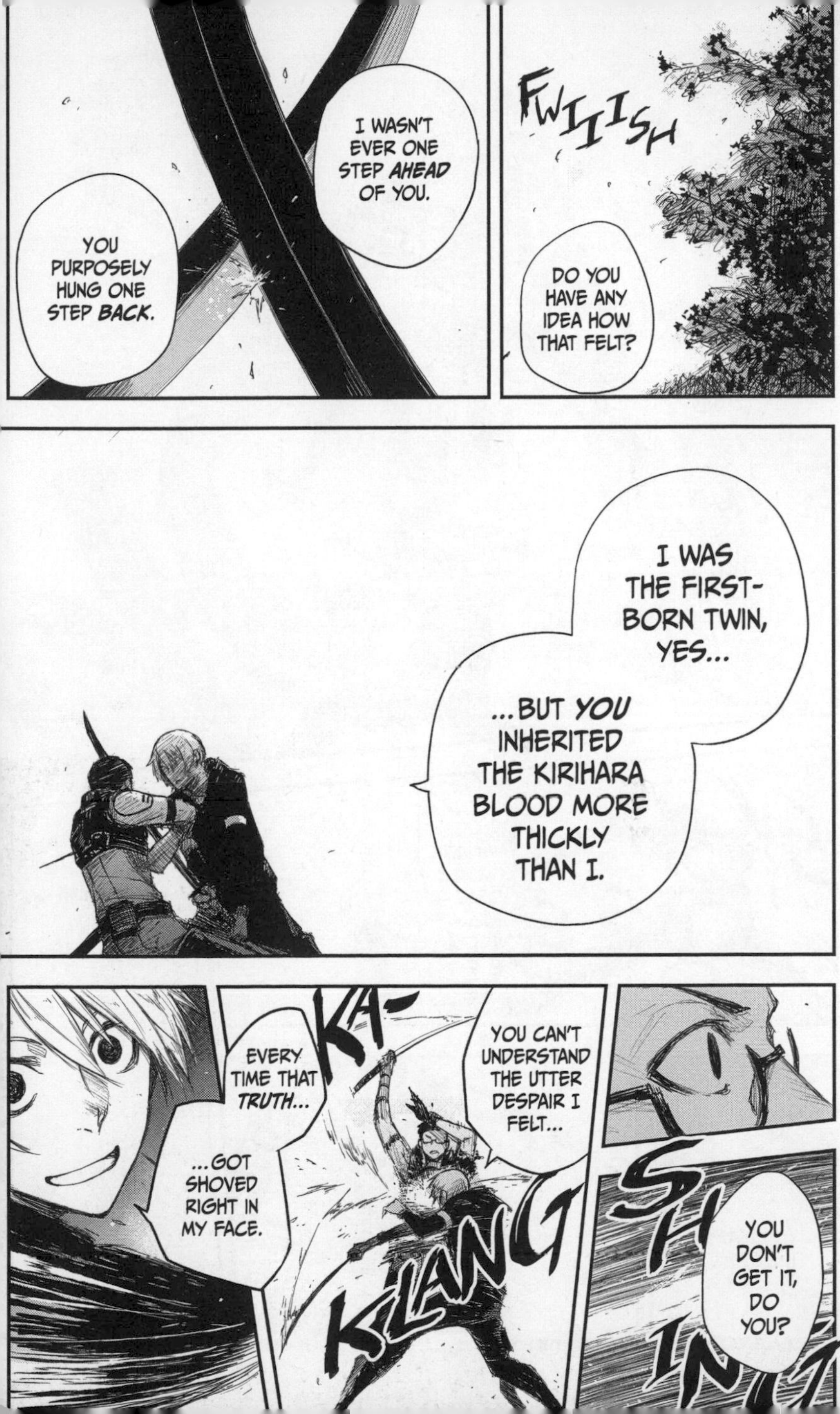
FWIIISH
DO YOU HAVE ANY IDEA HOW THAT FELT?
I WASN'T EVER ONE STEP *AHEAD* OF YOU.
YOU PURPOSELY HUNG ONE STEP *BACK*.
I WAS THE FIRST-BORN TWIN, YES...
...BUT *YOU* INHERITED THE KIRIHARA BLOOD MORE THICKLY THAN I.
SHING
YOU DON'T GET IT, DO YOU?
KA-KLANG
YOU CAN'T UNDERSTAND THE UTTER DESPAIR I FELT...
EVERY TIME THAT *TRUTH*...
...GOT SHOVED RIGHT IN MY FACE.

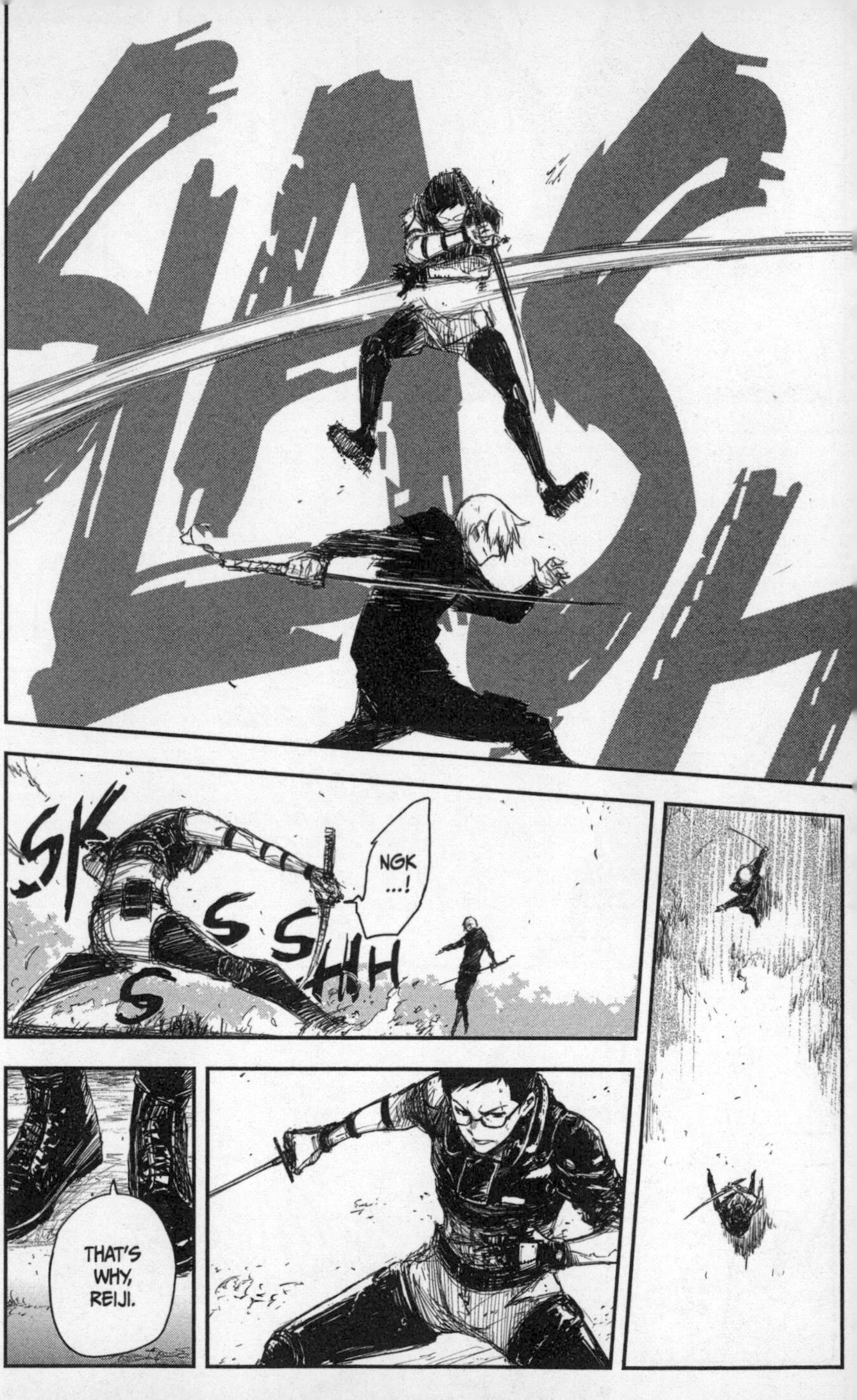
NGK ...!
SKSSSHH
THAT'S WHY, REIJI.

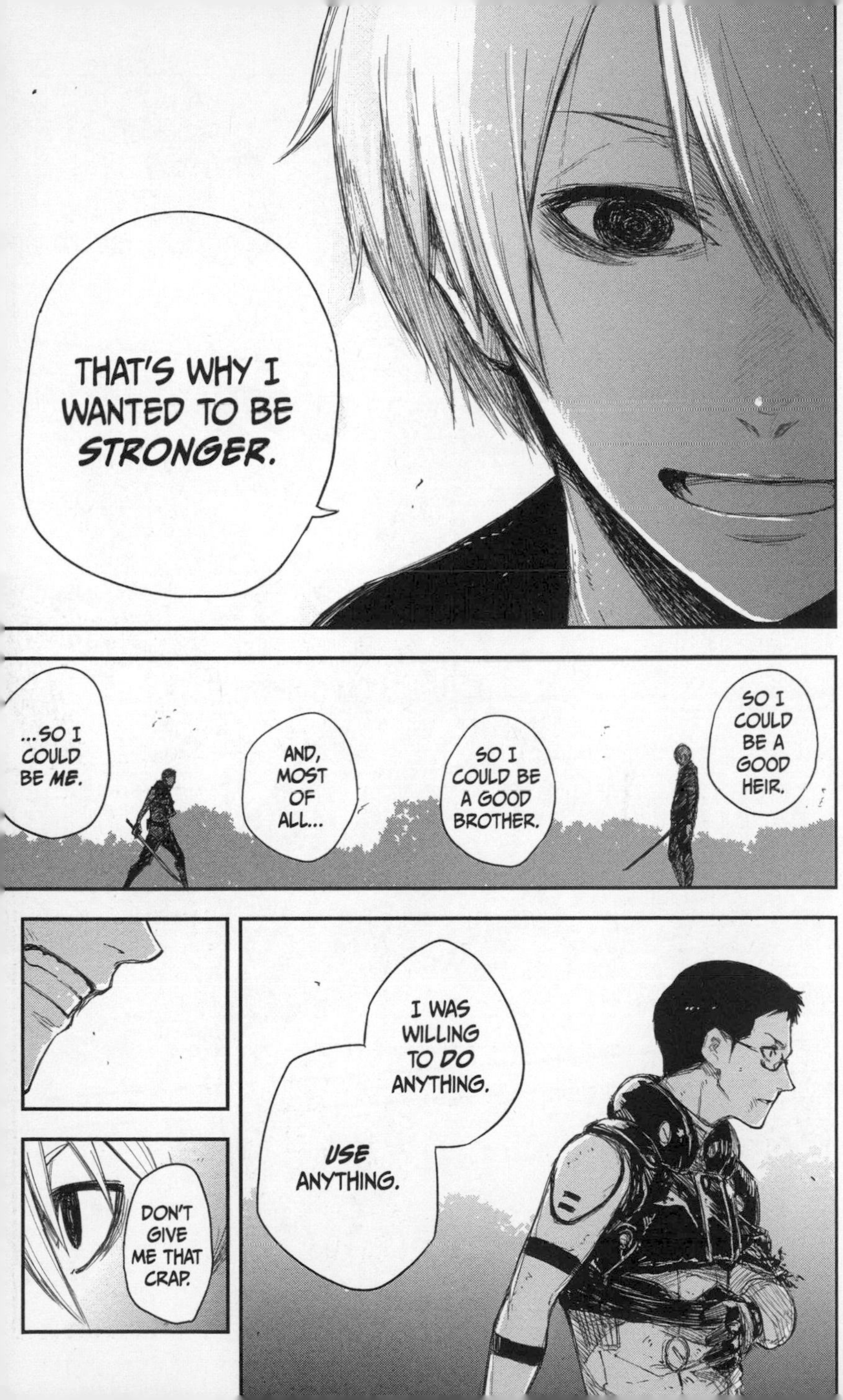
THAT'S WHY I WANTED TO BE STRONGER.
SO I COULD BE A GOOD HEIR.
SO I COULD BE A GOOD BROTHER.
AND, MOST OF ALL...
...SO I COULD BE ME.
I WAS WILLING TO DO ANYTHING.
USE ANYTHING.
DON'T GIVE ME THAT CRAP.

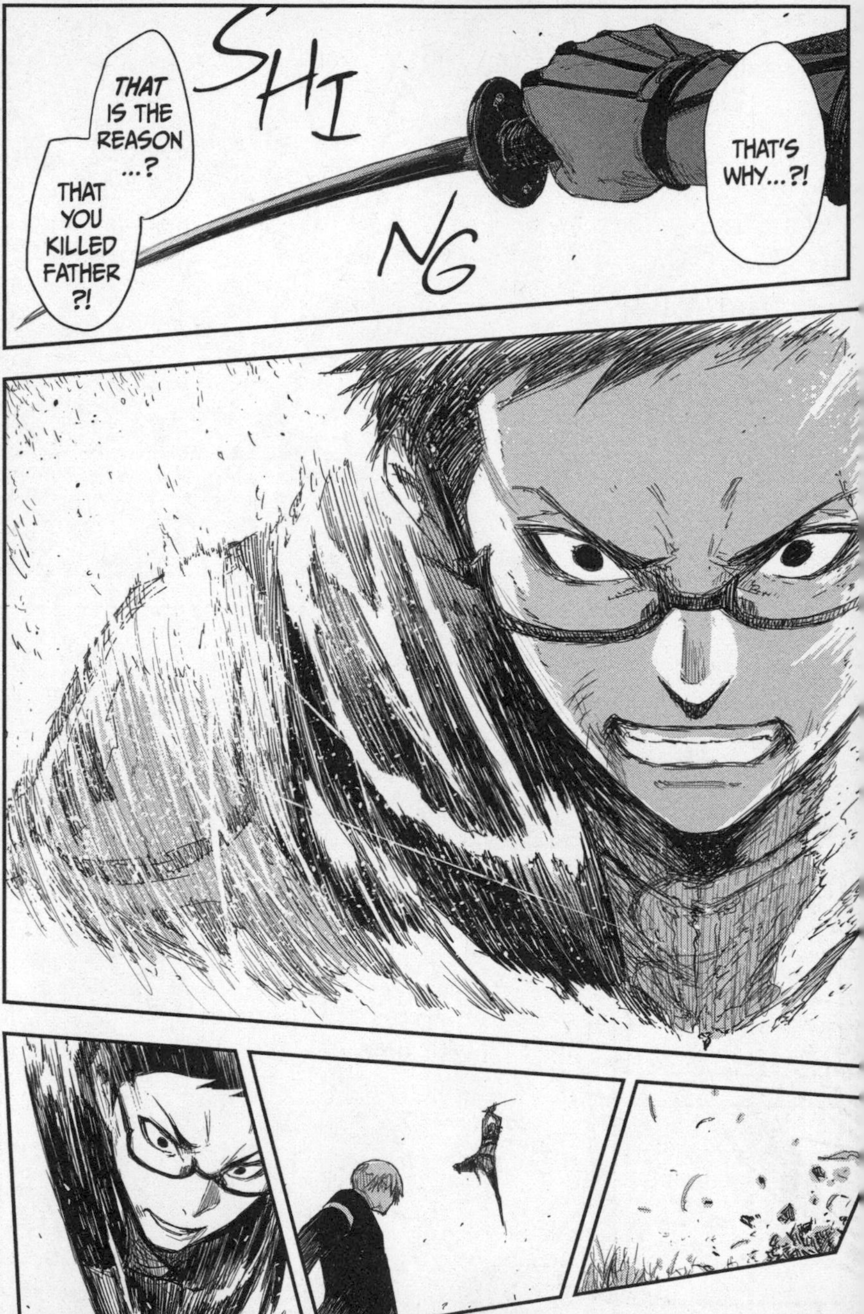
THAT'S WHY...?!
SHING
THAT IS THE REASON ...? THAT YOU KILLED FATHER ?!

GSH
KIRIHARA-RYU: ASSASSINATION ARTS—
FOOOM
ONI KUBIOTOSHI— OGRE SKULLSPLITTER!

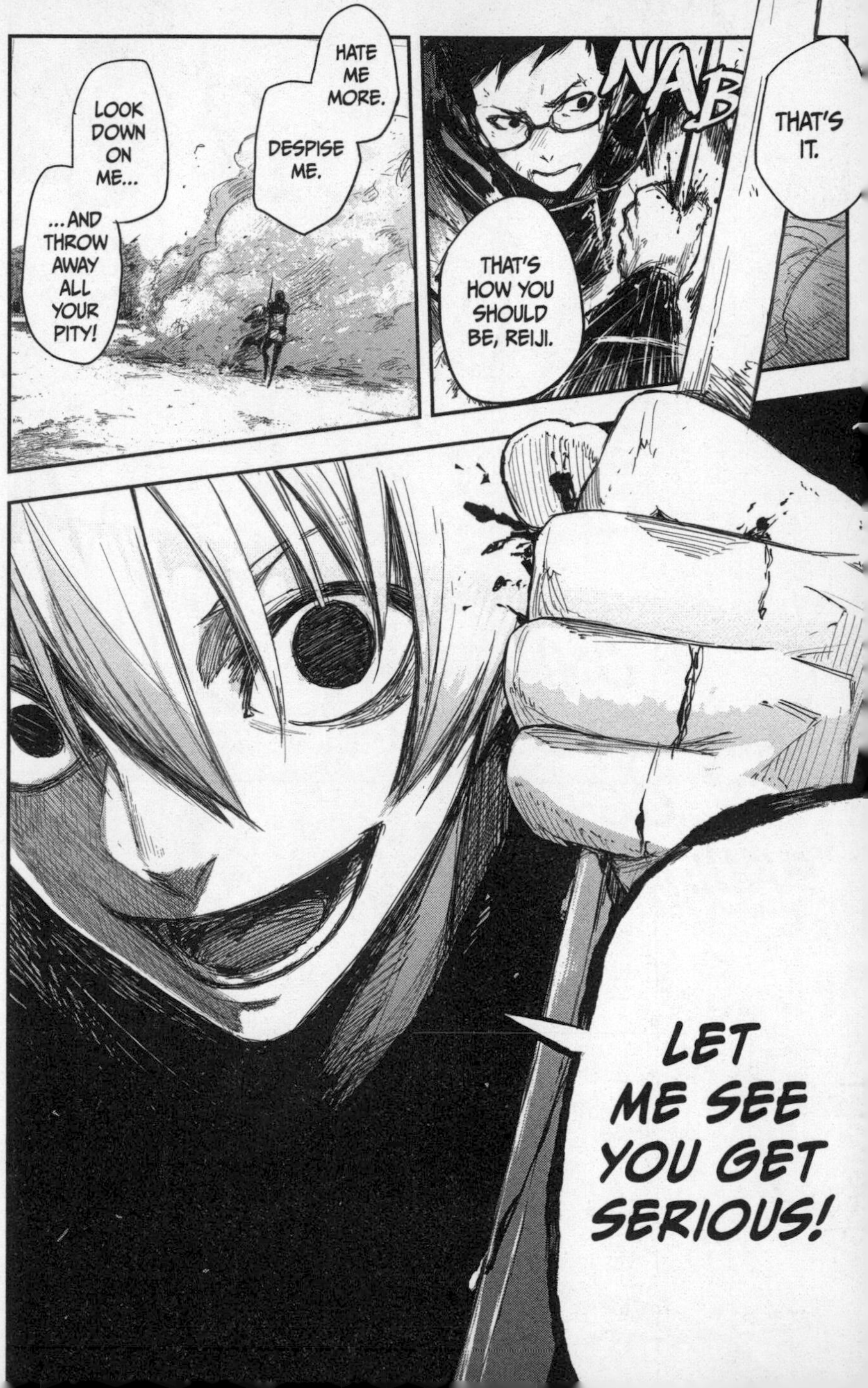
THAT'S IT.
NAB
THAT'S HOW YOU SHOULD BE, REIJI.
HATE ME MORE.
DESPISE ME.
LOOK DOWN ON ME...
...AND THROW AWAY ALL YOUR PITY!
LET ME SEE YOU GET SERIOUS!

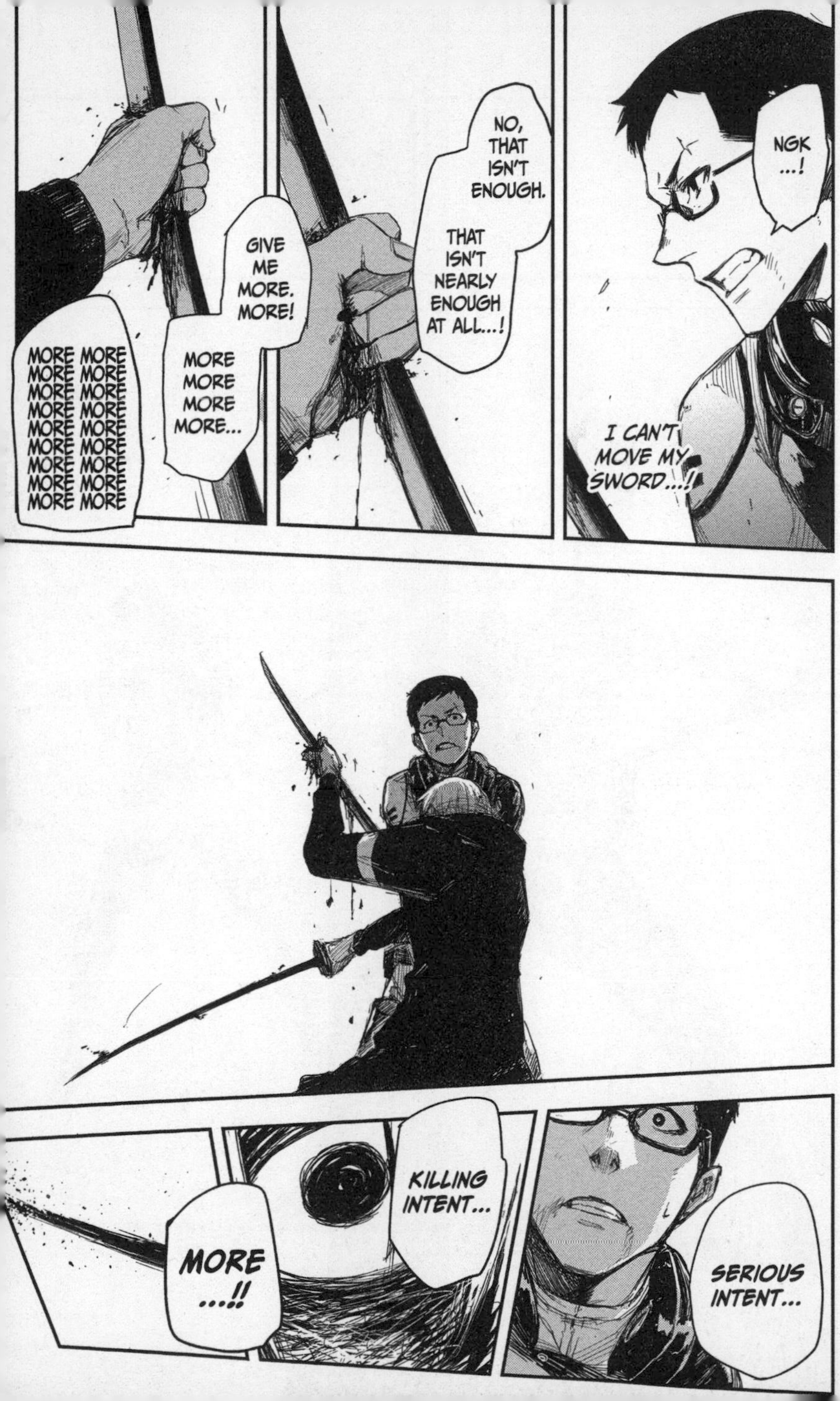
NGK ...!
I CAN'T MOVE MY SWORD...!
NO, THAT ISN'T ENOUGH.
THAT ISN'T NEARLY ENOUGH AT ALL...!
GIVE ME MORE. MORE!
MORE MORE MORE MORE...
MORE MORE MORE MORE MORE MORE MORE MORE MORE MORE MORE MORE MORE MORE MORE MORE MORE MORE
SERIOUS INTENT...
KILLING INTENT...
MORE ...!!

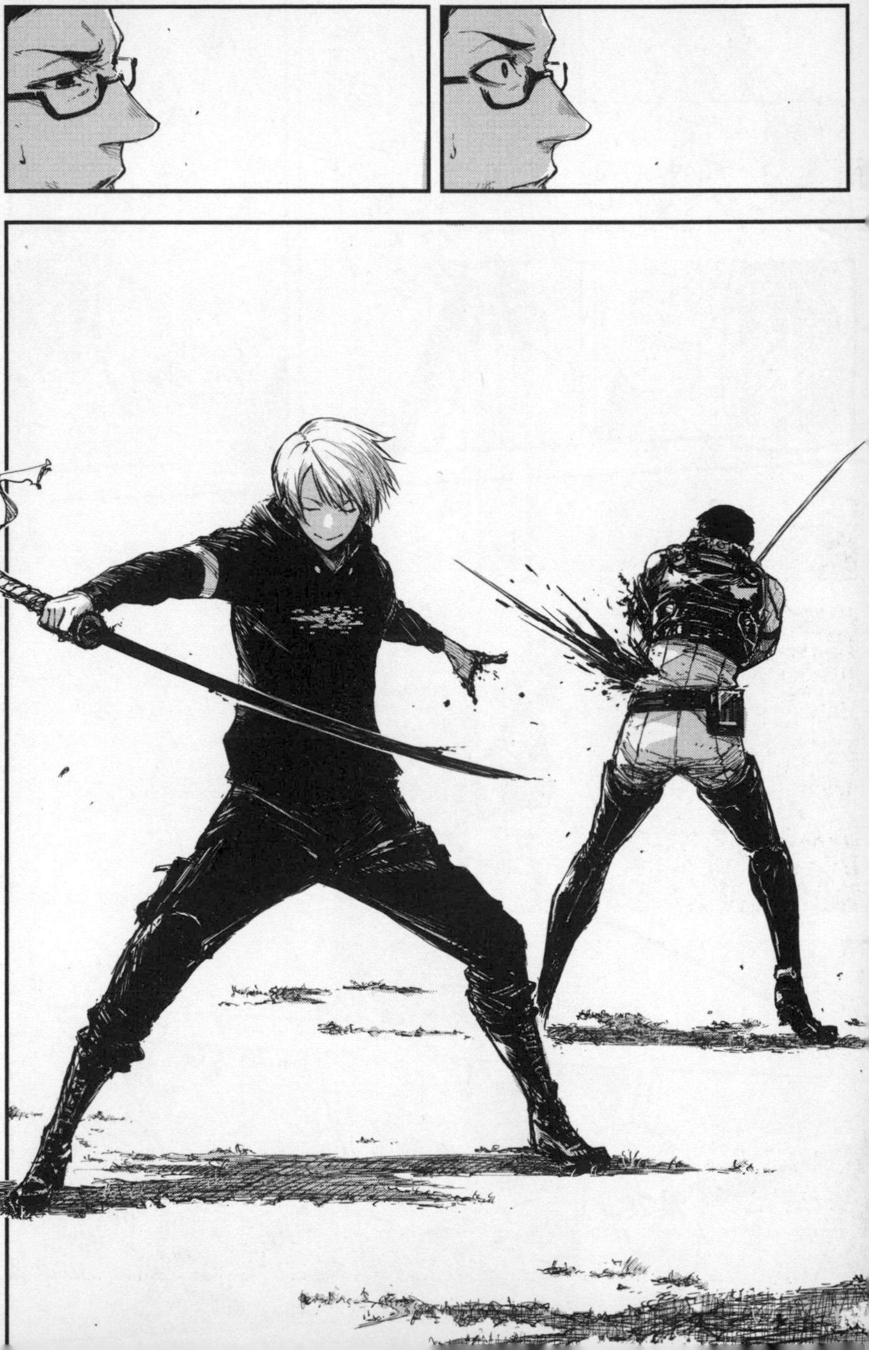

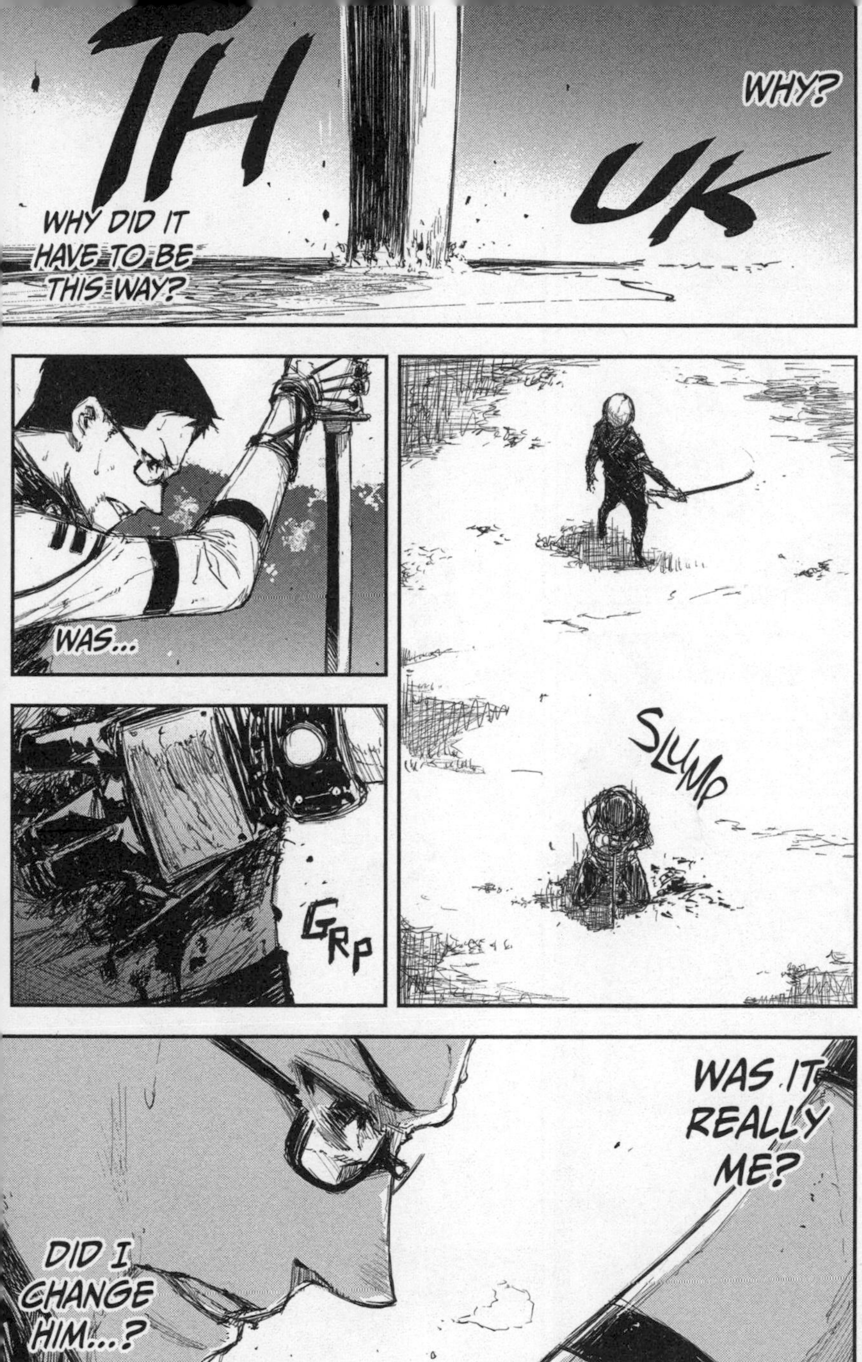
WHY?
THUK
WHY DID IT HAVE TO BE THIS WAY?
SLUMP
WAS...
GRP
WAS IT REALLY ME?
DID I CHANGE HIM...?

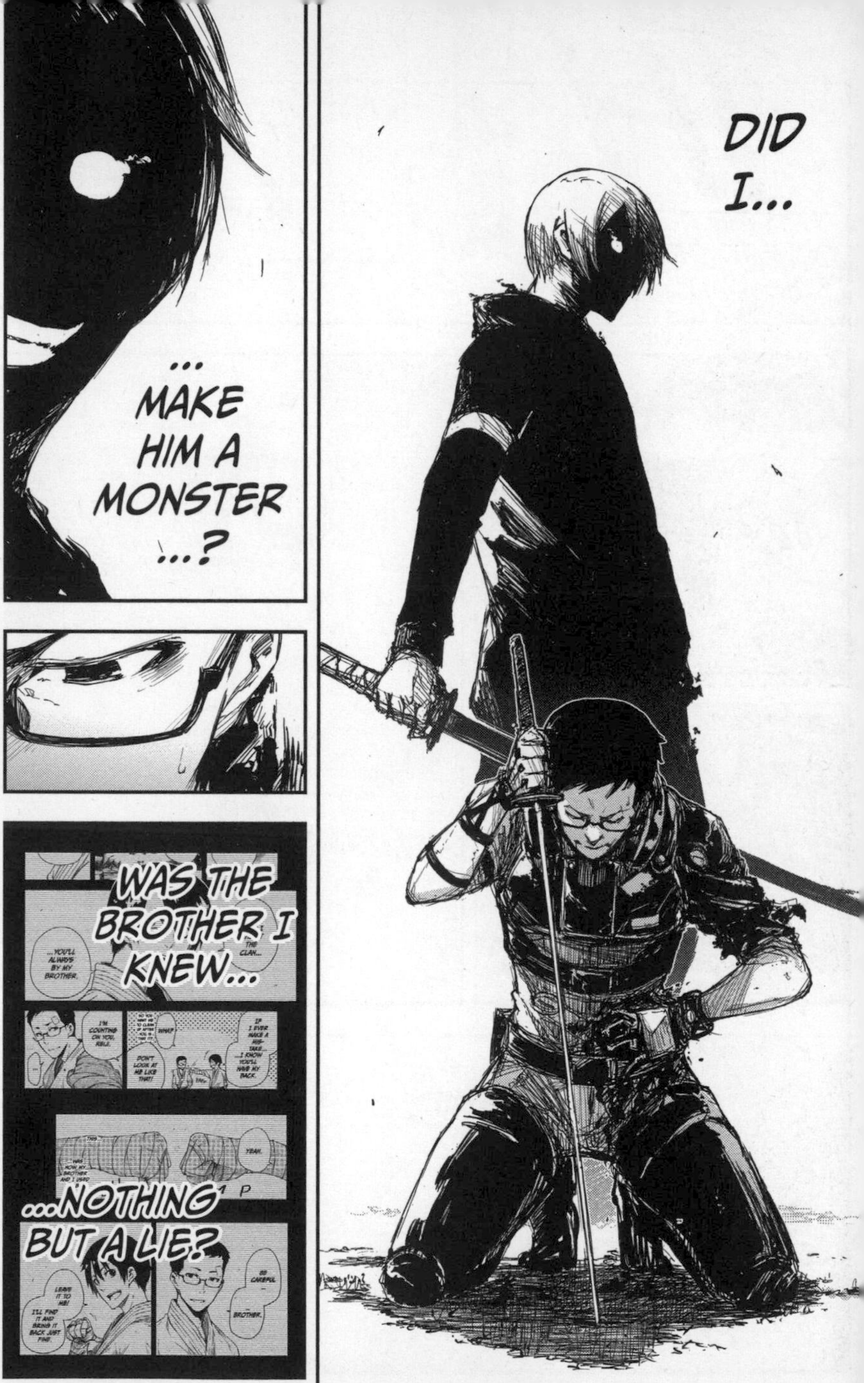
DID I...
...MAKE HIM A MONSTER...?
WAS THE BROTHER I KNEW...
THE CLAN...
...YOU'LL ALWAYS BY MY BROTHER.
IF I EVER MAKE A MIS-TAKE... ...I KNOW YOU'LL HAVE MY BACK.
WHAT?
DON'T LOOK AT ME LIKE THAT!
I'M COUNTING ON YOU, REIJI.
YEAH.
THIS...
...WAS HOW MY BROTHER AND I USED
...NOTHING BUT A LIE?
BE CAREFUL... BROTHER.
LEAVE IT TO ME!
I'LL FIND IT AND BRING IT BACK JUST FINE.

I ALMOST KILLED YOU.

TMP

SORRY ABOUT THAT, REIJI.

TMP

!

WHOOPS!

THAT WAS CLOSE.

TMP

TMP

THERE'S NO POINT TO KILLING YOU WHEN YOU'RE THIS SHAKEN AND CONFUSED THOUGH.

I'VE NOW TOLD YOU ALL THAT NEEDED TO BE SAID.

CHK

AH, WELL...

CH

ING

WE'LL CALL THIS GOOD FOR TODAY.

SO!

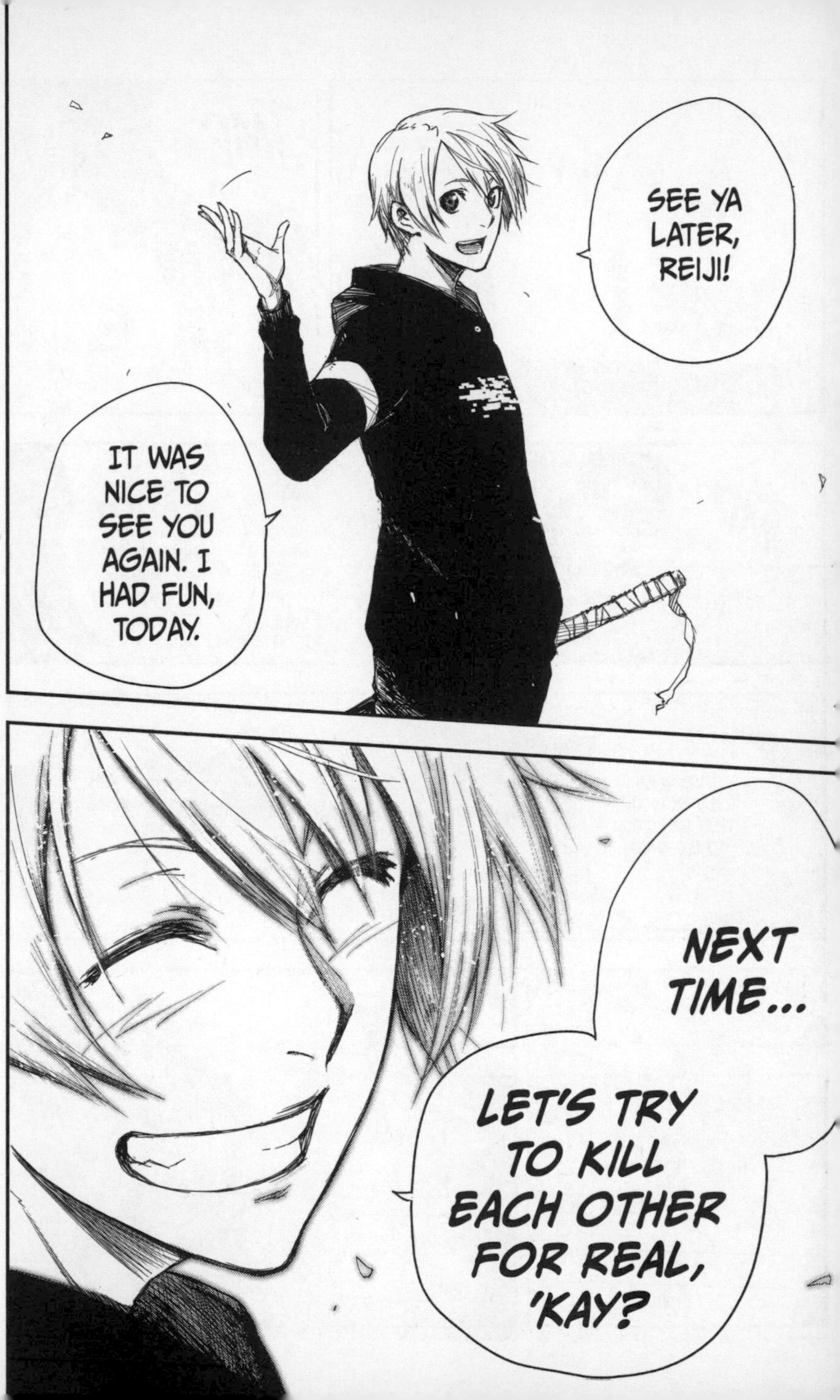
SEE YA LATER, REIJI!
IT WAS NICE TO SEE YOU AGAIN. I HAD FUN, TODAY.
NEXT TIME...
LET'S TRY TO KILL EACH OTHER FOR REAL, 'KAY?

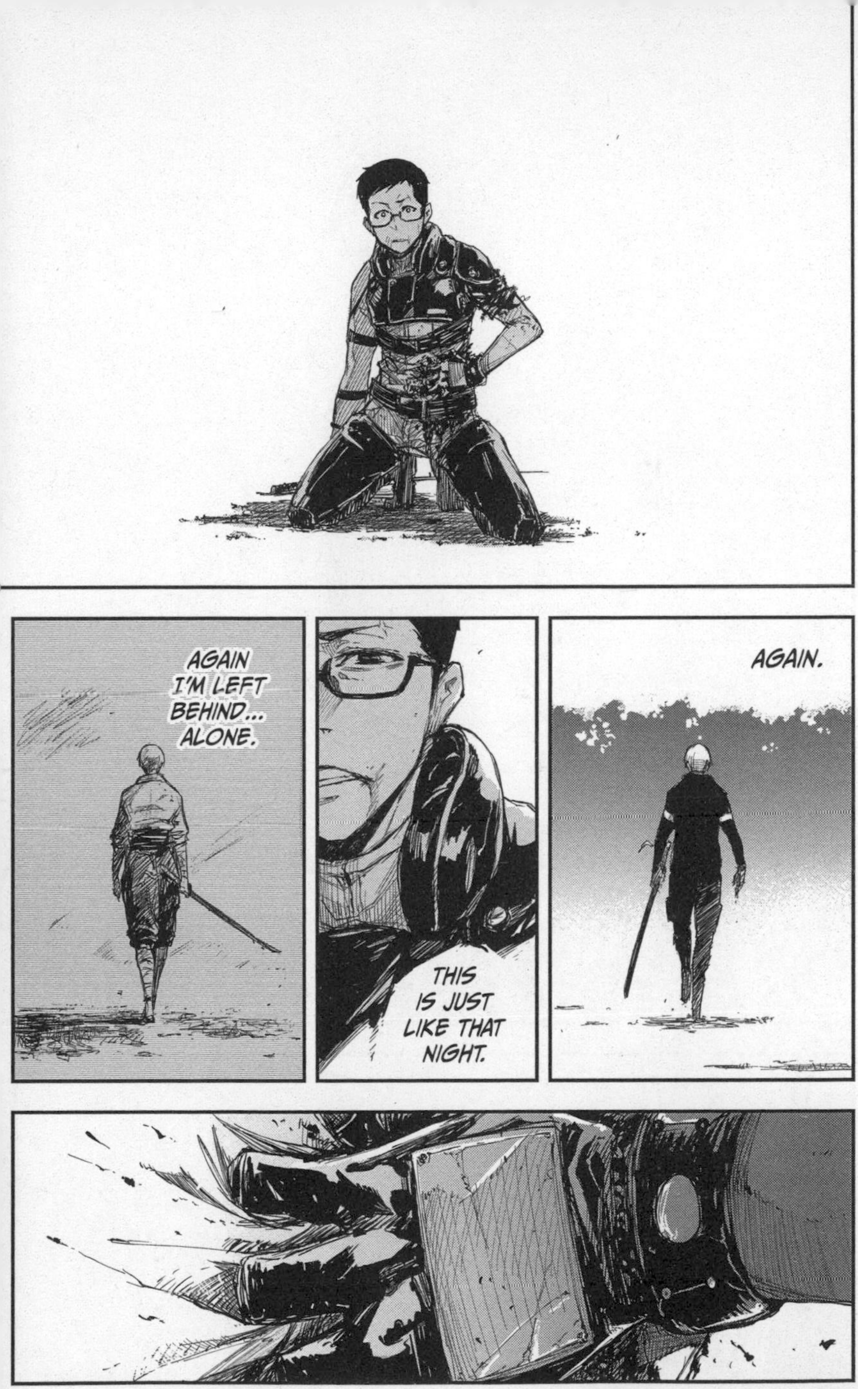
AGAIN.
THIS IS JUST LIKE THAT NIGHT.
AGAIN I'M LEFT BEHIND... ALONE.

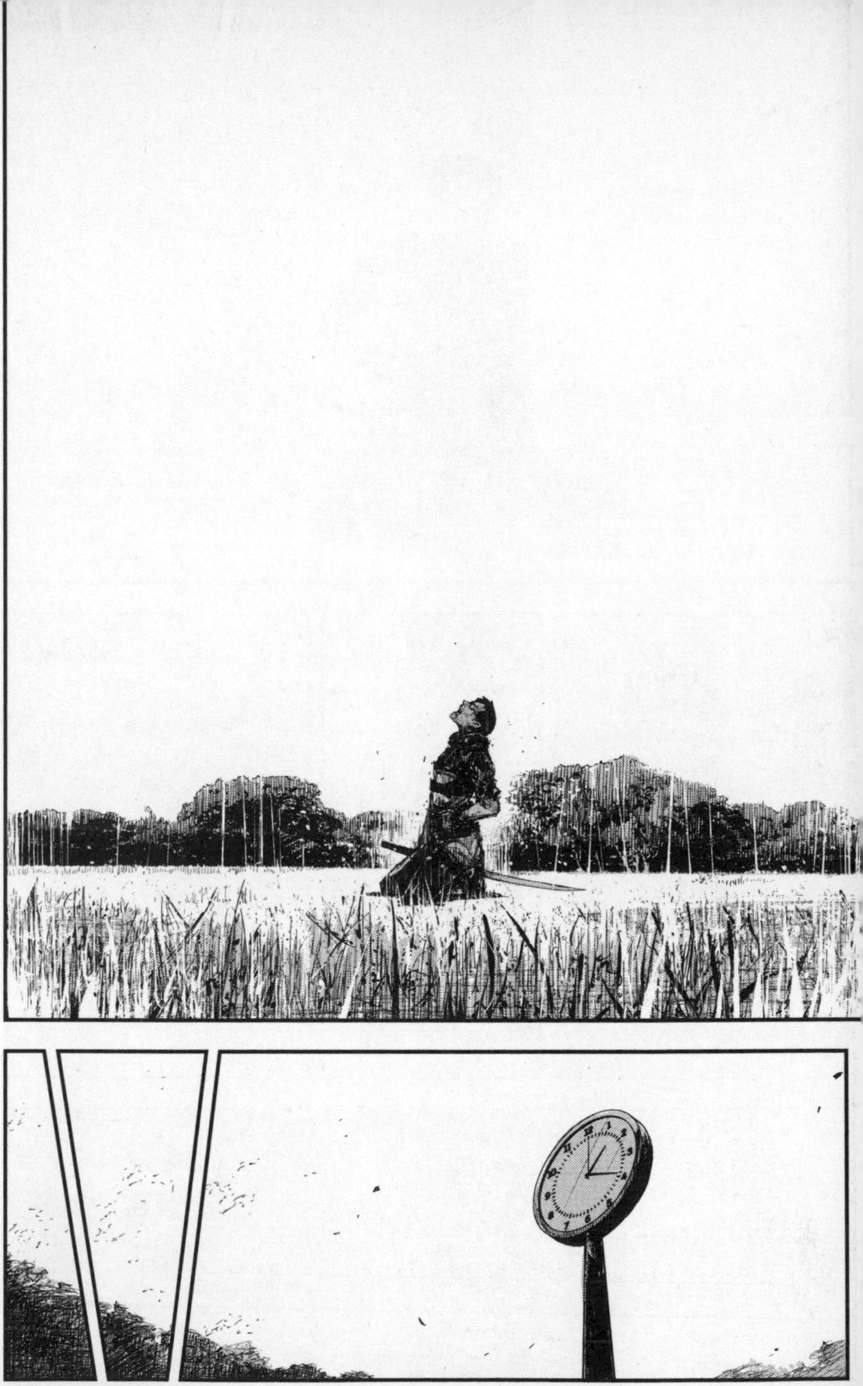

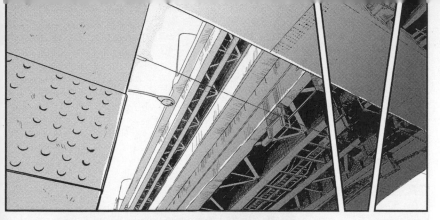

HUFF!

HUFF!

HUFF!

AAA-
AAA-
UGH!

DAMMIT,
THIS
SUCKS!

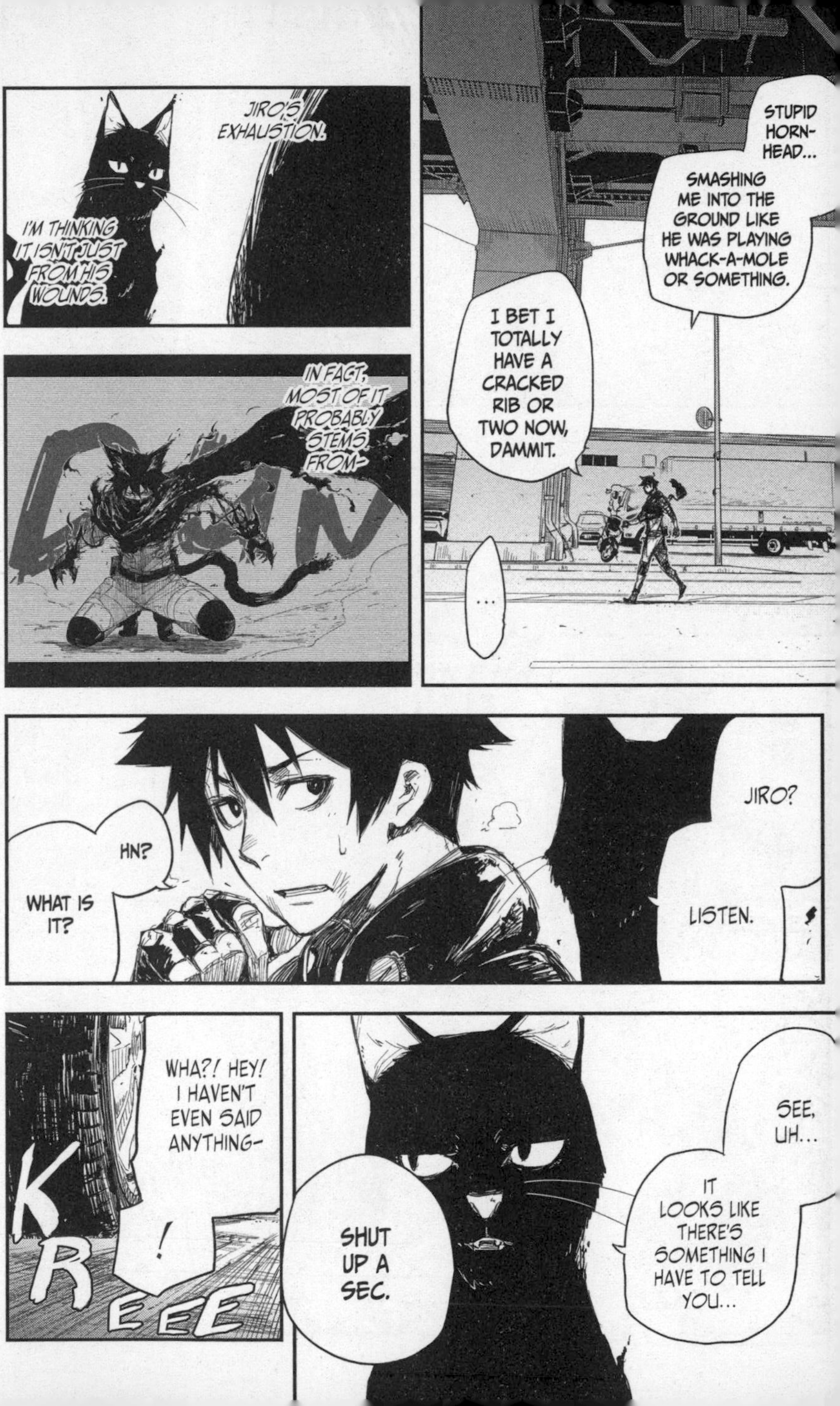
STUPID HORN-HEAD...
SMASHING ME INTO THE GROUND LIKE HE WAS PLAYING WHACK-A-MOLE OR SOMETHING.
I BET I TOTALLY HAVE A CRACKED RIB OR TWO NOW, DAMMIT.
...
JIRO'S EXHAUSTION.
I'M THINKING IT ISN'T JUST FROM HIS WOUNDS.
IN FACT, MOST OF IT PROBABLY STEMS FROM-
JIRO?
LISTEN.
HN?
WHAT IS IT?
SEE, UH...
IT LOOKS LIKE THERE'S SOMETHING I HAVE TO TELL YOU...
SHUT UP A SEC.
WHA?! HEY! I HAVEN'T EVEN SAID ANYTHING-
!
KREEEE

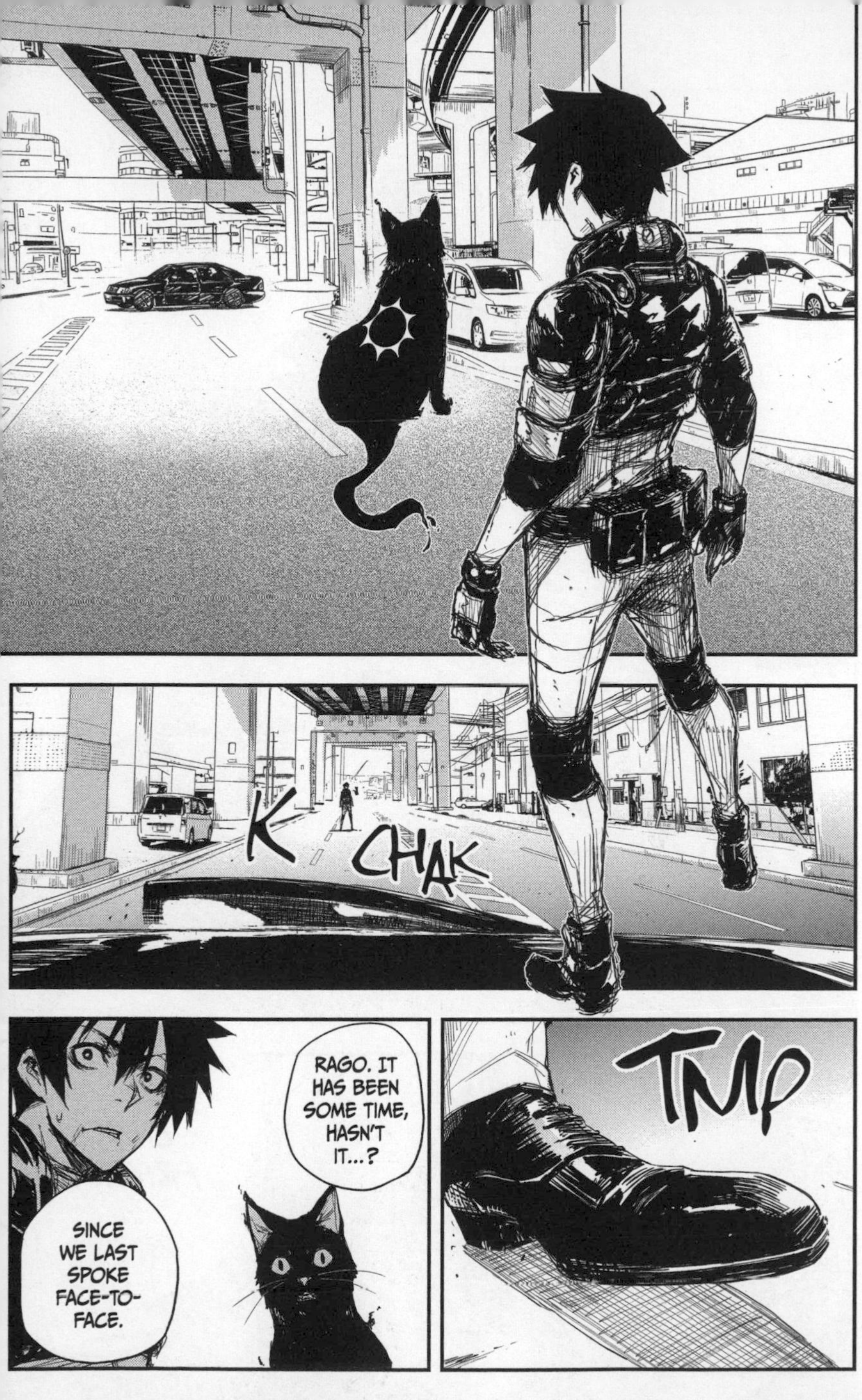
K CHAK
TMP
RAGO. IT HAS BEEN SOME TIME, HASN'T IT...?
SINCE WE LAST SPOKE FACE-TO-FACE.

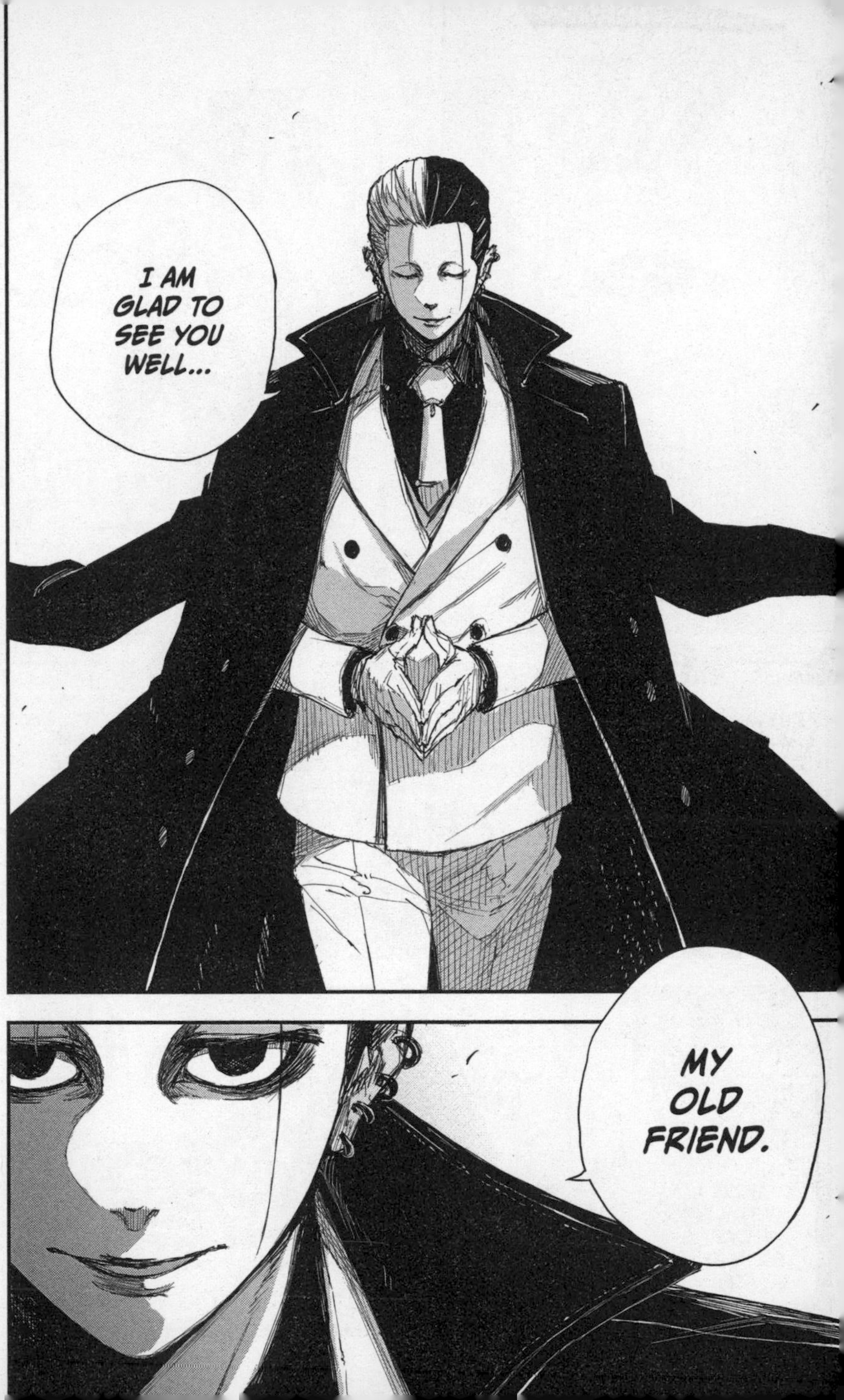
I AM GLAD TO SEE YOU WELL...
MY OLD FRIEND.

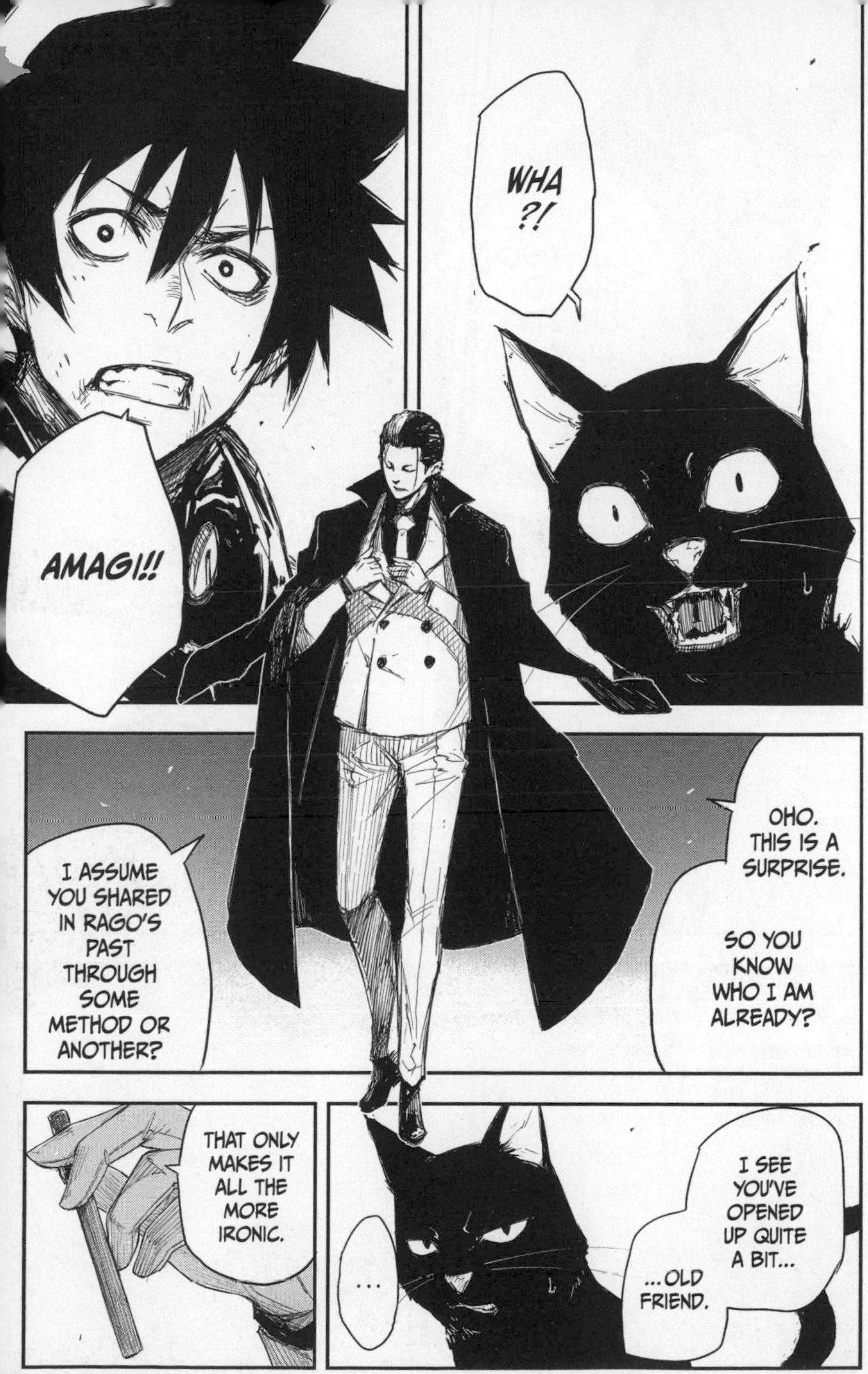
WHA ?!
AMAGI!!
OHO. THIS IS A SURPRISE.
SO YOU KNOW WHO I AM ALREADY?
I ASSUME YOU SHARED IN RAGO'S PAST THROUGH SOME METHOD OR ANOTHER?
I SEE YOU'VE OPENED UP QUITE A BIT...
...OLD FRIEND.
...
THAT ONLY MAKES IT ALL THE MORE IRONIC.

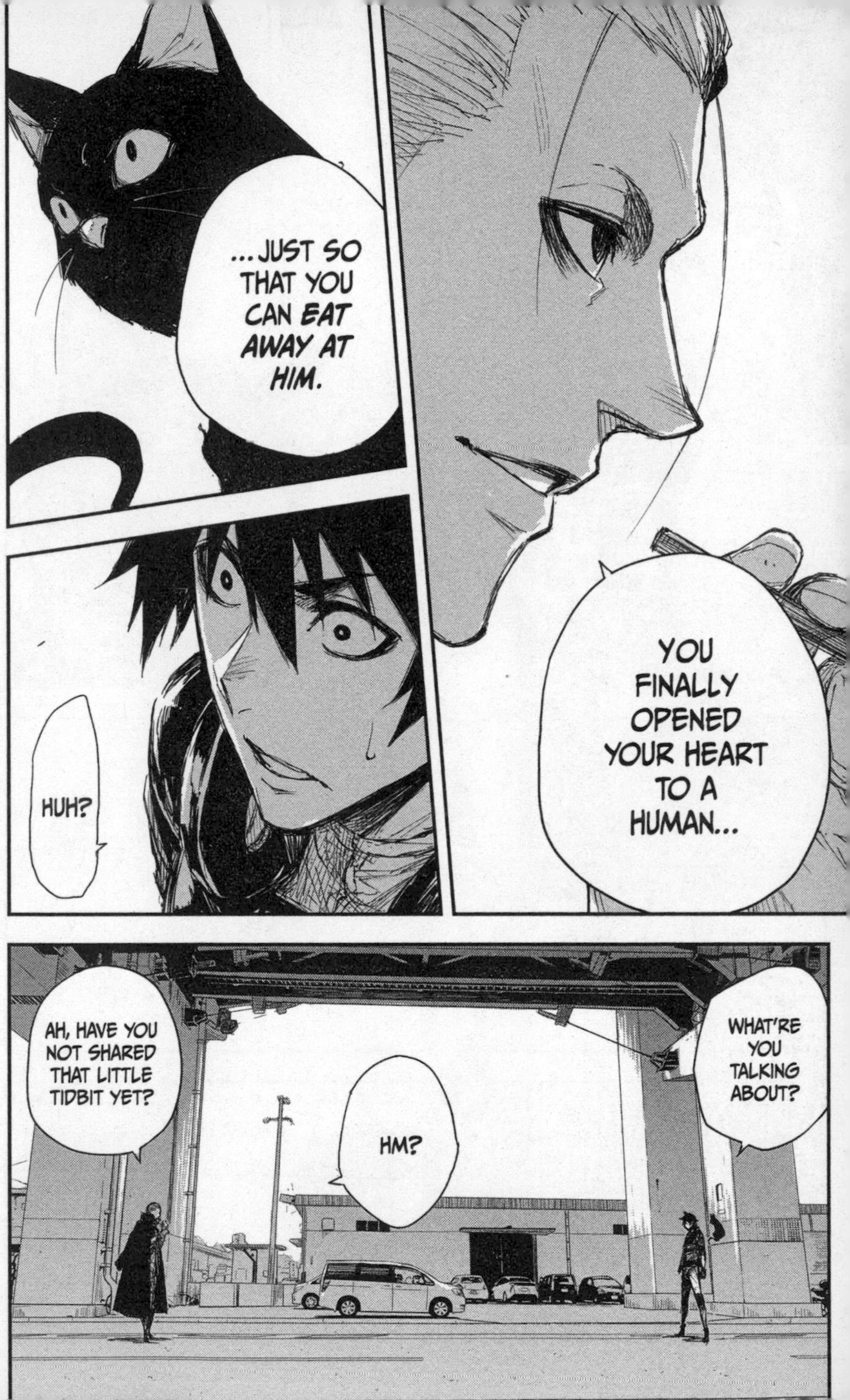
YOU FINALLY OPENED YOUR HEART TO A HUMAN...
...JUST SO THAT YOU CAN *EAT AWAY AT* HIM.
HUH?
WHAT'RE YOU TALKING ABOUT?
HM?
AH, HAVE YOU NOT SHARED THAT LITTLE TIDBIT YET?

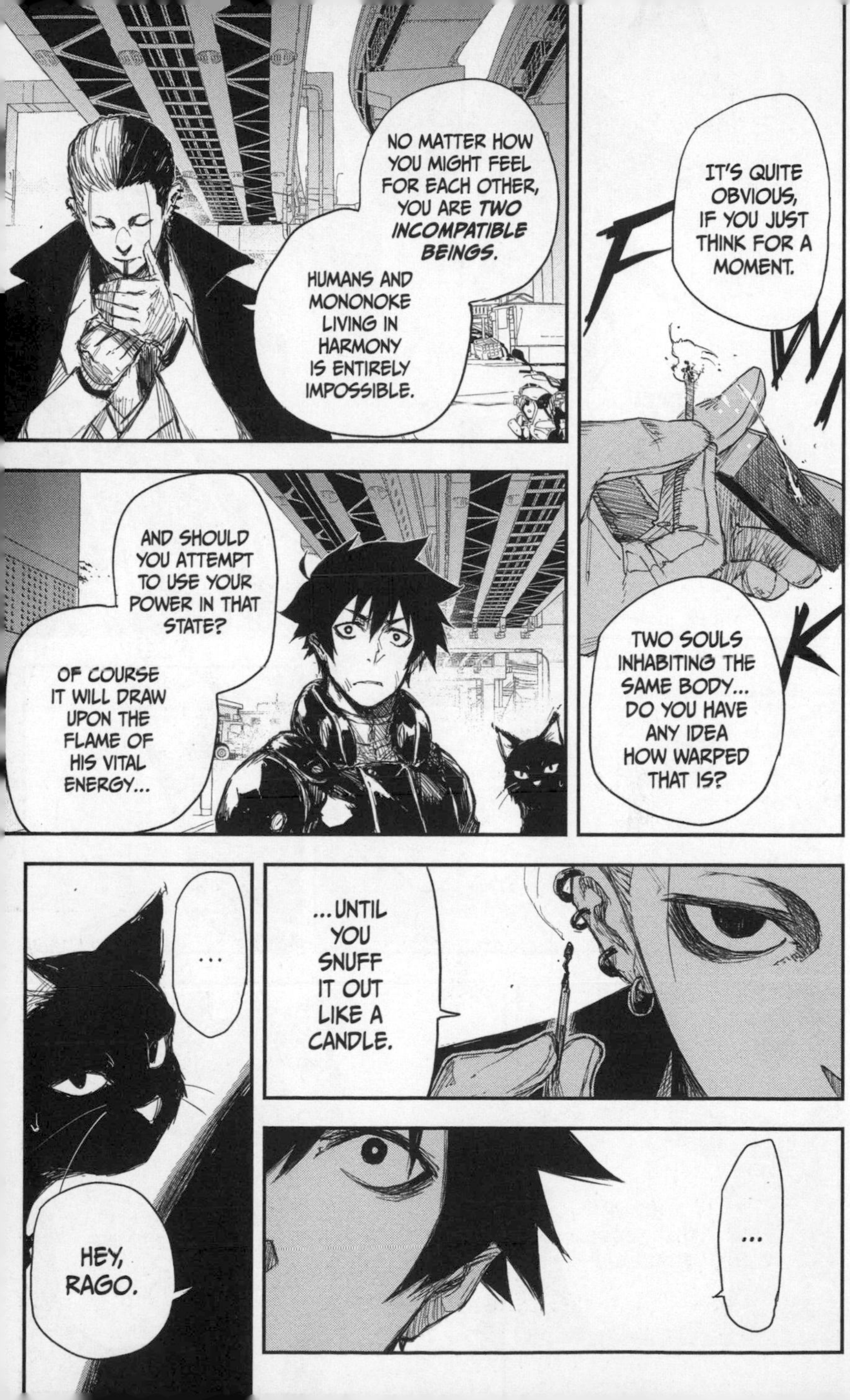
IT'S QUITE OBVIOUS, IF YOU JUST THINK FOR A MOMENT.
TWO SOULS INHABITING THE SAME BODY... DO YOU HAVE ANY IDEA HOW WARPED THAT IS?
NO MATTER HOW YOU MIGHT FEEL FOR EACH OTHER, YOU ARE *TWO INCOMPATIBLE BEINGS.*
HUMANS AND MONONOKE LIVING IN HARMONY IS ENTIRELY IMPOSSIBLE.
AND SHOULD YOU ATTEMPT TO USE YOUR POWER IN THAT STATE?
OF COURSE IT WILL DRAW UPON THE FLAME OF HIS VITAL ENERGY...
...UNTIL YOU SNUFF IT OUT LIKE A CANDLE.
...
...
HEY, RAGO.

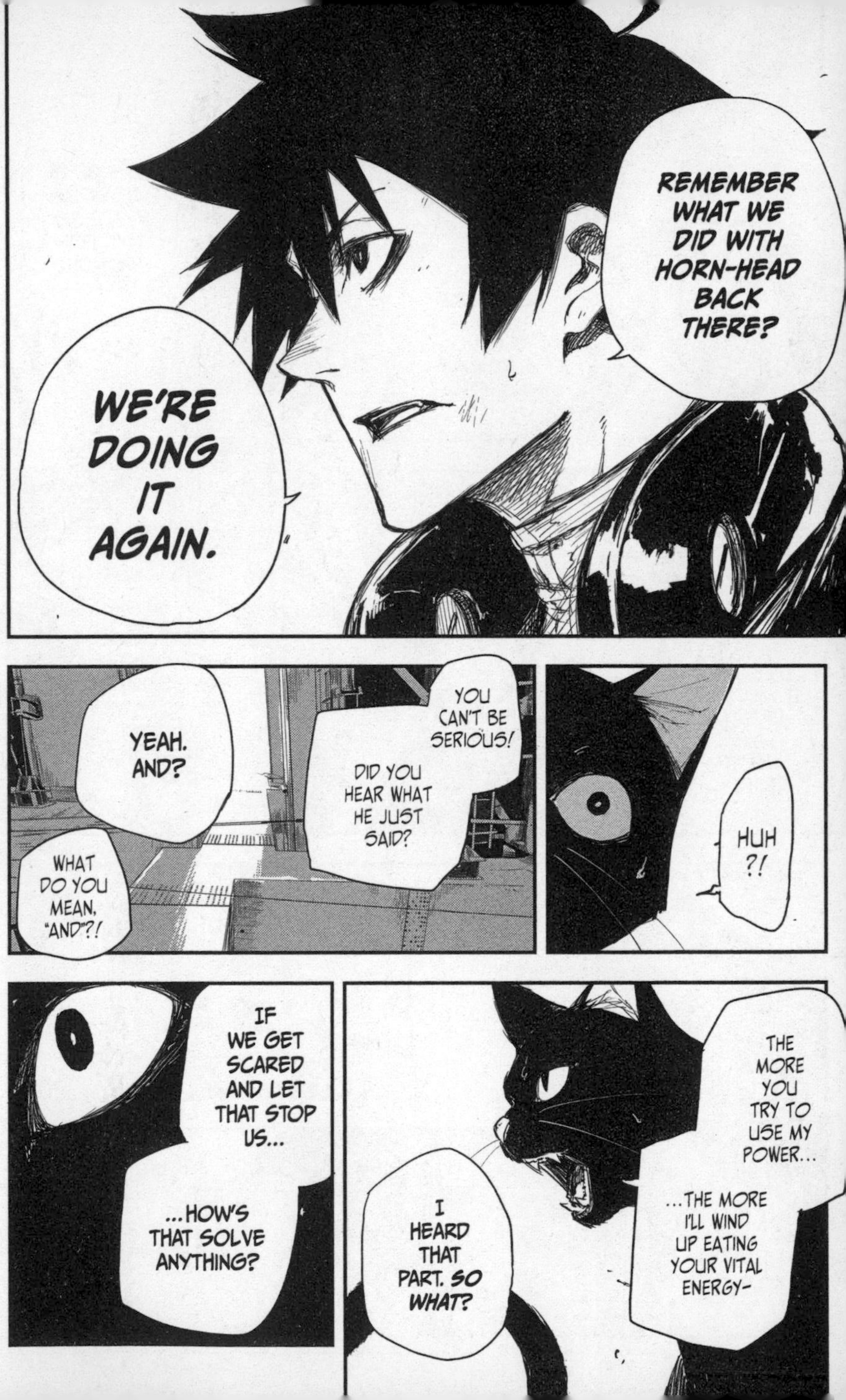
REMEMBER WHAT WE DID WITH HORN-HEAD BACK THERE?
WE'RE DOING IT AGAIN.
HUH ?!
YOU CAN'T BE SERIOUS!
DID YOU HEAR WHAT HE JUST SAID?
YEAH. AND?
WHAT DO YOU MEAN, "AND"?!
THE MORE YOU TRY TO USE MY POWER...
...THE MORE I'LL WIND UP EATING YOUR VITAL ENERGY-
I HEARD THAT PART. SO WHAT?
IF WE GET SCARED AND LET THAT STOP US...
...HOW'S THAT SOLVE ANYTHING?

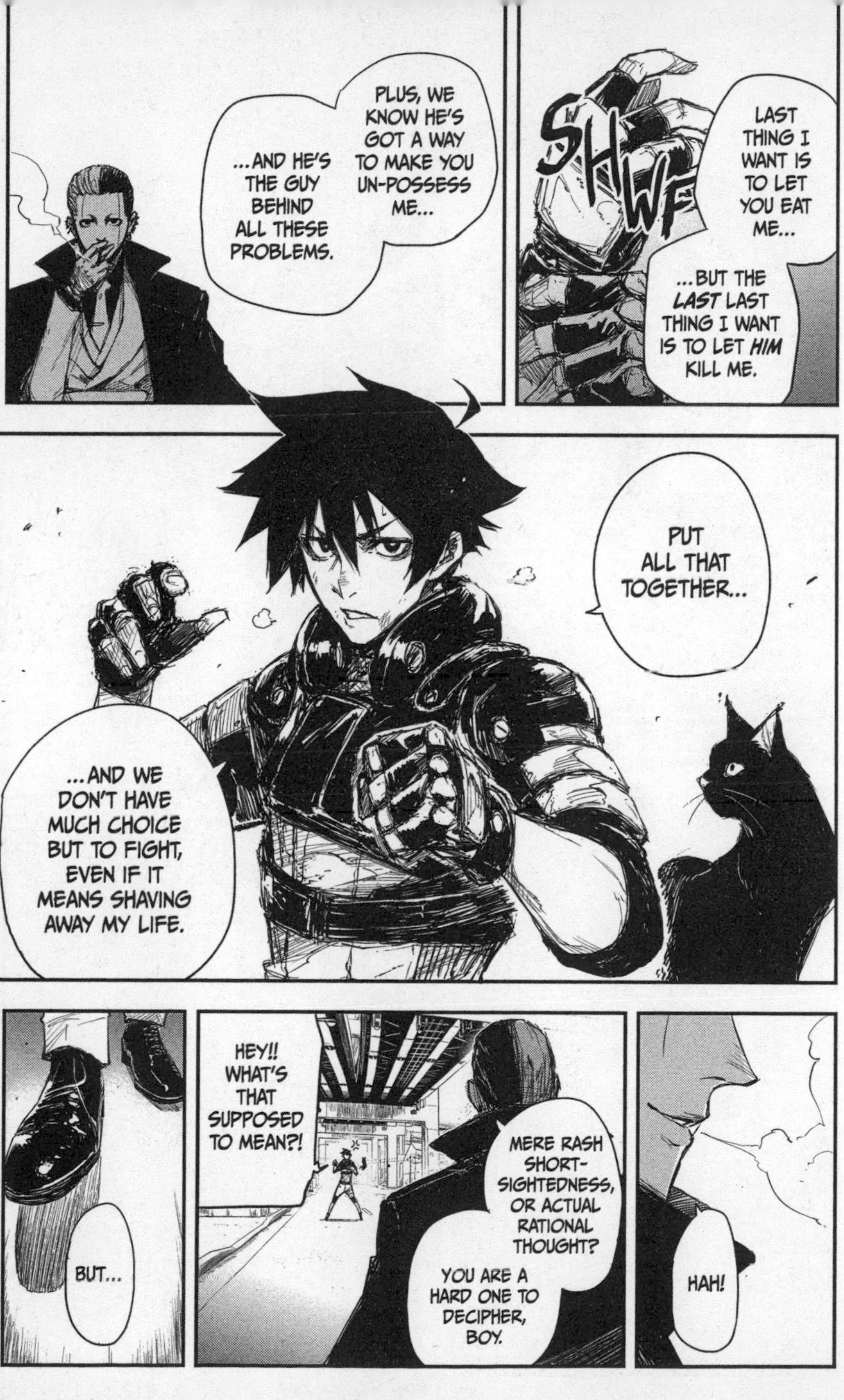
SHWF
LAST THING I WANT IS TO LET YOU EAT ME...
...BUT THE *LAST* LAST THING I WANT IS TO LET *HIM* KILL ME.
PLUS, WE KNOW HE'S GOT A WAY TO MAKE YOU UN-POSSESS ME...
...AND HE'S THE GUY BEHIND ALL THESE PROBLEMS.
PUT ALL THAT TOGETHER...
...AND WE DON'T HAVE MUCH CHOICE BUT TO FIGHT, EVEN IF IT MEANS SHAVING AWAY MY LIFE.
HAH!
MERE RASH SHORT-SIGHTEDNESS, OR ACTUAL RATIONAL THOUGHT?
YOU ARE A HARD ONE TO DECIPHER, BOY.
HEY!! WHAT'S THAT SUPPOSED TO MEAN?!
BUT...

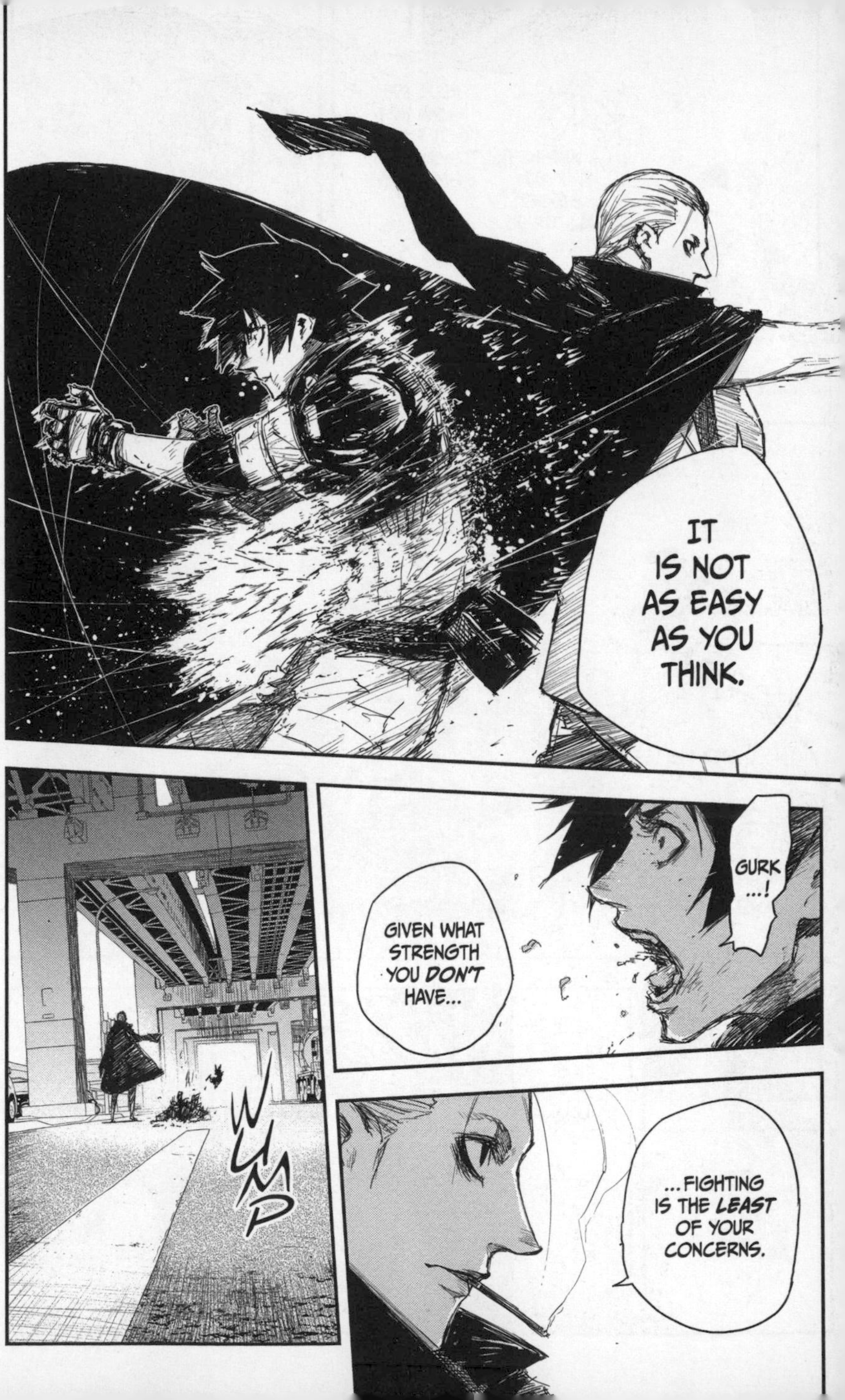
IT IS NOT AS EASY AS YOU THINK.
GURK ...!
GIVEN WHAT STRENGTH YOU *DON'T* HAVE...
...FIGHTING IS THE *LEAST* OF YOUR CONCERNS.
WUMP

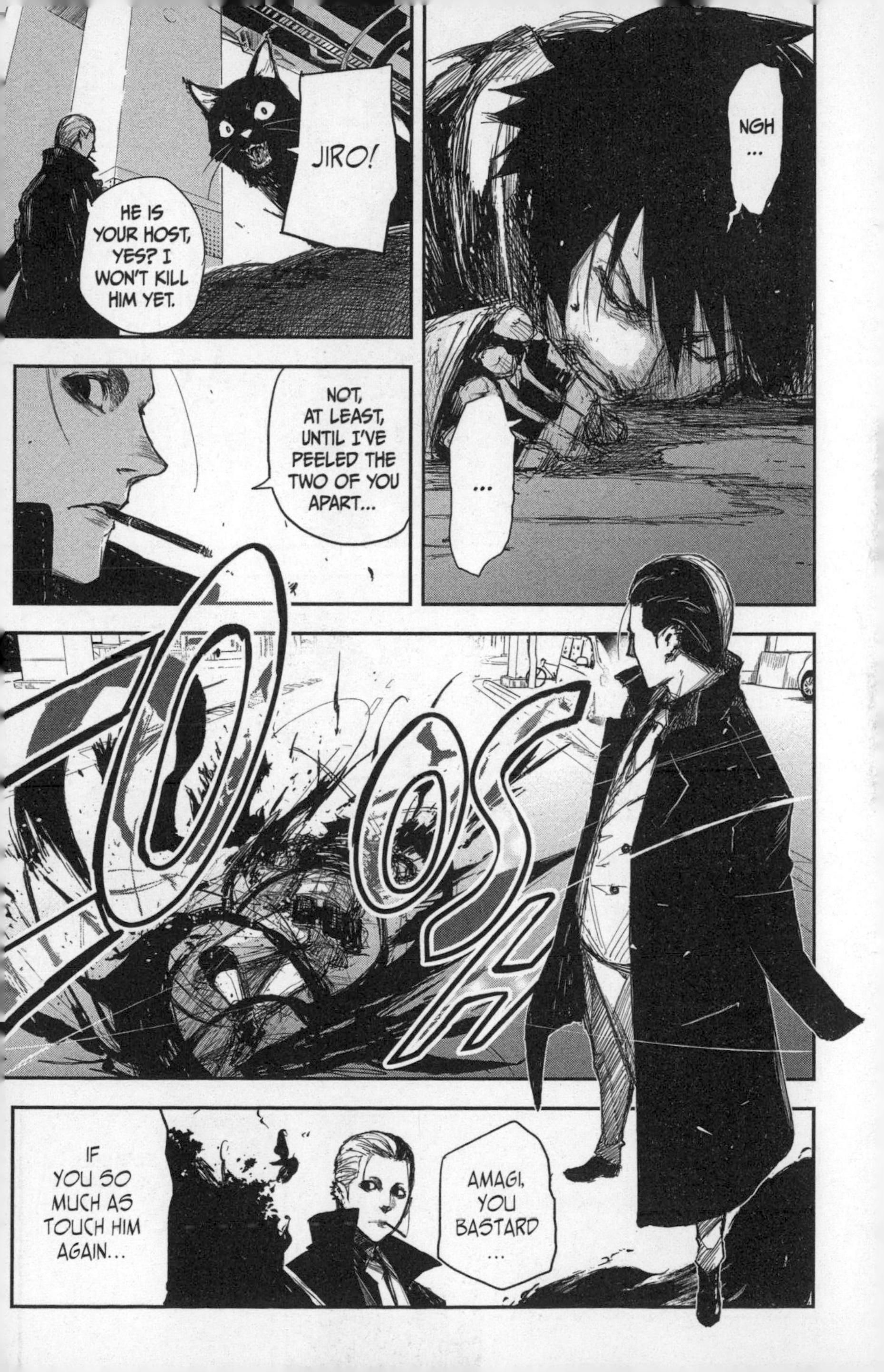
NGH ...
...
JIRO!
HE IS YOUR HOST, YES? I WON'T KILL HIM YET.
NOT, AT LEAST, UNTIL I'VE PEELED THE TWO OF YOU APART...
WOOSH
AMAGI, YOU BASTARD ...
IF YOU SO MUCH AS TOUCH HIM AGAIN...

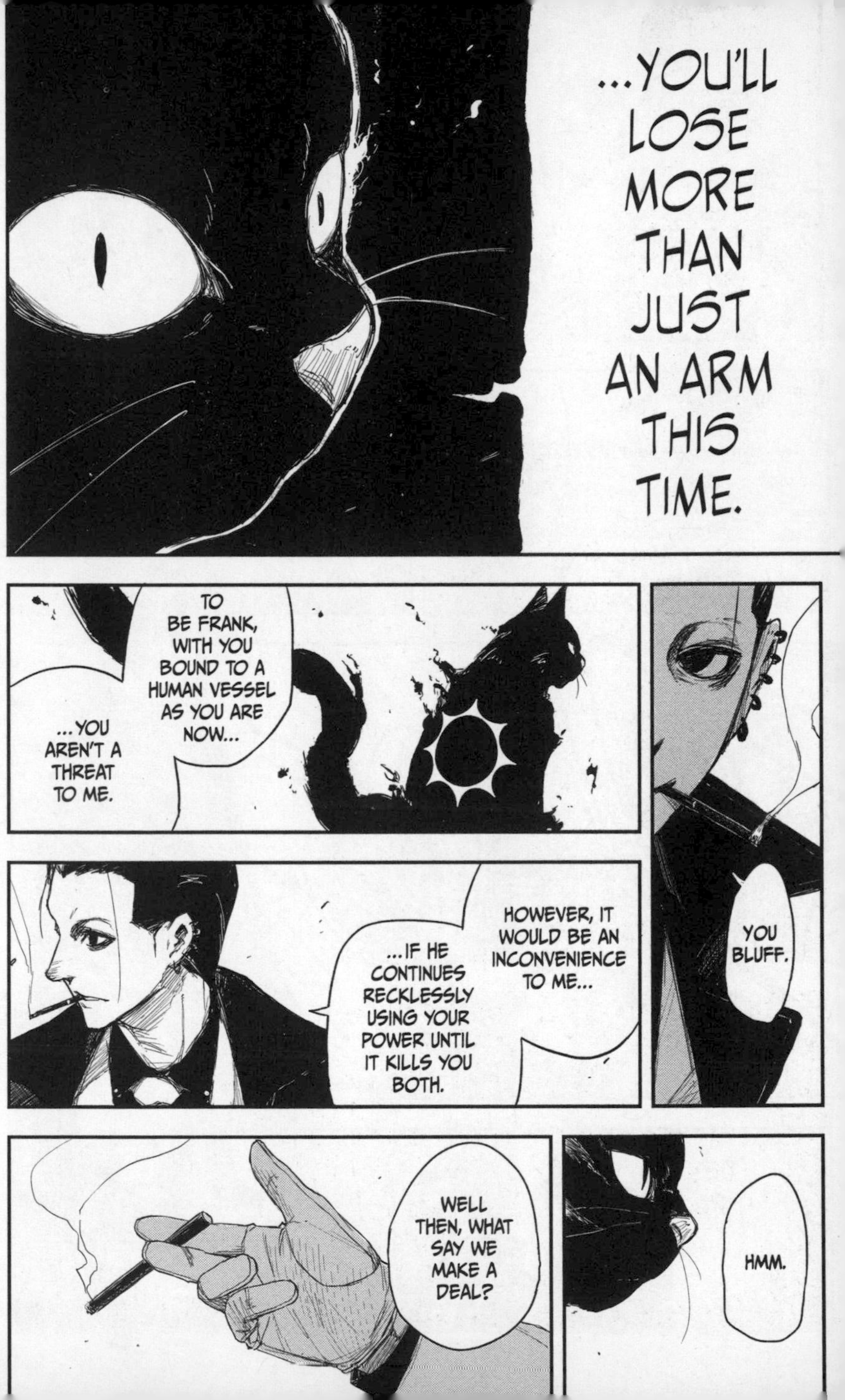
...YOU'LL LOSE MORE THAN JUST AN ARM THIS TIME.
YOU BLUFF.
TO BE FRANK, WITH YOU BOUND TO A HUMAN VESSEL AS YOU ARE NOW...
...YOU AREN'T A THREAT TO ME.
HOWEVER, IT WOULD BE AN INCONVENIENCE TO ME...
...IF HE CONTINUES RECKLESSLY USING YOUR POWER UNTIL IT KILLS YOU BOTH.
HMM.
WELL THEN, WHAT SAY WE MAKE A DEAL?

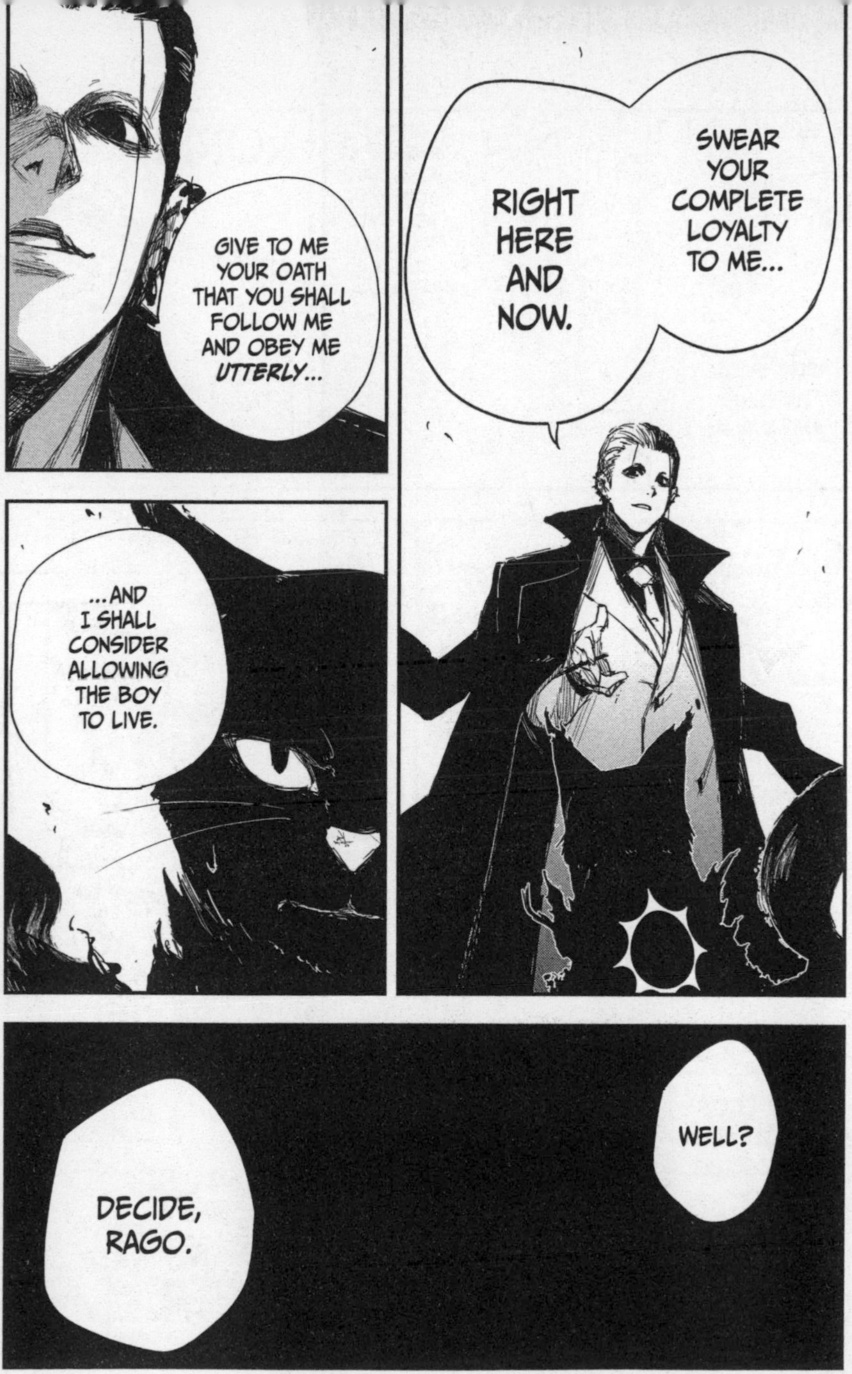
SWEAR YOUR COMPLETE LOYALTY TO ME...
RIGHT HERE AND NOW.
GIVE TO ME YOUR OATH THAT YOU SHALL FOLLOW ME AND OBEY ME *UTTERLY*...
...AND I SHALL CONSIDER ALLOWING THE BOY TO LIVE.
WELL?
DECIDE, RAGO.

TO BE CONTINUED!

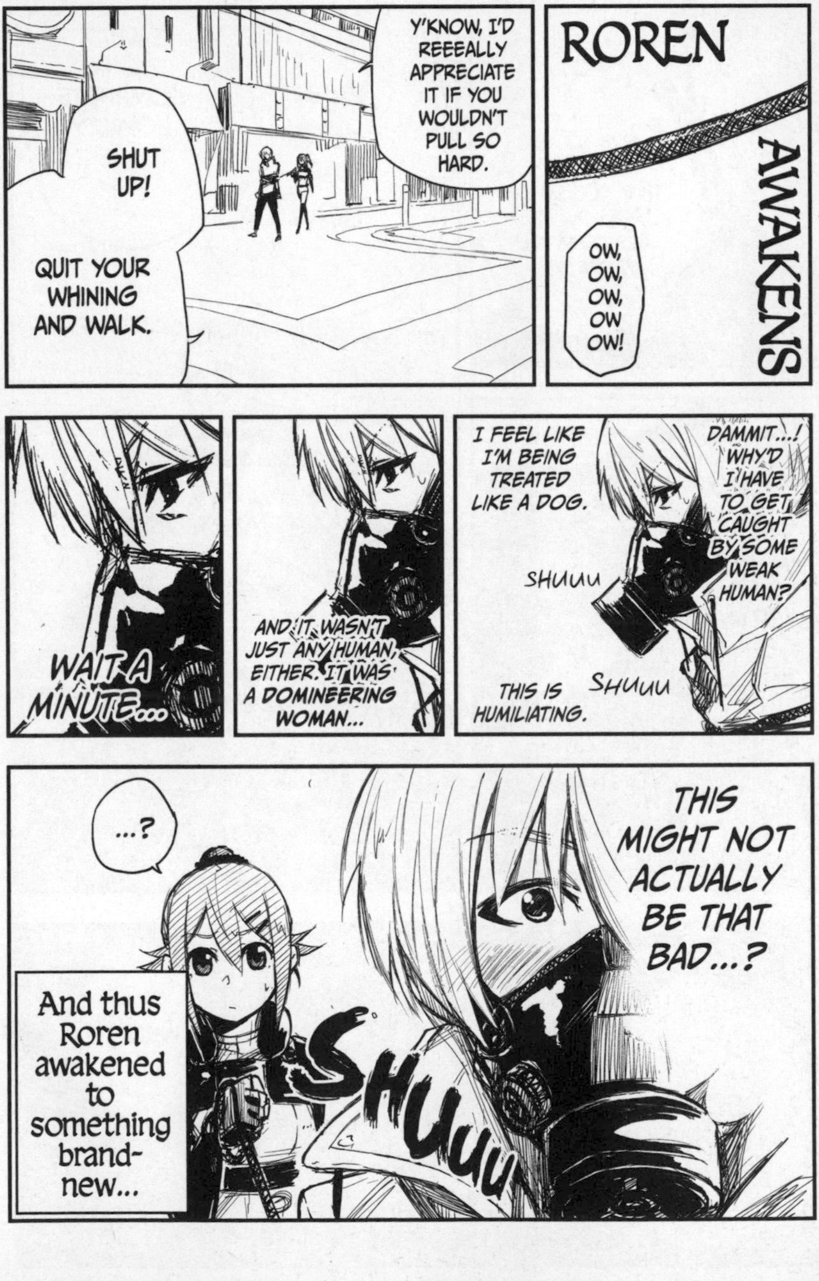
RORENAWAKENS
OW, OW, OW, OW OW!
Y'KNOW, I'D REEEALLY APPRECIATE IT IF YOU WOULDN'T PULL SO HARD.
SHUT UP!
QUIT YOUR WHINING AND WALK.
DAMMIT...! WHY'D I HAVE TO GET CAUGHT BY SOME WEAK HUMAN?
I FEEL LIKE I'M BEING TREATED LIKE A DOG.
SHUUU
SHUUU
THIS IS HUMILIATING.
AND IT WASN'T JUST ANY HUMAN, EITHER. IT WAS A DOMINEERING WOMAN...
WAIT A MINUTE...
THIS MIGHT NOT ACTUALLY BE THAT BAD...?
...?
SHUUU
And thus Roren awakened to something brand-new...

*The wire has strands of killing stone woven into it.

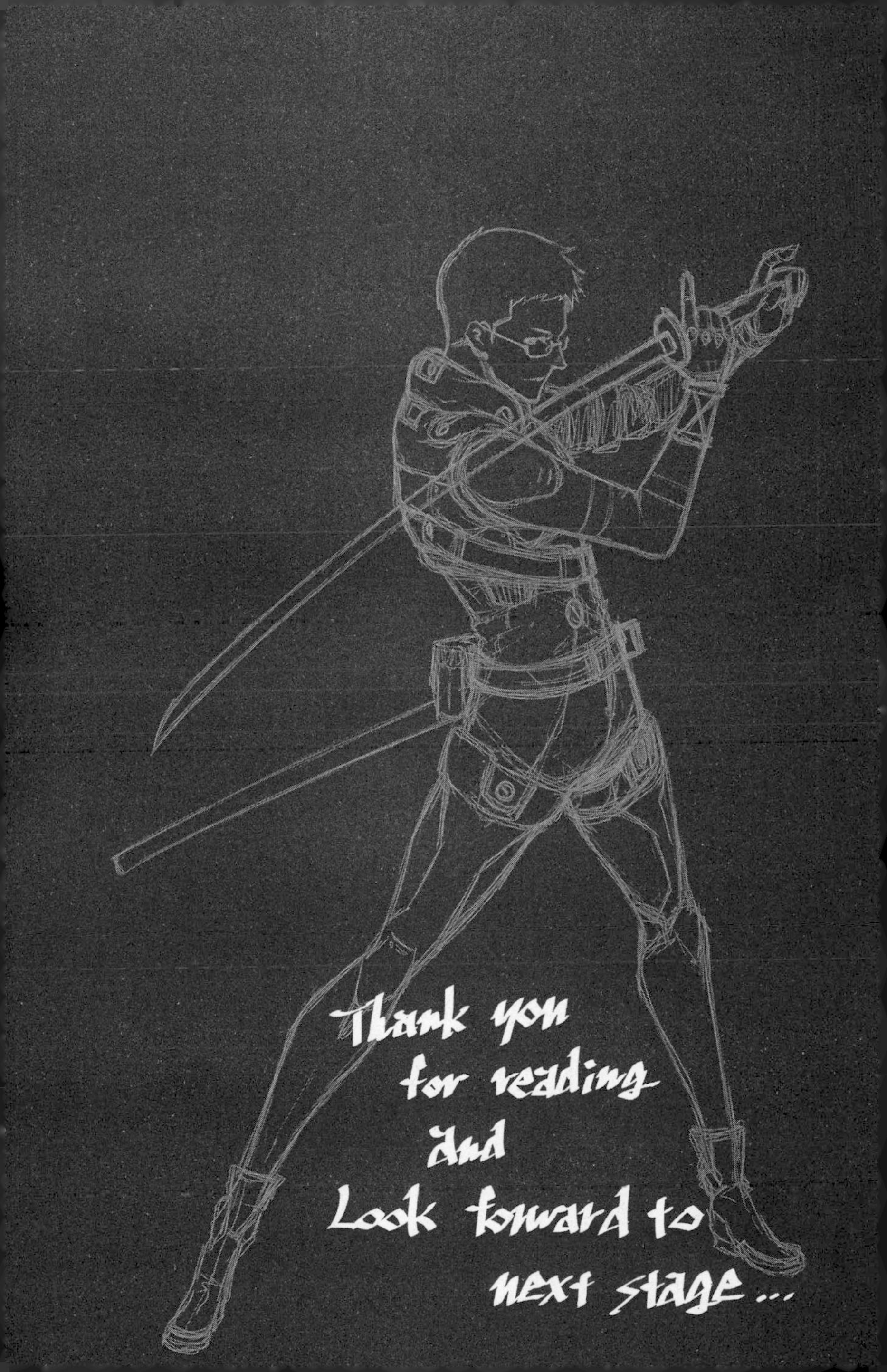
Thank you
for reading
and
Look forward to
next stage...

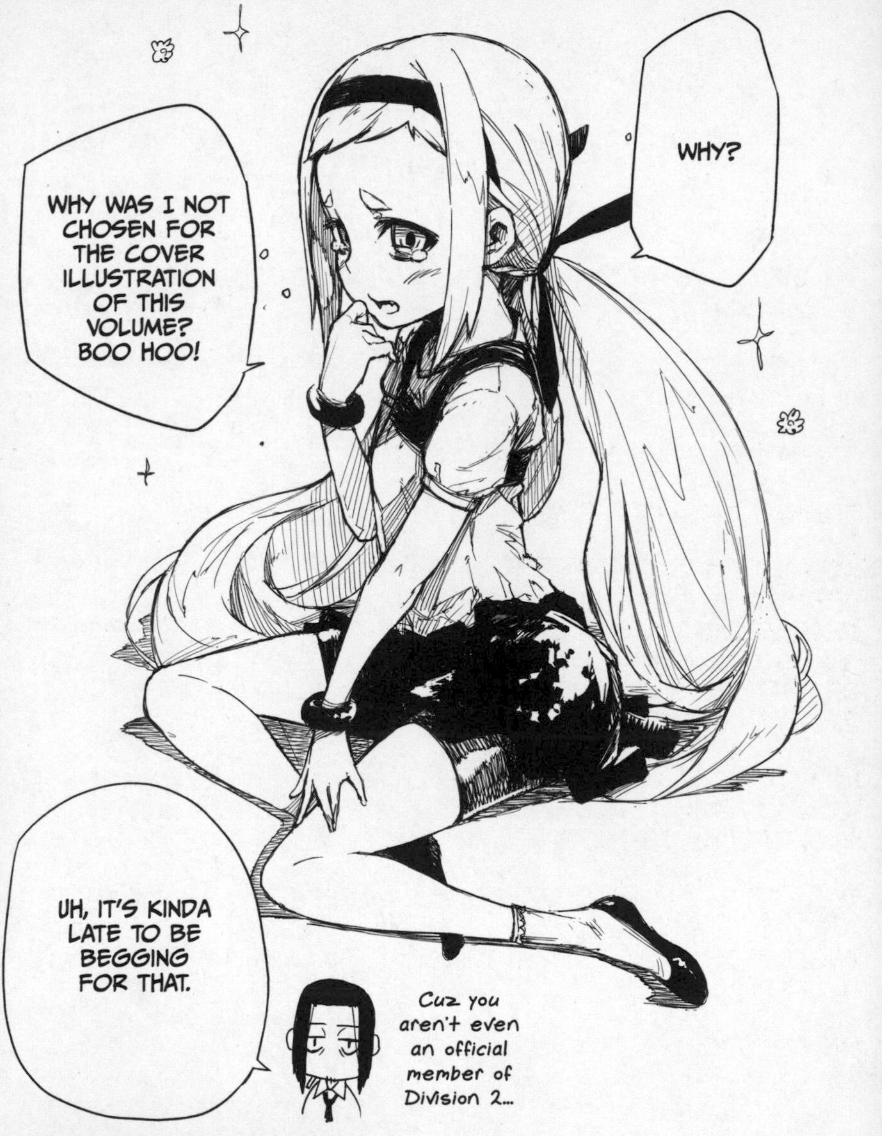
WHY?
WHY WAS I NOT CHOSEN FOR THE COVER ILLUSTRATION OF THIS VOLUME? BOO HOO!
UH, IT'S KINDA LATE TO BE BEGGING FOR THAT.
Cuz you aren't even an official member of Division 2...

BLACK TORCH 3

STORY & ART
TSUYOSHI TAKAKI

POORLY WRITTEN AFTERWORD!

THANK YOU FOR MAKING YOUR WAY TO THE END OF THE BOOK! I'M TAKAKI AND BOY, IT'S VOLUME 3 ALREADY? TIME FLIES FASTER THAN AN ARROW.

NOW THEN, THE TOPIC FOR THIS AFTERWORD IS "BEHIND THE TITLES FOR EACH CHAPTER." EAGLE-EYED READERS MAY HAVE ALREADY NOTICED, BUT EACH CHAPTER TITLE IS THE TITLE OF A SONG I LIKE. NOT ONLY THAT, MOST OF THOSE SONGS ARE FROM THE GENRE KNOWN AS "JAPANESE RAP." YES, I REALLY LIKE RAP.

"THUGGISH." "IN BAD TASTE." "JUST IMITATING BLACK PEOPLE."

THERE ARE A LOT OF PRECONCEIVED NOTIONS SURROUNDING JAPANESE RAP, BUT IF YOU LISTEN TO IT, YOU'LL FIND IT RUNS THE GAMUT FROM TRACKS THAT HAVE A POWERFUL MESSAGE TO ONES THAT ARE SO BAD THEY'RE FUNNY. SOME ALBUMS ARE EVEN CONSTRUCTED AS A STORY, LIKE MOVIES OR NOVELS. BASICALLY, THERE IS SUCH A WIDE VARIETY I FIND IT A VERY INTERESTING GENRE TO LISTEN TO. IT'S NOT JUST RAPPERS BRAGGING ABOUT HOW COOL THEY ARE OR SINGING THE PRAISES OF THEIR PARENTS.

I THINK, WHEN YOU FIRST ENCOUNTER SOMETHING, BE IT JAPANESE RAP OR ANYTHING ELSE, IT'S IMPORTANT TO PUT PREJUDICES AND PRECONCEIVED NOTIONS ASIDE AND JUST LOOK AT IT AND ACCEPT IT FOR WHAT IT IS.

BESIDES, THE MORE THINGS YOU FIND TO ENJOY IN THE WORLD, THE MORE FUN LIFE IS.

AAAND NOW THAT I'VE LOST TRACK OF WHERE I WAS GOING WITH THIS, I THINK I'LL JUST FINISH IT HERE.

I HOPE TO SEE YOU IN THE NEXT VOLUME!

Tsuyoshi Takaki

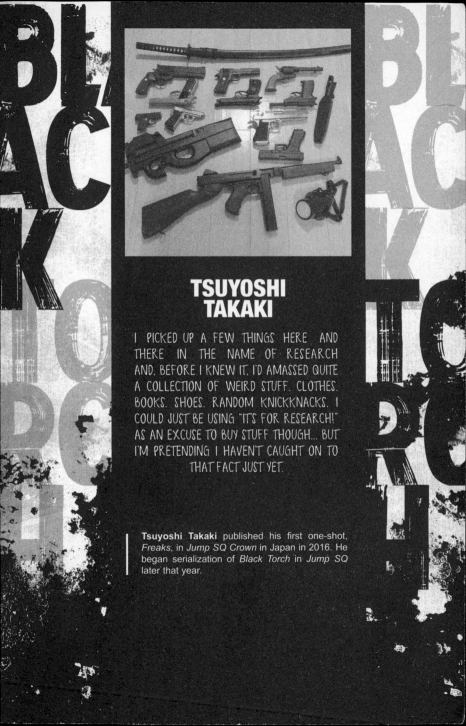

TSUYOSHI TAKAKI

I PICKED UP A FEW THINGS HERE AND THERE IN THE NAME OF RESEARCH AND, BEFORE I KNEW IT, I'D AMASSED QUITE A COLLECTION OF WEIRD STUFF. CLOTHES. BOOKS. SHOES. RANDOM KNICKKNACKS. I COULD JUST BE USING "IT'S FOR RESEARCH!" AS AN EXCUSE TO BUY STUFF THOUGH... BUT I'M PRETENDING I HAVEN'T CAUGHT ON TO THAT FACT JUST YET.

Tsuyoshi Takaki published his first one-shot, *Freaks*, in *Jump SQ Crown* in Japan in 2016. He began serialization of *Black Torch* in *Jump SQ* later that year.

BLACK TORCH

VOLUME 3

SHONEN JUMP Manga Edition

STORY AND ART BY **TSUYOSHI TAKAKI**

Translation/Adrienne Beck
Touch-Up Art & Lettering/Annaliese Christman
Design/Julian [JR] Robinson
Editor/Marlene First

BLACK TORCH © 2016 by Tsuyoshi Takaki
All rights reserved. First published in Japan in 2016 by
SHUEISHA Inc., Tokyo. English translation rights arranged by
SHUEISHA Inc.

The stories, characters and incidents mentioned in this
publication are entirely fictional.

Published by VIZ Media, LLC
P.O. Box 77010
San Francisco, CA 94107

Printed in the U.S.A.

10 9 8 7 6 5 4 3 2 1
First printing, February 2019

viz.com   shonenjump.com

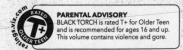

Black Clover
STORY & ART BY YŪKI TABATA
Asta is a young boy who dreams of becoming the greatest mage in the kingdom. Only one problem—he can't use any magic! Luckily for Asta, he receives the incredibly rare five-leaf clover grimoire that gives him the power of anti-magic. Can someone who can't use magic really become the Wizard King? One thing's for sure—Asta will never give up!
Black Clover
YUKI TABATA
STORY & ART BY YUKI TABATA
SHONEN JUMP MANGA
RATED T TEEN
SHONEN JUMP
VIZ media
www.viz.com
BLACK CLOVER © 2015 by Yuki Tabata/SHUEISHA Inc.

ONE-PUNCH MAN © 2012 by ONE, Yusuke Murata/SHUEISHA Inc.

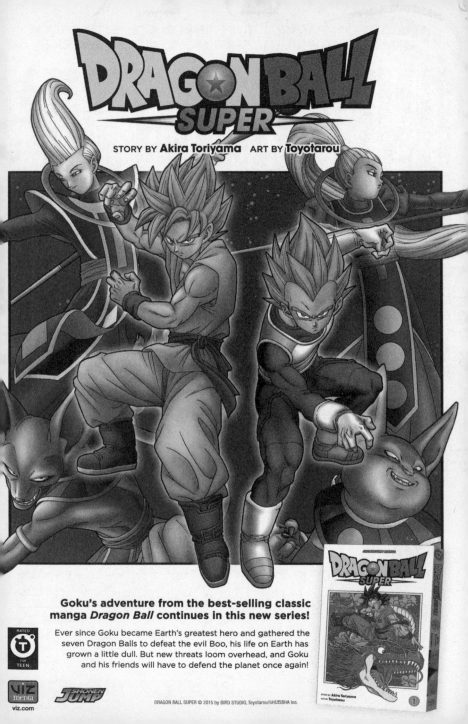

YOU ARE READING THE WRONG WAY

Black Torch reads from right to left, starting in the upper-right corner. Japanese is read from right to left, meaning that action, sound effects, and word-balloon order are completely reversed from English order.

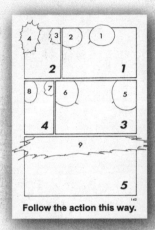

Follow the action this way.

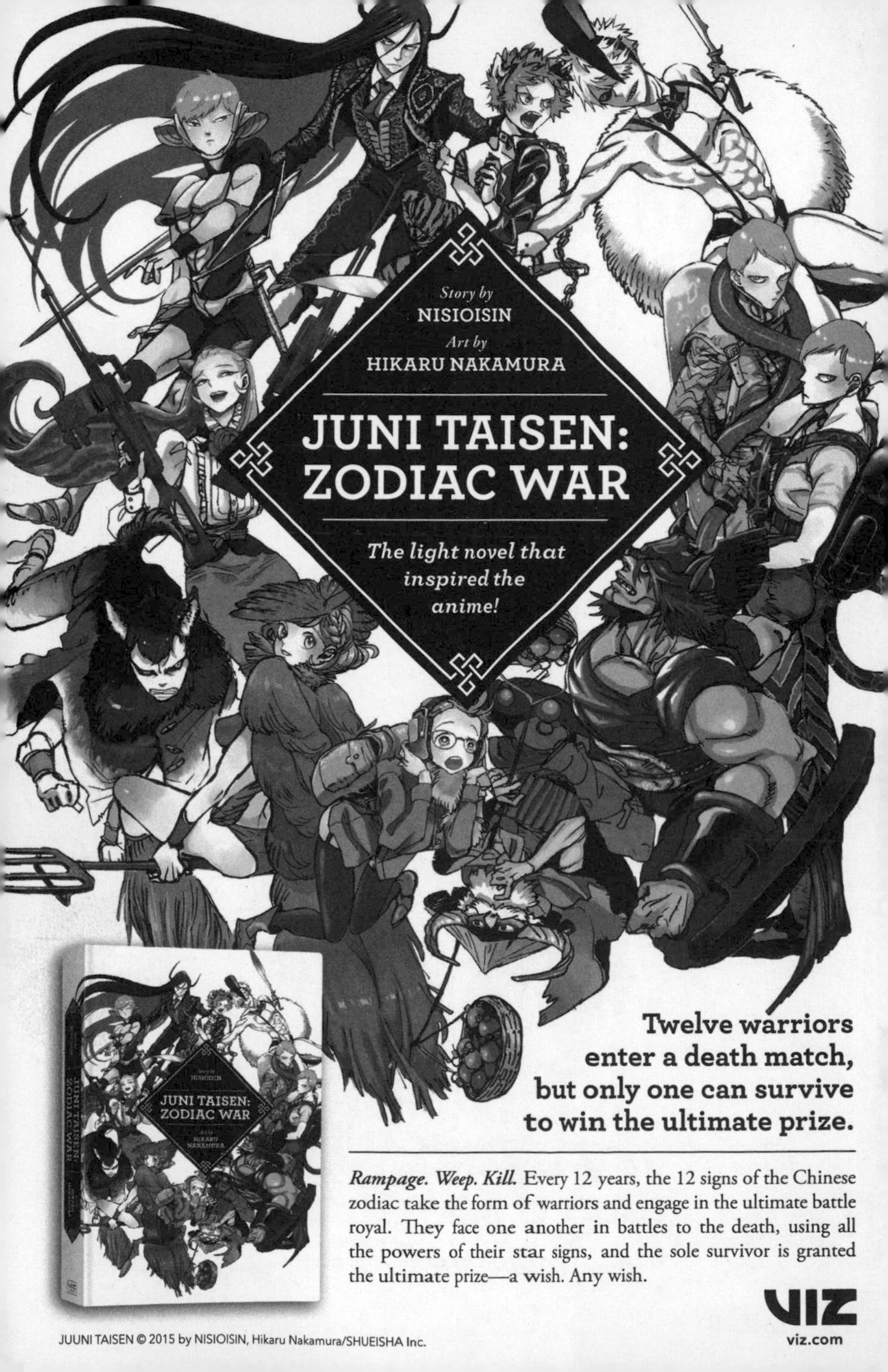

Story by
NISIOISIN
Art by
HIKARU NAKAMURA
JUNI TAISEN:
ZODIAC WAR
The light novel that inspired the anime!
Twelve warriors enter a death match, but only one can survive to win the ultimate prize.
Rampage. Weep. Kill. Every 12 years, the 12 signs of the Chinese zodiac take the form of warriors and engage in the ultimate battle royal. They face one another in battles to the death, using all the powers of their star signs, and the sole survivor is granted the ultimate prize—a wish. Any wish.
VIZ
viz.com
JUUNI TAISEN © 2015 by NISIOISIN, Hikaru Nakamura/SHUEISHA Inc.